3

𝔅lood of 𝔎ings

The Stuarts, the Ruthvens and the 'Gowrie Conspiracy'

For my students and colleagues at Bedford Modern School, 1987-2009:
'The best club in Bedfordshire' (D. G. Roberts)

Vera diu latitant, sed longo temporis usu,
Emergunt tandem, quae latuere diu.

'Truths which were long concealed emerge to light,
And controverted facts are rendered bright.'

(Inscription dating from the time of the Ruthvens, once borne on
a chamber brace at Huntingtower Castle, Perth)

Blood of Kings

The Stuarts, the Ruthvens and the 'Gowrie Conspiracy'

J. D. DAVIES

Ian Allan PUBLISHING

Blood of Kings
J. D. Davies

First published 2010

ISBN 978 0 7110 3526 3

Published by Ian Allan Publishing

an imprint of Ian Allan Publishing Ltd, Hersham, Surrey KT12 4RG.
Printed in England by CPI Mackays Ltd, Chatham, Kent ME5 8TD.

Visit the Ian Allan Publishing website at www.ianallanpublishing.com
Distributed in the United States of America and Canada by BookMasters Distribution Services.

Contents

Preface

This is a story about the violent killing of two young men in the immediate presence of the man who would become the first king of Great Britain. It is also the story of how those circumstances were interpreted, presented to the world and grossly distorted over four centuries. It is the story of the creation of two conflicting legends about the killings, and of the even more unsettling truths that both legends have successfully concealed from the world for all those long years.

I came to this so-called 'Gowrie Conspiracy', and the story of the bitter conflict between the Ruthvens and the royal house of Stuart, by a markedly roundabout route. I had been working for some years on the history of the Stepney family, baronets of Llanelli in Carmarthenshire, my home town. In itself, this was something of a change of direction from my usual academic focus as a naval historian specialising in the 17th and 18th centuries. As I worked through the voluminous Stepney papers in Carmarthenshire Record Office and Llanelli Library, I came across more and more references to the Ruthven family, Earls of Gowrie, and to the strange events that took place in Perth on 5 August 1600. It transpired that the Stepneys were the only direct descendants of the senior surviving line of the Ruthvens, which meant they were also the only descendants of the great artist Sir Anthony Van Dyck. The Stepneys believed that they were rightfully entitled to the lost titles of the Ruthvens, and pursued the claim from the 19th century until almost the end of the twentieth. They uncovered documents, corresponded with historians, renamed one of their Welsh houses after the grandest of the Ruthven castles, and got to the point where they were prepared to petition Queen Victoria for the restoration to them of the Ruthven titles; but it all came to nothing, in part because the two separate branches of the Stepney family could not agree on which of them had the superior claim to the titles, in part because the mysterious fate of the Ruthvens finally put too many obstacles in the way of their claim.

At first, I thought that the story of their Ruthven ancestry would make a chapter or two in my forthcoming book about the Stepneys, planned to coincide with the opening to the public in 2012 of their magnificent Georgian residence, Llanelly House. But it soon became apparent that this story demanded a book all to itself. North of Solway and Tweed, some eyebrows might be raised at the presumption of a Welshman in daring to write about one of the most infamous and mysterious events in Scottish history. But as I hope to show, the Gowrie Conspiracy has implications for the whole course of British History since 1600, and to an extent the wider history of the Ruthven family is a microcosm of the story of the tortuous relationship between Scotland and England in the second half of the 16th century. Moreover, I soon realised just how unlikely it was that Scottish or English writers who set out to work on the Ruthvens, working primarily in Scottish archives and on printed sources, would discover that a large archive of almost unknown material about the family and the so-called 'Gowrie Conspiracy' lay in little-known repositories hundreds of miles away in South Wales.* I subsequently discovered other relevant but comparatively unknown material in Scottish and English archives, and despite being all too aware of my own lack of grounding in many aspects of Scottish history, I knew that I would have to try and do my best by the long-dead Ruthvens and their nemesis King James VI of Scots, I of England.

The staffs of the National Library and National Archives of Scotland, Aberdeen and Edinburgh University Libraries, the Bodleian and British Libraries, the National Archives (Kew), and the county record offices in Gloucestershire, Kent and the Isle of Wight, all coped admirably with my demands for material of varying degrees of obscurity and inaccessibility. Particular thanks are due to the Institute of Historical Research, London, for providing probably the best collection of printed primary sources relating to Scotland to be found anywhere south of the border. In the Ruthvens' home town of Perth, the staffs of the Local Studies department at the A. K. Bell Library, and at Perth and Kinross Council Archives, provided exemplary assistance. Finally, I cannot praise highly enough the staff of Carmarthenshire Archives Service – even laying aside 'native bias' as much as possible, this must be one of the friendliest and most helpful repositories anywhere, even if some of the staff and many of the readers have a confusing tendency also to be called Davies!

Undoubtedly the most pleasant aspect of writing this book has been the excuses that it has offered for frequent and often extended visits to Scotland; not that I have ever needed excuses to spend as much time there as possible. I owe thanks to hoteliers, cottage owners, librarians, archivists and townspeople in many parts of Scotland. The visit that contributed the most to the genesis of this book was a week's stay in a cottage immediately adjacent to Huntingtower Castle, once the home of the Ruthvens, and briefly the

---

* An honourable exception was the late R. Ian McCallum (1920–2009), whose essay on Patrick Ruthven was published in the *Proceedings of the Society of Antiquaries of Scotland* in 2004; but then, McCallum was a doctor, not a historian.

prison of King James VI and I. Walking the few yards to the castle in harsh, frosty October dawns and dusks provided insights into the story told in this book that could never have been obtained from books and manuscripts alone. Thanks, too, to the bemused but helpful householder at Trochry, Perthshire, who finally put a hopelessly lost Welshman on the right track to finding the hunting lodge of the Ruthven family, but whose name I omitted to record because of my haste to see it.

I am very grateful to two direct descendants of the House of Ruthven for providing me with valuable information: namely, the current Earl of Gowrie and Mr Nicholas Howard, great-grandson of the last Stepney baronet and thus the senior surviving descendant of both the first Earl of Gowrie and of Sir Anthony Van Dyck. Thanks are also due to Dr Julian Goodare of the University of Edinburgh, who answered a number of queries, and Dr Steve Murdoch of the University of St Andrews, who provided information on the Ruthvens who served in foreign armies. I am also grateful to Mrs C. G. W. Roads MVO, Lyon Clerk and Keeper of the Records at the Court of the Lord Lyon, and to David Smith, archivist of Berkeley Castle, for responding to queries and providing information. As ever, Ann Coats, Richard Endsor, Frank Fox and above all Peter Le Fevre provided support and advice.

My partner, Wendy Berliner, cast her critical journalistic eye over all the drafts and redrafts of this book. Her constant emphasis on the 'story' element in 'history' has made this book considerably more readable than it might have been. Beyond that, though, only her encouragement, enthusiasm and unfailing support allowed the book to be written in the first place; and it would undoubtedly have been dedicated to her if she had not already been given that distinction in my first novel! As it is, much of the early work on this book was undertaken while I still had a 'day job' as a teacher and deputy headmaster. My former colleagues in the History and Politics departments of Bedford Modern School provided a down-to-earth mixture of moral support and irreverent chivvying, while my then headmaster, Stephen Smith, was always tolerant of my attempts to divide my time between the demands of the school and the exigencies of research and writing. Thanks, too, to Jo Newton of BMS for providing me with translations of French despatches. A special thank you is also due to all the students who kept me on my toes over so many years. I hope that the dedication of this book will satisfy all of those former students and colleagues who have demanded, at least half-jokingly, that they should have books dedicated to them individually!

J. D. Davies, *Bedfordshire, Dydd Gŵyl Dewi 2010*

Author's Note

Conventions

All dates are given in Old Style; that is, they follow the Julian calendar which was used in both England and Scotland until 1752. The exception to this convention is the second half of the Epilogue, which deliberately follows the dating in the Gregorian calendar. The Gregorian system was the one commonly used in Continental Europe during the period largely covered by this book, the sixteenth and seventeenth centuries. At that time, the Gregorian calendar was 10 days ahead of the Julian.

Although this decision might be criticised in Scotland, all spellings have been anglicised and modernised, except in those cases where retaining the original gives a better understanding of the circumstances or persons concerned. The royal family's surname, 'Stewart', was changed to the French form, 'Stuart', through the influence of the French-bred Mary, Queen of Scots. The original form has been used for most members of the Scots royal family and its many collateral lines; the French form for those born, or largely domiciled, in France, and for a few individuals who are more usually known by the French version of the name (eg, Lady Arbella Stuart and King James VI himself).

In the 16th century, the Scottish pound was worth about one-sixth of its English equivalent. All monetary values are given in pounds Scots, unless sterling is specified.

Matters of protocol

One important difference between the Scots and English peerages that recurs constantly in this book is the title given to the heir to any aristocratic title. In England, eldest sons and (if applicable) eldest grandsons are granted courtesy titles, which are effectively 'spare' secondary titles that the peer happens to possess in addition to his principal rank. Thus the title of the current owner of Woburn Abbey changed within six months from Lord Howland to Marquess of Tavistock and then to fifteenth Duke of Bedford. However, such titles cannot be bestowed on any other relation – for example, a Duke of Bedford's younger brother cannot be called Marquess of Tavistock, even if the Duke of Bedford has no children, as that title can only go to an eldest surviving son. In Scotland, however, the heir presumptive to any title automatically became 'the Master of ... ', regardless of his relationship to the incumbent. Thus in the eight-year period from 1566 to 1574, no fewer than three individuals (two brothers in succession, then an eldest son) bore the designation 'Master of Ruthven', as heir presumptive to the fourth Lord Ruthven.

References to 'abbots' and 'priors' in Scotland in the period after 1560 can be misleading. Even before the Reformation, it had become common practice for abbeys and other monasteries to be bestowed on laymen, who then drew the revenues of those institutions. Such individuals bore the titles of abbots or priors, but were actually laymen (technically known as 'commendators'). This was a useful way of providing for younger sons or brothers of great lords and the practice continued after the Reformation, long after the monks had been ejected and the monastic buildings had fallen into ruin. Nominally, then, even such an unlikely character as William, fourth Lord Ruthven and first Earl of Gowrie, was an abbot – Abbot of Scone – as was his eldest son, who obtained the office at the grand old age of two. Such individuals are called 'abbots' or 'priors' in the contemporary documents, and this style has been preferred to the clumsier term 'commendators', despite the fact that most historians now prefer the latter.

Another crucial difference between Scotland and England in the period under consideration is that women in Scotland generally enjoyed more rights and more legal independence than their English counterparts. One characteristic of this was the fact that Scots women retained their own surnames on marriage, as they did for many generations thereafter: thus when Lilias Ruthven married Ludovic Stuart, second Duke of Lennox, she became not Lilias Stuart, but Lilias Ruthven, Duchess of Lennox.

Finally, the family name of 'Ruthven' has always been pronounced 'Rivven'.

List of Abbreviations used in Notes

All books were published in London unless stated otherwise.
AKB – The A. K. Bell Library, Perth.
Arbuckle – W. F. Arbuckle, 'The "Gowrie Conspiracy"', *Scottish Historical Review*, 36 (1957), 1–24, 89–110.
BL – The British Library (Add. = Additional Manuscripts).
Border Papers – *The Border Papers : Calendar Of Letters And Papers Relating To The Affairs Of The Borders Of England And Scotland Preserved In Her Majesty's Public Record Office, London*, ed. J. Bain (Edinburgh, 1894–6).
Bruce, Papers – J. Bruce, *Papers Relating to William, First Earl of Gowrie, and Patrick Ruthven, his Fifth and Last Surviving Son* (1867).
CA – Carmarthenshire Archives Service, Carmarthen.
Calderwood – D. Calderwood, *History of the Kirk of Scotland*, ed. T. Thomson (8 vols, Edinburgh, Woodrow Society, 1842–9).
Cowan – S. Cowan, *The Ruthven Family Papers: The Ruthven Version Of The Conspiracy And Assassination At Gowrie House, Perth, 5th August 1600* (1912).
CSPD – *Calendar of State Papers, Domestic Series, 1547–1625*, ed. R. Lemon et al (12 vols, 1856–72).
CSPS – *Calendar Of The State Papers Relating To Scotland And Mary, Queen Of Scots, 1547–1603: Preserved In The Public Record Office, The British Museum, And Elsewhere In England*, ed. J. Bain et al, 13 vols (Edinburgh 1898–1969).
Donaldson, *Queen's Men* – G. Donaldson, *All the Queen's Men: Power and Politics in Mary Stewart's Scotland* (London, 1983).
Fraser – A. Fraser, *Mary Queen of Scots* (1969).
Guy – J. Guy, *My Heart is My Own: The Life of Mary, Queen of Scots* (2004).
Hewitt, *Morton*, – George R. Hewitt, *Scotland Under Morton* (Edinburgh, 2003).
HMC – Publications of the Historical Manuscripts Commission.
Juhala, 'Household' – A. L. Juhala, 'The Household and Court of King James VI of Scotland, 1567–1603) (Edinburgh University PhD thesis, 2000).

Keith – R. Keith, *The History of the Affairs of Church and State in Scotland: from the Beginning of the Reformation to the Year 1568* (The Spottiswoode Society, Edinburgh, 1844–50).

Knox – J. Knox, *History of the Reformation in Scotland*, ed. W. C. Dickinson (1949).

Lang – A. Lang, *James VI and the Gowrie Conspiracy* (1902).

NAS – The National Archives of Scotland, Edinburgh.

Nau – *The History Of Mary Stewart: From The Murder Of Riccio Until Her Flight Into England / By Claude Nau, Her Secretary. Now First Printed From The Original Manuscripts, With Illustrative Papers From The Secret Archives Of The Vatican And Other Collections In Rome; Ed., With Historical Preface, By The Rev. Joseph Stevenson, S. J.* (Edinburgh, 1883).

NLS – The National Library of Scotland, Edinburgh.

ODNB – *The Oxford Dictionary of National Biography* (2004 and subsequent electronic updates).

Pitcairn – *Ancient Criminal Trials In Scotland: Compiled From The Original Records And Manuscripts, With Historical Illustrations, Etc.*, ed. W. Pitcairn (3 vols, Edinburgh, Maitland Club, 1833).

PKA – Perth and Kinross Council Archives, Perth.

RGS – *Registrum Magni Sigilli Regum Scotorum: The Register Of The Great Seal Of Scotland, A.D. 1306–1668*, ed. J. M. Thomson et al (11 vols, Edinburgh 1882–1914).

RPCS – *The Register of the Privy Council of Scotland*, ed. D. Masson et al (14 vols, Edinburgh 1877–98).

RSS – *Registrum Secreti Sigilli Regum Scotorum*: The Register of the Privy Seal of Scotland, ed. M. Livingstone et al (6 vols, Edinburgh, 1908–date).

Scott – J. Scott, *A History of the Life and Death of John, Earl of Gowrie* (Edinburgh, 1818).

Spottiswood – J. Spottiswood, *The History of the Church of Scotland* (1656).

Spottiswoode – *The Spottiswoode Miscellany*, ed. J. Maidment, ii (Edinburgh, 1845).

Sprot Confessions – *The Gowrie Conspiracy: Confessions of George Sprot*, ed. A. Lang (Roxburghe Club, Edinburgh, 1902).

TNA – The National Archives (formerly the Public Records Office), Kew.

Turner – G. S. Turner, 'The Matter Of Fact: "The Tragedy Of Gowrie" (1604) And Its Contexts', Harvard University PhD thesis, 2006.

Weir – A. Weir, *Mary, Queen of Scots and the Murder of Lord Darnley* (2003).

INTRODUCTION:

THE DEATH OF KINGS (I)

Westminster, Tuesday, 5 November 1605. James I, King of England, should have been resplendent upon his throne in the House of Lords, addressing both Houses of Parliament. His queen, Anna of Denmark, should have been present at his side, as should the heir to the throne, the 11-year-old Prince Henry. In front of them should have been all the Lords and Commons of the realm. At that precise moment, if all had gone according to plan, every single one of them would have been blown to pieces by 36 barrels of gunpowder, secreted in the cellar beneath their feet.

As it was, one of the most audacious terrorist plots in history came to nothing. The powder had been discovered the evening before, during a supposedly routine search of the cellars. The man entrusted with setting it off was safely in custody. He claimed to be named John Johnson, but under interrogation he turned out to be a hard-bitten Yorkshire Catholic and Spanish army veteran called Guido Fawkes. His fellow plotters were being rounded up, their dreams of a Catholic *coup d'état* shattered. In truth, though, this 'Gunpowder Plot' had never involved much risk to the king and his parliament. The conspiracy had been infiltrated and monitored from early on. The government had been in control of events, and the exposure of the plot gave it the perfect justification for implementing a new security crackdown on English Catholics – *all* English Catholics, including the moderate and loyal majority, who were just as horrified as their Protestant neighbours at the actions of a tiny group of youthful fanatics. The great explosion that should have liberated Catholic England somehow became a damp squib that almost brought about its destruction.

At the time, virtually nothing of this was known to the MPs who gathered briefly in the Commons chamber on the morning of 5 November in an atmosphere of stunned disbelief, before dispersing in confusion back to their lodgings or the nearest taverns. The shock had only barely begun to dissipate by the following Saturday, the ninth, when the king came down to the Palace of Westminster to address his parliament on the subject of the plot. Not even the crown and his glorious red robes of state could transform the 39-year-old James Stuart into an entirely convincing figure of a monarch, and for the many who remembered his innately majestic predecessor, Queen Elizabeth, the contrast was particularly marked. His large, sad eyes, exaggerated cheekbones and greying beard made James look much older than his years. His gait was awkward and stumbling, and those who had seen him eat and drink commented unfavourably on his coarse habits. He was thought to be a coward, dreading the presence of cold steel and regularly wearing padded doublets to protect him against assassination attempts. James spoke with a broad Scots accent that embarrassed many of his adopted English countrymen. Yet those who judged the king by appearances alone seriously underestimated their man. Beneath the somewhat shambolic exterior, James Stuart was formidably intelligent, a brilliant debater, an astute political operator, and, when he needed to be, a brutally decisive head of state. Ruling the wild and fractious Scotland of the 16th century was a Herculean task, but on the whole James had made a success of it. He had certainly made a far better fist of the job than his mother Mary, Queen of Scots, who was driven out by her own people after making a series of catastrophic blunders, ending up as Elizabeth I's prisoner for 20 years before being beheaded as a threat to English state security.

The speech that King James delivered from the throne on Saturday 9 November was very different to the one that he had originally planned to give on the 5th, and it came from a perspective very different to that of his audience, the serried ranks of mightily relieved peers and MPs, shuffling uncomfortably in their places. Their lives had been miraculously preserved just this once. But as he addressed them from the throne, King James made it abundantly clear that this was not the first time that divine intervention had saved him from a violent and untimely death. It was not even the first time that God had saved his life on a Tuesday, the fifth of the month.

Consequently, the king's speech from the throne did not focus on the Gunpowder Plot alone. Instead, James deliberately compared the horrifying new plot to two previous attempts on his life. Some of his English listeners might well have been a little bemused by the king's suggestion that he had almost died 'before my birth, and while I was in my mother's belly', when a gun had been held to his pregnant mother's stomach. Some of them might have been a little sceptical of the king's claim that he had also been the target of an assassination plot five years earlier, in Perth, for that event was surrounded by mystery, and there had been not a few dark mutterings implying that James Stuart was really the instigator that day, not the victim. But on 9 November 1605, King James had no difficulty in drawing together what he regarded as the different threats to his life, calling the events at Perth in 1600 and the Gunpowder Plot 'these two great and fearful doomsdays'. He even hinted that although Guy Fawkes's conspiracy was on a greater scale, he, the king, had actually been in more direct personal danger five years before, on Tuesday 5 August 1600, and that the consequences for England if he had died that day would have been as incalculable as if he had been blown up in Parliament:

> I should have been baptized in blood, and in my
> destruction, not only the kingdom wherein I then was, but
> you also by your future interest, should have tasted of my
> ruin. Yet it pleased God to deliver me, as it were, from the
> very brink of death, from the point of the dagger[1]

Those members of his audience who knew anything at all of the king's history before he succeeded Elizabeth I on the English throne would have known that the two previous threats to which he alluded were directly connected, and in a very real sense connected by blood. For King James's 'crying sin of blood' was hereditary. The man whom he held responsible for almost terminating his life in the womb was Patrick, Lord Ruthven, a man commonly regarded as a malevolent warlock. It was the dying Ruthven who led the invasion of James's mother's chamber that culminated in the murder of her favourite and the pressing of the pistol to her belly, in what became one of most notorious and dramatic coups in British history. Two generations later, the men allegedly responsible for attempting to kill King James at Perth on 5 August 1600 were John Ruthven, third Earl of Gowrie, and Alexander Ruthven, his brother and heir. They were the grandsons of the same Patrick, Lord Ruthven. If James's version of events is to be believed, the Ruthven family came far closer to killing him than Guy Fawkes and the rest of the Gunpowder Plotters ever did – and not once, but several times.

****

Regardless of what might or might not have happened when he was still unborn, at Gowrie House in Perth on 5 August 1600 King James

Stuart was in very real danger of death *three times in one day*, during a barely explicable passage of events which culminated in the violent deaths under the king's eyes of the Earl of Gowrie and his brother.

Firstly, the unarmed king found himself alone for some time in a locked turret chamber with at least one armed man who had ample opportunity to kill him. This was the moment to which James alluded in his speech to Parliament: the moment when 'the point of the dagger' had supposedly been at his breast. On the hot afternoon of 5 August King James VI left his entourage to go to the upper floors of Gowrie House, the substantial Perth residence of the powerful Ruthven family and its head, John, third Earl of Gowrie. James went upstairs with just one companion, the earl's brother and heir Alexander, a very tall 19-year-old youth. Confusion followed. Royal courtiers, milling about in the street outside, heard a whispered rumour that the king had slipped out of Gowrie House by another exit, and was already riding out of Perth. They wondered whether they should take horse. The tall, dark and aquiline Earl of Gowrie seemed anxious and confused.[2] He called for his own horse, only to be told that it was at another of his residences, the palace of Scone, several miles away. His own porter was telling him that the king could not have left, for he had the keys to all the gates. In the midst of this uncertainty, the courtiers suddenly heard a familiar voice, and looked up. On the second floor of Gowrie House, a turret chamber jutted out over the street. There, at the half-open window, was the unmistakeable face of King James, red-faced with exertion, screaming 'Treason! Murder!' and the like. He seemed to be wrestling with his young companion. The king's friends immediately jumped to one conclusion: for whatever reason, Alexander Ruthven was trying to kill the King of Scots.[3] Indeed, one man eventually left that turret room as a corpse; but to the surprise and suspicion of many it was not the older and smaller of the two, King James Stuart, but the younger, taller and fitter, Ruthven, done to death thanks to the remarkably timely arrival of a small party of royal attendants.

Secondly, only moments later the Earl of Gowrie and his retinue charged towards that same turret chamber, stepping over Alexander Ruthven's dead body in the process, to launch a furious attack on the same small party of courtiers defending King James. This was a vicious and closely contested sword fight that could easily have gone either way, and one can only speculate about what a Gowrie maddened by the sight of his dead brother would have done to James had he laid hands on him.

Then there was the third and perhaps the most dangerous time of all, the several hours during which the Perth mob, enraged by the deaths of their beloved earl and his brother, surrounded Gowrie House, threatening to batter down its gates and bring up gunpowder to get at King James. Regardless of what the Ruthven brothers might or might not have planned to do that day, the enraged townspeople were far nearer to James in time and space than the gunpowder plotters ever came. The Westminster gunpowder was discovered the night before the planned state opening, and the plot was certainly compromised long before that. As he sat on his throne on 9 November 1605, looking out over his happily reprieved parliamentarians, King James VI and I was safe. He would have been equally safe if he had gone to Parliament on the fifth. It had been certain for several days, if not for much longer, that he would be safe. His ministers and spies had seen to that. There was no such predictability, and no such comfortable pre-emptive timescale, about the potentially explosive reactions of the Perth mob. That remained true even if one took the alternative view of what had happened at Gowrie House, as many Scots and Englishmen had, almost from the very day itself: the view that King James had deliberately engineered the deaths in his own presence of the Earl of Gowrie and his brother. If Fawkes had succeeded in lighting his fuse, there might have been more than a few good Scots Presbyterians who would have rejoiced at the success of this papist plot, as bringing down God's vengeance on the tyrant, hypocrite and murderer, James Stuart, for slaughtering the innocent Ruthven brothers.

****

The question 'What if the Gunpowder Plot had succeeded?' has fascinated historians and television producers for years. But the plot had virtually no realistic chance of success: a group of young zealots took on one of the most sophisticated intelligence systems in Europe in as gross a mismatch of amateurs against professionals as can be imagined. Leaving that aside, and allowing Guy Fawkes his 'big bang', the normal rules for writing 'alternative history' simply cease to exist, just as the entire English Parliament would have done. As King James rightly pointed out on 9 November 1605, hammering the point home to his quaking audience, the explosion would have wiped out *everyone*, every single one of them – the king, the queen, the heir to the throne, all the bishops, all the judges, all the Lords, all the Commons – in other words, the entire Protestant governing elite of England. Oddly, though, the one thing that a successful Gunpowder Plot would *not* have done would be to end the rule of the House of Stuart over England. Two of James's children were not intended to be at Parliament on 5 November. Princess Elizabeth, aged nine, was at Coombe Abbey in the Midlands. She was the Gunpowder Plotters' favoured candidate for the role of Catholic puppet monarch, had their plot succeeded. Meanwhile, Elizabeth's younger brother Prince Charles, Duke of York and Albany, aged five, was at the Palace of Richmond. The leading gunpowder plotter Thomas Percy planned to kidnap him, but this project had little support among his co-conspirators, and Charles seems to have been largely overlooked as a potential Catholic king. Perhaps his notoriously poor health led the plotters to feel there was no point in crowning a child who was bound to die sooner rather than later. Nevertheless, the facts remain the same. If Parliament had been blown up, the new government – be it Protestant or Catholic – would have had at least two Stuart heirs to choose from.[4] If male primogeniture won out, King Charles I would have become king of England and Scotland 20 years before he actually succeeded to those thrones. It is impossible to judge what might have happened in those 20 formative years, but if one accepts the argument for nature over nurture, Charles might still have made catastrophic political mistakes, brought about a civil war, and lost his throne and his head. With or without a successful Gunpowder Plot, British history might well have carried on along very much the same course.

But what if King James VI had died at Gowrie House on 5 August 1600, instead of John, Earl of Gowrie, and his brother? This creates a set of 'alternative histories' that are at once more clear-cut, and much more far-reaching, than those that stem from the fantasy of a successful Gunpowder Plot. Presumably James's elder son, the boy who should have been standing beside him on 5 November 1605, would have succeeded to the throne of Scotland as King Henry I, aged six. The Scots had a depressingly long tradition of having to crown infant monarchs, with James's grandfather having succeeded at the age of 17 months, his mother at the age of one week, and he himself at the age of 13 months; only one Scottish monarch since 1390 had succeeded at full age, and then only barely. The accession of Henry at such a tender age, with the prospect of a long regency under his mother, Anna of Denmark,* a Catholic convert, might have been of incalculable significance in

---

* Although in England it is still common to refer to the queen as 'Anne', she never used that name herself; and most historians now prefer to use the name that the Scots, and her own parents, always bestowed on her.

Scotland, where the balance between Protestant and Catholic was still precarious. But it would have been still more significant south of the border. Three years later, the child-king Henry of Scotland would hardly have been such an attractive potential king of England as his father undoubtedly was by that time, despite James's more dubious personal traits. If not James or Henry, then who would have succeeded Elizabeth I on the English throne?

This is the crux of the difference between the 'alternative histories' that stem from the 'Gunpowder Plot' and the 'Gowrie Conspiracy'. In 1605 the Stuarts were the only commodity on the market. James I had been duly crowned King of England, and even if he had only been on the throne for 30 months before being blown to kingdom come, the succession would have passed, by right, to his children. A Stuart would have ruled England still. But five years earlier, in 1600, the English succession was an auction. One contemporary discourse on the matter listed well over a dozen potential candidates for Elizabeth I's throne. To many people, James VI was the most attractive candidate on offer – adult, experienced, Protestant, and above all, male, following half a century of thoroughly unnatural female rule. But against that, he was a foreigner. English law specified that no foreigner could own land in England, so surely the same proviso applied to the country as a whole? Not only was he a foreigner, he was a Scot, and there were plenty of old Englishmen still alive who had fought against the Scots in formal wars or in the endemic casual violence along the border. To English law was added the complication of English history. Henry VIII's constant changes of mind over the order of succession as his marital saga progressed; the Wars of the Roses, which had torn up the rules of straightforward hereditary succession; the consequences of royal breeding all the way back to Edward III's notorious fecundity – all these legacies provided a long list of potential alternative candidates to the King of Scots, and every one of those candidates had their partisans.[5] None of that mattered once the English political establishment decided that it had to be James, if only as the 'least worst' option, and it mattered even less once James was crowned in Westminster Abbey. But if King James Stuart had been killed at Gowrie House on 5 August 1600, then the auction would have had to start all over again, with new favourites, new deals being done, and, inevitably, the emergence of a new king or queen of England on 24 March 1603.

If James had died in 1600, and the English political elite then rejected the seriously weakened claim of his Stuart children in favour of some suitable mediocrity, there would probably have been no civil war in the middle of the 17th century, with all that stemmed from it. After all, the outbreak of that war has often been attributed to the inadequacies as king of James's son, Charles I; but Charles was only King of England because his father had reigned there before him, and because his elder brother, the same Prince Henry who might have become King of Scots on 5 August 1600, died aged only 18. The many historians and politicians who see the origins of British parliamentary democracy in the civil war would presumably have to look elsewhere. If the Stuarts had never ruled England, would Scotland ever have lost her independence through an Act of Union, in 1707 or at any other time? In Ireland, King James VI and I was personally responsible for much of the 'plantation' policy in Ulster, encouraging English and Scottish Protestants to colonise large parts of the north of Ireland. The transformation of Derry into Londonderry occurred under James's direct auspices. So if James Stuart had never reigned in England, would Ireland ever have witnessed her tragically seminal events of the 17th century – the bloody rebellion of 1641, Cromwell's massacres at Drogheda and Wexford, and the Battle of the Boyne – with all their tortured and enduring legacies?

All of these events were able to come about *because James VI, King of Scots, did not die at Gowrie House on 5 August 1600*. In England, at least, the mindless little sectarian jamborees that take place every 'bonfire night', and the pointlessly enduring legacy of Guy Fawkes, ensure that there is no sense of proportion about the two great crises that James faced in the first five years of the 17th century. But as the man himself knew full well, James Stuart was in far more immediate danger, and in far more real and imminent risk of death, on 5 August 1600 at Perth than he was at Westminster on 5 November 1605 at the hands of Fawkes and his manipulated, misled and ultimately incompetent fellow plotters. Despite the fact that it commemorates a complete non-event, and for all its political incorrectness and nightmarish 'health and safety' implications, Bonfire Night lives on, while the arguably far more significant events of 5 August 1600 are virtually forgotten. Even in Scotland, the memory of the 'Gowrie Conspiracy' has faded; Perth's museum is strong on innocuous social history, but has literally nothing on display to mark probably the most important event that ever took place in the town.[6] If modern history books refer to the Gowrie affair at all,[7] they usually dismiss it in a few sentences or paragraphs as a bungled attempt at an aristocratic coup, mounted by two naïve and inept young men. But what happened on 5 August 1600 at Gowrie House, *or what could have happened*, was far more significant than that. The fact that King James Stuart did not die that day, when the odds were stacked heavily in favour of his dying, changed the history of the British Isles, for better or worse.

****

The 34-year-old King James rode into Perth at about one in the afternoon of 5 August 1600, hot from a vigorous morning's hunting in glorious weather in the royal park of Falkland in Fife. He came at the invitation of Alexander Ruthven, known as Sandy, who, as his brother's heir, held the courtesy title of Master of Ruthven.[8] At breakfast time, just before the hunt was due to begin, Sandy had told James the tale of a mysterious stranger he had come across the night before, in a field near Perth. This stranger supposedly held a cloak over his mouth to conceal his face, but Sandy Ruthven and his entourage quickly discovered that the cloak concealed a large pot of gold coins. They took the stranger back to Gowrie House, where he remained under close guard. Ruthven urged the king to come at once to Perth to view the find and interview the stranger. Unsurprisingly, King James found the tale too tall for his liking, especially when Sandy Ruthven claimed that his brother knew nothing of it, and that if he found out, the earl would immediately seek to deprive the king of his right to the treasure trove. Despite the young man's insistence that he should come to Perth at once, James decided to carry on with the hunt. It was a particularly hard and lengthy chase that ended only when the buck had brought the royal party almost full circle, back to the neighbourhood of Falkland Palace, where it met its death. Only then did King James agree to set out for Gowrie House with a small party that included his cousin, Ludovic Stuart, Duke of Lennox, and John Erskine, Earl of Mar, most of them still wearing their green hunting garb, and only lightly armed. It was now about 11 o'clock in the morning. Having already sent a servant ahead to forewarn his brother, Sandy Ruthven rode off in front of the main party, ostensibly to ensure that his brother had made all ready for the royal visit – even though that brother was still allegedly ignorant of the true reason for King James's visit to Perth.

During the ride across Fife and south Perthshire, James speculated about the nature of the mysterious treasure with the Duke of Lennox, the only person in whom he confided the secret of the pot of gold. Lennox was immediately sceptical about such a far-fetched tale, but even if it eventually turned out to be a fantasy, any rumour of the miraculous appearance of large amounts of bullion was bound to interest a king who always spent far more money than he possessed. In the Scotland of 1600, though, gold coins might mean far more than a welcome boost for the ever-precarious royal finances. Scotland was nominally a Protestant country, but the Catholic faith was still strong, and Spain had already made several attempts to buy the support of Scots noblemen for a restoration of the old religion. King James and Sandy Ruthven had already agreed that the mysterious stranger was most likely to be a Jesuit, one of the feared 'stormtroopers' of the Counter-Reformation. But there was one other power with an obvious interest in spending gold in Scotland to further its own ends. In 1600 Queen Elizabeth I of England was an old woman, her life bound to be drawing towards its close. Her closest living relative and most obvious successor was James, King of Scots. James VI had been king for all but one of his 34 years, and by 1600 he had a reputation as a competent and successful monarch. Even so, there were many in England who did not want a Scottish king, no matter how impressive his track record, and there were many in Scotland who did not want their king abandoning them to take control of the larger and wealthier southern kingdom, Scotland's traditional enemy for many centuries. So in the Scotland of 1600, a pot of gold was not necessarily an innocent windfall. A pot of gold was the stuff that potentially changed the religions of entire countries, or altered the destinies of crowns.

The king's party approached Saint John's Town of Perth from the south. The broad River Tay flowed due south down the town's east side before turning sharply east under Kinnoull Hill, flowing out into a wide firth before eventually spilling into the sea beyond Dundee. The river was still navigable as far as Perth, which had a bustling harbour. The royal party would have approached the town across the South Inch, one of the two broad open spaces that flanked it. By far the tallest structure in sight would have been the tower of St John's Kirk, Perth's parish church. King James was fascinated by history and genealogy, so presumably he would have known that the kirk contained the mortal remains of both his great-grandmother, Queen Margaret Tudor, and his great-great-great-great-grandfather, King James I. The sixth King James derived his claim to the English throne from Margaret, the colourful but sexually erratic elder sister of King Henry VIII of England. The memory of his namesake might have been less welcome to James: on the night of 20–21 February 1437, the first King James

Stewart was brutally stabbed to death in the sewers beneath Perth's Dominican monastery, the culmination of a noble plot to overthrow a strong and successful monarch. As he neared the walls of Perth, perhaps James VI allowed himself a moment's reflection on the possibility of history repeating itself.

On the South Inch, James was greeted by the Provost (in English terms, the mayor) of Perth. John Ruthven, third Earl of Gowrie, was 22 years old, highly educated, cultured and handsome. He was also the son and successor of the first earl, who had once kidnapped the same James VI and held him captive, and the grandson of the man who had almost caused Mary, Queen of Scots, to miscarry. James's natural wariness of the Ruthven family and his initial scepticism about the 'pot of gold' story can only have been exacerbated by the reception that he received. Gowrie himself seemed nervous and uneasy, despite having apparently had ample warning of the royal party's approach. The earl would have led the king into Perth through the Spey Port, near the southwest corner of the town wall. This led into the Spey Gate, a street that ran virtually north-south and merged into the Water Gate.* These streets ran, and still run, virtually at right angles to the two main streets of the town of Perth, South Street and High Street. Spey Gate is now occupied chiefly by a car park, while Water Gate is run down and partly derelict. Then, the two streets formed one of the most desirable residential districts in Scotland. Perth stood at the edge of the Highland line, close to the palace at Stirling and the royal hunting park at Falkland, with excellent communications in all directions. The Scottish Parliament and Kirk assemblies often met at Perth, which was far more central than Edinburgh or Glasgow. Scone, across the Tay and a couple of miles to the east, had been the ancient crowning place of Scotland's kings.

The destination of young John Ruthven and his monarch stood where Spey Gate intersected South Street. Gowrie House occupied the plum site in Perth, occupying the south-eastern corner of the walled town. An L-shaped, three-storey mansion, it had been built in 1520 and was purchased by the crown in 1526, with the Ruthvens swiftly becoming hereditary custodians of this 'king's lodging'. Gowrie's father modernised it in the early 1580s, giving it the name by which it would become notorious. The first earl also laid out delightful gardens and orchards running down to the town wall on the

---

* In sixteenth-century Scotland, a 'port' was a gate, a 'gate' was a street.

south side and to the Tay on the east. On the first floor, the first Earl of Gowrie installed a grand gallery, with large windows looking out to the south, across his garden, towards the sun and the river Tay. At the west end of the same floor, an anteroom or gallery chamber led to two small pepperpot turrets, after the French fashion, that jutted out over the Spey Gate.

****

After the royal party entered Gowrie House, there was no immediate interrogation of the stranger, no urgent examination of the pot of gold. According to the logic of Sandy Ruthven's story, he and James would have to await an opportunity to slip away, unnoticed by the Earl of Gowrie. In the meantime, the king expected to be served a decent dinner. But the earl continued to seem uneasy. He took an unconscionable time to organise any hospitality for his guests, despite the early warning of their arrival that he had supposedly received; in fact, despite this forewarning he had already dined early, between about noon and one, with a small group of friends who were visiting the house. Now servants had to hurriedly scour Perth for a makeshift royal banquet, and between them, they managed to scramble together a grouse, a hen, a shoulder of mutton and some strawberries.[9] A late lunch was served, first to the king in one room at about two, slightly later in another to Lennox, Mar, and the rest. The earl remained with James, but remained nervous, responding to the king's chatter with barely coherent mumbling. When Gowrie finally went out of the king's dining room to attend properly to his other guests, Sandy Ruthven suggested to James that the time was right for them to go and inspect the treasure, keeping the earl ignorant of their intentions. Without explanation, the king and the Master of Ruthven passed the feasting noblemen, crossed the hall to the main staircase, and disappeared into the upper rooms of the building. Sandy told some of James's attendants that the king wanted no one to follow them, and he locked the doors behind them as they went.

After a while, the Earl of Gowrie and some of the king's party went out to the garden, where they wandered among the apple trees. They nibbled cherries and killed time until one of Gowrie's attendants, and then the earl himself, suddenly attempted to convince them that the king had already left by another exit. The party went through the house and out of the yard to the front gate (see Plan A), where Gowrie's porter abruptly announced that the king could not have left: the other gate was locked, and he had the key. Gowrie went back into the house,

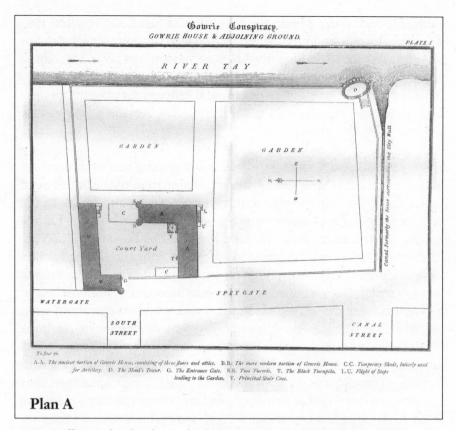

Gowrie Conspiracy.
GOWRIE HOUSE & ADJOINING GROUND.

PLATE I

RIVER TAY

GARDEN

GARDEN

Canal formerly the Fosse surrounding the City Wall

Court Yard

WATERGATE

SPEY GATE

SOUTH
STREET

CANAL
STREET

To face 70.

A.A. The ancient portion of Gowrie House, consisting of three floors and attics. B.B. The more modern portion of Gowrie House. C.C. Temporary Sheds, latterly used for Artillery. D. The Monk's Tower. G. The Entrance Gate. S.S. Two Turrets. T. The Black Turnpike. I.U. Flight of Steps leading to the Garden. Y. Principal Stair Case.

Plan A

supposedly to check where the king was, and emerged to confirm that he had indeed started to ride out of Perth. The earl called for horses, but was reminded that his own horse was at Scone, another of his houses, some three miles away. As the confusion mounted, the royal head appeared at the turret window: 'I am murdered! Treason! My Lord of Mar, help me!' Sir Thomas Erskine, a kinsman of Mar's and another member of the hunting party, grabbed the Earl of Gowrie and cried 'Fie, traitor, this is thy deed. Thou shalt die!' But an apparently bewildered Gowrie simply said 'I know nothing about it'.

Meanwhile, Lennox, Mar and some of the other green-coated retinue had run back into the house and tried to get to the upper gallery from the main stairway, but the final door was locked against them from the inside, and for half an hour it resisted all the increasingly frantic attempts to break it open. One of James's courtiers, John Ramsay, was outside in the stable, and noticed from there that a door was open at the foot of a separate turnpike stair, which led directly to the gallery from the outside of the house. Despite having a hawk perched incongruously on his arm, Ramsay raced up the turnpike and reached the turret room. There he found the king wrestling for his life with the Master of Ruthven, who was bearing a dagger and was seemingly intent on killing the king. A mysterious third man, armed and in armour, stood in the room, watching silently. Unhesitatingly, Ramsay stabbed Sandy Ruthven in the neck, and the king pushed the dying youth down the stairs. Other courtiers, including Sir Thomas Erskine and the king's club-footed doctor, Huw Herries, were now running up the turnpike stair in response to the shouts from King James and Ramsay. They rushed past the bleeding Master of Ruthven, stabbing him yet again for good measure. The dying Sandy Ruthven's last words echoed his brother's protest of a few minutes earlier: 'Alas, I had no blame of it'.

Outside, the Earl of Gowrie had escaped the clutches of Erskine and others loyal to the king, and ran out into the High Street of Perth. As the town's alarm bell rang out, and the street cries proclaimed treason and murder at Gowrie House, the earl donned a steel bonnet and drew the two swords that he kept in one scabbard, Italian-style. He gathered a small force of retainers and townsmen, and ran back to his house. Seeing his brother's bloodied corpse at the foot of the turnpike, the furious earl shouted 'Up the stair!' The avenging Ruthven gang raced up the steps, but the courtiers were ready for them. A bitter swordfight ensued at the top of the turnpike and in the gallery chamber. Erskine was wounded in the hand and Herries lost two fingers. The king saw nothing of this, for his men had locked him in the turret room for his safety. The struggle was brought to a sudden end when Ramsay's blade found its mark for the second time. John, third and last Earl of Gowrie, fell dead on the turnpike stair, close to the corpse of his brother. The stair was to be remembered by posterity as the Black Turnpike.

Outside, an angry mob was gathering in the streets. The Ruthvens were loved in the town and had provided its provosts since time immemorial. Townsmen grabbed whatever weapons they could, others called for gunpowder, and the would-be avengers of the Ruthven brothers advanced on Gowrie House. Abuse was shouted at the 'green coats' who had murdered Perth's beloved provost, and at the king himself. For a time, perhaps as long as several hours, it seemed likely that the enraged townspeople of Perth would sweep into Gowrie House, kill the king and avenge their dead provost. A James Stewart, King of Scots, had died violently in Perth before, and in the afternoon of 5 August 1600, there seemed every chance that history would repeat itself. But the gates of Gowrie House held firm. Leaderless, the townspeople became confused. The anger dissipated. The king's followers were able to take control. The mob slowly dispersed. That evening, King James VI was able to ride back to Falkland, allegedly to spontaneous popular applause from the townsfolk of Perth. As a consequence of his deliverance, some 32 months later he was able finally to succeed Queen Elizabeth on the English throne, becoming James I, King of Great Britain.

Surely, then, on 5 August 1600 a dastardly plot to murder God's lieutenant on earth had been foiled, the perpetrators had been justly put to death, and the sacred life of King James had been preserved. Rejoicing was ordered throughout the land for the miraculous deliverance of Scotland's anointed monarch, and for the downfall of the treacherous Ruthven brothers.

Such, at least, is the gist of the official narrative of what happened that day at Gowrie House. From the very beginning, there were many who simply never believed a word of it.

****

Despite the fact that the alleged would-be assassins were dead, Scots justice had to be seen to take its course. A suitably terrible example had to be sent out to any others who might be inclined to plot against the country's divinely ordained king. Consequently, the bodies of the Earl of Gowrie and the Master of Ruthven were transported from Perth to Edinburgh. Under an obscure but singularly gruesome refinement of Scots law, their corpses were propped up in an Edinburgh courtroom and the decomposing Ruthven brothers were duly found guilty of high treason.[10] The honours and titles of the family were forfeited and literally stricken from the record. The earl's lands passed to the king, who wasted little time in distributing them to those who had saved him that day in Perth, as he claimed. In due course, the monarch's defenders accumulated suitably exalted titles to go with their new lands: such were the rewards of loyalty. But for the Ruthvens, the penalties for alleged disloyalty were heavy. The family lost not only its lands and its titles, but also its very name; 'forasmuch as the surname of Ruthven has been so naturally bent ... to attempt most high and horrible treasons against his majesty and his most noble progenitor [Mary Queen of Scots]', it was ordered to be obliterated, and never to be borne again in Scotland.[11] Gowrie House was to be demolished and a memorial to the king's miraculous deliverance erected in its place. The two surviving Ruthven brothers, William and Patrick, were driven into exile, guilty by association of the treasons of their bloodline during three generations.

In practice, though, King James's bark proved to be far worse than his bite. Throughout his reign, the surname 'Ruthven' crops up many times in Scottish records. The more prominent Ruthvens simply ignored the injunction, and it was overturned in any case less than 40 years later. Members of the family went on to play notable parts in history under their own names. Patrick Ruthven, Earl of Forth and Brentford, served as captain-general of the Royalist armies in England during the civil war, and perhaps if he had remained in the chief command and not been replaced by King Charles I's impulsive nephew, Prince Rupert of the Rhine, then that war might have had a very different outcome.[12] That might also have been the case if a nephew of the last Earl of Gowrie and Sandy Ruthven had sustained perhaps one of the most brilliant military campaigns in European history: for one of their sisters was the mother of James Graham, Marquess of Montrose, one of Britain's greatest soldiers and the man who almost won Scotland for King Charles. Much later, a Ruthven won the Victoria Cross in the Sudan campaign of 1898, and became the highly respected Governor-General of Australia throughout World War II.[13] In 1945 he was rewarded with the restoration of the notorious title, becoming the first Earl of Gowrie of a new creation.[14] Deeply aware of his family's history, the earl fully appreciated the irony of the fact that he spent his later years as the governor of Windsor Castle, entrusted with protecting the Royal Family that his relatives might have tried (allegedly) to destroy; he even presided over the burial of King George VI, the great-grandson at eight removes of the king who might have tried (allegedly) to destroy the Ruthvens.[15] Even more ironic was the fact that to his close family, the new earl was known by a name with just a little resonance: they called him Sandy Ruthven.

In seventeenth-century Perth, the order to demolish Gowrie House was either never issued or was simply forgotten, although the turret chamber itself was removed some time after 1617 and the Black Turnpike was taken down before the 1750s.[16] King James himself revisited the house in 1617; his son, Charles I, was liberally entertained there in 1633, followed by his grandson Charles II in 1650.[17] At the end of the 17th century, Gowrie House even came within a hair's breadth of becoming the centrepiece of a relocated

University of St Andrew's. In 1697–8 the university seriously contemplated moving to Perth, which was less isolated, did not reek of decomposing herrings, and did not have townspeople with an 'aversion and hatred ... to learning and learned men', but the negotiations fell through.[18] The building later passed briefly into the ownership of James's notorious great-great-great-grandson, the Duke of Cumberland (the 'butcher of Culloden'). It then became an artillery barracks, and was for some time the headquarters of the Board of Ordnance in Scotland.[19] It was finally demolished in 1806–7, the stones going to shore up the embankment on the River Tay. The site was eventually filled not by some grand memorial to the preservation of King James, but by a set of somewhat bland Regency court buildings.[20] A faded bronze Victorian commemorative tablet, obscured by a large road sign indicating the way to the M90, now marks the spot where British history very nearly changed.

Even the remaining Ruthven brothers, the siblings and heirs of Earl John and Master Sandy, survived to tell the tale. William and Patrick escaped to England after the calamity at Gowrie House, but James seemed to pursue them like an avenging angel. One of his very first executive acts as King of England – on 27 April 1603, long before he even reached London – was to order the sheriffs of every county in the land to look out for, and arrest, the surviving Ruthven brothers.[21] Twenty-year-old William vanished, but 19-year-old Patrick was indeed duly arrested by the English authorities. Not for him, though, the traitor's death that might have been expected. Instead, Patrick Ruthven spent a reasonably comfortable 19 years in the Tower of London, and even obtained a substantial pension from both James and his successor. He became one of the most prominent alchemists of his day, corresponding on equal terms with some of the greatest intellectuals of the age, and after his release he moved in the highest circles of court life. By the 1640s, Patrick Ruthven was evidently considered respectable enough to address the English House of Lords on behalf of his infant and orphaned grand-daughter, the only child of his brilliant son-in-law, Sir Anthony Van Dyck, Charles I's court artist. A few years later, despite being in his mid-sixties and poverty stricken, Patrick even thought himself safe enough to contemplate signing a legal document with the title that he clearly believed by then to be rightfully his: 'Earl of Gowrie'.

But the corpses of Patrick's eldest brothers met with no such leniency. Instead, they suffered the traditional fate prescribed for traitors, regardless of the somewhat inconvenient fact that they were already dead.

The bodies were hanged, drawn, and quartered at the Mercat Cross in Edinburgh. The Edinburgh treasurer's records provide a chilling insight into the macabre process: 53s 4d for the poles on which the remains would be impaled, 21s 4d to the executioner for dismembering the bodies and sticking Edinburgh's chosen quarters (the heads) on their distinctly expensive poles, 12s 8d for a barrel of salt to preserve the quarters that were to be taken to Dundee, Stirling, and naturally enough, to Perth.[22] The quarters of the Ruthvens remained *in situ* for half a century,[23] a gruesome reminder to all who surveyed them of what had passed on 5 August 1600 in Gowrie House; or, at least, of what had allegedly passed there. There were to be other reminders of the 'official version' of the story, too. A royal proclamation ordained that for ever after, 5 August should be kept as a day of solemn commemoration for the deliverance of the king.[24] Of course, from 5 August 1603 it became official policy to commemorate it throughout England as well, notably by means of sermons delivered at court and Paul's Cross, but also through prayers in every parish church in the land.[25] The leading modern authorities on ceremony and ritual in 17th century Britain assume that the insistence on this was personal to James alone, and disappeared rapidly after his death. Perhaps it did in England (although the Anglican form of prayer for 5 August remained part of the liturgy until 1859), but in Scotland the custom was restored with Charles II; until well into the 1680s, the guns of the Scottish royal castles boomed out every August to commemorate the events at Gowrie House.[26] Thus the remembrance of what became known as 'the Gowrie Conspiracy' lived on alongside that of the other miraculous deliverance of King James from a devilish scheme to assassinate him, the 'Gunpowder Plot' of 5 November 1605.

****

The apocalypse at Gowrie House had not materialised out of thin air. Throughout the four decades before that afternoon in Perth, the relationship between the House of Stuart and the House of Ruthven had been fraught and murderous. Patrick, third Lord Ruthven, led the invasion of Mary Queen of Scots' private apartment that culminated in the murder of Rizzio. Patrick's son and successor, William, first Earl of Gowrie and Lord Treasurer of Scotland, like his father a staunch champion of the Presbyterian Kirk, had been one of the principal architects of the Queen of Scots' abdication and imprisonment. Then, in 1582, he dramatically kidnapped the 15-year-old King James in the so-called 'Raid of Ruthven' and held him under house arrest for almost a year, becoming the effective ruler of Scotland during that time. His first major act was to force James to exile the man who might have been his first homosexual lover, his cousin Esmé Stuart, first Duke of Lennox, perhaps the one man at that time who could have engineered the return of Scotland and its king to the Catholic faith. The first Earl of Gowrie was also the last known owner of 'the Casket Letters', the mysterious and long-sought-after documents that allegedly proved Queen Mary's complicity in the murder of Henry, Lord Darnley – her alcoholic and psychotic second husband, and the legal father of her son, James VI. In 1584 the first Earl was executed after being tricked into confessing to treason by a devious and amoral enemy. The 'Casket Letters' disappeared, and the originals have never been seen since.

Vengeance for the judicial murder of their father, the first Earl, by James VI's regime is one of the most plausible explanations for John and Alexander Ruthven concocting a conspiracy against the king. But other possible explanations for what happened in Perth on 5 August 1600 have been almost legion, have been circulating almost from that same day, and vary from the plausible to the surreal. Perhaps Gowrie sought to kidnap the king and seize control of the government, just as his father had done 18 years before. Perhaps he was supported in his plot by England, which was said by some to have provided a warship to assist. Perhaps the plot actually centred on the Queen, who was close to the Ruthvens: two of her ladies in waiting and closest confidantes were sisters of the two murdered youths. Or maybe Alexander, Master of Ruthven, hatched some sort of desperate scheme of which his brother knew nothing, so that when the Earl of Gowrie proclaimed his ignorance to Sir Thomas Erskine, he was actually telling the truth.

Then there are the alternative versions, the ones that make the king the villain rather than the victim, the Ruthvens the innocent targets of royal malice. Perhaps the king sought to cancel in one desperate stroke enormous debts that he owed to the Ruthven family. Maybe he wished to eliminate once and for all an overly powerful and arrogant dynasty of aristocrats who had publicly crossed him once too often, most recently when the Earl of Gowrie opposed extra taxes to bankroll an army intended to further the king's most cherished ambition of all, his succession to the English throne. Perhaps James believed that Gowrie or Alexander had been having an affair with the Queen, and was simply a cuckolded husband seeking revenge. Maybe he had made Alexander the target of his next homosexual dalliance, and been rebuffed. Perhaps James had been persuaded to bring down the Ruthvens by those who stood to benefit most, their own immediate neighbours, who coveted their extensive lands. William Murray, laird of Tullibardine, was said to have danced for joy when he learned of the slaughter at Gowrie House, and he became one of the greatest beneficiaries of their downfall.[27] For many of the direct descendants of the surviving Ruthvens, and those historians who supported their cause, there was no doubt in the matter: there was no 'Gowrie Conspiracy', only a conspiracy by King James to rid himself of the Earl of Gowrie and all the Ruthvens. For over 300 years there was no objective study of the events at Gowrie House. Those who wrote on the subject took sides, for or against the Ruthven brothers or the king, in an ongoing partisan battle. Even in the spring of 1944, as his adopted countrymen's troops fought their way through the jungles of New Guinea and his native country's troops prepared for D-Day, Lord Gowrie, the Governor-General of Australia, found time to state categorically that 'a grave injustice was done to the Gowries', this in response to a correspondent who had condemned 'this bloody minded assassin, James VI'. Three years later, Gowrie castigated the BBC for broadcasting an innocuous 20-minute children's programme about the conspiracy that was too favourable to the king's version of events for Gowrie's liking.[28]

Conspiracy theories are always attractive, and even in the 17th century, a conspiracy theory that connected royalty, sex, murder and the illegitimacy of the entire Stuart bloodline proved irresistible to many. But then, perhaps one of the greatest historians of them all, Lord Macaulay, whose opinion of the matter is given here for the first time, had the right of it by suggesting that on 5 August 1600, there was actually no conspiracy on either side, merely a disastrous misunderstanding:

> the King, whose cowardice and want of veracity was
> proverbial, became suddenly frightened, probably
> without sufficient cause, and for this reason or some
> other trifling circumstance finding himself separated
> from the rest of his suite and exaggerating danger to
> himself he called out for assistance[29]

There is evidence that can be brought forward to support each and every one of these theories, and all of it will be considered in due course. But in terms of firm, eye-witness evidence of what took place in the upper rooms of Gowrie House that day, the essential problem of the 'Gowrie Conspiracy' immediately presents itself. One, or maybe two, of those who knew what had happened were dead on the turnpike stair. Another of those who might have known, the motionless man in armour, was perhaps an invention, perhaps a stooge, or perhaps something else entirely; the question of his identity and role will be one of the keys to unravelling the truth about the events at Gowrie House. The penultimate first-hand witness, John Ramsay, would have known what he saw when he first entered the turret room, but he had a very obvious vested interest in presenting himself as the hero of the hour, and in agreeing with the version of events presented by the last, best, but ultimately least reliable witness of them all: King James VI himself.

Then there are the darker legends, some of which hovered on the fringes of the story of the Ruthvens even in their own days, long before 5 August 1600. Perhaps there was an elaborate Catholic plot to reconquer Scotland, and perhaps the Ruthvens were not quite the loyal sons of the Kirk that they seemed to be. Perhaps the two young Ruthven brothers were the puppets of far more powerful and unscrupulous forces: for example, Queen Elizabeth of England, the ageing 'Gloriana' herself, and her devious chief minister, Robert Cecil, who in 1600 were certainly pursuing their own secret agendas in Scotland. Perhaps the truth lies in those themes not normally considered in 'respectable' histories. Each of the last three heads of the House of Ruthven was accused of dabbling in the black arts, and the suspicions levelled at the last Earl of Gowrie were particularly damning. Papers bearing strange cabalistic symbols were found on his corpse, and he had been educated at the University of Padua, a hotbed of both the respectable sciences and their darker offshoots. The earl's younger brother, Patrick, certainly became an accomplished alchemist in due course. Perhaps magic and legend went hand in hand with freemasonry, then in its infancy in Scotland, which hovered secretively on the fringes of the Gowrie affair.

And perhaps, in the final analysis, there are still more sinister potential explanations for the events at Gowrie House, explanations which strike at the heart of the current British royal family's right to the throne and at the whole course of European history over the last 400 years.

****

Inevitably, the drama and mysteries surrounding the events of 5 August 1600 soon attracted the attention of writers, as they have done ever since: they even became the unlikely basis of an Icelandic saga.[30] In 1604 the English theatre company, the King's Men, staged two performances of a play called *Gowrie*. This was immediately banned by jittery Privy Councillors, presumably because it touched nerves that were still too raw. Shortly afterwards, the company's resident playwright and possible author of *Gowrie* (who might himself have played King James in that lost drama) drew once again on the events of 5 August 1600 as a principal source of inspiration for a new play. The premiere might even have taken place before the king himself, to mark the sixth anniversary of the royal deliverance. The playwright employed a number of themes apparently modelled on the official narrative of the 'Gowrie Conspiracy'. Following an invitation, a wise and well-loved king rides unexpectedly to the home of a nobleman who is treacherously plotting to kill him. The nobleman's family has a history of conspiracy against monarchs. The plotter rides ahead of the king, allegedly to see that all is in good order for his arrival. The king finds that hospitality is slow to appear, and when the feast finally takes place, the host's behaviour is peculiar, the atmosphere strained. A porter plays an important but ambiguous part in the action. Then a cry is heard: 'Murder! Treason!' As the king is killed, his noblemen mill around in confusion, eventually trying to rush the doors. Finally, and above all, in both fact and fiction we have a common motivation for the central character's actions. The noble conspirator has been driven to attempt the life of his king by a malevolent dark power: witchcraft.

This time, the playwright concealed these influences rather more deeply within his plot, and evidently did so with rather more subtlety than in *Gowrie*. Consequently, the new play ran no risk of being banned and never performed again, especially as both fact and fiction shared one influential character with the same name.

The name of the character was Lennox. The name of the play was *Macbeth*.[31]

CHAPTER ONE

THE WORD OF A KING

As the royal party rode back to Falkland in the evening of 5 August 1600, it is said that King James regaled all and sundry with his story of the pot of gold and the struggle in the turret chamber. The Laird of Moncreiff is alleged to have listened dutifully: 'A very wonderful story, your majesty', he said, 'if it be true'.[32] When five of the most respected Presbyterian ministers of Edinburgh heard the royal version of events on the following morning, they flatly refused both to believe it and to preach it from their pulpits.[33] From the very beginning, the royal version of the events in Perth suffered from a credibility problem of staggering proportions.

To counter such immediate and widespread scepticism, the spinning of the 'Gowrie House affair' began within hours. That night, in the run-down, crumbling surroundings of Falkland Palace, King James and his clerk, David Moysie, worked into the small hours to produce the first official account of the murderous events. This was sent in a letter to the secretary of the Privy Council, James Elphinstone, and reached Edinburgh by nine in the morning of the following day, Wednesday 6 August. The council immediately ordered a public proclamation of thanksgiving, which took place at one in the afternoon, followed by bells, bonfires, the firing of the castle guns, and 'the youths of the town gone out to skirmish for joy'.[34] Apart from any consequences of youthful skirmishing, the day was marred only by the ministers' point-blank refusal to follow the official line in their sermons, but James and his ministers temporarily had more urgent matters to attend to than the doubts of a bunch of obstreperous clerics. The king's letter to the Council no longer exists, but Elphinstone gave a verbal summary of it to George Nicolson, the English agent in Scotland, who in turn passed on the report in the letter he wrote later that afternoon to Robert Cecil, Queen Elizabeth's chief minister.[35] Nicolson's account provides all the essentials of the king's story: Sandy Ruthven speaking about the treasure trove to the king before the hunt; the arrival at Gowrie House; Sandy surreptitiously taking the king to the turret chamber, locking the doors behind him; the presence of the armoured man in the chamber. Then, Nicolson stated, Sandy grabbed the king:

> and drew his dagger, saying he had killed his father, and he would kill him! The king with good words and means sought to dissuade him, saying he was young when his father was executed … that he was innocent thereof; had restored his brother; and for amends, made him greater than he was; that if he killed him, he could not escape nor be his heir. That he presumed Mr Alexander had learned more divinity than to kill his Prince; assuring him, and faithfully promising him, that if he would leave off his enterprise, he would forgive him, and keep it secret, as a matter attempted upon heat and rashness only. That to these the Master replied, what was he preaching, that should not help him; he should die. And that therewith, he struck at the king, the king and he both going to the ground, that the Master called to the man there present to kill the king. That the man answered, he had neither heart nor hand; and yet is a very courageous man. That the king having no dagger, but in his hunting clothes with his horn, yet defended himself from the Master; and in struggling, got to the window, where he cried Treason.[36]

Nicolson went on to describe the death of Sandy, Gowrie's fight in the gallery and his death, and the townsmen's assault on the house. However, the Englishman's account of the later sequence of events is briefer and more confused than his summary of the earlier exchanges in the turret chamber. His letter is coloured by the fact that it is a secondhand recounting of a verbatim summary by another, and unsurprisingly Nicolson chose to concentrate on the aspects that his readers – Cecil, and, inevitably, Queen Elizabeth – would find the most intriguing: the alleged motive for the alleged murder attempt, and the performance *in extremis* of a fellow anointed monarch who also happened to be the likely next ruler of England. Even allowing for these issues of journalistic provenance, though, there are a number of problems and contradictions that emerge from the Nicholson letter, especially when it is compared with the other tellings of the story that emerged in the following days and weeks. Firstly, Nicolson makes no mention of the mysterious stranger and his 'pot of gold', found in a field by Sandy Ruthven; instead, his letter states that the treasure was found in a room of Gowrie House by the earl himself. This is astonishing, for both at the time and since, every single commentator on the events of 5 August has found the 'pot of gold' story one of the most memorable and stunningly implausible details in the story. If it had been in the original letter, Nicolson would surely have passed it on, rather than recounting an entirely different and equally unlikely version of the 'treasure' story: *which means that the king's first explanation of the day's events completely contradicts the reasons that he and others later gave for his going to Perth in the first place.* Secondly, Nicolson makes no mention of Sandy Ruthven's supposed insistence on his brother's ignorance of the treasure – how could he, if Gowrie himself had discovered it? Finally, Nicolson raises immediately one of the central mysteries of the 'Gowrie House' affair: who was the man in armour, and why did he refuse to help Sandy Ruthven kill the king? Above all, if no one – least of all James – actually knew who the armoured man was, how could the king claim that he was 'yet a very courageous man'?

For all the potential difficulties of Nicolson's letter, its chosen emphasis undoubtedly reflects King James's own, and that emphasis pervades the gathering of evidence, and the further recountings of the story, that took place in the following weeks and months. Quite simply, the James of the Nicolson letter is the hero of the day. He tries to face down his murderer with logic, kingly dignity and magnanimity; when that fails, he fearlessly engages his assailant in a combat to the death. From the very beginning, this interpretation raised more than a few eyebrows. But it set the parameters for the evidence-gathering that followed, for contradicting the king's version of events could have been interpreted as *lèse-majesté*, or worse. Above all, it explains why the armoured man was so crucial to the king's story. Whoever he was, he was the only witness to what was said and done in the turret chamber: therefore, only he could corroborate the whole of the king's version of events, and James's heroic portrayal of himself. But for those who have damned King James over the years, it has proved very easy to extend this argument to its logical but cynical conclusion. James needed a third man in the turret chamber, for without corroboration from such a witness, it would be perfectly possible for people to visualise the king's motives for being alone with Sandy Ruthven: they ran the gamut from male rape to premeditated murder. *Ergo,* whispered the cynics, James had to have a witness in the right place at the right time, to listen to the 'right' version of events and recount them in the 'right' way; in other words, there had to be a man in armour, even if he had to be invented. Consequently, the five days immediately following the slaughter at Gowrie House saw an increasingly frantic search to establish the identity of the armoured man.

As Edinburgh celebrated on 6 August, and Nicolson sat down to write his letter to Cecil, the king's control of the information agenda was already weakening. In Perth, the town council could not have known of James's Falkland letter, on which Nicolson based his, so they were probably largely ignorant of his version of events when they assembled to interview a crucial witness. This was Thomas Cranstoun, who described himself as a servant of the dead Earl of Gowrie; in fact, he had been the earl's master stabler. Cranstoun was the man who told Gowrie, Lennox, Mar and the others that the king had left Gowrie House and was riding back to Falkland: plainly, if there really had been a plot to kill the king, this attempt to confuse and misdirect his attendants would have been central to it, so Cranstoun was a prime suspect. Cranstoun claimed that his report of the king's departure was merely passing on a rumour he had heard in the house. However, he could not deny that he had then helped Gowrie to free himself from a fight with some Murrays at the gate, although according to him, he had assumed that the earl was the victim of an unprovoked attack. Gowrie then told him 'he would go in to his own house, or die by the way', but as they reached the turnpike they saw Sandy Ruthven at its foot, 'whether dead or hurt he knew not'. According to Cranstoun, Gowrie shouted 'Up the stair!', and they ran up to find themselves facing Sir Thomas Erskine, John Ramsay and Dr Herries, all with their swords drawn. Cranstoun admitted that he and Gowrie had fought the king's men, but he claimed ignorance of any prior knowledge of a conspiracy, stating that he had not seen the brothers for the fortnight before 5 August.[37]

On the following day, Thursday 7 August, the Privy Council convened at Falkland Palace. The likes of the Earl of Montrose, Lord Chancellor and Lord President, and the Elphinstone brothers, Alexander and James, Lord Treasurer and Secretary respectively, had hurried there from Edinburgh to join Lennox and Mar. The government of Scotland was coming together in a crisis: after all, who could guarantee that the events at Gowrie House had not been simply the first move in a larger game, and that there was not still an ongoing threat to the king? Access to James had already been restricted, and the security around him increased. The minutes of the 7 August Privy Council meeting made the inevitable denunciation of 'a most horrible and traitorous conspiracy', from which

James had been delivered 'most miraculously'. More practically, they proceeded to order the preservation of the bodies of Gowrie and the Master of Ruthven, a ban on anyone named Ruthven approaching the royal presence, the confiscation of Gowrie House and the other Ruthven properties, and the placing of the Ruthven estates under royal control until a decision had been taken about their future.[38] Royal agents must have searched the Ruthven residences during the following days, but they evidently discovered no incriminating evidence within them. Nevertheless, the immediate and necessary reactive measures had been taken, the government was back in control, and the enquiry into what had actually happened at Gowrie House could now begin.

On Saturday, 9 August, the councillors then present at Falkland interrogated James Wemyss of Bogie, a cousin of the two dead Ruthven brothers. Wemyss had been hunting with the earl in Strathbraan during July, and was presumably called before the Council in the hope that he might have heard treasonable words uttered by his cousins during that time. In this respect, Wemyss disappointed: he had seen and heard nothing that suggested a conspiracy. However, he provided titbits that proved vital to the gloss that the crown and its propagandists were to place on the posthumous reputation of the last Earl of Gowrie. One day, Wemyss said, they had come across a dead adder, and the earl remarked that if it had not been dead, he would have been able to immobilise it simply by uttering a magical Hebrew word. On another occasion, Gowrie had apparently foretold the death by hanging of a man who had insulted him. Wemyss claimed that he warned the earl of the dangers of such practices, but was told 'he would speak them to none, but to great scholars ... [he] would not reveal the same again, seeing he knew they would be evil interpreted amongst the common sort'.[39] James Wemyss had provided James and his government with another piece of their jigsaw: if Wemyss was telling the truth, then the Earl of Gowrie had not been the staunchly Presbyterian darling of the Kirk that he had seemed to be, but a practitioner of satanic black arts. The story possessed an attractive inner logic of its own, for Gowrie's father and grandfather had both been accused of being warlocks, and it placed the events at Gowrie House firmly in the context of one of King James's most passionately-held beliefs, the extermination of witchcraft in Scotland.

****

On Monday, 11 August, King James VI returned in triumph to his capital city. He rode from Falkland to the Fife shore, crossed the Firth of Forth by ship, and landed on the sands of Leith. The population came out to meet him 'in arms, with great joy and shooting of muskets and shaking of pikes'; the councillors came down to Leith in their best armour (or paid a £20 fine if they did not) and paid for drummers to precede the royal party.[40] James made a glorious ceremonial entrance into Edinburgh itself, and at the city's market cross, he sat down to listen to the Presbyterian minister Patrick Galloway preach a sermon on the 124th Psalm. In fact, the psalm itself was secondary to Galloway's and James's purpose, for this sermon was to be the second public exposition of the king's story of Gowrie House, duly expanded with corrections, clarifications, and one almighty new bombshell. Presumably using Wemyss's testimony as his evidence, Galloway denounced the Earl of Gowrie as a sorcerer, and added an entirely new dimension to the unfolding story by accusing Gowrie of being a secret Catholic. Or as Galloway put it: 'A deep dissembled hypocrite! A profound atheist! An incarnate devil, in the coat of an angel! … a conjurer of devils [who had lived] out of the country, in haunting with papists, yea the Pope himself … '.[41] Galloway then told the story of the events of the previous Tuesday, beginning with Sandy Ruthven's arrival at Falkland. This time, there was no explanation for Sandy enticing James to Perth – no mention of treasure at all, be it in a field or in Gowrie House. Otherwise, Galloway added a few domestic details for his audience of townsfolk, such as the fact that the meal belatedly laid on for the king at Gowrie House had been 'a cold dinner, yea, a very cold dinner!' Then there was the high drama to horrify the listeners:

> As an innocent lamb, he was closed up between two
> hungry lions, thirsting for his blood; and four locks
> between him and his friends … Alexander had taken him
> by the gorget, and had held the dagger to his breast, not
> two inches from it, so that there was scarce two inches
> between his death and his life[42]

Of course, Galloway's King James was no coward, and was not fazed by such mortal danger; and even if he actually had been a fazed coward on 5 August, Galloway was hardly going to say so on the 11th, when the same king was sitting a few feet away from him and had presumably dictated much, if not all, of the sermon's content. So Galloway went on to elaborate on the original account's version of what James had said to Sandy Ruthven. According to the minister, the king reminded Sandy of his Christian upbringing, warning him that Robert Rollock, his old tutor at Edinburgh University, would have looked on regicide with disapproval.[43] Then Galloway let slip another possible and momentous motive for the Ruthven brothers' actions, in words that King James was supposed to have said to Sandy: 'suppose you take my life, neither you nor your brother will be king after me; yea, the subjects of Scotland will root you out, and all your name!' In Galloway's version of the story, the royal words softened the heart of the traitor, who begged forgiveness. Sandy then left to seek advice from Gowrie, who was implacable and 'from whom he received commission to dispatch him [James] quickly'.[44] Perhaps even some of the listeners in Edinburgh's market square immediately realised the implications of Galloway's new sequence of events. Firstly, the king must have been alone for a short time in the turret chamber with the mysterious armoured man. Secondly, it was now Gowrie himself who provided the direct order to kill the king: in the Falkland letter, there had been no direct evidence of treason on the earl's part. The body of the earl was being preserved at Perth specifically so that it could be propped up in a treason trial.[45] If Gowrie himself had been a traitor, rather than just his brother, the Ruthven lands could be forfeited and redistributed to others, but for that to happen, there would need to be rather more evidence of treason against him than the king's letter and the depositions of Cranstoun and Wemyss had so far provided.

Galloway's next remarks also differed from, or added to, the version in the Falkland letter. In the sermon, Sandy returns to the chamber and declares that the king must die after all. He has brought garters with him to bind James's hands, 'to the intent, no doubt, that he being bound, they might have strangled him' and dumped his body in a pit prepared for the purpose.[46] Once again, the king plays the melodramatic hero: 'I was born a free prince! I have lived hitherto a free prince! I shall never die bound!' – and with that, the king wrestles with and overcomes the villainous Master of Ruthven, who is therefore subdued *before* John Ramsay bursts into the room and stabs him. Even Galloway must have realised that his audience would find this difficult to swallow, given the ungainly and knock-kneed appearance of the monarch sitting directly in front of them, so he admitted that Sandy was 'an able young man' with twice or three times the king's strength and brazened it out by attributing James's victory to a miracle, thereby explicitly turning those who doubted the royal narrative into doubters of divine intervention itself.[47] Galloway went on to describe the attempt to mislead the rest of the hunting party by claiming that James had already left Gowrie House, and the Earl of Gowrie's desperate ascent of the black turnpike and his assault on the courtiers in the gallery. A new detail was added: as Gowrie fought John Ramsay, the latter cried out ' "Fie upon thee, cruel traitor! Have you not done evil enough else? Thou has gotten the king's life else, and would thou have ours too?" At which speech, he drew a little back; and in back-going, he got the strike whereof he died.'[48]

This was all good, dramatic stuff, delivered by a consummately professional sermoniser. But it was as nothing to the peroration, and the card that Patrick Galloway had up his sleeve. Almost certainly, he and the king would have realised that at least some in the audience (not to mention the world at large) were still sceptical, and thinking such thoughts as 'But what about the armoured man? Come to that, just who was the armoured man?' In the five days since the king's letter had reached Edinburgh, speculation about his identity had been rife. At first, he had been identified as Robert Oliphant, 'a black, grim man', but it had been proved that Oliphant was not in Perth that day. Then the armoured man was thought to be someone called Leslie, and then Younger, a servant of Gowrie's, but the latter had been in Dundee on the fifth. He was on his way to Falkland to prove his innocence when he ran into a search party seeking to arrest him: they pursued him, and killed Younger in a cornfield.[49] James was said to have been angry that was not taken alive.[50] This is plausible, because the king desperately needed to produce the armoured man to corroborate his story; but he needed an 'armoured man' who could be relied upon to do just that, and it is equally possible that Younger died because his mouth was not quite reliable enough. Galloway knew all this, and he knew that his audience knew. As he admitted at the very end of the sermon, there were 'rumours that go [around], that the king was a doer, and not a sufferer; a pursuer, and not pursued'. But Galloway had the answer. His bombshell was ready, and now he delivered it: *he knew who the armoured man was.*

> This is the very truth of the fact, which I have received
> (not by the King's Majesty) but by him who should have
> been the doer of the turn. He is living yet; he is not
> slain; a man well enough known to this town: Andrew
> Henderson, chamberlain to my Lord of Gowrie.[51]

Galloway could do better still. Not only did he know it was Henderson, he had a letter from him to prove it, and he even invited sceptics to come and examine the handwriting. Galloway then quoted at length from Henderson's letter. The chamberlain claimed that Gowrie had commanded him to ride to Falkland with Sandy Ruthven, and later that morning, Sandy told him to go back to Perth to tell the earl that the king was coming. At Gowrie House, the earl ordered Henderson to put on armour and follow the Master of Ruthven's instructions. Sandy took him up the black turnpike, through three second-floor rooms, and locked him in the turret chamber. According to Galloway's account of Henderson's alleged words, he now became suspicious that there might be 'some evil against the king', and took to his knees to pray. Soon afterwards, the Master entered the chamber, and from then on, Galloway said, Henderson's account followed that which he had already given, except for the manner of the 'armoured man's' escape: while James and Sandy were wrestling, Henderson had slipped down the black turnpike.

If James and Galloway hoped that the sudden production of Andrew Henderson would swing public opinion in their direction, they were rapidly disappointed. To begin with, Galloway was generally regarded as a 'flattering preacher', a royal chaplain and thus a royal mouthpiece, and could be condemned as a turncoat to boot; he had once been the minister of Perth, and a supporter of the newly dead Earl of Gowrie's long-dead father. Galloway also knew Henderson of old, and it was immediately suspected that Henderson had volunteered to come forward in return for a promise of pardon.[52] Moreover, Henderson's supposed account raised more questions than it answered – for example, why was he there in the first place, why did he know nothing of what was to happen, and above all, why did he do nothing when it happened? Then there was the need to corroborate the account of the corroborator, or even his very existence: in other words, someone needed to have seen Henderson, either in the turret chamber or making his escape, because if he went down the black turnpike, he would surely have encountered John Ramsay, at least, coming up it, even if he did not encounter any of the other courtiers on the stairs or in the yard. But these problems were as nothing alongside the two perceived flaws in identifying Henderson as the man in armour. Firstly, the initial description of that man had been categorical: he was black and grim. Henderson was short, red-faced, brown-haired and hangdog. Secondly, King James had not known the identity of the armoured man – that much was clear from his own Falkland letter. According to one account, he was asked categorically during those few days after 5 August 1600, when many names were being bandied around Scotland, ' "whether Henderson was the man?" Answered, that "It was not he, [for] he [James] knew that smaick [= *face*] well enough" '.[53] But if Andrew Henderson was not, or could not have been, the armoured man in the turret chamber, why was he suddenly saying that he was, and why were King James VI and his ministers so keen to agree with such a pathetically implausible candidate for the role?

****

Tuesday 12 August was exactly one week after the cataclysm at Gowrie House, and it was the day on which the full, majestic panoply of Scottish government and law was deployed against plotters and doubters alike. The Privy Council met at Holyrood Palace, and denounced several of Gowrie's friends and retainers for treason: George Craigengelt, the steward of Gowrie House; Harry and Alexander Ruthven, the earl's cousins; Hew Moncreiff and Patrick Eviot, kinsman and neighbour respectively; and finally, Andrew Henderson, the reputed armoured man himself. The five Presbyterian ministers of Edinburgh, who had doubted the veracity of James's story from the beginning, were to be silenced. They were not to speak in public on pain of death, and were to remove themselves to at least 10 miles from Edinburgh within 48 hours.[54] On the following day, a similar injunction was issued against anyone who bore the surname of Ruthven, though the mind boggles at the enforcement issues involved in checking that no one within a 10-mile radius of the capital bore the reviled name.

A few days later, the next series of witness depositions were taken, and these were followed in short order by the trials of those regarded as the Ruthvens' chief accomplices. On 16 August, George Craigengelt was examined at Falkland, having presumably surrendered himself to the authorities. He began his testimony by swearing that he had never heard the Earl of Gowrie suggesting that he wished to avenge his father's death; indeed, he and the earl's tutor, William Rynd, had agreed to persuade him to keep the king's favour, 'in respect of jealousy that was among them'. Craigengelt denied that any messenger had come to the Earl of Gowrie with messages from court, and that he had provided a meal for such a man. This denial was undoubtedly in response to the rumours that Patrick Galloway had mentioned in his sermon, the rumours which made James the instigator of the events at Gowrie House. It was being whispered that letters had been sent to summon the Ruthvens to Falkland; if Sandy Ruthven had gone there by royal command, the king's story simply could not be true, and therefore James VI, King of Scots, had to be a murderer. Craigengelt claimed that he knew nothing of Sandy and Henderson going to Falkland, and that he had been woken from his sick bed by other servants who told him that the king had come to Perth. As steward of Gowrie House, the preparation of a meal was Craigengelt's responsibility, but he found the kitchen empty of meat. He recounted how he frantically gathered together enough food to provide a respectable meal, and how he then met Sandy Ruthven on the stairs. Craigengelt asked him where he had been, and Sandy replied 'An errand not far off'. When Craigengelt asked why the king had come to Perth, he was told 'Robert Abercromby, that false knave, had brought the king there, to cause his Majesty [to] take order for his debt'. Abercromby was James's saddler: the idea of the King of Scots running an errand as his saddler's debt collector is as ludicrous as the 'pot of gold' story, but perhaps Sandy Ruthven thought it was a tale good enough to silence his inquisitive steward. Craigengelt then claimed that he was dining with the Erskine servants when they heard a tumult outside. Craigengelt armed himself with a two-handed sword from Gowrie's chamber, and ran out into the yard. There, he met the earl, who was running back towards the house with some 10 or 12 men at his back, all with their swords drawn. Craigengelt responded to Thomas Cranstoun's cry of 'keep the gate!' by rushing to secure the back entrance into the yard.[55]

His actions, and especially his wielding of the sword, doomed George Craigengelt. On 22 August, he, Cranstoun, and John Barron or MacDuff, the steward of the Ruthven hunting lodge at Trochrie, were put on trial at Perth. Craigengelt was accused of having 'besieged' the king in Gowrie House for over two hours, the time that he had held the back gate with the assistance of 'ten or twelve rascals'. Cranstoun was accused of spreading the rumour that the king had left, and of fighting the king's men in the gallery. Barron was charged with telling Gowrie that his brother was dead, inciting him to go back to the house, and then with taking part in the fight in the gallery. There was ample eye-witness evidence that all three men had been carrying drawn swords in the vicinity of the king. Under several acts of the Scottish Parliament, their actions were undoubtedly treason, and the verdicts were never in doubt.[56] On the following day, a Saturday, the three men were hanged in the market square of Perth. Cranstoun is reported to have made a speech from the scaffold:

'I have been taken', he said, 'for a traitor, but I thank God, I am not one. I was stabbed through with a sword, at this last tumult; and now I am to be hanged'. He conceived a fervent prayer, at what time, in the midst of a cloudy darkness, glanced a sudden brightness, to the astonishment of the beholders.[57]

****

As more and more information emerged, so the doubts about the royal story increased. As Nicolson, the English ambassador, noted on 21 August, 'the more the king deals in the matter, the greater do the doubts rise with the people what is the truth of the king's part'.[58] The royal government urgently needed to produce strong new evidence, both to support its case and to find proof of treason against the Earl of Gowrie, and James's ministers were attempting to do exactly that. At Falkland on the previous day, a group of privy councillors headed by the Chancellor, Montrose, interrogated two particularly crucial witnesses. William Rynd had been Gowrie's personal tutor since he was a child. He had schooled him at Perth, attended on him at Edinburgh University, and then accompanied him to Padua. If anyone knew what was in Gowrie's mind, it should have been William Rynd. He was asked first about the sinister 'magical' papers that were found on the earl's body. Rynd testified that Gowrie always carried these close to his person, and when Rynd had asked him what purpose they served, the response had been a testy 'Can you not let them be? They do you no evil.' The tutor tried to hide the papers and even considered burning them, but he had feared the earl's reaction if he did so. The interrogation then moved on to the events at Perth. According to Rynd, on the evening of Monday 4 August Gowrie held a conference with his brother, Rynd, and Andrew Henderson. However, Rynd had no idea that Sandy Ruthven and Henderson had subsequently gone to Falkland, and claimed that he believed Gowrie was lying to him when he claimed to have no prior knowledge of the king's arrival at Perth.

in his opinion, the Master could not have drawn the king to my lord's house, without my lord's knowledge; and that when he heard the tumult, he was resolved in his heart the Master had done his Majesty wrong; and that no true Christian can think otherwise, but that it was an high treason attempted against his Highness by the Master and the Lord.[59]

The distinguished interrogators moved on from Rynd to Andrew Henderson. His testimony was potentially the most crucial piece of evidence of all, for the 'armoured man' was the only witness to what had been said and done in the turret chamber. Henderson was first asked what Gowrie had said to him in the evening of 4 August. He stated that the earl ordered him to go to Falkland with the Master of Ruthven and another servant, Andrew Ruthven, and to ride back with whatever message Sandy gave him. They left Perth at about four in the morning, reaching Falkland about three hours later. On arriving, Sandy Ruthven went immediately to speak privately with the king, and then told Henderson to ride back to Gowrie House to warn the earl that James would be coming. Henderson duly got back to Perth at about ten and reported to the earl, passing on the Master's request that he should prepare a dinner. Gowrie was keen to know how James had got on with his brother, and was told that the king had placed his hand affectionately on Sandy's shoulder. Gowrie also wanted to know the size and composition of the hunting party that accompanied the king, and was told that the Duke of Lennox was part of it. At about eleven the earl told Henderson to put on his armour, 'for he had a Highland man to take'; Henderson believed that this was a man named Mackildouy, who was to be captured at Archibald MacBreck's house in the Shoegait. Henderson then claimed that at about noon, he had been seconded to serve dinner to Gowrie and his house guests, as Craigengelt was ill. This he did, but when the second course was being served, Sandy Ruthven came into the hall. Gowrie and 'the whole company' then rose and went out to the South Inch: 'and he [Henderson] followed my lord to the Inch, and returning back with his Majesty to the lodging, being directed to get drink'. According to Henderson, Sandy Ruthven then sent him to William Rynd to get the key of the gallery chamber; Gowrie spoke to Sandy; Gowrie sent Thomas Cranstoun with an order for Henderson to go up to the gallery and the turret chamber beyond, followed by a direct order from the earl for Henderson to do his brother's bidding. This, Henderson claimed, was how he found himself in the turret chamber, where Sandy locked him in with the words 'You must go in here, and tarry until I come back; for I will take the key with me.'[60]

In this testimony, Andrew Henderson made no mention of what he thought or did while waiting for the Master of Ruthven to return. However, his account of what happened when Sandy and the king entered the chamber corroborates the king's account. Sandy covered his head, held a dagger to James's breast, and said that the king must die. But according to Henderson, the dagger was his own, that Sandy Ruthven had snatched from him, and Henderson claimed that he then knocked it out of Sandy's hand. (When told of this contradiction, King James was said not to have any recollection of Henderson doing this.)[61] Henderson then recorded the king's attempt to mollify the Master of Ruthven's anger, followed by Sandy's departure to consult with his brother – *trusting Henderson, the man who had supposedly just knocked the dagger out of his hand, to guard the king*. When they were alone, James asked Henderson 'what he was', and was told 'a servant of my lord's'. The king asked if Gowrie intended to harm him, to which Henderson said he replied 'As God that judge my soul, I shall die first'. Sandy Ruthven then returned, bearing a garter and saying that the king must die after all. Henderson claimed that he had snatched the garter from Sandy's hand, had tried to pull the Master off the king as they wrestled, and that he had then opened the window, allowing the king to call out for rescue. Henderson saw John Ramsay enter the chamber and strike Sandy Ruthven, but he then hurried 'privily' down the Black Turnpike and made his way home. His wife asked him 'What the fray meant?' to which Henderson said he replied, 'That the King's Majesty would have been twice sticked *[= stabbed]*, had not he released him'.[62]

On 22 August, William Rynd was re-examined and asked two further questions. Had the Earl of Gowrie ever given his opinion about 'the duty of a wise man in the execution of a high enterprise'? Such a seemingly bizarre question, completely unconnected to Rynd's previous testimony, can only have been asked because his interrogators already knew the answer, but wanted it recorded under oath for public consumption. Rynd replied that while they were abroad, Gowrie had commented on this very issue several times, and had once said that 'he was not a wise man, that having intended the execution of a high and dangerous purpose, communicate the same to any but to himself; because keeping it to himself, it could not be discovered or disappointed'. The second question that Rynd was asked was rather less opaque. He was given Andrew Henderson's deposition to read, and was then asked if it tallied with his memory of events. Rynd declared 'upon his salutation, that he believes Andrew Henderson has declared the circumstances truly'.[63]

These testimonies of Rynd and Henderson are problematic on several counts. Firstly, Calderwood and the English ambassador, Nicholson, were almost certainly right in assuming that Rynd had been tortured beforehand: according to Calderwood, he had been 'tortured in the boots ... so that his legs were crushed'.[64] This might have a particular bearing on his answer to the supplementary question about Gowrie's attitude to conspiracies. Regardless of whether Rynd was speaking the truth or saving himself from further torture by following a script, the result was the same. By emphasising Gowrie's secrecy, the government now had a plausible explanation for the complete failure to find any evidence of accomplices and co-conspirators of the Ruthven brothers; alternatively, of course, if the government for its own purposes wanted to conceal the inconveniently powerful identities of genuine accomplices, then Rynd's testimony served the purpose equally well. Secondly, both Rynd and Henderson had strong motives for saying exactly what their distinguished listeners wanted to hear. Rynd would have been desperate to clear himself of any prior knowledge of the plot: as Gowrie's confidante and mentor, he was plainly a prime suspect to have been a leading light in any deep-rooted conspiracy. If Henderson was indeed the man in the turret chamber, he had every incentive to clear himself of treason, and to agree with the version of events that the king had already given; in the event, Henderson went much further, transforming himself into the king's heroic deliverer. Thirdly, though, Henderson certainly did not agree wholly with the king's story. His suggestion that the king *had* actually left Gowrie House, albeit briefly, and that he, Henderson, had taken first the dagger and then the garter out of Sandy's hand, seemed flatly to contradict the official line.

Finally, both Rynd's and Henderson's emphasis on the earl's foreknowledge of Sandy's intentions indicates the subtle shift that had taken place, over a fortnight after the slaughter at Gowrie House. As in all murder cases down the centuries, the initial emphasis was on rounding up the suspected accessories, getting to the bottom of what had happened, and trying to discover why it had happened. Given the exalted nature of the intended 'murder victim', there had been other initial emphases, too: the need to ensure that the king and his government were fully in control of the country, and then the perceived need for a monarch to be seen to act decisively against treasonable conspirators. (Hence the rapid executions of Craigengelt, Cranstoun and Barron: James needed a few quick hangings to maintain a reputation for toughness in his own country, among his fellow royals throughout Europe, and among those in England who might be judging his credentials to be their next monarch.) But by 20 August, other priorities were becoming more important. For one thing, the king's story had to be shored up in the face of rampant scepticism, and the evidence of Rynd and Henderson provided additional support to the official narrative, despite the strong doubts about their veracity. Rynd's second examination, where he corroborated Henderson's account under oath, might well have been an attempt to gloss over the more problematic aspects of the latter; Rynd's insistence that the Ruthvens had no accomplices also had the incidental (or deliberate?) effect of exculpating Andrew Henderson, whose self-proclaimed ignorance of what was to happen in the turret thus became just a little less incredible. The other priority governing the thoughts of the king and his ministers was the need to convict the Earl of Gowrie of treason. Only by doing so could they take over the Ruthven lands and distribute them to deserving allies, so Rynd's and Henderson's testimonies about the earl's foreknowledge were godsends. Even if no treason at all had been committed at Gowrie House, it was now politically essential to prove that it had been.

****

At the end of August, the official narrative of what was said to have happened at Gowrie House belatedly appeared in print, under the title *Gowrie's Conspiracie. A Discourse of the Unnaturall and Vyle Conspiracie, attempted against the King's Majesties Person, at Sanct-Johnstoun, upon Twysday the Fifth of August 1600.*[65] This pamphlet, which James's government attempted to elevate into 'a kind of quasi-biblical truth',[66] drew together the evidence that had already emerged, cleared up some of the perceived inconsistencies, but also raised a number of new questions. According to *Gowrie's Conspiracie*, it was with 'a very dejected countenance, his eyes ever fixed upon the earth' that Sandy Ruthven told the king of the stranger with the pot of gold. James initially proposed sending a commission to the Perth magistrates to look into the matter, but Sandy insisted on him coming in person. James thought about the matter during the hunt, ignoring Sandy's insistence that he should ride to Perth at once. When they eventually began the journey towards Gowrie House, Sandy suggested that the king should send back all his attendants, especially Lennox and Mar, and go on with just a handful of servants. James was now becoming suspicious, especially when Sandy told him to tell no one about the treasure and to come alone to the room where the 'Catholic agent' and the 'pot of gold' had been concealed. Despite his growing doubts – according to himself, at any rate – the King of Scots rode on, 'betwixt trust and distrust'.[67]

Again according to the published narrative, at dinner the Earl of
Gowrie seemed nervous and preoccupied, often leaving the room
briefly or muttering to servants. Sandy then got the king to send
Gowrie away to toast the rest of the hunting party. After the earl left,
Sandy led the king out into the hall and up the stair, ignoring James's
order to send for Sir Thomas Erskine to accompany them. They went
through the second floor rooms, with Sandy locking each door behind
them, until they reached the turret chamber, where a man 'with a very
abased countenance' was standing, a dagger at his belt.[68] The following
sequence of events, and the words spoken, corresponded to the versions
that had already appeared, up to the moment when Sandy Ruthven left
the room. Then, so *Gowrie's Conspiracie* claimed, James asked the
armoured man if he was there to kill him. 'As the Lord should judge
him', 'Henderson' replied, 'he was never made acquainted with that
purpose, but that he was put in there perforce and the door lockt upon
him a little space before his Majesty's coming'. James asked him to open
a window, which he did. Sandy Ruthven now returned, and so began the
fight between the Master of Ruthven and the King of Scots. The door
between the turret and gallery chambers had been left open by Sandy
when he returned, and the fight spilled out into the larger room. It was
there that John Ramsay found them, and there that he stabbed the
Master of Ruthven. According to this narrative, the wounding of the
Master was 'Henderson's cue to scuttle to safety down the Black
Turnpike'.[69] Henderson's own deposition was printed as an appendix,
along with those of Rynd and Wemyss of Bogie. Knowing full well that
readers would immediately spot the discrepancies between Henderson's
deposition and the king's version, the editor confronted the issue head
on: 'he may understand the same to be uttered by the deponent in his
own behalf, for obtaining of his Majesty's princely grace and favour'.[70]
In other words, even the definitive official account of the events at
Gowrie House had to admit that Andrew Henderson was exaggerating
his role in order to obtain a pardon; and as cynics remarked at the time
and since, if Henderson made up his 'disarming' of the Master of
Ruthven, what else had he invented? The French ambassador in
London, de Boissize, reported the response to the official narrative in
Scotland and London: 'ministers preach that it was a set-up to rid
himself of the said earl and his brother because they were among the
most zealous in their religion'. The common people of Scotland were
openly voicing their disbelief, while even Queen Elizabeth herself told
James's envoy that she found his version of events simply unbelievable.[71]

Royal solidarity went only so far, and besides, Elizabeth had greatly liked the Earl of Gowrie.

****

Over five days, from 23 September onwards, an extraordinary spectacle was played out within the walls of St John's Kirk in Perth. From seven until nine in the morning, then from ten until midday, and finally from two until six, a steady procession of men made their way into the church. Quarter by quarter, suburb by suburb, every male inhabitant of Perth was summoned by beat of drum to attend a special commission drawn from their own town council. By the end of the five days, depositions had been taken from some 355 men. Taken together, they provided a record of what every man in Perth was doing on the afternoon of 5 August 1600.[72] They also provided the evidence for the last, and perhaps most dangerous, threat to King James's life on that day: the attempt by the Perth mob to storm Gowrie House.

The questions posed by the commissioners were hardly neutral. First, the witnesses were asked if they had any foreknowledge of the Ruthven brothers' 'wild and unnatural treason', and if they went to Gowrie House in armour 'to assist that filthy act'. The tribunal wanted to know of any 'irreverent' comments about the king or his servants, and if anyone was in any doubt about the definition of irreverence, they provided helpful examples: 'Green-coats! Bloody butchers! Traitors! Murderers! You shall all die! Give us forth our Provost!' Had anyone cried for fire or powder? Had anyone seen a roof-beam being brought to batter down the door of Gowrie House? Finally, there was a catch-all: did anyone know anything else at all about what had happened that day?[73] Unsurprisingly, it is difficult to read the responses of Perth's townsmen without suspecting that some, at least, were attempting to present themselves retrospectively as unimpeachably loyal supporters of the king. John Lawrie, for example, claimed that all the townspeople were crying 'The king is well', and that he replied 'God be thanked', but Lawrie had good reason to establish his royalist credentials: the gunpowder that Gowrie's supporters tried to use to blow their way through the gate had been 'stolen' from his shop.[74] Other townsmen of Perth were probably being distinctly 'economical with the truth', and some undoubtedly saw this as a perfect opportunity to settle old scores with neighbours they disliked. Even so, the assembled testimony is so extensive that it creates a vivid picture of what must have happened in the streets of Perth on the afternoon of Tuesday 5 August.

There was the constant ringing of the town bell, its alarm signal summoning the citizens to defend their king against their provost, or vice-versa.[75] There were the rumours, spreading like wildfire: the king was dead; Gowrie was dead; the 'green coats' had killed the provost. There was Alexander Ruthven of Freeland, running through the streets with his sword drawn, breaking into John Lawrie's shop, and crying 'Fie for powder! He is dead! He is slain!' and 'Thieves! You are unworthy of such a provost! ... If he [the king] lives, he shall remember this day!' Then there were the bailiffs of Perth, trying desperately to restrain and disperse the mob (or so they said). There were the cries of women, too, such as the screams that Violet Ruthven directed towards the king's hunting party: 'Bloody butchers! ... Thieves! Limmers! Traitors! and Bloody Thieves! ... Bloody traitors, that have murdered the innocents! Green coats!' There were those who cowered in their houses, like Alexander Peebles, who watched Gowrie's servants arming, heard the women shouting, and testified that either Thomas Bissett or James Bower had cried, ' "Green coats! We will have amends of you!" wagging their hands up, saying "you shall pay for it!" ' There were the moments of farce in the midst of tragedy. Andrew Gellatlie heard the bell and went to get his weapon, but his wife had the house key, and by the time he found her, it was all over. Thomas Elgin, Andrew Gibb and John Robertson slept through the whole of the most dramatic event in the history of their town; Robertson was a maltman, so his slumber might have been induced by over-zealous sampling of his product.[76]

The most important evidence came from those townsmen who were either in Gowrie House to begin with, or who had witnessed some of the events inside. Thomas Robertson was helping to prepare the dinner in Gowrie's kitchen, and confirmed that Henderson had served the first course. Robertson later went out into the yard, saw the Master of Ruthven lying dead at the foot of the Black Turnpike, and watched as the Earl of Gowrie and his servants stepped over his body to rush up the stair.[77] William Robertson, notary, also saw Sandy Ruthven's dead body at the foot of the stair, but he also provided crucial corroboration of Henderson's story: he claimed to have seen the 'armoured man' come down the stair and step 'over the Master's belly', to have asked him 'Chamberlain, Jesus! What means the matter?', and to have received no reply from Henderson.[78] Soon afterwards, William Rynd, namesake of Gowrie's tutor, went up the turnpike. He saw Patrick Eviot with a drawn sword, and Hew Moncreiff wielding the short pike known as a Jedburgh-staff.[79] Meanwhile Archibald MacBreck witnessed Sir

Thomas Erskine's scuffle with Gowrie; the earl broke free almost in front of MacBreck's house, where he drew his two swords. John Brown, notary, also saw Gowrie fighting Erskine, and heard the latter saying "'Oh traitor! This is thy deed!" Or the like term'.[80]

The inquisition at Perth seems to have been a cathartic moment for the town. On 30 September, three days after the statement-taking was completed, bonfires were lit in Perth, as in all of Scotland, to celebrate the preservation of King James's life. Perhaps Perth also had good cause to celebrate its own preservation. Over many decades, the Ruthvens had built up a strong alliance with the burgesses and powerful craft guilds of the town: if Perth as a whole was found to have been overtly or covertly supportive of Gowrie's plot, the consequences could have been disastrous.[81] As it was, Perth's great and good acted speedily to proclaim their fulsome and unqualified loyalty to the crown. Their rigorous enquiry into the actions of the townspeople on 5 August seemed to establish beyond doubt that the attack on Gowrie House had been carried out by a small clique of Ruthvens and their allies, acting in a way that was totally abhorrent to the loyal and law-abiding majority of the citizens. Perhaps this was so, but it undoubtedly served the purposes of both Perth's own authorities and the royal government that the town which had been Scotland's capital, and where James VI's ancestors had been crowned and buried, should not have been guilty of some sort of 'corporate treason'. The consequence was the elaborate series of rituals played out on 15 April 1601, when King James VI returned to Perth. At the market cross, James was installed as a burgess of the town and as its provost, succeeding the dead Gowrie. The king reaffirmed the town's charter, and in the junketing that followed, an enormous bowl of wine was drunk dry.[82] Somewhere overlooking the scene, stuck on a pike, were dismembered body parts of the two young men who had died in Gowrie House eight months earlier.

****

Late in October 1600, a grizzly procession set out from Perth. The bodies of John, Earl of Gowrie, and Alexander, Master of Ruthven, were making their last journey, escorted by a strong body of soldiers. King James was taking no chances. Perhaps he was concerned that the Ruthvens' friends might spirit the bodies away to bury them secretly and respectfully. Perhaps he was worried that if there were no corpses, the Ruthvens might turn into the stuff of legend, folk heroes who would return, like King Arthur or Sir Francis Drake, to save their people in the hour of need – *Gowrie quondam, Gowrie futurus.* But there was a more prosaic reason for guarding the bodies so well. If the corpses went missing, their treason trial could not proceed; and if they could not be found guilty of treason, the Ruthven estates could not be forfeited and promptly redistributed to those who had allegedly saved the king's life at Gowrie House. And so for the last time, the Ruthven brothers went to Edinburgh.

CHAPTER TWO

THE FALL OF THE HOUSE OF RUTHVEN

The Parliament of Scotland convened in Edinburgh on 11 November 1600. The 'riding of Parliament' battled its way through heavy snow and frost, uphill from the Palace of Holyrood to the Tolbooth, where the proceedings were to be held.[83] The procession had been turned, quite deliberately, into the triumphal cavalcade of the heroes of Gowrie House. After the initial group of office-holders and lords, the five trumpeters, and the eight heralds in their gloriously colourful tabards, the Earl of Mar struggled through the snow bearing Scotland's sword of state. Then came the Chancellor, the Earl of Montrose. Behind him, King James VI himself fought his way up the hill in his state robes. By tradition, the Earl of Erroll should have been on James's right hand, but that place was now taken by Sir Thomas Erskine, one of the central figures in the events of 5 August. Immediately behind the king came that other key player at Gowrie House, the Duke of Lennox, with Scotland's two new Marquesses, Hamilton and Huntly, on either side of him. Following Scotland's greatest lords came the other 'heroes' who had saved their king: Sir James Erskine, Sir William Stewart, and the newly-knighted Sir Hew Herries and Sir John Ramsay.[84] This symbolic linking of the Parliament with the events at Gowrie House was only appropriate, for the main business of the following session would be the trial of the dead Ruthven brothers, their inevitable posthumous condemnation for high treason, and the forfeiture of their estates.

****

In the days preceding the state opening of Parliament, the final elements of the crown's case were put in place. Strictly speaking, treason charges had been laid against six living individuals: William Ruthven, brother and heir of the dead Earl of Gowrie and Master of Ruthven; their cousins Alexander and Harry Ruthven; Patrick Eviot; Hew Moncreiff; and

Andrew Henderson, the only one of the accused who was actually in custody. Between 8 and 10 November, 32 depositions were taken from most of the remaining key witnesses to what had happened at Gowrie House on 5 August 1600. Protocol dictated that the first witness to be sworn was the highest in the social order, Ludovic Stuart, Duke of Lennox, the king's cousin. The duke's testimony was critical to James, for there were parts of the royal story that only Lennox could corroborate. The first of these was the information which Sandy Ruthven had given the king at Falkland. According to Lennox, after the hunt ended in Falkland Park, James told him that they were going to ride to Perth to talk to the Earl of Gowrie. After the duke had changed horses and caught up with the king, James steered him out of earshot of the main party and babbled excitedly, 'You cannot guess what errand I am riding for! I am going to get a poise* in Perth; and Master Alexander Ruthven has informed me, that he has found a man that has a pitcher full of coined gold of great sorts'. James then asked Lennox what he thought of Sandy Ruthven – perhaps a strange question, as Sandy was well known about the court, but as his erstwhile brother-in-law, Lennox presumably knew him far better than did the king. The duke stated that 'he knew nothing of him but an honest discreet gentleman'. James then told Lennox the story of the man in the field that the Master of Ruthven had supposedly told him. The duke's reaction was sceptical: 'I like not that, sir, for that is not likely.' James was already having doubts, for as they rode past the Bridge of Earn he told Lennox to accompany him when the Master of Ruthven took him to view the prisoner and the gold, contrary to Sandy's express insistence that James should come alone.[85]

Lennox's testimony then followed the already well-known outline of the story until the end of the dinner, when Lennox rose to attend on the king. However, Gowrie told him that 'his Majesty was gone up quietly upon some quiet errand', and took Lennox, the Abbot of Lindores, Dr Herries and others out into the garden.[86] Shortly afterwards, Thomas Cranstoun came to them with the word that the king had left, and was riding back over the South Inch.

> And then the Earl of Gowrie cried, 'Horses! Horses!'. And the said Master Thomas Cranstoun answered to him, 'Your horse is in Scone', which the Earl of Gowrie made not to hear, but cried again, 'Horse! Horse!'. And the

---

* Poise = a treasure

deponent [Lennox] and the Earl of Gowrie came forth of the garden, through the hall, to the close, and came to the outer gate; and this deponent asked the porter, 'If the king was forth?' Who answered, that 'he was assured that his Majesty was not come forth of the place'. Then the Earl of Gowrie said, 'I am sure he is forth; nevertheless stay, my lord duke, and I shall go up and get your lordship the verity and certainty thereof'. And the said Earl of Gowrie passed up, and incontinent came down again to the close, and he affirmed to this deponent, that 'the King's Majesty was forth at the back gate and away'.

Lennox, Mar, Gowrie and the rest walked out into the High Street, where the duke claimed that he heard the king's shout. He said to Mar, 'This is the king's voice that cries, be where he will'. They looked up and saw James's face at the window, 'wanting his hat, his face being red, and a hand gripping his cheek and mouth'. The king cried 'I am murdered! Treason! My Lord of Mar, help! help!'[87] Lennox, Mar and the rest then rushed to the chamber door, which they found locked, and even furious hammering could not break it open; the door was only opened from the inside, after the two Ruthven brothers had been killed. Gowrie's men were still fighting to get into the chamber from the Black Turnpike. Lennox recognised only one, Alexander Ruthven of Freeland, who cried to him, 'For God's sake, my lord, tell me how my Lord of Gowrie does?' Presumably realising that the truth might only have inflamed Ruthven, the duke lied that Gowrie was well, and told Ruthven to go home. Gowrie's men went back down the stair to the yard, and from the window Lennox recognised a few faces that had been at the dinner: Harry and Alexander Ruthven of Freeland, Hew Moncreiff, Patrick Eviot, George Craigengelt. He watched a beam being brought up to batter down the door, and ended his testimony by stating that the tumult outside Gowrie House lasted for 'two hours and more'.[88]

John Erskine, Earl of Mar, the late Earl of Gowrie's godfather, was sworn next, but his testimony is remarkably brief. It occupies just over seven lines in the printed edition of the depositions, and contains only a very few minor variations from Lennox's account, the most important being the fact that Mar did not catch up with the king until he reached the Bridge of Earn.[89] Some have regarded Mar's brevity as suspicious, but it need not have been: as he was virtually continuously in Lennox's company from the Bridge of Earn onwards, his account would naturally have been similar to the duke's, and there was little point in wasting breath and paper in simply reiterating Lennox's account. The same could be said of many of the other November depositions. John Graham of Orchill 'conforms to the Lord Duke of Lennox and Earl of Mar, in all things', except that when he was dining in the hall of Gowrie House, he saw King James and Sandy Ruthven pass through to go up the stair; when Graham and some others made to follow, Ruthven called out, 'Gentlemen, stay, for it is his Highness' will'.[90] Another John Graham, of Balgowan, again agreed with Lennox in all things, but he added the detail that he was the man who picked up the garter that Sandy Ruthven had allegedly used to tie the king's hands.[91] A number of the king's servants testified, but added little beyond corroboration of the movements of the key players. Several Perth men testified, some of them for the second time in two months, to prove the treasonable actions of Gowrie's friends and attendants, but they added nothing about their actions that had not already emerged from the depositions taken at Perth in September.

Most of the 'green coats' from the royal hunting party duly gave their evidence. James Drummond, Abbot of Inchaffray, had met his distant cousins Sandy and Andrew Ruthven at Falkland at seven in the morning of 5 August, and saw Sandy speaking to the king for about a quarter of an hour. Drummond invited the Master of Ruthven to breakfast, only to be told 'he might not tarry, by reason his Majesty had commanded him to wait upon him'. The abbot then set off for his eponymous estate, but was overtaken on the road by the royal party, riding for Perth, so he joined them.[92] Drummond's testimony concerning what happened at Gowrie House simply confirmed other statements. His fellow 'abbot', Patrick Leslie of Lindores, had witnessed the exchange between the Earl of Gowrie and his porter, Robert Christie. Leslie's testimony closely corroborates that of Christie himself, who stated that he had been in Gowrie's employment for only five weeks prior to 5 August 1600. According to Leslie, Gowrie asked Christie, 'If the King's Majesty was gone forth?' The porter replied, 'He was not passed forth'. Gowrie insisted that 'He was passed forth at the back gate', but received the categorical reply, 'That can not be, my lord, because I have the key of the back gate'. Leslie then witnessed the struggle between Gowrie and Sir Thomas Erskine, ending when the earl dramatically drew his two swords from their single scabbard and cried 'I will either be at my own house, or die by the gate!'[93] The last of the *ersatz*-clerics to testify was George Hay, the 20-year-old Prior of Charterhouse. Crucially, he had been with the

Earl of Gowrie before the king's arrival, having gone to Gowrie House to discuss some business with him. Hay witnessed Andrew Henderson's arrival and Gowrie's question to him, 'Who was with his Majesty in Falkland'? This was the strongest, indeed virtually the only, evidence confirming Henderson's own story that he had ridden to Falkland and back that morning. According to Hay, Gowrie then took Henderson aside for a private conversation. When he returned, he brusquely sent Hay away, saying that he had other things to do that day.[94]

Sir Thomas Erskine's testimony began with him hearing the king's desperate cries from the turret chamber: 'Fie! Help! I am betrayed! They are murdering me!' Erskine said nothing at all about his activities before that time. He testified that he had grabbed the Earl of Gowrie by the neck and said to him, 'Traitor, this is thy deed!' to which Gowrie replied, 'What is the matter? I know nothing!'[95] Gowrie's men pulled him away, and Erskine went through to the yard, where he met Doctor Herries (incidentally and intriguingly, the good doctor never testified). Erskine heard John Ramsay shout from the top of the Black Turnpike, 'Fie! Sir Thomas, come up this turnpike, even to the head'. Five steps up, Erskine ran into Sandy Ruthven, who was bleeding from the face and neck. Erskine shouted to Herries, 'Fie! This is the traitor! Strike him!' They stabbed Ruthven again, and as he fell, he turned to them and cried 'Alas! I had no wyte [= knowledge] of it!'[96] When Erskine reached the gallery at the top of the turnpike, he found only John Ramsay and the king standing there. He said to James, 'I thought your Majesty would have concredited more to me,* than to have commanded me to await your Majesty at the door, if you thought it not meet to have taken me with you'. The king replied, 'Alas! The traitor deceived me in that, as he did in the rest; for I commanded him expressly to bring you to me, which he promised to me to do, and returned back as I thought to fetch you, but he did nothing but shut the door'.[97] The conversation was curtailed by the arrival of Gowrie and Thomas Cranstoun, swords in hand and thirsting to avenge the dead Master of Ruthven. Erskine fought Cranstoun and was wounded in the hand. He saw Gowrie struck down by John Ramsay. He also swore that there were more men in the chamber, supporting the earl and Cranstoun. He recognised none of them, although he thought that a dark-skinned man might have been Hew Moncreiff, the Laird of Moncreiff's brother.[98]

---

* ie, given me more credit.

The deposition of Sir John Ramsay, the killer of the two Ruthven brothers, began in the spirit of Stanley Holloway, with Ramsay fastening a hawk on his hand. The bird had just been presented to the king by John Murray, and Ramsay took charge of it so that Murray could eat his dinner.[99] Ramsay claimed that he was missing the king, so he asked John Moncreiff, the swarthy Hew's brother, where James was. They looked in the room where he had dined, then in the yard, before Moncreiff took Ramsay up 'to a fair gallery, where this deponent was never before'. There they studied the Earl of Gowrie's paintings, little realising the drama that was being played out two doors away, past the gallery chamber. Instead they went back down to the yard, where they heard Thomas Cranstoun proclaiming that the king was 'away upon horseback at the Inch'.[100] Ramsay left Moncreiff and went to the stable to get his horse. As he got ready to saddle up, he heard the king call out from the turret chamber, though he could not make out what he said. Ramsay saw that the door at the foot of the Black Turnpike was open, so he raced up the stair. When he reached the door at the top, he heard the sounds of a struggle beyond, so 'he ran with his whole force' at the door and burst into the gallery chamber – still, incongruously, with the hawk on his hand. He saw the king and Sandy Ruthven wrestling, 'his Majesty having Master Alexander's head under his arm, and Master Alexander being almost on his knees, [with] his hand upon his Majesty's face and mouth'. On seeing Ramsay, James cried out 'Fie! Strike him low, because he has a pyne doublet* upon him'. Ramsay freed the hawk, drew his dagger, and struck Sandy Ruthven, who was then shoved down the turnpike by the King of Scots. Ramsay went to the window and called out to Sir Thomas Erskine, in exactly the words that Erskine included in his testimony. Meantime, King James put his foot on the hawk's leash, and secured the bird until Ramsay came over and put it back on his hand. Ramsay's final sentences seem almost like an irrelevant afterthought:

> when this deponent entered first within the chamber, he
> saw a man standing beside his Majesty's back, whom he
> no ways knew; nor remembers what apparel he had on;
> but after this deponent had struck Master Alexander, he
> saw that man no more.[101]

---

* A shirt of chain mail concealed under his ordinary clothing.

Inevitably, 'that man' was the other key witness to give his testimony in the bitterly cold Edinburgh of November 1600. For the second time under oath, Andrew Henderson told his story of his part in the tragedy of Gowrie House. This time, he provided more detail about the meeting between himself, the Earl of Gowrie, and Sandy Ruthven, after supper on 4 August. The earl told him that the next morning,

> you must ride to Falkland, in company with my brother
> Master Alexander, and take Andrew Ruthven with you;
> and that you be ready to ride, by four hours in the
> morning; and haste you back with answer, as my brother
> directs you, by writing or otherwise; and let Andrew
> Ruthven remain with my brother.[102]

Henderson's statement then adhered very closely to the version he had given in August, up until the moment when he found himself alone in the turret chamber, locked in by the Master of Ruthven. At that point, though, the two accounts began to diverge. Henderson claimed that he spent half an hour alone in the chamber: 'all this time, this deponent, fearing some evil to be done, sat upon his knees and prayed to God'. Then Sandy Ruthven came in with the king, took Henderson's dagger, and held it to the king's breast, saying 'Sir, you must be my prisoner. Remember on my father's death! … Hold your tongue, sir, or by Christ you shall die!' Once again, Henderson claimed that he had knocked the dagger out of Sandy's hand, but he then went on to provide a very different account of the exchange between the king and the Master. After James told Sandy that he could not become king, and that James's friends would avenge him, the young man swore an oath and protested 'it was neither his life nor blood that he craved'. James asked why Sandy was disrespectfully wearing his hat, at which the Master obediently removed it. The king then said, 'What is it you crave, man, if you crave not my life?' Sandy replied, 'Sir, it is but a promise'. James answered, 'What promise?', and Sandy said, 'Sir, my lord my brother will tell you.' James told him to fetch Gowrie, and promised not to cry out or open the window while he was away.[103]

According to Henderson's new account, the king now turned to him and asked why he was there. 'As God lives, I am shut in here like as a dog', Henderson replied. James asked him to open the window, thereby not breaking his word to Sandy Ruthven, but Henderson opened the window 'that looked to the Spey Tower': 'Fie!' cried the king, 'the wrong window, man!' Henderson went to open the other window, but then

Sandy returned, saying 'By God, sir, there is no remedy!' and carrying a garter to bind James's hands. Henderson then related the struggle between the king and Sandy Ruthven, his opening of the correct window, and the king's cry for help. He claimed that Sandy, trembling with emotion, said to him, 'Is there no help with you? Woe with you, you will cause us all die.' Henderson watched as the king and the master, locked together in mortal combat, tumbled out into the gallery chamber. He claimed that he went to the door leading into the Black Turnpike and turned the key, opening it so that he could get out and (so he claimed) the king's servants could get in.[104] No sooner had he done so than John Ramsay came through the door, his hawk on his hand. As Ramsay drew his dagger, Andrew Henderson slipped out of the chamber and down the Black Turnpike. He hid at home until the king left Perth, then walked aimlessly on the bridge for an hour or so. He reported his conversation with his wife almost exactly as he had given it in August, but to his boast about saving the king's life, he added a pathetic rider: 'Woe is me, for the thing that has fallen out!'[105]

****

Far from ending all discussion of the events at Gowrie House, the new witness statements served only to increase the doubts about the king's story. Key witnesses, especially Henderson, seemed directly to contradict their own earlier depositions; and the doubts about Henderson's credibility only increased when James had his name removed from the treason indictment just before Parliament heard the case on 15 November. There were other discrepancies with the earlier accounts. In November, William Robertson, notary of Perth, testified only that he had seen the Earl of Gowrie in the street, wearing a steel bonnet and armed with a sword in each hand. The sight frightened Robertson, who hurried away 'and knows no more of the matter'. But in September, Robertson testified that he had gone into the yard, seen Sandy Ruthven lying dead at the foot of the stair, and then seen Andrew Henderson stepping over the corpse to emerge from the turnpike. Robertson had thus provided the vital (indeed, almost the only) corroboration of Henderson's presence in the upper floors of Gowrie House, but two months later Robertson was strangely silent on the presence of the 'armoured man'.[106] As for Henderson's new deposition, this put crucially different words into Sandy Ruthven's mouth: the Master's intention now seems to have been to make the king his prisoner, not to kill him. John Ramsay's testimony also raises awkward questions. Why did he make, and recount in detail, a tour of the house with John Moncreiff (whose own testimony mentioned no such tour)? Above all, Ramsay's and Henderson's statements seem directly to contradict each other on two vital and related points. According to Henderson, he opened the door to the Black Turnpike, and must have been almost face to face with John Ramsay as he came through the open door. According to Ramsay, he had to break through a locked door, and barely registered Henderson's presence at all.

Contemporaries were also quick to comment on the fact that the depositions had been taken over two months *after* the publication of the official narrative: the pressure to conform to the king's version must have been compelling and insidious, or so the sceptics assumed.[107] The same charge could be levelled at the process of giving testimony, too. Lennox made his statement first, and it would have taken a very brave or a very foolish man to contradict the tale told by the king's cousin, Scotland's (indeed, Britain's) only duke. As it was, witness after witness gave testimony that began by conforming entirely to Lennox's deposition, adding only a few additional points of detail from each witness's perspective. To modern eyes, too, the questions that were put to each of the witnesses hardly smack of disinterested legal process.

> First to enquire, if they knew that the sometime earl directed the said Master Alexander, Andrew Henderson, and Andrew Ruthven to His Majesty, to Falkland, to persuade him to come to Saint John's Town?
>
> … If they saw the said Andrew Henderson and Andrew Ruthven, before the king's coming, come to Gowrie and speak secretly with him? If they knew that Gowrie commanded Andrew Henderson to put on his armour?
>
> … If they saw his Majesty push out his bare head and arm out of the window of the turret above the gate, and cry 'Treason! Help! I am murdered!' The said Master Alexander having his hand at his Highness' face and his throat?[108]

Modern defence lawyers would be raising objection after objection against questions seemingly designed blatantly to lead the witnesses. But judging the legal processes and social mores of other ages by the standards of our own is always perilous. The loaded questions posed to Lennox and the rest actually explain much about the nature of the evidence that they provided, and the apparent contradictions with earlier accounts. Essentially, the November witness statements had nothing to do with establishing 'the truth' in a modern legal or philosophical sense. They had even less to do with reinforcing the king's story of 5 August: the official narratives had been in print for over two months, the unofficial myths in circulation for over three, and no amount of new evidence was going to convince the remaining doubters. The new depositions were taken for two specific and related purposes alone: to condemn Gowrie's alleged accomplices for treason, and thus to justify the forfeiture of the Ruthven estates. For that to happen, the witnesses needed to establish treasonable words and deeds on the parts of the Earl of Gowrie and the Master of Ruthven, deceased, and Hew Moncreiff, Patrick Eviot, and Harry and Alexander Ruthven of Freeland, extant. Strictly speaking, everything else was irrelevant. Consequently, the witnesses simply did not need to recount everything they had seen or heard; they needed only to confirm or elaborate on what they knew about the movements and actions of the key players. Alexander Peebles, burgess of Perth, provided a quite exemplary deposition, as far as the very limited aim of the proceedings was concerned:

> [He saw] the Earl of Gowrie enter in at the gate, with two drawn swords, one in each hand; and a servant put a steel bonnet on his head. And a certain space thereafter, the deponent saw Hew Moncreiff come forth of the place, with a bloody [sword] held, and Patrick Eviot's man, likewise bloodied. And also, saw Patrick Eviot come forth of the gate; but remembers not if he had a sword in his hand. And saw Alexander Ruthven also come forth, with a sword drawn in his hand.[109]

Men with swords in their hands, so close to the king's presence, were guilty of high treason. Nothing else mattered.

Because the purpose of the November statements was entirely different to that underpinning much of the evidence gathered in August and September, and was in any case produced so much later, omissions and apparent contradictions should only be expected, not held up as apparent proof of a sinister royal cover-up. Writers who thought of the

Ruthven brothers as slaughtered innocents even conjured up the notion that the November statements constituted mass perjury by everyone from Lennox downwards.[110] Leaving aside *pro tem* the apparent discrepancies between Henderson's two statements, the November evidence provides nothing concrete to undermine the king's story, which was already old news by that time. William Robertson's failure in November to mention the meeting with Henderson that he described in his September statement has been viewed as suspicious, but in November the witnesses were asked specifically whether they had seen Henderson *in the turret chamber*, and were asked about their knowledge of the Master of Ruthven's actions *while he was alive*, so as to establish his treason. In September, Robertson had admitted to seeing Henderson and the body of the Master at the foot of the turnpike; but then, back in September he had been asked the much more general catch-all question of whether he knew anything else not contained in the questions he had already been asked. No such all-embracing final question was asked in November, simply because it did not need to be. Robertson's sighting of the Earl of Gowrie was relevant to the forfeiture of his lands; his sighting of Henderson and the dead Master was not. Robertson evidently interpreted the questions he was asked in November more narrowly and literally than did some of the other witnesses, but that has always been the case when those caught up in criminal cases consider the questions before them. It is human nature, not proof of some dark conspiracy.

If James and his ministers had set out to create a cast-iron cover story for their own devious machinations, the November witness statements backfired on them spectacularly. For example, Robertson's new evidence actually weakened the crown's case, as did Henderson's new account of a Master of Ruthven who simply sought to extract a promise from the king, not to kill him. But almost all of the apparent contradictions become explicable if we accept that by mid-November, the crown was no longer particularly interested in strengthening its public case, merely in assembling sufficient evidence to persuade Parliament to forfeit the Ruthven estates. Moreover, the November statements provide a mass of tiny human details that strengthen the case for the witnesses' veracity. Lennox's admission that he found the 'pot of gold' story highly unlikely, and told the king so, is at once very human, very plausible, and puts the gullible James in a bad light, hardly the action of a perjurer concerned to reinforce the royal story at all costs. Sir Thomas Erskine heard Gowrie say something as he burst into the gallery chamber, but could not make out the words[111] –

even though a convenient recollection of them might have strengthened the posthumous treason charge against the dead earl, and guaranteed Erskine even more lavish rewards than the ones he received. Henderson's admission that he wandered aimlessly on Perth bridge for an hour is irrelevant to the central question of whether or not he was the 'armoured man', but it is surely entirely natural as the confused reaction of a little man caught up in something far beyond his comprehension, desperate to get some air, clear his head, and collect his thoughts. There were moments of low farce, too, and these also ring true, especially as they simply would not have needed to appear in statements that had some hidden ulterior motive: Andrew Henderson's opening of the wrong window, and the king's exasperated command for him to open the right one; John Ramsay's hawk, and the king treading on the leash to stop the bird flying away.

****

Despite the many doubts about the consistency and credibility of the November witness statements, they served their purpose. On 15 November, Parliament duly passed a series of draconian decrees against the dead Ruthven brothers and their entire kin. 'The name, memory and dignity' of the House of Ruthven was 'to be abolished and extinguished'. The lands, goods, and titles of the Earl of Gowrie and his brother were forfeited to the crown. Other members of the family were barred from owning property. The coat-of-arms of the Ruthven Earls of Gowrie was formally torn to pieces in Parliament, and later at the market cross of Edinburgh. All those who bore the hated Ruthven surname would be forced to change it for another before the following Whitsun. The name of Ruthven Castle was changed, too: to celebrate the king's favourite pastime, it became Huntingtower, the name that it bears to this day.[112] The fifth of August was declared a day of thanksgiving 'in all times and ages to come'. Finally, on Monday 19 November 1600, the decomposing bodies of John, Earl of Gowrie, and Alexander, Master of Ruthven, were dragged through the streets of the capital before being solemnly hanged and dismembered by the common hangman at Edinburgh Cross. Their heads were then stuck on iron pins on the roof of the same Tolbooth where Parliament had met to condemn them.[113] Later that evening at Dunfermline Palace in Fife, James VI's queen, Anna of Denmark, was delivered of the couple's fifth child and second son.[114] He was duly christened Charles, and created Duke of Albany; but the child was puny, sickly, and not expected to live.

****

To the victors, the spoils. James VI did not keep the Ruthven lands in his own possession for very long. They were rapidly distributed to new owners, for the 'heroes' of Gowrie House and other loyalists had to receive their just rewards. Indeed, there had been a veritable feeding frenzy of anticipation in the weeks leading up to the meeting of Parliament, with avaricious courtiers eyeing up their favourite Ruthven lands and soliciting all and sundry to secure them. There was a minor panic when it was suggested that the last Earl of Gowrie had never been formally invested in his lands; if he never legally owned them, they could hardly be parcelled out to others.[115] In the end, the Act of Parliament that forfeited the estate was carefully worded to cover all eventualities, and the redistribution began. The Ruthvens' old Perthshire neighbours, the Murrays, swiftly became the greatest beneficiaries of their downfall. William Murray of Tullibardine obtained the Ruthvens' hereditary sheriffdom of Perthshire, holding it until such offices were abolished in 1748.[116] He later became the second Earl of Tullibardine; in turn, his son became the first Murray Earl of Atholl, and William Murray's descendants are still Dukes of Atholl, commanders-in-chief of Europe's last private army (despite being South African). Tullibardine's distant kinsman Sir David Murray, comptroller of James VI's household, succeeded the last Earl of Gowrie as provost of Perth. In 1604 James made him Lord Scone, granting him that rich estate of the Earls of Gowrie, along with the great house that the first earl had built on the site of Scone Abbey. In due course David, Lord Scone, became the first Viscount Stormont, and his descendants, the Earls of Mansfield, still live in Scone Palace. The other major Perthshire residence of the Ruthvens, newly rechristened Huntingtower Castle, also went to the Murrays, ending up as a property of the Atholl line.

Inevitably, the chief actors at Gowrie House fared well, at least in the short term. Sir Hew Herries gained the Ruthven barony of Cousland, but did not live very long to enjoy it.[117] Sir Thomas Erskine was promised Dirleton Castle at the death of the dowager Countess of Gowrie. When James went to England, Erskine accompanied him and soon replaced the disgraced Sir Walter Raleigh as captain of the Yeomen of the Guard. In 1604 he became Lord Dirleton, and in 1619 was created the first Earl of Kellie. Erskine married two wealthy English widows in succession, but his lack of real power and riches embittered him. He also became increasingly isolated and unpopular south of the border: many despised him as an archetype of the hated Scottish courtiers who surrounded King

James, depriving deserving Englishmen of plumb offices and royal patronage (or, as one embittered *Sassenach* put it, 'sucking at the breasts of the state').[118] Perhaps there was also an additional and specific reason for the English to dislike Erskine. Not long after James arrived in his new kingdom, the 13-year-old Lady Anne Clifford noted that she and her party 'were all lousy by sitting in the chamber of Sir Thomas Erskine'.[119] When the old king died, Erskine slipped into an obscure retirement, finally dying in 1639. His cousin, the Earl of Mar, fared rather better. In 1603 he was appointed to the English Privy Council, and (like Lennox and Kellie) he became a Knight of the Garter. He eventually became Lord Treasurer of Scotland, but died in 1634 after falling over his dog.

The actual killer of the Ruthven brothers, John Ramsay, had become a knight at the age of 20, but he had to wait a little longer for further honours. In June 1606 he became Viscount Haddington: his new coat of arms included a right arm bearing a sword, and the motto *Haec dextra vindex principis et patriae* ('This right arm saved the king and the nation').[120] In 1608 Ramsay made a grand marriage to the daughter of the Earl of Sussex, one of England's greatest aristocrats. In 1621 he became Earl of Holdernesse, and every 5 August for the last four years of James's life, he bore the English sword of state before the king. John Ramsay died without heirs in 1626, but as befitted the man who had supposedly 'saved the king and the nation', he was given an impressive funeral in Westminster Abbey.[121] There he joined Ludovic, Duke of Lennox, who had gone to his grave two years earlier. Of vaguely royal status, laden with great offices and titles, but possessing virtually no real power, Lennox had long been a grand and decorative nonentity, despite possessing one of the most impressive beards at King James's hirsute court and a dubious track record of marrying colourful but wholly unsuitable women.

****

Sinister or unlikely stories emanating from governments are often challenged by persistent lone critics who pursue the truth long after others have given up, heedless of abuse, derision and intimidation; or else, depending on one's point of view, by obsessive cranks with a grudge. In King James's case, his would-be nemesis wielding the sword of truth was the Reverend Robert Bruce. James and Robert Bruce were old enemies: in 1599 the minister took the king to court for cancelling his pension, and won (despite the king's blatant intimidation of the judges). Bruce was one of the five Edinburgh ministers who from the very beginning refused to believe the official narrative of Gowrie House. On 12 August 1600 the five met the king in person, and Bruce told James to his face that he could not possibly preach on the subject, as the initial accounts seemed so contradictory.[122] Within a month, four of the ministers satisfied themselves of the truth of the 'Gowrie Conspiracy', and only the diehard Bruce held out. On 11 September, he appeared before the king again, and was asked if he was convinced at last. Bruce's response was categorical: he would only be satisfied if Andrew Henderson was hanged as a traitor, and died penitently.

> 'Then,' said the king, 'I see you will not trust me, nor
> the noblemen that were with me, except you try me … I
> see, Mr Robert, that you would make me a murderer. It
> is known very well that I was never bloodthirsty. *If I*
> *would have taken their lives, I had causes enough; I needed*
> *not to hazard myself so.*'[123]

Bruce was banished from Scotland, returning in September 1601. In the following April, James summoned him to another face-to-face conference, this time at Brechin. Bruce's first answer must have stunned and gratified the king: when asked if he now agreed with the official story, Bruce said 'Yes'. Mar and Erskine had convinced him of the sequence of events in and around Gowrie House; he only retained doubts about what had happened in the turret chamber. ' "Doubt ye of that?" said the king. "Then you could not but account me a murderer!" ' Bruce disagreed, saying that for all he knew, 'you might have some secret cause' for wanting Sandy Ruthven dead. James then told Bruce his story of 5 August, and listened 'gently' as the cleric explained his remaining doubts. Finally, Bruce agreed to sign the declaration concurring with the official story of 5 August. If James thought the matter was settled, he had reckoned without Bruce's particularly tender Presbyterian conscience. Bruce now believed the king, and would sign a declaration to that effect – but he would not preach it from his pulpit, saying that he 'ought to preach nothing but the word of God', rather than comment on secular matters. This sudden change of direction clearly exasperated James, who resorted to sarcasm and bullying. 'I would lay a wager, there is no express word of King James the Sixth, in the Scripture … the whole Kirk has done it already, you must not be singular!'[124]

The two men met again at Perth on 24 June, and fell immediately into the same arguments. Could the king order Bruce, or any minister, to preach what was effectively a political speech from his pulpit? Was

James truly innocent of the murder of the Ruthven brothers – or, as Bruce put it, 'what can I or any many say, what your Majesty had before your eyes? Or what particular [cause] you had?' Astonishingly, James agreed with him, and allowed Bruce to subject him to a point-by-point interrogation: the closest that King James VI would ever come to making his own witness deposition. Bruce asked,

'Had you a purpose to slay my lord [Gowrie]?'

'As I shall answer to God', said the king, 'I knew not that my Lord was slain till I saw him in his last agony; and was very sorry, yea prayed in my heart for the same.'

'What say you then concerning Master Alexander?' said Mr Robert.

'I grant,' said the king, 'I am art and part of Master Alexander's slaughter; for it was in my own defence.'

'Why brought you him not to justice?' said Mr Robert, 'seeing you would have had God before your eyes?'

'I had neither God nor the devil, man, before my eyes,' said the king, 'but my own defence!' Here the king began to fret … he 'was once minded to have spared Master Alexander; but being moved, for the time, the motion prevailed.'

Farther, Mr Robert demanded of the king, 'If he had a purpose, that day, in the morning, to slay Master Alexander?'

The king answered, 'Upon his salvation, that day in the morning he loved him as his brother!'

Bruce concluded that James was not guilty of setting out to kill the brothers, but had acted in the heat of the moment; in his opinion and in modern parlance, Robert Bruce decided that the King of Scots was innocent of premeditated murder, but guilty of manslaughter. The public letter that Bruce finally agreed to sign damned his monarch with faint praise. 'I am resolved of his Majesty's innocence and the guiltiness of the Earl of Gowrie and his brother, according as it is declared by the Act of Parliament'.[125]

The dogged minister met his king one last time. His colleagues in the Kirk considered it essential for Bruce to be part of the delegation sent to congratulate James on his recent accession to the English throne, so early in the morning of 5 April 1603 Bruce was ushered into the royal bedchamber at Holyrood. James was already booted for the ride to England, and circled the room impatiently as the minister spoke. Bruce delivered his prepared speech of congratulations, which tactfully avoided any mention of the events at Gowrie House, and the king responded with platitudes. Afterwards, when the new – and first – King of Great Britain had mounted his horse in the palace yard, Bruce approached him again, and was warmly received. Those standing nearby heard the king say, 'Now all particulars [= quarrels] are past between you and me, Master Robert.'[126] But there was no happy ending. Bruce continued to act the maverick, ignoring royal injunctions and his own Kirk's decrees. He was eventually banned from preaching, spent long periods imprisoned in Edinburgh and Inverness Castles, and died in comparative poverty in 1631.

****

John, Earl of Gowrie, and Alexander, Master of Ruthven, were survived by two younger brothers. William, aged about 17, notionally became the rightful fourth earl on 5 August 1600. He and Patrick, aged about 16, were at school in Edinburgh. When news of the tragedy at Gowrie House reached them, presumably shortly after it came to Edinburgh on the morning of 6 August, they rode east to join their mother Dorothea, the dowager Countess, at Dirleton Castle. James's councillors in Edinburgh immediately despatched a posse to arrest them, commanded by the Master of Orkney and Sir James Sandilands. A courtier named Kennedy forewarned the boys and their mother just in time, and that same evening, with half an hour to spare, the young Ruthvens bolted for the English border. The old countess received the king's agents 'soberly' in her castle, but then one of them disastrously attempted to reassure her that the boys would suffer no harm, as the intention was only to commit them to the custody of the Chancellor, the Earl of Montrose. At that, Dorothea burst out in a harangue against her family's old enemy, even though Montrose's heir was now her son-in-law: 'Ah, ah, false traitor, thief! Shall my bairns come in his hands?'[127] Dorothea, dowager Countess of Gowrie, probably never saw her two youngest sons again. She lived on in her dower property, Dirleton Castle, mourning her executed husband and her murdered sons, grieving for her absent children, and knowing that on her death, this last great Ruthven estate would pass to the hated Sir Thomas Erskine. In October 1600, King James VI sent her a letter; its contents are unknown. In the following month, she begged Secretary Elphinstone to intercede with the king, praying for support for her 'very desolate' daughters and for some relief from the intolerable burden of her husband's debts to the crown, incurred during his time as treasurer over 20 years earlier.[128] She was involved in a series of legal cases in 1605, but after December of that year, there is no further record of her. She was dead by 1608, and Sir Thomas Erskine duly took possession of the Dirleton estate.[129]

Meanwhile, on 11 August 1600, six days after the slaughter at Gowrie House, a disguised William and Patrick Ruthven slipped through the massive new fortifications that guarded Elizabethan Berwick-upon-Tweed, and entered England's northernmost fortress. The deputy governor, Sir John Carey, immediately reported to London:

> they only desire that their lives may be safe, and they
> may have a little oversight here, till the truth of their
> cause may be known. And the pitiful case of the poor old
> distressed good countess, has made me the willinger to
> give my consent for their stay here a while, till I may be
> your honourable means, know the Queen's Majesty's
> pleasure whether they shall stay here, or go somewhere
> further into the country? For they only desire the safety
> of their lives, and the old countess's case is pitiful and
> lamentable … the poor gentlemen stole into the town
> this morning closely, and I could not well turn them out
> again, seeing they came for refuge to save their lives.[130]

The young refugees stayed in their chamber for weeks, never venturing out. Carey discussed their future with their tutor, who agreed that it would be better if they went further away from the border, 'that the king might not so easily hear of them'.[131] On 4 September Carey reported that 'the young Earl of Gowrie and his brother' had finally left Berwick.[132] They sent to their mother for some maintenance, but she could send none; partly because she could not trust any of her servants, partly because 'if it should be known that she did any manner of way either gave them succour or maintenance or any manner of help, she should presently forfeit and be thrown out of all she has'. Countess Dorothea was evidently in hiding, and search parties were everywhere in southern Scotland, so 'no friend either dare or can travel between them … almost no man can travel in their country, but he is searched'. Carey believed that if he sent them away sooner, they would probably be killed or taken, so he delayed, risking the wrath of both his queen and the king of Scots, and finally sent them off to Durham with one of his own men and some of his own money. They were to stay at Durham for three weeks before passing on to Cambridge with their tutor, 'there to study for a time'.[133] King James was furious that Elizabeth's officials on the border had granted shelter to the fugitive brothers, and so he remained.[134] In 1601 it was rumoured that he had commissioned an assassin to poison the two boys, and in December 1602, believing that they had either returned covertly to Scotland or sought to do so, James issued a draconian proclamation condemning as traitors anyone who attempted to communicate with William and Patrick, or else assisted them in any way.[135] The plight of the young Ruthvens plucked some unlikely hearts: in 1602 Theodore Beza, the leader of European Calvinism, offered them asylum in Geneva.[136]

Following James's accession to the English throne, a frantic hue and cry for the Ruthven brothers took place across the length and breadth of England. Inevitably, there were false alarms and cases of mistaken identity.[137] In the event, Patrick was captured quite by accident, in the unlikely surroundings of an isolated country pub in the north of England. On 21 June 1603 Francis Wandesford, of Durham, came to Christopher Mawlam's inn at Kirkby Malzeard, on the edge of the Yorkshire moors near Ripon.[138] There, he saw a youth who reminded him of one of the Ruthven brothers; he had seen them when they passed through his home town three years earlier. Wandesford started talking to him, and became suspicious when the youth mispronounced the name of the Durham village where he claimed to have been born. Wandesford asked more questions, heard more contradictions, and watched the young man become so distressed that he started to cry. Wandesford then got Mawlam to detain the youth, and the innkeeper tricked him into confirming his identity by seemingly accepting a bribe to help him escape. Wandesford sent for a justice of the peace, Sir William Ingilby of Ripley Castle, who duly arrested the young man: the only possessions he had on him were a satchel crammed with books, 'a few pothecary confections' and King James's proclamation against the Ruthven brothers.

The story of Patrick Ruthven's arrest begs one question above all others. Why should he have fetched up in Kirkby Malzeard, of all places? The village is hard enough to find today, concealed from the wider world by winding lanes and unhelpfully minute signposts. The most plausible explanation for Patrick Ruthven's presence in Yorkshire must be that he was trying to make his way home to Scotland, and his mother, by back roads, calculating that his chances of safety increased with every mile that he put between himself and the vengeful James Stuart. On the other hand, perhaps he had never carried out his intention of going to Cambridge, and remained in the north of England throughout the last years of Queen Elizabeth's life. Sir John Carey had suggested Ripon, along with Richmond and Hull, as potential hiding places for the Ruthven boys not long after they first crossed the border, and his selection suggests that there was some specific rationale behind suggesting these three towns and omitting (say) York.[139] Patrick would have needed board and lodging in the home of a sympathetic, like-minded protector. So Francis Wandesford's summoning of the nearest available Justice of the Peace might have had more profound implications than Wandesford could possibly have envisaged.

Sir William Ingilby, a keen amateur physician, would have been a highly suitable candidate for the role of the scientifically-inclined Patrick Ruthven's guardian.[140] His home at Ripley Castle was an ideal 'safe house', although Patrick would presumably have had to move out temporarily to ensure that he did not cross the path of Ingilby's recent house guest, King James, who made Ripley one of his many stops en route to London. As a fugitive and a possible target for assassins, Patrick Ruthven would have been safest in the company of people who coped with such circumstances on a daily basis, and the north of England was full of them. England's Catholics had become accustomed to the arts of concealment and outwitting the authorities, and despite his nominal respectability as a JP, Sir William Ingilby was at the head of a great Catholic dynasty. Ripley Castle contained a 'priest hole', and Ingilby's brother had been executed simply for being an ordained priest. Patrick Ruthven certainly converted to Catholicism at some point in his life: what could have been more natural than for this to have been triggered by the kindness of Catholic hosts, especially when it was so evident that the Presbyterian God of the Ruthvens had forsaken them? Ultimately, there is no proof that Patrick was sheltered by the Ingilbys. But even if Sir William Ingilby's role in his life went no further than that of arresting officer, it still provides an astonishing direct link between the two great plots against King James Stuart. For Ingilby had three nephews in Worcestershire, his sister's sons. Their surname was Winter. They were among the leaders of the Gunpowder Plot.

****

Patrick Ruthven was safely lodged in the Tower of London by July 1603, when the Ruthven brothers became the only exceptions to the general pardon issued by the new King James I.[141] His detention has surprisingly modern resonances: he was never charged with any crime, he never faced a trial, and as he was a citizen of what was still an independent foreign country, there was never a basis in law for detaining him indefinitely in England. William Ruthven escaped the same fate as his brother, but what actually became of him was long a mystery. According to some optimistic American genealogists, William sailed to Virginia in 1635, changed his name to Ruffin to conceal his identity, and, in his mid-sixties, married and fathered a family. The obvious biological implausibilities in this tale are as nothing to the historical ones. By 1635 no Ruthven needed to conceal his or her identity in Britain, and they certainly would not have needed to do so in the New World. The truth is far sadder. William disappears from the record after King James succeeded to his English throne; if he had stayed in England he would certainly have become a well-documented state prisoner, like his brother, and if he had remained at large for only a short time, he would equally certainly have become the object of yet more ferocious proclamations to sheriffs and mayors throughout the land. The conclusion is inescapable. Very quickly, King James and his ministers knew that, one way or another, William Ruthven, the 'fourth Earl of Gowrie', was beyond their reach.

Writing decades later, Bishop Gilbert Burnet claimed that William Ruthven went 'beyond the seas', became a great chemist, and discovered the 'philosopher's stone'. But Burnet was often unreliable, and probably confused William with his brother Patrick. In fact, Patrick himself provided the solution to his brother's fate; in a document written between 1622 and 1631 he stated categorically that William had died in France, and Patrick's own subsequent claim to the Ruthven titles suggests he had firm evidence that William had no male heirs.[142] Perhaps the 'fourth earl of Gowrie' was already dead by 1608, when King Henri IV interceded on behalf of Patrick Ruthven and referred to the latter explicitly as the rightful Earl of Gowrie.[143] In any event, the outcome is beyond doubt. Patrick, the youngest son of the first earl, was now the *soi-disant* fifth earl, the last of the Ruthvens.[144]

CHAPTER THREE

THE DARK LORDS

When he delivered his thunderous sermon at Edinburgh's market cross on 11 August 1600, Patrick Galloway sensationally denounced the Earl of Gowrie as nothing less than an agent of the Antichrist. According to Galloway, John Ruthven was 'a studier of magic, and a conjurer of devils, and to have had so many at his command'.[145] When the dead earl's clothes were searched, charms and papers bearing strange symbols were discovered. Charms were relatively commonplace and usually innocent, but in the heightened tensions and suspicions on 5 August and in the days that followed, it was inevitable that a sinister interpretation was placed on Gowrie's possession of such items.[146] It was said that a parchment found on Gowrie's body made up the word 'Tetragrammaton', and that while he carried it, his blood could not be spilled.[147] Other reports that reached England's agents in Scotland within a week of the 'Gowrie House affair' suggested that some of the inscriptions were love charms, but that another was *'contra potestatem divino majestatis'* (= against the divine power of kings).[148] Two of the first witnesses examined by the state testified to Gowrie's supposed obsession with the dark arts. James Wemyss of Bogie, his hunting companion in Strathbraan, told of the earl's boasts that he could immobilise a snake by uttering a mystical Hebrew word, that he had foretold a man's death, and that humans could be created by other than natural means.[149] William Rynd, the earl's old tutor, stated that he saw the charms found on Gowrie's body while they were at Padua, that some were in Hebrew and some in Latin, that Gowrie always kept the charms about his person, and that when Patrick Galloway showed him the papers taken off the dead earl, he confirmed they were the same ones that he had seen before.[150] The very fact that Gowrie had spent so long in Italy was suspicious in itself, for the peninsula was alleged to be a hotbed of necromancy and neoplatonism.[151]

Indirect confirmation of the Ruthven family's interest in the esoteric can also be adduced from the subsequent career of Gowrie's younger brother Patrick, who was imprisoned in the Tower of London from 1603 onwards. In 1608 James flatly turned down Patrick's request for maintenance or permission to go abroad, but in other respects, his condition was remarkably comfortable.[152] In August 1605 the lieutenant of the Tower summarised the condition of his prisoners, observing that 'the young gentleman Gowrie' was sometimes visited by his sister, and this sibling contact obviously continued on a regular basis; in May 1614, he was even allowed out of the Tower briefly to visit Barbara, who was 'very dangerously sick'.[153] Patrick had his own rooms, and they contained a bedstead, bed, bolster, rug, blankets, sheets and a canopy. He seems even to have had his own study, and he had his own servant for at least some of the time.[154] The Lieutenant of the Tower was allowed £3 a week to feed him (this at a time when a labourer earned about 8d a day), 20 shillings per annum to do his washing, £10 per annum for new clothes, and the same amount for the services of a reader.

In these relatively comfortable circumstances, Patrick spent his time furthering his knowledge of chemistry, medicine, and alchemy in the company of such illustrious fellow prisoners as Sir Walter Raleigh.[155] For an obviously bookish young man, then, the conditions of his imprisonment might not have been too onerous: quite the opposite, in fact. By the time of his release, Patrick Ruthven's 19 years of virtually uninterrupted study had made him an accomplished practitioner across a range of scientific disciplines, some of them rather less orthodox than others. His commonplace book of alchemy survives, and although it dates from several years after his release from the Tower, it provides a fascinating insight into Patrick's mental world.[156] The book contains long extracts from various classical and scientific works, drawings of alchemical symbols, and lengthy quotations from prominent alchemists. The book also suggests that Ruthven was corresponding with some of the great European minds of the day, notably John Napier, his fellow Scot and the inventor of logarithms. Throughout the centuries, alchemy has centred on the endless quest for the 'philosopher's stone', the magical substance that would turn base metal into gold. Patrick Ruthven spent much of his life in pursuit of the elusive stone, judging by the many references to the interaction of metals in his commonplace book, and his interest in such mysteries as a strange box with three key holes, last seen at Ramsey Abbey in the Fens.

Until he opened Ramsey's mysterious box, or otherwise located the philosopher's stone, Ruthven had to earn a living. For much of the 17th century science remained a conveniently fluid concept, not yet broken down into rigidly defined academic subjects. Thus Patrick Ruthven, alchemist, saw the practice of medicine as a natural extension of his studies: the commonplace book contains his remedies for the plague, leprosy and 'all fiery diseases, and other infirmities that vex mankind', though modern medical opinion might well baulk at his reliance on the likes of the powdered skin of a serpent bathed in moonshine.[157] An eclectic collection of Patrick Ruthven's remedies was published a couple of years after his death, under the title 'The Ladies Cabinet Enlarged and Opened'.[158] This included his cures for deafness (an oil made from chopped adders), toothache (washing the mouth with white wine every morning), the French pox and sea sickness. His method for ascertaining whether a patient would die of the plague involved placing frogs on the sores. If they burst, the patient would survive; if not, he or she would die. ('Some say a dried toad will do it better', Ruthven observed with impeccable scientific detachment.) To make a child urinate, Ruthven advocated giving the retentive infant a quart of ale containing three or four dried and powdered bees. All in all, though, purely medical matters took up only a fraction of Ruthven's posthumous tome, which was otherwise essentially a recipe book – the educated 17th century mind would have seen no intrinsic intellectual barriers between curing the plague, turning base metal into gold, making one's own wine, and preparing such delights as steak pie, sausages, gooseberry fool and mallard stew, just a few of the favourite recipes of the would-be 'fifth Earl of Gowrie'.

Whatever modern 'experts' might make of Patrick Ruthven's ideas on cookery and medicine, in his own day he built up a substantial reputation as a medical practitioner. Even while still in the Tower, he was able to correspond with patients across Britain, such as Sir John Oglander, of Nunwell on the Isle of Wight, to whom he sent some 'aloe pills' and advice on taking them:

> You shall take them always once in six days, half an hour
> or an hour before supper, and, presently, after the pill, you
> shall take 10 or 11 grams of ambergrease in panad, or any
> such liquid thing that may help to convey it the better into
> the stomach. It will work next morning, but so gently that
> you may go where you list and eat whatsoever your

appetite affecteth, abstaining only from cheese, vinegar and such other meats as are of astringent quality ... I hope you shall find much good of it, but that you must not expect presently but after some continuance of time.

Oglander wrote at the foot of the letter, 'The letter was sent me from Patrick Ruthven, who was brother to the Earl Gowry in Scotland, that conspired to have killed the King'.[159] In 1639 Ruthven treated the wife of Sir Henry Slingsby, who described Patrick as 'a Scottish gentleman of the family of Lord Gowrie, who had made it his study in the art of physic to administer help to others, but not for any gain to himself'.[160]

The charges of sorcery levelled against the last Earl of Gowrie were undoubtedly given credibility in the eyes of posterity by the subsequent career of his brother Patrick and by the fact that his two immediate predecessors had been accused of exactly the same offence. His father, the first earl, had been charged with consulting a sorcerer; but the diabolic credentials of his grandfather, Patrick, third Lord Ruthven, were more substantial still. After all, Mary Queen of Scots did not live in fear of too many of her nobility on the grounds that they were warlocks.

****

The Scottish Reformation effectively began at Perth on 11 May 1559 when a Protestant mob, responding to a fiery sermon preached by John Knox in St John's Kirk on the previous day, ransacked the town's churches and monasteries. Knox had been invited to speak by Perth's provost: Patrick, third Lord Ruthven, head of one of the most powerful dynasties in Perthshire but a man widely distrusted owing to his propensity for changing sides and for once attempting to sell Perth to an invading English army.* His sponsorship of Knox transformed Ruthven's position, and by the autumn of 1559 he was one of the leaders of the 'Lords of the Congregation', the group of Protestant nobles leading the resistance against the Catholic Regent Marie de Guise, who ruled in the name of her daughter Mary, Queen of Scots, and the French garrisons that supported her. Ruthven was an active military commander in the campaigns of 1559–60 against the French, and in 1560 he helped to facilitate the entry into Scotland of an English army. The death of Marie de Guise in June was followed in

* See Appendix A.

short order by the withdrawal of the French troops. With their departure, the 'auld alliance' that had endured for 265 years came to an end, and the triumph of Ruthven, his fellow Lords of the Congregation, and of England, appeared to be complete.

Then, on 19 August 1561, two French galleys sailed into the Water of Leith, the port of Edinburgh. A strikingly beautiful, red-haired, and very tall young woman of 18 years disembarked from one of them. Mary Stuart, Queen of Scots, Queen dowager of France, and in the eyes of many, rightful Queen of England, had returned to her native land after 15 years in exile and eight months of widowhood. The return of Mary meant that for the first time in almost two decades, Scotland had a resident, adult monarch once again. That fact alone would have been enough totally to transform the political landscape for the likes of Patrick, Lord Ruthven: dealing with a regent was a very different proposition from dealing with a divinely ordained sovereign, even one still only in her eighteenth year. But for Ruthven and Scotland's other leaders, four obvious facts about their new ruler threatened to make their immediate futures markedly problematic. First, the queen was more French than Scottish; she signed herself in the French manner, 'Marie', and preferred the French version of her surname, 'Stuart'. Secondly, Protestant lords like Patrick Ruthven knew all too well that Mary was a Catholic, returning to a Scotland that had just become officially Protestant. The queen's early months in her homeland coincided with the last session of the Council of Trent, which redefined Catholic doctrine, reformed abuses, and gave the Church of Rome a mission to win back ground that it had lost to Protestants. John Knox's violent reaction against the queen when he first met her suggests that, deep down, he feared there was a real danger of Scotland going precisely that way.[161] Quite apart from religious considerations, such a counter-revolution would have been economically disastrous for those who had benefited directly from the downfall of the Catholic Church in Scotland. Like many of his fellow Lords of the Congregation, Patrick Ruthven had successfully snapped up prime church land – in his case, some of the abbey lands, woods and fishing rights of Scone Abbey, destroyed by the Perth mob on 27 June 1559 but granted to Ruthven in November 1560.[162] Ruthven and the others like him had ample cause to resist any move to take Scotland back to the pope, and to resist the queen if she tried to do so.

Particularly anglophile nobles like Lord Ruthven would certainly have been well aware of the third troublesome aspect of their new queen. For many English and European Catholics, Mary was not merely Queen of Scots: she was also the rightful Queen of England as well. For Catholics, Henry VIII's divorce from Catherine of Aragon had never been valid. Thus his second marriage, to Anne Boleyn, had never been legal at all as far as Catholic Europe was concerned, and the child of that marriage, Elizabeth Tudor, was consequently a bastard and a usurper. But the fourth obvious fact about the queen was perhaps the most significant of all: the fact that she was a woman. In a patriarchal age, many would have agreed with the central thesis of Knox's ferocious diatribe, *The First Blast of the Trumpet Against the Monstrous Regiment of Women*, namely that it was unnatural and ungodly for women to rule over men.

The inconvenient young queen's first task was to decide on the composition of her government, specifically the membership of the Privy Council.[163] In practice, the most important figure on the council was Lord James Stewart, soon to be Earl of Moray, the queen's 30-year-old half-brother. He was one of 12 Protestants who sat alongside four Catholics. Patrick Ruthven first served on the council in April 1563, but after attending two meetings he did not turn up again until December, and had another prolonged absence through the summer of 1564. After that, though, he became an ever-present attendee, indeed one of the most regular of all.[164] However, his fellow Councillors and Lords of the Congregation did not trust a man who had changed sides rather too often, and their opinion was soon shared by the Queen, albeit for rather different reasons. Ruthven once offered her a ring as a peace offering, but a few years later Mary reminded him that Moray had wanted him punished, perhaps even executed, for giving her this gift. Ruthven protested that it 'was but a little ring with a pointed diamond in it'. Mary said, 'Remember you not that you said it had a virtue to keep me from poisoning'? Ruthven had to admit that 'I said so much, that the ring had that virtue', but went on in time-honoured political tradition to claim that his remarks had been taken out of context.[165] John Knox corroborated the story by claiming that Mary said Ruthven was 'one I cannot love (for I know him to use enchantment) and yet is he made one of my Privy Council'.[166] The antipathy between Ruthven and the queen only increased in December 1563 when Ruthven made an ill-judged attempt to defend Knox, whom Mary had finally put on trial for treasonable incitements to violence. Ruthven argued that Knox gathered people together quietly and legally for the purpose of prayers and sermons, but Mary furiously snapped at him 'Hold your peace!', and Ruthven had to back down.[167] Nevertheless, Ruthven's defence of Knox, and his earlier part in the Perth riots, ensured that he remained the darling of the Kirk, which either did not know of, or else simply rejected, the imputations of witchcraft that clung to him.

In September 1564 Matthew Stewart, thirteenth Earl of Lennox, was finally permitted to return to Scotland after spending almost 19 years in exile. Lennox – a descendant of King James II – was regarded by some as Mary's rightful heir, and he had reinforced his claims by marrying Lady Margaret Douglas, the daughter of Queen Margaret Tudor by her second marriage. Therefore Matthew and Margaret of Lennox, and their children, had strong claims to both the Scottish and English thrones, and Elizabeth I's ever-present paranoia about potential rivals for her crown had led to them spending four years in the Tower of London.[168] Lennox's return to Scotland created a new focus for those who disliked the dominance of Moray. For Patrick, Lord Ruthven, the decision to throw in his lot with Lennox was more personal, for after all, Lady Margaret Douglas, Countess of Lennox, was the half-sister of his first wife, and the friendship between the two families went back many years. By March 1565 the English ambassador was reporting that Ruthven was one of Lennox's faction, despite the fact that they were of different religions, and Ruthven hoped that a Lennox ascendancy would bring him the office of Lord Treasurer.[169] Lennox's rise was cemented by the fact that at last, in the early summer of 1565, Mary, Queen of Scots, finally settled on her choice of a second husband. Fatally for all concerned, she settled on Lennox's elder son, the 19-year-old Henry Stewart, Lord Darnley.

Darnley was tall, handsome, athletic and musical, so at least he looked the part of a royal consort, and of course he was also Mary's cousin. Lord Ruthven was soon identified as one of the driving forces behind the Darnley marriage. In May 1565 the English ambassador, Randolph, noted that he 'stirs coals as hot as fire to have these matters take effect, to his utter shame and contempt of all godly or honest'.[170] But Randolph undoubtedly tended to equate 'godly and honest' with 'complying precisely with the whims of Queen Elizabeth', and despite her own direct responsibility for allowing the Lennox family to return home in the first place, the English monarch was furious when she realised that Mary and Darnley were to marry.[171] After all, a marriage of Mary and Darnley would unite the claims of Elizabeth's two closest potential heirs and rivals for the English throne. Ruthven claimed to have no fear of England's queen, telling Mary 'that if she will follow his advice and such as he will take to him, he will both quiet this country [Scotland] and make England be content with reason'.[172] It was probably no coincidence that the convention of the nobility, summoned to ratify Mary's decision to marry, met in June at Perth, Ruthven's private fiefdom; and it was Ruthven who bore most responsibility for thwarting an apparent plot by Moray to kidnap the queen, Darnley and Lennox as they passed through the Pass of Dron, south of Perth, on 1 July.[173]

On 29 July 1565 Mary, Queen of Scots, was married to Henry, Lord Darnley, in the Chapel Royal of Holyrood Palace. Scotland had a new king, if only as a consort: Henry Stewart, by the grace of God, King of Scots. The new dispensation was clearly to the advantage of the Lennox family's close ally, Lord Ruthven. In the summer of 1565 Patrick twice entertained Mary, Queen of Scots, at Ruthven Castle. She stayed there from 25 to 27 June while attending the convention of the nobility, and she and Darnley also spent two days of their belated honeymoon there in September.[174] But within months, it all turned to dust. Patrick Ruthven fell ill some time in the autumn or winter of 1565. He was still up and about at the start of November, and he attended Privy Council meetings in Edinburgh regularly throughout December and January, but after attending on 25 January he never appeared again.[175] At some point, presumably around that date, he took to his bed, suffering from what he later described as 'an inflammation of the liver and a consumption of the kidney'; he claimed that he was 'scarcely able to walk twice the length of his own chamber', and was tended by the queen's French doctor, among others.[176] Patrick, Lord Ruthven, was a dying man. While his illness grew on him, the situation at court altered dramatically. The Queen was pregnant, but she was also fast falling out of love with her husband, whose rather less attractive character traits were increasingly apparent. Darnley may have been physically handsome, but he was also a weak, vain, indecisive, selfish, arrogant, childish, petulant, violent alcoholic. According to some sources, Lord Ruthven himself caught a glimpse of Darnley's true colours, some time before Darnley's marriage to the queen took place. Apparently, Ruthven was the messenger chosen by the Queen to inform Darnley that she was delaying his elevation to the dukedom of Albany until she knew how Queen Elizabeth had reacted to her blunt message that she intended to marry him, regardless of England's opposition. Although the delay was arguably in Darnley's interests, he reacted with blind fury and drew a knife on Ruthven, the blameless messenger.[177] Despite this, and despite 'King Henry's' other equally obvious inadequacies, he and his supporters were desperate to obtain for him the Crown Matrimonial, which would have given him full rights as co-sovereign rather than just the decorative status of a consort. The Crown Matrimonial would also mean that Darnley could succeed Mary if she died before they had any children. Once she discovered his true measure, though, Mary became equally determined to resist her husband's demand for the title, which would instantly make her both superfluous and expendable.

By the end of 1565, there was another festering cause of discord between the King and Queen of Scots. Some four years earlier, an embassy from the Duke of Savoy had arrived at the Scottish court to pay its respects to the newly returned queen. Among the ambassador's entourage was an ugly, bombastic little man with an exquisite singing voice: David Riccio, or Rizzio. Shortly after the embassy's arrival, the queen needed a bass to fill in at short notice in the quartet of singers that regularly entertained her. Rizzio volunteered, the queen was impressed by his voice, and the embassy returned to Savoy without its star musician, who was quickly employed by Mary as a gentleman of the privy chamber. In December 1564 he became additionally her secretary for French correspondence. The queen's obvious favour for a low-born foreign upstart, a 'stranger varlet',[178] naturally created resentment among the Scottish nobility, as did Rizzio's brashness in flaunting his position. Rizzio initially supported the Darnley marriage, and the two men were very friendly; indeed, there were rumours that they were homosexual lovers.[179] Now 'King Henry's' cronies quickly poisoned his mind against the Italian. They insinuated the idea that Rizzio was so constantly in the Queen's company that perhaps he was her lover; worse, they cast doubt on the paternity of Mary's unborn child. The more assertive pro-Catholic policy that Mary began to pursue in January 1566 was also blamed on Rizzio, who became that classic scapegoat of political history – the 'evil counsellor' who was deluding a well-intentioned monarch. The fact that he was also seen as a jumped-up arrogant foreigner, and a papist spy to boot, made him even more perfect.[180] What the conspirators needed now was someone prepared personally to lead the actual assassination of Rizzio. What they needed was a convinced Protestant with a reputation for violence; a man totally committed to the cause of the House of Lennox; and ideally, a man who had little to lose. That man could only be Patrick, Lord Ruthven. After all, who could have less to lose than a dead man walking?

****

By the start of March 1566 Ruthven's fatal illness was well advanced, and he knew it. Only a supreme effort of will allowed him to play what became his one great dramatic part in history, and it suggests the depth of his feelings against the 'papist agent' Rizzio and for the Lennox family. Ruthven, his ally the Earl of Morton (head of the mighty Douglas family), and other Protestant lords, including the exiled Moray, signed a bond with Darnley, by which the King agreed to pardon them for any crimes and to guarantee the religious status quo.[181] In return, the lords would ensure that Darnley obtained the Crown Matrimonial and would be recognised as Mary's heir. Ruthven probably thought that if he became one of the key instruments in granting Darnley such glittering prizes, the grateful king in turn would shower the family with rewards, even if Patrick Ruthven himself did not live long enough to enjoy them. Ruthven probably also knew that the English government was fully aware of, and entirely complicit in, the plot against Rizzio – and being in good credit with that government might again bear fruit for the Ruthvens if and when Mary, Darnley, or their child, inherited the English throne.

The murder was carefully planned for the night of Saturday 9 March, but it was to be much more than the simple killing of one man. The moment of Rizzio's death would be co-ordinated with the return to Edinburgh of Morton and above all of Moray, who was waiting at the English border, ready to cross into Scotland on the following morning. Rizzio's death would also be co-ordinated with the seizure of the loyal noblemen in the palace, namely the Earls of Bothwell, Atholl and Huntly. Moreover, the Italian's death would provide the excuse for the cancellation of the Parliament that had opened on 7 March – a parliament at which it was widely expected that Mary would legalize public attendance at the Catholic Mass. In the midst of this far-reaching political revolution, even the actual death scene of the man David Rizzio would have multiple resonances, for Rizzio was not going to die in some private corner. Seemingly at Darnley's own insistence, Rizzio was going to die in the queen's presence. At the very least, this would be a suitably terrifying warning to Mary (who was now six months' pregnant) not to cross her lords and her husband again – even if the intention was not to eliminate Mary herself, and that was by no means inconceivable. What was more, Rizzio was also to die in the king's presence. The conspirators had decided that personally and directly involving Darnley would ensure his adherence to them; by March 1566, not even his own friends particularly trusted 'King Henry' any more, as shown by their insistence that he sign an additional bond indemnifying the lords for eliminating 'a stranger Italian called Davie … to cut [him] off immediately, and to take and slay [him] whenever it happeneth'.[182] Thus it was Darnley who led Patrick, Lord Ruthven, and one of his servants, through the darkened rooms of Holyrood Palace, their way illuminated by candles. They climbed the private staircase that led to the two levels of royal apartments and emerged through a secret door into the queen's bedroom.

The layout of the queen's chambers at the Palace of Holyroodhouse has remained essentially unaltered since the night of Rizzio's death. Several doors led off the queen's bedchamber. The attendant ran to one, the door to the presence or outer chamber, and opened it, admitting those who had come from that direction via the main staircase – the Earl of Morton and some 80 Douglas, Lennox and Ruthven retainers, among them Patrick's son William, the Master of Ruthven, and Patrick's younger brother, Archibald Ruthven of Freeland. Darnley went to another door, the one that led directly into the small chamber where Mary was having supper with a group of five friends, including Rizzio. Darnley went across to speak to the queen and put his hand on her waist. This diversionary tactic gave time for Lord Ruthven to get from the staircase to the supper chamber, for by his own admission the dying lord could walk only slowly and painfully, even when in ordinary dress. That night, his costume was anything but ordinary. When he finally appeared in the door of the chamber, the effect must have been terrifying. By the flickering light of the palace candles, Ruthven's face, ravaged by months of terminal illness and the exertions of the long climb to the chamber, appeared lined, deathly pale and cadaverous. He was dressed in full armour, worn incongruously under a long nightgown. Sir Walter Scott's imagination found the image irresistible:

> There comes the fierce fanatic Ruthven, party hatred
> enabling him to bear the armour which would otherwise
> weigh down a form extenuated by wasting disease. See
> how his writhen features show under the hollow helmet,

like those of a corpse tenanted by a demon, whose
vindictive purpose looks out at the flashing eyes, while
the visage has the stillness of death.[183]

When the astonishing spectre that was Patrick Ruthven finally spoke,
his purpose was equally chilling: 'It would please your Majesty to let
yonder man Davie come forth of your presence, for he has been
overlong here'.[184]

Like almost all of the Stuarts, Mary was certainly no coward. She
stood up to the bizarre apparition of Lord Ruthven, demanding to
know what offence Rizzio had committed. Ruthven replied,

Madam, he has offended your honour, which I dare not
be so bold to speak of. As to the King your husband's
honour, he hath hindered him of the Crown
Matrimonial, which Your Grace promised him ... he has
been the destroyer of the commonwealth, by taking
bribes, and must learn his duty better.

'Leave our presence under pain of treason', Mary demanded, but
Ruthven was determined. He told Darnley to take care of the queen,
but when she stood, Rizzio cowered behind her, holding on to her
skirts for dear life. Mary's friends and servants tried to grab Ruthven,
who now drew his dagger, crying 'Lay not hands on me, for I will not
be handled!' Now the advantage swung back to Ruthven, for at this
moment, Morton and his party burst into the room. The conspirators
were now able to get at Rizzio, who screamed in Italian, 'Justice!
Justice! Save my life, Madame, save me!' Ruthven bundled Mary into
Darnley's arms, damningly incriminating her husband by saying 'all
that was done is the King's own deed and action'. Andrew Ker of
Fawdonside briefly held a pistol to the queen's pregnant belly to stop
her helping her secretary. Ruthven later denied that the queen was
threatened with a pistol, or that Rizzio was struck by knives in her
presence, but by then he had good reason for denying that such acts
took place, and other sources amply prove that Ruthven was being
economical with the truth. In the end the Italian was manhandled into
the outer chamber, where the plotters fell on him in a fury. Over 50
stab wounds ended his life, and the last dagger to be stuck in the
corpse was that of Henry Stewart, Lord Darnley, King of Scots
(although Darnley himself did not wield it).

With Rizzio dead, Lord Ruthven proceeded to give Mary a piece of his mind: 'I beseech your Majesty to be of good comfort, to entertain your husband and use the counsel of the nobility, and then your government will be as prosperous as in any king's days'. Either before or after he said this, according to the varying accounts, Mary turned to Darnley and demanded 'Why have you caused to do this wicked deed to me ... what offence have I made you that you should have done me such shame'? Darnley ranted about how she had denied him his conjugal rights, preferring the Italian's company instead.[185] Reduced to a mere spectator at this domestic soap opera, Ruthven found his infirmities, the weight of his armour, and the exertions of the evening, all catching up with him. He abruptly demanded a drink and a seat, and when he was brought a glass of wine, he downed it in one. The queen asked caustically, 'Is this your sickness, Lord Ruthven?', and Ruthven replied, 'God forbid Your Majesty had such a sickness'. Then Mary spoke to him once more, with a chilling finality that might yet have had a sequel years later, when Ruthven's grandsons met their end at Gowrie House: 'If I or my child die, you will have the blame thereof', and one source claims she warned Ruthven that the child growing in her belly would one day be avenged on his progeny.[186] More immediately, she threatened him with the catalogue of those who would avenge her against the House of Ruthven: King Philip II of Spain ('her great friend'), the Holy Roman Emperor Maximillian II ('likewise'), her brother-in-law King Charles IX of France, the Cardinal of Lorraine and her other Guise relations, and last but not least, the pope himself. With self-deprecation and perhaps some irony, too, Ruthven replied that 'these noble princes were over-great personages to meddle with such a poor man as he was'.

Lord Ruthven had no time to contemplate the queen's threats, for news soon arrived that Bothwell and Huntly had managed to climb out of a window and escaped through the palace's lion enclosure. This was a disaster for the plotters: it meant that a powerful noble faction was at large, one that could call on large numbers of armed men, was ferociously loyal to the person of the queen and her unborn child, but which was also hostile to all the elements of the fragile and mutually suspicious coalition of Darnley, Lennox, Moray, Morton and Ruthven. In this atmosphere of crisis the plotters discussed what to do next, and now Ruthven's sheer ruthlessness came to the fore. It was proposed to move the queen to Stirling, where her child could be born. If any resisted, said Ruthven, 'we will throw her to them piecemeal, from the top of the terrace'; but in any case, 'I feel certain, and I will stake my life on it, that the baby is only a girl, and there will be no danger'.[187] He warned Darnley that he should follow their advice and not talk to the queen alone. But, frightened by the attitude of his erstwhile friends, Darnley was already wavering, only hours after Rizzio's death. To ensnare him, Mary even feigned a miscarriage, which, in turn, forced Morton and Ruthven to reinstate her ladies of the bedchamber, her communication channels to the outside world. Mary knew her man well by this time, and was playing on Darnley's weakness in a skilful attempt to turn him against his former erstwhile allies. As she had said to a confidante within hours of Rizzio's death, 'No more tears. I will think upon revenge'.[188]

The queen's counter-attack, and the downfall of Lord Ruthven and the rest of the coalition ranged against her, was stunningly rapid. Within hours of Rizzio's death she had managed to get notes out of the palace via her ladies to the Earls of Bothwell and Huntly. And then there was the queen's brother himself, for Moray's return to Edinburgh on the night of 10 March paradoxically gave Mary a glorious opportunity to divide her enemies. She welcomed her brother gladly, promised him pardon, and complained about her treatment at the hands of his allies. Meanwhile she continued to work on Darnley, even promising to have sex with him that night. He promptly boasted of this to all and sundry, and Ruthven waited in the king's dressing room for Darnley to come and resume marital relations with his wife. The king never appeared, for as Mary had probably anticipated, he got so drunk celebrating their imminent coupling that he passed out before he got there. Ruthven gave up and went to sleep himself. When Darnley finally emerged the next day, Ruthven said 'You did not keep your promise to the Queen's Majesty to lie with her all that night'. Darnley sheepishly admitted that he had slept too deeply, but would go up straightaway. Ruthven quipped 'I trust she shall serve you in the morning as you did her at night!' Which is precisely what Mary did. When Darnley got to her bedchamber, she feigned sleep; when she 'woke', she feigned illness. Now that she had Darnley where she wanted him – alone – she worked on his weakness and his vanity. When Darnley returned to his co-conspirators, he 'very merrily' proclaimed that he had everything under control: Mary would pardon the exiled lords, who would ensure that he obtained the Crown Matrimonial in the next parliament. But when he went back to Mary, she told him bluntly that once Moray and the rest were pardoned, they would no longer need Darnley; after all, why should they acquiesce in his receiving the Crown Matrimonial, when that would be so detrimental to their own power? Moreover, his so-called friends were all Protestants; for how long, exactly, would the likes of Patrick Ruthven be prepared to tolerate a Catholic king? Slowly, the very stupid Darnley crumbled before her relentless logic and considerably greater intelligence. Slowly, the very naïve King of Scots gave way to a Queen of Scots who had been brought up, as her enemies like Ruthven knew all too well, in the most politically sophisticated and devious court in Europe, by probably the most able and ruthless politicians at that court – her maternal family, the Guises.

Mary continued to pursue her escape strategy throughout the next day, 11 March. She convinced the lords around her that she was suffering labour pains and needed a freer environment; she assured them that they would have royal pardons, in writing, for the murder of Rizzio, but mysteriously delayed applying her signature to them; simultaneously, she continued to work on her hapless husband. Ruthven strongly suspected the truth of what was happening, or at least, he subsequently claimed that he did. He warned Darnley 'that what end followed thereupon, or what blood was shed for the same, that it should come upon the king's head and posterity, and nought upon theirs'. Finally, at midnight on 11/12 March, Mary and Darnley escaped from Holyrood. They made their way down the same staircase that had admitted Darnley and Ruthven two nights before, got out into the abbey precincts unobserved, and almost fell over the freshly dug grave of David Rizzio.[189] They rode fast to Dunbar Castle, 25 miles away, where they assembled an army before returning to Edinburgh in triumph on 18 March. After making a feeble attempt to get Mary to sign their promised pardons, Ruthven and Morton realised that the queen was dividing her opponents by forgiving those lords who had been in England on 9 March, but 'the queen … [would] bare her Majesty's whole rage against them that were with the king at the slaughter of Davie'. Patrick Ruthven, his son William and the Earl of Morton, all fled to England. Ruthven himself rode hard down Teviotdale, crossing the English border at Wark Castle and reaching Berwick on 20 March.[190] The last act of the newly exiled lords was to send Mary the bond that they and Darnley had signed – the bond that proved beyond doubt the complicity of her husband in the murder of her favourite. As Ruthven put it in his account, written only days later, 'they have done nothing without the king's command'. Mary had been convinced from the start that the murder in the supper chamber had actually been part of a plot against herself and her unborn child, and the revelation of the bond's existence only strengthened her intention to take revenge on the plotters, including the King of Scots, her weak and duplicitous Darnley.

However, she had no need to pursue the leader of the murderers. The third Lord Ruthven used the first days of his exile to write letters to the English authorities, and followed these by compiling his own account of his part in the death of Rizzio, signing it at Berwick on 28 March. Inevitably, this was largely self-justificatory, and was written very much for English consumption; Ruthven showed no remorse whatsoever, insisting that he had acted only in defence of the wronged and cuckolded King Henry, whom he identified as the instigator of the entire conspiracy.[191] Patrick, Lord Ruthven, died at Newcastle on 13 June 1566. Exactly six days after his death, the child of Mary and Lord Darnley was born in Edinburgh Castle and named James.

****

In death, as in life, opinion about Patrick Ruthven was divided. Claude Nau, the 'ghost writer' of the memoirs that Mary Stuart composed in her English prison some 10 years later, summed up well the death of the man regarded by many in the Kirk as a hero, and regarded by others – including the Queen of Scots – as a demon incarnate:

> Before his death Lord Ruthven showed great repentance
> for his wicked life. He thanked God for having given
> him the opportunity and the inclination before He
> called him to Himself, to pray for mercy and the pardon
> of his sins. Others say that he died like a madman,
> exclaiming that he was paradise opened, and a great
> company of angels coming to take him. It is probable
> that these were diabolical illusions, wrought by evil
> spirits, who wished to delude him as he was passing
> away, that he might not escape them, for during his life
> they had possessed him with the art of magic.[192]

Of course, Nau was not actually present at Ruthven's deathbed, but Morton was. The Douglas earl recorded the event rather differently, claiming Patrick Ruthven's end was 'so godly that all men that saw it did rejoice'.[193] Even Nau admitted that he 'showed great repentance for his wicked life'. So died Patrick, third Lord Ruthven, a man with a fearsome and unholy reputation even before he took the leading part in Rizzio's death. It is difficult to build a case for Patrick Ruthven, even if one treats with scepticism the limited evidence linking him with the black arts. His career was unprincipled and opportunistic, but in that, he was hardly unique among the Scottish nobility of his day. On the other hand, Ruthven was clearly deeply attached to his family and wider kin, and much of what he did was plainly done to promote the interests of the House of Ruthven as he saw them. Even his part in Rizzio's murder becomes explicable when seen in the context of kin loyalty: Lord Darnley, the King of Scots, was his kinsman, a kinsman who had been wronged and shamed by his wife, and it was Ruthven's duty to obtain redress for him. There might also have been an element of male chauvinism here, deep in the mindset of a Scottish aristocrat (and follower of John Knox) who undoubtedly preferred to deal with a male monarch, however inadequate, than with a half-French queen regnant.

However, it is surely impossible to defend Ruthven's treatment of Mary during the critical 48 hours after Rizzio's death. His apparent lack of concern for her safety, and that of her unborn child, is shocking enough, and seemingly contradicts the opinion of those historians who argue that the plotters did not intend to do away with Mary (as to do so before she had granted Darnley the Crown Matrimonial would surely have defeated their purpose). But such an assumption ignores the realities of the Scottish succession. If Mary Stuart and her child had died on 9 March 1566 then the throne would almost certainly have passed to Matthew Stewart, Earl of Lennox, Lord Darnley's father; unless, of course, he resigned his claim to his son, who already bore the title of king. Lennox was in Edinburgh (unlike the other likely contender, Moray); the conspirators were acting on his son's behalf; and Lord Ruthven was his kinsman and friend. The debates about the Crown Matrimonial would have been entirely academic if the Lennox Stewarts had secured the throne of Scotland itself, so Ruthven might have calculated that his family's interests could not possibly lose, whatever the fate of Mary Stuart. Unfortunately for him, he underestimated the abilities and native cunning of Mary, Queen of Scots, and he certainly underestimated the feebleness and fickleness of his own kinsman, Henry, King of Scots. Even Lord Ruthven's apparently total certainty that their offspring would be a girl was proved to be utterly wrong, and in the end, as Mary had allegedly predicted, the son growing in her belly on 9 March 1566 would wreak a final and complete revenge on the House of Ruthven on 5 August 1600.

****

The undisputed facts of Ruthven involvement in the dark arts gave rise to legends galore, and they still do. The Internet carries unsourced suggestions that Patrick, Lord Ruthven, and his two successors, were all worshippers of Satan, and among the leaders of a secret diabolic cult in Scotland.[194] Rather more certain is the dramatic intervention by Archibald Ruthven at the wedding in 1570 of Euphemia McCalzean, daughter and heiress of one of the senators of the College of Justice, to the son of another prominent lawyer. Archie, a brother of the first Earl of Gowrie who was briefly Master of Ruthven in the early 1570s before he embarked on a calamitous career as a mercenary general in the Baltic,[195] provided every bride's worst nightmare about what might happen when the minister asks the time-honoured question about 'just cause and impediment': he proclaimed loudly that the wedding was invalid because he had the first promise of Euphemia's hand and had already acted on this promise by sleeping with the bride. The wedding degenerated into a riot, with assorted Ruthvens and lawyers brawling through the streets of Edinburgh.[196] Archie Ruthven died in a Swedish prison a few years later; Euphemia McCalzean was burned alive on Edinburgh's castle hill in 1591, the most prominent casualty of the North Berwick witch-hunt of that year.[197]

The Ruthven tradition of indulging in science and sorcery (and perhaps occasionally sleeping with witches) extended well beyond the heads of the family, and was not confined to the men alone: Lilias Ruthven, Lady Drummond, the first Earl of Gowrie's aunt, owned a book of astrology.[198] Then there was George Ruthven of Perth, born in about 1546, who presumably knew the dreaded third lord well. His exact relationship to the main Ruthven family is unknown, but was clearly close; his favourite chair bore the Ruthven court-of-arms.[199] Young George became a respected physician and lived well into his nineties. In the 1620s or 1630s the poet Henry Adamson made him the subject and alleged author of several poems that were later published as *The Muse's Threnodie*. Ruthven was suspected of involvement in the 'Gowrie House affair', and Adamson also hinted that he had been accused of witchcraft.[200] Nevertheless, Ruthven kissed King James's hand at Perth on 15 April 1601, a sure sign that he had been forgiven for any direct part in the alleged conspiracy. In reality, George Ruthven's role in the affair was most likely indirect but disastrously formative. John Ruthven, third Earl of Gowrie, and his younger brother Patrick clearly picked up their interest in science and the occult somewhere, or from someone. Both their father and grandfather had been accused of dabbling in the black arts, but their grandfather was long dead and their father was executed when John was six, perhaps before Patrick was even born. The Ruthven boys grew up surrounded by women and had precious few male role models from their own family. But their old relation George, whose house in Perth was literally around the corner from Gowrie House, must have been an exotic and irresistible mentor, surrounded by potions and regaling them from his vast fund of esoteric knowledge.

The lives of both George and Patrick Ruthven demonstrated that the boundaries between 'science' and 'magic' (and astrology, and alchemy, and necromancy) were blurred. They were part of a wider tradition of interest in the dark arts among the Scottish elite, but it was easy for the ignorant and credulous to charge those with intelligent, enquiring minds with straying too far into the black arts, especially during the hysterical witch-craze of the 1590s.[201] In the circumstances, it would only have been surprising if those would-be regicides, the Ruthvens, had *not* been condemned as warlocks, in league with Satan.

****

The demonic reputations of Patrick, third Lord Ruthven, and of his family as a whole, might perhaps have had one more witting or unwitting consequence for posterity. During that mythic occasion in literary history, the stormy night in June 1816 at the Villa Diodati on the shores of Lake Geneva, Lord Byron, Percy Bysshe Shelley, Shelley's bride-to-be Mary and Byron's physician John Polidori famously competed with each to write horror stories that would outdo those of the others. By far the greatest product of the night was Mary's story of resurrected corpses that became the basis of *Frankenstein*. But Polidori's work, too, was published and became a sensational success in its own time. Polidori's *The Vampyre* is widely regarded as the model for most of the stories of the undead that have been written since that time, including Bram Stoker's *Dracula*. The glamorous, devious and cold-bloodedly amoral character of *The Vampyre* was plainly based on Lord Byron, and Polidori even appropriated the same name that Byron's jilted lover Lady Caroline Lamb had used for her similar portrayal of the poet in the novel *Glenarvon*. If the derivation of the character traits is obvious, it is still interesting to speculate on exactly how and why Lamb and Polidori struck on their choice of name: for the name of *The Vampyre* was Lord Ruthven.

CHAPTER FOUR

GREYSTEIL

The various versions of King James's account of what happened at Gowrie House were unanimous. The Ruthven brothers were intent on a simple crime driven by a simple motive: murder born of vengeance. From the night of 5 August 1600 onwards, James himself publicly stuck to the idea that the Ruthvens' intention had been revenge for their father's execution. The last public account he ever gave of the conspiracy, during his return visit to Perth in 1617, claimed that Sandy had said to him, 'Now Sir, you must know, I had a father, whose blood calls for revenge, shed for your sake'.[202] This line was parroted in all the hellfire sermons delivered by James's tame preachers: the events at Gowrie House were an attempt to assassinate the king, to commit regicide, nothing more and nothing less. Murdering the king to avenge the first Earl of Gowrie has a simplicity and logic that most of the other explanations of the 'Gowrie House affair' lack. Conversely, if James wanted to conceal the truth of what was really said and done in the turret chamber, attributing to Sandy Ruthven a desire to avenge his dead father provided a simple and believable 'cover story', and an assassination plot provided a neat, black-and-white rationale for charges of treason and for forfeiting the Ruthven estates. It also avoided awkward questions about what else the brothers might have had in mind, and about any mysterious accomplices who might have been sheltering behind them. However, its credibility as an explanation for the events at Gowrie House hinged in turn on the answer to another question: exactly how plausible was the claim that King James VI had judicially murdered William Ruthven, first Earl of Gowrie?

****

William Ruthven was 24 years old when his father died in 1566. He should then have become the fourth Lord Ruthven, but there seemed little realistic prospect of that. The victory of Queen Mary, Moray and Bothwell over the murderers of Rizzio seemed to ensure that Ruthven would never succeed to his title and lands, which were rapidly forfeited to the crown. But William Ruthven's career amply demonstrated the unpredictability of sixteenth-century Scottish politics. During the second half of 1566, while William remained in exile, events moved rapidly in his favour. Above all, relations between the queen and Darnley were going from bad to worse. During November Mary lay dangerously ill at Craigmillar Castle, south of Edinburgh. If Mary died then the infant Prince James would become king, but his unstable father would have a strong claim to rule on his behalf, and most of Scotland's nobility simply could not contemplate that. Eventually it was whispered that the only way to deal with Darnley was to eliminate him once and for all. Of course, the risk in getting rid of Darnley was that the Lennox Stewarts could still potentially mobilise a formidable force against the 'Craigmillar lords'. That risk would be greatly reduced, Mary was told, if the Lennoxes' potential allies, the exiled murderers of Rizzio, were pardoned and brought into the grand alliance of potential murderers of Darnley. So, on Christmas Eve 1566, and presumably not without much swallowing of both pride and bile, the Queen of Scots duly issued pardons to the exiles.[203] William Ruthven returned to Scotland, and on 19 March 1567 he was confirmed in his ownership of his ancestral lands.[204] Nine days later the natural order of things was restored in Perth: William, now fourth Lord Ruthven, entered into his family's traditional office, becoming the town's provost.[205]

During the first 10 weeks of 1567, then, William Ruthven's main concern was to ensure that he was legally confirmed in his estates, and this probably explains why he seems not to have become directly involved in the plot to murder Darnley at Kirk O'Field in Edinburgh on 10 February 1567. However, Mary's subsequent marriage to the Earl of Bothwell, the alleged murderer of Darnley, was too much for Ruthven and many others to stomach. Noblemen began to sign bonds pledging to defend Prince James and to bring to justice the murderers of Darnley (an obvious euphemism for 'Bothwell'). Prominent among these 'confederate lords' was William, Lord Ruthven, and in June 1567 he commanded part of the confederate rearguard when Mary surrendered at Carberry Hill.[206] The confederate lords now no longer had any real use for Mary, for they had an obvious replacement monarch to hand in the shape of her son. Ruthven was one of the two lords chosen to escort her to Lochleven Castle and then to keep her under close guard; they arrived at the castle on 16 June.[207] Lochleven seemed the perfect prison. Occupying virtually the whole of an island in the middle of the vast loch, it would plainly be difficult for the queen's friends to mount a surprise rescue bid. But as the Queen of Scots began her confinement, her old charms worked their magic even on the fourth Lord Ruthven. Early in July 1567, English sources reported that Ruthven was to be replaced because he was becoming too affectionate towards the queen.[208] Mary, too, subsequently claimed that he had made advances towards her, writing her an inappropriate letter and coming to her one morning, 'throwing himself on his knees near her bed, [and] promised that he would free her if she would love him'. Any ambitions that Ruthven might have harboured to become the queen's fourth husband were short-lived, and on 24 July he stood over her as she signed the instrument of abdication, bluntly threatening her with death if she refused to sign it.[209] Ruthven brought the document to Stirling on the 29th, swore disingenuously that the queen had signed it of her own free will, and attended the hastily-arranged ceremony that took place in the Church of the Holy Rude later that day: the coronation of James VI, by the grace of God, King of Scots, aged 13 months.

Inevitably, the new regime was barely in place before some began to plot against it. They engineered Mary's escape from Lochleven on 2 May 1568, and the queen immediately declared her abdication null and void, so Scots faced a choice of sides: the King's Men, or the Queen's Men? William Ruthven's allegiance was never in doubt, and when the two armies faced each other at Langside (near Glasgow) on 13 May, he was one of the chief commanders on the side of king and regent, who won the battle decisively. Mary panicked and fled to England, where her cousin Elizabeth placed her under house arrest. In Scotland, though, the civil war raged on. Lord Ruthven continued to be one of the most prominent leaders of the King's Men, and was rewarded with lands and offices from the regent, Moray. On 23 January 1570, though, James, Earl of Moray was assassinated at Linlithgow, and William Ruthven found himself one of the eight lords bearing the regent's coffin to its grave in St Giles' Cathedral.[210] The king's party was now in crisis, with more and more lords and towns declaring for the queen.[211] In desperation, the leaders of the 'king's men' turned to a new regent, the one man who could potentially guarantee them the English military support that they needed: on 12

July Matthew Stewart, Earl of Lennox, was sworn in as regent of Scotland.[212] Lennox's elevation inevitably benefited Ruthven, who maintained his family's long tradition of loyalty to the Lennox Stewarts. Equally, Lennox needed to guarantee his power base by rewarding his loyalists, and his generosity to Lord Ruthven was spectacular: on 24 June 1571 Lennox appointed Ruthven Lord High Treasurer of Scotland for life. On 4 September, though, the Regent Lennox was killed in Stirling during a lightning attack on the town by Mary's forces. Among those who died at the regent's side was George, Master of Ruthven, Lord William's brother and heir.[213]

Lord Ruthven's value to the 'King's Men' was also demonstrated by his active career as a military commander and diplomat throughout the civil war. He commanded several successful operations and undertook independent negotiations, although he spent most of the war assisting with the interminable siege of Edinburgh Castle.[214] In April 1573 Ruthven signed the agreement that brought an English artillery train against Edinburgh Castle. The fortress finally surrendered on 28 May, thanks partly to the English guns, and its fall signalled the end of the civil war.[215] Meanwhile Ruthven also fulfilled an old obligation, perhaps one inherited from his father. On 24 November 1572, he attended the deathbed of John Knox. Solicitously, Ruthven asked 'If there be anything, sir, that I am able to do for you, I pray you charge me with it'. Curmudgeonly to the last, the old firebrand replied, 'I care not for all the pleasure and friendship of the world'.[216]

****

While Scotland warred with itself, the family of William, Lord Ruthven, grew prolifically. Between 1562 and 1584 his wife Dorothea bore him at least 14 children: an apparently unbroken succession of daughters, followed by an apparently unbroken succession of sons. The eldest child, Mary, must have been born in 1562, and was naturally named after Scotland's newly returned queen, who served as her godmother. After her, and in approximate order of age, came Lilias, Dorothea, Margaret, Sophia, Jean, Isabel, Beatrix and Barbara. The first surviving son, James, Master of Ruthven, was not born until about 1574, and was named in tribute to Scotland's sovereign and his latest regent, the Earl of Morton.[217] The next son, John, born in about 1577, was named after John, Earl of Atholl, the old ally of the Ruthven family. Alexander, William and Patrick followed between 1580 and 1584.

While his family grew, William Ruthven embarked on an ambitious programme of building, rebuilding and refurbishment at his various properties. Partly, this might have been driven by the need to accommodate his growing brood; partly, it might have been inspired by the perceived need for a great lord to live in a grand style that made an impressive statement to all. Partly, though, the building programme was undoubtedly driven by Lord Ruthven's own passionate interests in architecture, the fine arts, gardening and the land. Ruthven Castle, nominally still the family's chief seat, was too cramped and old-fashioned for major development, but at Dirleton Ruthven could give full rein to his architectural ambitions. He built a spacious new Renaissance residence, just inside the gatehouse, and this remains known as the Ruthven Lodging. He and Dorothea were also mainly responsible for the laying-out of the magnificent formal gardens that still survive, partly as they planned them, and which feature in *The Guinness Book of Records* by virtue of possessing the longest herbaceous border in the world. The lodging was carefully positioned to give an uninterrupted view out over the gardens.[218] The Ruthvens were also building at two of their other properties. In 1579 they installed a fashionable new long gallery at their town house in Perth, a gallery that would loom large in the downfall of both William Ruthven and his sons.[219] Finally, there was their newest property, the Abbey of Scone. The Ruthvens had acquired certain rights on Scone land in 1559, but in 1571 William Ruthven took full ownership of the property. By 1580, he had begun construction of an impressive new two-storeyed palace on the site of the medieval abbey buildings, incorporating elements of the old abbot's lodging.[220] Parts of Ruthven's building still survive, incorporated into the structure of the extant 19th century palace. Above all, Ruthven's glorious long gallery is still there, having survived such indignities as being iced over so that Queen Victoria could watch a curling demonstration.[221]

Like his predecessors, William, the fourth Lord Ruthven, was an astute builder of kinship, friendship and marriage alliances that placed his family at the heart of Scotland's political elite. Unlike his father, though, he was equally determined to enhance his family's prosperity, transforming his estates into a grand display of the power, prosperity and good taste of the House of Ruthven. All of this was neatly summed up by one observer in 1577: 'The Lord Ruthven, of the same surname, Sheriff of Perth by inheritance ... a baron of good living ... The house of Ruthven have been always very loyal to their estate, wise, and men hardy. Not many of their surname, but of good power by their friends and alliances'.[222]

****

In October 1572 the forceful, uncouth Earl of Morton, the old ally and kinsman of William Ruthven's father, became regent of Scotland. Unsurprisingly, Ruthven continued to prosper under Morton's regime, receiving several grants from the regent.[223] Above all, he continued to serve as Scotland's Lord Treasurer. In one respect, this was a thankless task: Scotland's royal finances were always precarious, and treasurers were usually selected on the basis of their capacity to bail out the royal coffers. Ruthven faced particularly onerous burdens, notably the cost of rebuilding Edinburgh Castle after the civil war. On the other hand, being Lord Treasurer of any early modern state supposedly presented the officeholder with considerable opportunities for personal enrichment, and many contemporaries believed that rewards were sticking surreptitiously to Ruthven's fingers. Perhaps the extravagant building programme that he pursued during the 1570s and 1580s suggests that they might have been right.[224] Even so, from about 1576 onwards Ruthven was in increasing difficulties, for he had to use increasing amounts of his own capital to remedy the pitiful state of the treasury. By 1580 he was owed some £40,000 from the Crown, and had obtained £26,000 on the security of his own estates. These vast debts had not been repaid when William Ruthven died.[225]

In 1574 there was some talk of Morton losing his place as regent. Lord Ruthven was mentioned as a possible successor, albeit in tandem with three others, but nothing came of it.[226] Nevertheless, at much the same time Ruthven was said by one English commentator to be 'of blood to the king, especially friended [ie to England], and of credit and valiant', all of which made him worth a retainer of £100 sterling from the English crown. Morton was worth £500.[227] By 1577, though, the first cracks were appearing in the seemingly impregnable alliance between Lord Ruthven and the Regent Morton. William Ruthven had many neighbourhood and kinship loyalties that could pull him away from his usual alignment with the House of Douglas, and probably the most important of these was the Ruthvens' friend, neighbour and kinsman, John Stewart, fourth Earl of Atholl. When Atholl and the Earl of Argyll formed an alliance that aimed to bring down Morton, Ruthven threw in his lot with them.[228] They won over the young king, and on 12 March 1578, Morton was forced to resign the regency. Atholl became Lord Chancellor, and the 12-year-old James VI was declared nominally old enough to rule in his own right.[229] Lord Ruthven received the surrender of Edinburgh Castle from the ex-regent.[230] Morton survived, and even staged a partial comeback a few months later, effectively becoming head of the government again, though without the title of regent. Indeed, he also quickly rebuilt his relationship with Ruthven.

****

In April 1579, the earls of Atholl and Morton dined together at Stirling; a few days later, Atholl died in agony. Inevitably, there were rumours of poisoning, and Atholl's family and friends naturally blamed Morton. Soon afterwards, Atholl's widow and her neighbours Lord and Lady Ruthven hatched a plan for another marriage alliance between the two families. The new Earl of Atholl, a 16-year-old youth, married Mary, the eldest of the Ruthvens' many daughters, at Perth on 24 January 1580. One English commentator remarked:

> The Earl of Atholl doth marry the Lord Ruthven's
> daughter. It is a question whether by that marriage the
> Lord Ruthven will draw the Earl to the devotion of
> Morton, or the Earl will draw the Lord Ruthven to his
> devotion, who is as yet an enemy of Morton.[231]

The answer became apparent a few months later, although the young Atholl was hardly responsible for it. On 1 November 1580 a wedding party led by Lord Ruthven was attacked by the Master of Oliphant and some of his followers. There had been bad blood between the Ruthvens and Oliphants for centuries, and one of the Ruthven party was shot dead. Lord Ruthven demanded that Oliphant be tried for murder, which he duly was; but Morton sided with the Master, whose father-in-law was Morton's cousin, and he was acquitted.[232] Ruthven was furious, and the Oliphant murder seems to have heralded his final breach with Morton.

The Earl of Morton's many enemies were gathering for a final reckoning. On New Year's Eve 1580 Morton was attending a meeting of the Privy Council when he was suddenly and publicly accused of complicity in Darnley's murder. Ruthven allegedly knew of the plot against Morton, but decided not to warn him about it. The earl's trial was held at his own stronghold, Dalkeith, in May 1581. Although

Ruthven attended the preliminary discussions, he did not sit on the jury, partly because he suddenly fell ill 'so that his face and whole body broke out in blisters and swelling'. There were inevitable rumours of poisoning, but Ruthven actually seems to have been laid low by a particularly bad batch of Dalkeith beer.[233] Inevitably, a jury composed almost exclusively of his enemies condemned Morton to death, a sentence carried out at Edinburgh Cross on 2 June 1581. The manner of his end was particularly apposite: Morton had introduced to Scotland an early form of the guillotine, nicknamed 'The Maiden', and he perished by his own invention. Ruthven benefited spectacularly from the distribution of honours that inevitably followed Morton's downfall. In August 1581 the lands of Scone Abbey were elevated into the territorial basis for a new earldom, and William Ruthven was created the first Earl of Gowrie. In October 1581 William was belted by the king at Holyrood Palace.[234] The new Earl of Gowrie was still not 40, he had healthy sons to succeed him, and more were still to be born. The future for the House of Ruthven must have seemed rosy indeed.

****

In September 1579, King James VI's cousin Esmé Stewart, Seigneur d'Aubigny, appeared at Holyrood Palace. He had come from his native France at James's invitation, and his arrival at the drab northern court caused a sensation, not least because he brought with him 40,000 gold pieces and all the latest French fashions.[235] Witty, cultured and exotic, the 37-year-old Esmé immediately captivated his 13-year-old cousin, perhaps triggering the sexual ambivalence that James VI and I demonstrated ever after. The arrival of the Catholic Aubigny might have seemed to run completely counter to the public position of the Ruthven family over three generations, but it was all far more complex than that; for Esmé was a Lennox Stewart, the new head of a line to which the Ruthvens had been loyal for decades. Esmé Stewart's father John was a brother of the Regent Lennox, Darnley's father, and had gone out to take over the French estates when the previous line of Aubigny Stewarts died out in 1543. Thus Esmé was one of the young king's very few close living relations, and, indeed, debatably his closest heir. The timing of Esmé's trip to Scotland, in the wake of James's invitation, undoubtedly stemmed from his wish to establish his claims to both the Lennox earldom and the royal succession itself.[236] As far as William, Lord Ruthven, was concerned, his family's traditional loyalty to the Lennox Stewarts, along with a weather eye on the reversionary interest should James die, ensured that the future Earl of Gowrie rapidly cultivated the friendship of the new royal favourite.

Esmé's rise was rapid and spectacular. In March 1580 James made him Lord Darnley and Earl of Lennox, the titles that had been held by the king's father and grandfather. By October 1580, Esmé was Great Chamberlain of Scotland and first gentleman of the bedchamber, responsible for a sweeping reorganisation of the royal household.[237] On 5 August 1581, and presumably to the chagrin of most of the country's old nobility, the royal favourite became Duke of Lennox, the only duke in Scotland (and England, come to that). Inevitably, many nailed their colours to the mast of the new favourite even more emphatically than William Ruthven. Contemporaries quickly identified Lennox's closest ally: Captain James Stewart, a younger son of Lord Ochiltree. Stewart had been a soldier in Sweden, Germany and Russia, and he already had a reputation as a dashing, ruthless, arrogant man of action. He was soon a gentleman of the bedchamber, and in 1581 he became captain of the royal guard. Stewart and Lennox were the prime movers behind the Earl of Morton's final downfall and execution, and Stewart was subsequently created Earl of Arran, receiving his earl's belt from the king at the same time that William, Earl of Gowrie, received his. The title of Earl of Arran was traditionally borne by the head of the House of Hamilton, and there was already an incumbent earl, albeit an insane one. But the Hamiltons had been crushed by Morton in 1579 and the earl's brothers were in exile, so the pathetic Arran was compelled to resign his title to the man who had recently and conveniently become his guardian – Captain James Stewart.

Arran was hated not only by the Hamiltons. The downfall of Morton was accompanied by the disgrace of the House of Douglas as a whole, and its new head, the Earl of Angus, had fled to England. Within a few months, therefore, Arran had successfully alienated what had long been the two most powerful families in Scotland, the Hamiltons and the Douglases. He also found a wife who was, if anything, even more rapacious and arrogant than he was. Elizabeth Stewart was a daughter of the Ruthvens' old friend, the fourth Earl of Atholl, and was described by one contemporary as 'a lewd, fascinating woman'.[238] In 1578, aged about 24, she married Esmé's aged uncle Robert Stewart, Earl of Lennox and Bishop of Caithness. The highly sexed Elizabeth soon found the dashing young Captain Stewart more to her taste, and she was already pregnant by him when in May 1581 she divorced her elderly husband, now Earl of March following his resignation of the Lennox title to Esmé, on trumped-up grounds of impotence (or, as one writer memorably put it, 'because his instrument was not good').[239] Six weeks later she married her lover, the new Earl of Arran, thus achieving some sort of improbable record as the countess of three separate earldoms in less than three years. Elizabeth's high-handed behaviour at court, and her all-too-apparent lust for fine clothes and jewels, offended most of those who encountered her. She earned the nickname Lady Jezebel, and was soon accused of consorting with witches. It is hardly surprising that some 20th century scholars saw Arran and his countess as possible models for two of the best known characters in English literature: the Macbeths.[240]

****

The Duke of Lennox converted to Protestantism in 1581, but many doubted the sincerity of his conversion and saw him as the obvious focus for a Catholic revival in Scotland. During 1581–2 there was much discussion of schemes that would have involved the release of Mary, Queen of Scots, who would mount Scotland's throne again, in joint sovereignty with her son. Lennox would have had much to lose from such an arrangement, so he was at best ambivalent about such suggestions, but even so, many wrongly associated him with a restoration of Scotland's Catholic queen.[241] Similarly, many Protestants became convinced that the Kirk was in danger, perhaps because both Lennox and Arran had little time for the pomposity of the ministers and insulted them to their faces. Then there were those who hated Arran, and damned Lennox by association: but before the end of 1581, Lennox and Arran had fallen out decisively following a series of bitter arguments over control of access to the young king.[242] Perhaps a better politician than Lennox could have turned the new situation to his advantage, but he blundered on, oblivious to the dangers. Depending on one's point of view, therefore, the Duke of Lennox was either a French (and/or Spanish, and/or papal) agent, a threat to the king and to Protestant Scotland, or else he was a blithering incompetent. Either way, he had to go.[243]

Behind the scenes, as always, and working hard to manipulate the opinions of Scotland's elites, were the agents of England. Their fundamental problem was that they were not always entirely certain of the direction in which they were meant to be manipulating those opinions, for in her policy towards Scotland, as in so many other ways, Elizabeth I was idiosyncratic, inconsistent and infuriating. She did not want to see a full-blown restoration of Mary, Queen of Scots; but on the other hand, Mary was her cousin and a legitimate sovereign, one of God's anointed (like Elizabeth herself, of course), and in that sense James VI was a usurper, placed on the throne following an illegal coup which provided an uncomfortable model for the Virgin Queen's own discontented subjects. Elizabeth was suspicious of Lennox because he was French and, perhaps, still a Catholic too;[244] but on the other hand, she was pursuing a friendly policy towards France when Lennox was in power. Finally, whatever policy Elizabeth wanted in Scotland, it had to obey the one cardinal rule of English foreign policy: it had to cost as little as possible, and preferably nothing at all. It was in these circumstances, in October 1580, that William Ruthven had a long conversation with the English ambassador, Robert Bowes. Ruthven professed his personal loyalty to Queen Elizabeth's cause, and his willingness to support a marriage for King James that would meet with the queen's approval. Moreover, Ruthven sought to allay Elizabeth's doubt about Lennox's motives: he had no aim, Ruthven claimed, other than to serve the king, 'honour the Queen of England, and maintain the amity'. In any case, he could hardly pursue a very different policy, as he relied on the support of the nobility, and the majority of them would never stand for a change of direction.[245] Bowes was impressed, and continued to regard the soon-to-be Earl of Gowrie as one of the main advocates of Elizabeth's cause in Scotland, although both he and the queen continued to doubt his assessment of Lennox's innocence.[246] So, too, did many of Gowrie's peers.

By the summer of 1582, a group of noblemen had come together to plot a *coup d'état*, and as was usual in Scottish plots, they signed a bond setting out their purpose.[247] This was simple: they would seize the king, govern in his name, and drive out of Scotland both the Duke of Lennox and the Earl of Arran, adding to the latter's name the ominous rider, 'in case he escaped with his life'. Gowrie probably came to the plot late, and only after he was warned that Lennox intended to have him killed at the first opportunity.[248] Gowrie's initially good relationship with the duke had collapsed following at least two serious arguments which culminated in both sides toughing it out in the streets of Edinburgh, the Earl of Huntly and his men escorting Lennox, Atholl and 'others of the town of Perth' escorting Gowrie.[249] However, Gowrie's breach with Lennox might not have been entirely spontaneous. The new English ambassador, Thomas Randolph, had been instructed by Elizabeth's chief minister, Lord Burghley, to use all means possible to detach Gowrie (then still Lord Ruthven) from Lennox's faction. At first Randolph despaired of achieving this end, claiming in February 1581 that Ruthven had 'so far failed in honesty that now he is past shame where profit may be had', but by the spring of 1582 Gowrie was so restored in England's regard that Elizabeth I herself wrote to James on his behalf, noting that the earl had been the victim of 'evil offices' (presumably Lennox's), and commending him as a man 'by birth, courage, sufficiency, and other good qualities … very fit to be about your person and to do you service'.[250] Quite apart from his personal quarrels with Lennox and his concern to ensure the survival of a Protestant Scotland, Gowrie's office of Lord Treasurer undoubtedly provided him with other reasons to take action against the royal favourite. Firstly, and perhaps cynically, he was still owed large sums by the Crown from the 1570s, perhaps as much as £33,000, and seizing control of the state might have seemed a desperate but essential way of ensuring that he got at least some of it back.[251] Indeed, a tax levied by his regime in April 1583 was designed primarily to repay some of the debt due to him. Secondly, and more disinterestedly, Gowrie seems to have been alarmed at the extravagant spending that Lennox had encouraged. Court entertainments had mushroomed to lavish proportions, partly due to the fact that in 1580 James VI learned how to dance, and the debt increased from £36,000 to £45,000 in a few months – although it has to be said that one of the most lavish entertainments of all was the marriage on 11 November 1581, at Holyrood, of Gowrie's daughter Jean to James, Master of Ogilvie, a ceremony that was accompanied by spectacular festivities and fireworks.[252] Thus one of the few consistent and successful policies that Gowrie's government would implement in the limited time available to it was a serious cutting back of expenditure in the royal household.

As usual, the coalition of plotters that aimed to bring about yet another political revolution in Scotland was a diverse collection of former friends and enemies, some with very different agendas. Some apparently believed that Lennox and Arran were turning the young king into a moral degenerate: 'they fostered him in his bawdy talk, provoked him to the pleasures of the flesh, and all kind of licentiousness', or as the ministers of the Kirk believed, 'the Duke goes about to draw the king to carnal lust'.[253] Equally worrying for some, though perhaps not for Gowrie, was Lennox's apparent wish to be declared heir to the throne, which, the conspirators' manifesto claimed, would have put James 'daily in hazard of his life, in the company of this double dissembled hypocrite, of these murderers of his father and regent'.[254] Then there was Archibald, Earl of Angus, successor to the Earl of Morton as head of the House of Douglas. As ever, the Douglases had their own agenda: Angus, who was still in exile in England, was determined to overturn the disgrace of the family, and the forfeiture of its lands, that had followed the execution of his uncle, Morton. He also wanted an honourable burial for Morton's head, which was still stuck on a spike on the Edinburgh Tolbooth.[255]

The timing of the 'Raid of Ruthven' was carefully calculated. In August, many of the Raiders' likely opponents would be away from the king, holding the regular justice ayres in their different shires. Lennox himself would be so employed, first at Edinburgh in his chamberlain's court, then at Glasgow for the Lennox lands, which sprawled around Loch Lomond.[256] James was on his way back from hunting in Atholl, and had left Dunkeld en route to Stirling when he received Gowrie's invitation to come to Ruthven Castle. There would have been nothing to excite suspicion in this; indeed, James had stayed at Ruthven a few days earlier, on his way north to Atholl, and had also been in Perth in July, when he held the justice ayres there in person.[257] He returned to Ruthven on 22 August to find himself surrounded by Gowrie, the Earl of Mar and their followers, who immediately removed supporters of Lennox and Arran from the royal presence. A thousand armed men ringed Ruthven Castle. James was not allowed to leave, and the Master of Glamis suggested to the 16-year-old king that he should forget thoughts of real horses and real hunting, and get back instead to his hobby horse. Later, after the 'Ruthven Raiders' had taken James back to Stirling under close escort, Glamis roughly prevented him from leaving the castle by sticking his leg across a door. James's tears prompted the famous and bitter response from the hirsute Master, 'better bairns should weep than bearded men'.[258]

Once he learned of the coup Arran rode at once for Ruthven, hoping to gain access to the king and win guarantees of his position and his safety. Fighting his way out of an ambush, he got into the castle and tried to make his way to James.[259] He was saved either by the intervention of Gowrie's wife, the Countess Dorothea, who allegedly pleaded on Arran's behalf, or else by one George Auchinleck, a former servant of the Regent Morton, who stayed Gowrie's hand as he was about to drive his knife into James Stewart.[260] Arran was imprisoned, but gave evidence against Lennox and was released by Gowrie after the duke left Scotland.[261] Another sign of Gowrie's remarkable leniency to his enemies was that he soon appointed Arran's sidekick Colonel William Stewart as captain of the king's guard, hoping thereby to divide the two Stewarts.[262]

****

As with all leaders of coups, the Ruthven Raiders immediately promulgated a declaration setting out their public aims.[263] Letters were also sent out to well-affected or neutral nobles and lairds, explaining the reasons for the Raid and summoning them to Stirling to show their support for the change of regime.[264] The king appeared in public, assuring all and sundry (especially the English and French ambassadors) that he was well content with the actions of those around him, and that he remained a free man. On 28 August the Privy Council met at Perth and rubber-stamped James's declaration of approval for the Ruthven Raid.[265] Privately, though, King James was sad and bitter. He made his feelings very clear to all who would listen, and determined to free himself from the Raiders as soon as he could.[266] Particularly galling for the king would have been the torrent of abuse that now poured forth against his cousin, favourite and prospective heir. Lennox was accused of an eclectic range of crimes that included importing Jesuits, corrupting the royal morals, being obnoxious to the Kirk, imposing extortionate customs duties on Dutchmen and being unacceptable to Elizabeth I. Finally, there was the most heinous charge of all: that Lennox had encouraged James to write to his mother.[267] The charges against Arran and Colonel Stewart were simpler. They were 'the most godless and cruel men in the country, who have committed sundry odious murders with their own hands'.[268]

The Duke of Lennox left the country slowly and reluctantly, but finally, on 21 December, he set out for the English border.[269] Esmé Stewart died only six months later, at Paris on 26 May 1583, refusing to admit Catholic priests to his deathbed and proclaiming that he died in the faith of the Kirk.[270] Naturally, there was talk of poisoning, but others pointed to a lethal combination of depression, dysentery and gonorrhea. His heart was embalmed and sent to James VI, who was inconsolable. The duke's last letter to his cousin expressed the wish that James would provide for his children. The elder son, Ludovic, was brought to Scotland in November 1583 and was duly installed as second Duke of Lennox; he remained a firm royal favourite for the rest of his days, and was one of the most important witnesses to the mysterious events at Gowrie House on 5 August 1600.[271]

With Lennox gone, Gowrie's regime could start to implement its chosen policies, but these proved to be disappointingly limited. Ironically, the Raiders' regime did far less for the Kirk than had the hated duke, whose rule had seen the subscription of the first Covenant and important moves to improve clerical pay. Above all, the new government faced the perennial problem that had plagued Scotland's rulers for five centuries or more: England. In December 1582 Gowrie wrote to Queen Elizabeth's minister, Lord Burghley, requesting 'a further acquaintance and intelligence betwixt us', and he also corresponded with the powerful secretary of state, Francis Walsingham.[272] In reality, though, England did little to help the Ruthven government, and its indifference proved fatal to the regime's prospects. Elizabeth refused to return to James the English lands of his father's family, the Lennox Stewarts, and further alienated the Scots by resurrecting the scheme for joint sovereignty between James and his mother. Her treasury did provide a loan of £1,000 to pay for James's royal guard, and finally, in May 1583, a regular subsidy of £3,000 was agreed. It was too little, too late: the Raiders' rule ended in the following month.[273] Elizabeth simply had other priorities, and was too parsimonious to contemplate the sort of military support or massive subsidy that the Raiders desired. As a result, Gowrie's government ended up with the worst of both worlds: receiving no worthwhile backing from England, yet tarred with the brush of being nothing more than a coterie of English puppets.[274] Perhaps it was hardly surprising in the circumstances that Gowrie at least listened to the tempting overtures from the French ambassador, who allegedly promised him a pension of 2,000 crowns, another 10,000 in ready money, and the settling of his debts as Lord Treasurer, in return for Gowrie's acquiescence in finding James a wife acceptable to Henri III, rather than to Elizabeth I.[275]

In June 1583, James persuaded the Raider lords to allow him to go from Falkland Palace to St Andrews Castle to visit his Lennox great-uncle, old Earl-Bishop Robert. In reality, this was a pretext suggested by the captain of the guard, Colonel Stewart, for waiting near St Andrews were the leaders of the anti-Ruthven faction, the earls of Argyll, Crawford, Huntly, Marischal, Montrose and Rothes. The Raiders made a feeble attempt to retake St Andrews and the king, but they were easily repulsed.[276] However, it seems that Gowrie himself might have triggered the end of his own regime: he either knew in advance of James's defection, or else decided immediately afterwards that his best course was to fall on the king's mercy and apologise for his actions of the last year.[277] Gowrie's behaviour is not quite as perverse as it might seem. It was not difficult for any reasonably intelligent Scot to realise that King James was now 17, and Gowrie presumably also realised that it would be increasingly hard for him (or anyone else) to restrain an adult king, especially when the anti-Ruthven party was so powerful and when James was manifestly a highly intelligent young man. Scottish royal minorities had a long history of ending with a pogrom against those who had tried to rule in the king's name. Moreover, during the spring of 1583 Gowrie had been involved in a series of arguments with other members of his regime and members of the extended Stewart family.[278] All of these considerations might have led Gowrie to see the writing on the wall. He fell on his knees before the king at St Andrews Castle, obtained royal forgiveness, and even persuaded James to pay a return visit to Ruthven Castle, where the earl again publicly apologised for the indignities he had heaped upon the monarch in his 'unhappy house'. James was forgiving, but he also requested that Arran be allowed to return to court. Fatally for himself, Gowrie agreed.[279] This abrupt change of sides, submission to the king, and leniency to Arran doomed William Ruthven, first Earl of Gowrie. From that point on, his former colleagues among the Raiders stopped trusting him – and Arran was the last man to display any gratitude.[280]

At first, though, there was little sign that Gowrie would suffer because of his leading role in the Raid. The English ambassador noted that the earl was part of the new regime, but Gowrie soon started to doubt the security of his position.[281] He remained on the Privy Council until 23 August 1583, but when the council sat at St Andrews on that day, Arran, too, was present.[282] It proved to be Gowrie's last meeting, and the start of Arran's dominance in Scotland. He soon began to push James back into a more conservative, pro-French policy that thoroughly alarmed England. Prompted by Arran, James also adopted a far harsher policy against the former Raiders.[283] Increasingly damning indictments of the raid were published, and those involved in it were compelled to seek royal pardons. Gowrie himself was peremptorily summoned to court and told that he had to obtain full remission from the king for the Ruthven Raid. Gowrie was furious, refusing to accept pardon 'for that which his conscience testifies to be good', and stormed off back to Perth.[284] In due course Angus was exiled to the north of Scotland, Mar and Glamis to Ireland. This left Gowrie dangerously isolated, and there was soon talk that he would be arrested for his part in the Ruthven Raid.[285] During the autumn and winter of 1583 Gowrie lived in precarious retirement on his estates, spending at least some of the time in his eyrie-like tower of Rohallion, high on Birnam Hill overlooking Dunkeld.[286]

****

On 27 December 1583, at Coupar Angus, the Earl of Gowrie did what people have always done with a New Year fast approaching: he wrote out a long list of 'things to do'.[287] Most immediate would be the 'rings and tablets for New Year gifts'. However, most of Gowrie's *'memoria'* were concerned with plans for his various properties. The spring of 1584 would see much planting of trees and hedges at Ruthven and Scone, pear trees at Dirleton, and strawberries at all four of the earl's houses, including the newly-christened Gowrie House in Perth. Apple and pear trees were to be brought from France: a modern display board at Dirleton enquires, only half-jokingly, whether Gowrie might have been the man responsible for introducing Golden Delicious into the British Isles. The earl wrote himself an *aide memoire* to ask 'the best gardeners in the country if the Banks of Ruthven will serve for planting of fruit trees', and in the meantime, Ruthven Castle was to get an avenue of elm and ash leading up to its entrance. There was also to be much interior decoration, with notes to remind him about tapestries, gold leaf and chandeliers. There were letters to be written, to the likes of Colonel Stewart and the Earl of Atholl. There was a reading list, too. Gowrie wanted the 'Acts of Parliament in the King's time', a prayer book, and Bibles in both English and Latin for his son and heir, James, the eight-year-old Master of Ruthven. Gowrie's educated, cultured background can also be seen in the Greek motto that adorns these *'memoria'*, and in his note to himself to get hold of the *Cosmography* of 'Erlebus Mensleius' [sic; probably Boethius, the 6th century philosopher]. There were some intriguing asides: 'to commit him to God and his own good guiding'; 'how unwilling I am that they which fears their own estate possess his person'; and 'that I have rather periled a good cause nor to tyn [sic] a good king'. Finally, Gowrie made one note that suggests he was not unappreciative of the sporting potential of the coastal lands around Dirleton Castle, which would eventually contain some of Scotland's greatest links courses: he wrote a reminder to himself to get 'two dozen of golf balls'.

Meanwhile, 'the party of the banished lords' were plotting a counter-coup to overthrow Arran and restore them to power and their estates. Elizabeth I and her ministers gave tacit backing to the plot. Gowrie was not involved: he had retired to his estates, and in any case the banished lords did not trust their erstwhile colleague. One writer noted caustically of William Ruthven at this time, 'as he was hated by the one party, so he was scarce pitied by the other. He repents his repentances, condemns his condemning of the fact of [the Raid of] Ruthven'.[288] Another sneered, 'But what society could be sure with the Earl of Gowrie's so often changing? If his changing proceeded from fraud, who could join with him? Or if it were from fear, what sure hold could they have of one so fearful?'[289] Even so, Gowrie knew that something was afoot, and took steps to protect his family. He obtained royal permission to go into exile abroad, hoping to avoid being charged with complicity in the plot, and signed over much of his land to his son, James, Master of Ruthven.[290] In this way Gowrie clearly hoped to preserve his estates for his family, even if he was condemned or forced to remain in exile. But he was not sanguine about his prospects. In March 1584, shortly after Gowrie had received a royal order to act on his permission to go abroad and to leave the kingdom within fourteen days, his kinsman David Hume of Godscroft visited him at Gowrie House.[291] Hume found the earl:

> greatly perplexed, solicitous about his estate, the affairs
> of the kingdom, and greatly afraid of the violence of the
> courtiers. Looking pitifully upon his gallery, wherein we
> were walking at the time, and which he had lately built
> and decorated with pictures, he broke out into these
> words, having first fetched a deep sigh, 'Cousin, is there
> no remedy? *Et impius haec tam culta novalia miles habebit?
> Barbarus has segetes?*'

William Ruthven evidently knew his Virgil well: 'And shall an impious soldier have these well cultivated fields? Shall a barbarian seize on these standing corns?' He also knew that it was too late. The barbarian, Arran, was already at the gates.

In March or early in April, the banished lords finally brought Gowrie into their confidence. Their plan was to seize Stirling Castle and use their control of it to force James to dismiss Arran and effectively restore the previous Raider regime. Despite their mistrust of him, Gowrie's control of nearby Perth and his network of family alliances in Perthshire made him vital to the plot's prospects.[292] William Ruthven was now faced with a dilemma, but regardless of his choice of course, the plot would not come to fruition before the royal deadline for him to leave the country expired. Gowrie tried desperately to cover all eventualities, but ended up appearing uncertain and vacillating, perhaps proofs of an 'over slow' nature.[293] He moved to Dundee, as though to board a ship for the Continent, but in reality to await news of the plot's success. If the timings worked, Gowrie could return from Dundee, join the 'Stirling lords', and resume his place at the heart of government. In reality, though, the 1584 plot was doomed before it began, for the chief protagonists were simply too far apart.[294] Mar and Glamis did manage to take Stirling Castle on 17 April, but their success was short-lived. The 'Stirling lords' had greatly overestimated the potential support for another coup; as usual, English backing went no further than encouraging words; and even those who detested Arran could not argue with the fact that the army he now led against Stirling was acting legitimately in the name of a free, adult King of Scots. What was more, it was an army of at least 12,000 men, with a King of Scots himself at its head for the first time in over 40 years. Faced with such an impressive display, the rebellion collapsed with almost farcical speed. After no more than a week in control of the castle, the 'Stirling lords' skulked out of its gates at night, and became once more the 'banished lords'.[295]

It was all too late for William, Earl of Gowrie. Arran stood at the head of an excellent intelligence system. He soon knew that Gowrie was at Dundee, isolated from his potential co-conspirators and from his own heartland around Perth, where he might have been able to resist any attempt to seize him. Incredibly, Gowrie had actually returned briefly to the safety of Perth, allegedly to attend to some of his own affairs before departing abroad, but perhaps to make contact again with the plotters; then he returned once more to Dundee, a town that had always been hostile to the Ruthvens.[296] Arran quickly despatched a hundred men under Colonel William Stewart, the captain of the guard whom Gowrie had promoted. On 15 April, two days before the rebel standard was raised at Stirling, Stewart's men attacked the house in which Gowrie had barricaded himself. The fighting lasted some 12 hours, but at the end of it, Gowrie was a prisoner.[297]

With Gowrie in custody, the Earl of Arran's essential problem was that not even the most rigged court was likely to find Gowrie guilty of treason. After all, he had not been caught performing any treasonable act, unless the definition of treason was suddenly extended to embrace sitting in a house in Dundee. What Arran needed was a confession, and his enemies later claimed that he went to Gowrie to persuade him to sign one. William Ruthven would confess to prior knowledge of the Stirling plot in return for a promise of royal pardon. If the story is true, Gowrie believed naively that because Arran effectively owed him his life, he would deal truthfully with him. The report sent to England has Gowrie saying of the proposed confession,

> That policy is very perilous, for where I know myself so clear of all crimes against his Highness, I should by that means make my own dyttie [indictment], and not being sure of my own life nor how the king will accept my excuse, incur the danger of forfeitry for confessing treason, to the tynsell [loss] of my life, and the defamation and utter ruin of my house.

Arran replied baldly,

> Notwithstanding all these dangers which you seem to fall into by that confession, thus far I will certify you, that whether such things be or no, you must confess the foreknowledge of them or else it is concluded you must die.

> Gowrie was despondent. 'Goes it so hard with me? If there be no remedy in case I had an assured promise of my life, I would not stick to prove the device of the letter.' Arran replied, 'I will then, upon my honour, faithfully promise you that your life shall be in no danger if you do so'. Gowrie signed the confession, his own death warrant ...[298]

Gowrie was formally tried at Stirling on 4 May.[299] He conducted his own defence, even though 'it is very hard for me, not being acquainted with the form of law, to dispute for my life, with such an experienced and practised lawyer [as the prosecutor, the Lord Advocate], the time being so short, and so sudden'.[300] He was charged, firstly, with claiming to be of royal blood, and yet of having conspired against the king during the Raid of Ruthven. Gowrie protested that he had received a full remission for the Raid, and as for claiming to be related to the king,

> truly, albeit I am not in name a Stewart, nor a disturber
> of the commonwealth, bringing both the king and the
> country in hazard; yet am I as near in sibness, and hath
> done better, and ofter service to his Majesty, then he
> who thirsts for my blood, by this cowardly revenge.

The judge then raised the subject of his confession. Gowrie protested that he had the king's promise of pardon, but when Arran was interrogated under oath, he promptly denied all knowledge of any promise. Seeing the way the wind was blowing, Gowrie commented sardonically, 'This is a strange matter, that neither law nor promise can avail'. Then the circumstances of his capture at Dundee were raised, and finally a charge with resonances from the days of William Ruthven's father: 'you are accused of witchcraft, and conferring with MacLean, a sorcerer'. Gowrie was incredulous, and accused the court of jesting with him: 'This is no just accusation, but a malicious slander, and I know by whom devised … if there be any witchcraft, I think it be nearer the court', and he named the Countess of Arran. Perhaps he and the tribunal were aware of the rumour that Countess Elizabeth had consulted 'Highland oracles' who told her that Gowrie would fall, so she 'helped forward that prophesy the best she could'.[301] So ended the Earl of Gowrie's examination; the jury proceeded to its deliberations.

The jury of 15 contained hardly any friends of the Earl of Gowrie. Even so, the English ambassador reported that several members had tried not to serve, and when it came to a vote, they tried to avoid condemning him.[302] Before the sentence was declared, Arran made a disingenuous speech acknowledging how much he had loved the Earl of Gowrie, stressing quite how much he (Arran) had done for Gowrie in the past. William Ruthven was duly condemned on the basis that he had been informed of the Stirling plot in February by servants of Mar and Angus, that he had agreed to take part, and that he had not informed the authorities. Almost as an afterthought, he was also found guilty of failing to surrender quickly enough to Colonel William Stewart. The accusation of involvement in the black arts had been quietly dropped. Gowrie 'smiled, and sat down and called for drink, and taking the cup, drank to sundry, did shake hands with others'. He managed to speak to an onlooker,

> desiring to commend him to his wife, and to conceal his
> death from her, requesting also, that his friends might
> comfort her, and put her in good hope of his life till she
> were stronger in body, for she was even at this instant
> weakened through the delivery of his child.[303]

Then, before sentence was passed, he turned to the court.

> Well, my lords, since it is the king's contentment that I
> lose my life, I am as willing now to do it, as I was before
> to do him service; and the noblemen who have been
> upon my assize will know the matter better hereafter.
> And yet, in condemning me to die, they have hazarded
> their own souls, for I had their promise. God [grant]
> that my blood be not upon the king's head.

Gowrie claimed to be sick of the royal court and of politics, and finally
returned to his greatest concern, his family and his estates:

> My Lord Judge, since these are but small oversights
> whereupon I am condemned, I pray you, so would I
> desire you not to make the matter so heinous, as to
> punish it by the penalty of forfeitry. My sons are in my
> lands many years since, and have all their rights
> confirmed by the king; and failing the eldest, the second
> is to succeed, and is assigned to all my causes.

According to a note that he scribbled in prison, Gowrie had intended
to make an even more heartfelt plea to be allowed to enjoy his
precious lands unmolested: 'What pity it were to take me from my
parks and policy!'[304]

The plea fell on deaf ears. The Earl of Gowrie received the
customary sentence for a traitor: beheading, followed by the forfeiture
of his titles, lands and possessions.[305] He responded by saying 'I pray
God my blood may satiate and extinguish the bloody rage and ire of
the courtiers, and bring the country to quietness'. Gowrie shook hands
with many in the courtroom, said prayers with a minister in a nearby
chamber, then went out to the place of execution, the market square

of Stirling, below the castle walls. Gowrie played the part of the martyr to perfection, dying as a 'devout Christian, and a resolute Roman'.[306] Two different accounts of his valedictory speech from the scaffold exist. In both, he reiterated his innocence of any crime against the king, commended the welfare of his wife and children, and protested that he had not implicated anyone else in the crimes that he had been accused of. In one of the accounts, though, he could not resist a final dig at his nemesis, the Earl of Arran. After all, William Ruthven was only the second Scottish earl in over a century to die on the scaffold: the first had been Morton, only three years earlier, both of them dying at the instigation of James Stewart, Earl of Arran, who would take the lion's share of both their lands. Gowrie said,

> he feared not for the flesh, wishing at God as well that
> his innocent blood were not laid to his Majesty's charge,
> as that the thirst and cruelty of the procurers thereof
> might be sated and slackened therewith; so that they
> attempted no further; and herefor prayed to God to
> send the king's majesty such a counsel as should be more
> careful of God's glory, and of his majesty's standing, than
> of their own promotion, by seeking noblemen's blood,
> whereof the practice they might see in his person.

Then Gowrie prayed, lay down on the block, and at about 8.30 in the evening, the axe fell. His head fell into a scarlet cloth that he had specifically requested; later, his family saw to it that the head was sewn back on before the body was decently buried.[307] The countess and one of their daughters were reported to be 'dead also with sorrow'.[308]

Gowrie's elaborate attempts to ensure that his posterity's inheritance would be saved proved fruitless. In 1584 the Scottish Parliament, wholly dominated by Arran, passed an act which permitted the disinheriting of the children of traitors, specifically those of the Earl of Gowrie.[309] The Ruthvens' lands were duly distributed to Arran and his cronies. Arran himself got the plum estate of Dirleton; Scone went to the Earl of Crawford; Ruthven itself to the Earl of Montrose, the new Lord Treasurer.[310] Gowrie's son-in-law, Atholl, was arrested simply because he would not put away his Ruthven wife and sign over her dowry to Arran.[311] With her husband, lands and income all gone, Dorothea Stewart, Countess of Gowrie, tried desperately to reach the king to beg some relief for herself and her many children. Calderwood, the historian of the Kirk, recorded what happened on 22 August 1584, when the royal party was going in procession through Edinburgh to the opening of Parliament:

> The Lady Gowrie sat down on her knees, crying to the king for grace to her and her poor bairns, who never had offended his Grace. Arran would not suffer her to come near, but thrust her down, and hurt her back and her hand. She fell [in] a swoon, and lay in the street till they were in the Tolbooth, and then was taken in to a house. This was the reward she received for saving Arran's life at the Raid of Ruthven.[312]

An English agent added more detail about this treatment of 'the poor Countess of Gowrie, who, since her husband's death, is wasted with grief and affliction':

> Arran, going between her and the king, led him hastily by her, and she reaching at his cloak to stay his Majesty, Arran putting her from him not only overthrew her, which was easy to do in respect of the poor lady's weakness, but marched over her … even their [ie Arran and his wife's] most affectionate friends utterly condemn and cry shame of this inhumanity.[313]

****

Among those who did not mourn for William Ruthven, first Earl of Gowrie, was a living ghost, far away from Scotland. In her captivity at Sheffield Castle, the sickly and ageing Mary, Queen of Scots expressed grim satisfaction that Gowrie was dead, 'upon some ancient quarrel of Lochleven'.[314] In the ongoing and uneasy relationship between the Houses of Ruthven and Stuart, another old score had been settled.

CHAPTER FIVE

GOWRIE AND THE DEVIL

The plight of Dorothea Stewart, Countess of Gowrie, and her vast, fatherless brood touched some unlikely hearts after she was trampled underfoot by Arran and the courtiers. Above all, the Queen of England herself intervened directly on their behalf, and in December 1584 Elizabeth I wrote to James VI. Her letter has been quoted here at length, partly because it records the queen's unsubtle attempts to pressurise James, partly because it reveals much about the Ruthvens themselves, their kin and their attitudes.[315]

> Understanding the long and faithful service of old of your
> trusty cousin, the late William, sometime Earl of Gowrie,
> who, as he was one of the chief instruments to put the
> royal crown upon your head, so did he constantly persist,
> without shrinking, in maintaining of that cause, against the
> murderers of your dearest father *[Darnley]*, grandfather
> *[Lennox]*, and uncle *[Moray]*, of noble memory; … and
> hazarded his own life and his friends at sundry times …
> We are the rather, of pity and conscience, moved to
> interpone our credit, earnestly to solicit that your ire,
> incensed against his poor wife and thirteen fatherless
> children, may be assuaged with his own execution; and to
> extend your royal clemency and compassion towards them,
> whose offence, as it could not merit, so could not their
> innocence bear your indignation, nor their youth be
> thought worthy of your wrath. That they being restored to
> enjoy their father's lands, rents and possessions, under your
> obedience and protection, some monument of that ancient
> house may abide with the posterity, and that name be not
> rooted out from the face of the earth, through the private
> craft and malice of their private adversaries, contrary [to]

your good nature ... So, we hope his earnest affection well known to the promoting of true religion, and good liking to the continuance of the amity between us both and the people, shall be no small furtherance to the accomplishing thereof, according to your good pleasure. So, reposing upon your gracious and favourable answer, we take our leave.

Elizabeth R

There is an unusual amount of personal feeling and emotional power in the queen's appeal, hardly what one might expect from a monarch interceding on behalf of foreigners whom she barely knew. In fact, these aspects of the letter, and its detail about Gowrie's family and services, can be attributed to the simple fact that Elizabeth was actually plagiarising the words of another: the dead Earl of Gowrie himself. In the previous month, Gowrie's younger brother Alexander Ruthven wrote to Elizabeth's secretary of state, Walsingham, 'being mercifully delivered ... from the dangerous and pitiful shipwreck of an ancient house of my country'. Before his execution, the earl had commanded Alexander to convey 'his last will and words' to Walsingham as a safeguard against 'the malice and craft of certain of the king's majesty's councillors who sought the utter ruin of his house and surname'. The rest of Alexander's letter faithfully recorded Gowrie's plea for his family, and with only minor amendments – presumably the work of Walsingham himself – they were the same words that Elizabeth allowed to be sent, under her name and seal, to King James.[316]

Elizabeth's intercession brought no immediate results. However, the Earl of Arran over-reached himself within months and was ousted from power in his turn. James VI was more lenient to him than Arran had been to Gowrie and Morton, sending him into internal exile. Stripped of his earldom, he reverted to being plain Captain James Stewart and lived in obscurity for over a decade, caricatured by his enemies as Lord Quondam and constantly plotting to regain his dominance over king and country. But his enemies had very long memories. In 1596 Stewart set out for Ayrshire on a road that took him through the heartland of the Douglases. On 1 December, at Symington near Biggar, he was ambushed by James Douglas, a nephew of the same Earl of Morton whom Stewart had put to death 15 years earlier. Douglas's men hacked Stewart to death, and Douglas triumphantly stuck the erstwhile Earl of Arran's severed head on the end of his lance. The remaining body parts were left at the roadside, where they were duly consumed by the dogs and pigs of Lanarkshire. The Regent Morton was avenged, and so, too, was William Ruthven, Earl of Gowrie, both in his own right and as the son of a Douglas mother.[317] As for Arran's rapacious countess, she had preened herself for years on account of a witch's prediction that one day she would become the greatest woman in Scotland. In 1595 a fatal attack of dropsy made her body swell to gargantuan proportions, so in one sense, the manner of her death fulfilled the old crone's prophecy.[318]

Arran's downfall brought the remaining Ruthven Raiders back to power, and once more, the victors received the spoils. On 10 December 1585, the parliament that met at Linlithgow formally overturned the forfeitures of Angus, Mar and the rest, as well as obtaining redress for the widow and children of their old friend, the Earl of Gowrie. The Parliament duly restored his family to their estates and rights.[319] A few months later the title itself was restored, and its new holder entered into his birthright. At the age of 12, James Ruthven became the second Earl of Gowrie. The Earls of Montrose and Crawford had to give up their brief tenures at Ruthven Castle and Scone Palace; the young earl was soon denouncing Montrose in Parliament for the damage he had allegedly caused to the family's eponymous castle.[320] Of course, the erstwhile Earl of Arran had already forfeited Dirleton Castle, which seems to have resumed its old role as the dowager Countess of Gowrie's favourite residence. Countess Dorothea was now one of the most powerful women in Scotland. She was tutrix and governess to her son, administering one of the finest estates in the country. Meanwhile Earl James's eldest sister Mary Ruthven, Countess of Atholl, might have been mourning her dead godmother, Mary, Queen of Scots, who was beheaded at Fotheringhay Castle on 8 February 1587 after becoming implicated in one last, forlorn attempt to escape and return to her native land. Soon she had another to mourn. In 1588 Earl James died, aged just 14, and was buried in the Ruthven vault of St John's Kirk, Perth. The second son, John, was now the third Earl of Gowrie, aged 10. The third son, Alexander, aged seven or eight, became the Master of Ruthven.

****

The political world that surrounded the new third earl was vastly different to the one that his father had left only four years earlier. The great constant of William Ruthven's time had been the problem of Mary, Queen of Scots; but the headsman's axe ended all of that. In its place came the new reality of war between England and Spain, a war that created threats or opportunities galore for Scots, depending on which side of the religious fence one sat. The Spanish Armada was famously defeated more by bad weather than by the guns of the English fleet, but as the 'Protestant wind' drove it first along the east, and then the north and west coasts of Scotland, Scots feared or hoped that it might regroup and invade their own land. Armada ships did indeed come onto the Scottish coast, but only as wrecks. Nevertheless, those who wished to resurrect Catholic Scotland took encouragement from the lesson: if a Spanish fleet could reach Scotland unintentionally, it could also do so premeditatedly. Then there was the new constant that loomed ever larger in the minds of both Scots and Englishmen. In 1589 Elizabeth I of England was 56, the same age that her father, Henry VIII, had been when he died. If Elizabeth expired, her nearest blood relative was James, King of Scots. For centuries many had worked, fought and died for the day when one man would rule both England and Scotland: but relatively few of them had been Scots. The prospect of a 'union of the crowns' under James would hardly have been unwelcome to the House of Ruthven, for half a century probably the most consistently anglophile great family in Scotland. An English report of September 1589 summed up the new third Earl of Gowrie succinctly: 'though he be but young, yet is he ruled by your [ie, England's] friends'.[321] However, Gowrie's and England's 'friends' were an eclectic bunch. They included the likes of Gowrie's brother-in-law, the Earl of Atholl; Gowrie's godfather the Earl of Mar, the first earl's old friend and fellow Ruthven Raider; and James Stewart, second Earl of Moray, the son-in-law and successor of James VI's first regent. Their number also included a new and wholly unpredictable figure on Scotland's political scene, albeit one who bore an old and familiar title, with dark resonances of other days: the Earl of Bothwell.

Francis Stewart was born in 1562. His father was one of King James V's legion of illegitimate sons; his mother was the sister and heir of James Hepburn, Earl of Bothwell, Queen Mary's third husband and nemesis. Bothwell was intelligent and cultured, but like his predecessor in the title, he could also be unpredictable and violent, as shown in 1584 when he personally hacked to pieces one of the Homes.[322] Even his generally sympathetic biographer calls him 'a murderer, rapist, wife-beater, pirate, thief and liar'.[323] Despite his massive personal faults, Bothwell's status made him a key political player. He did not wholeheartedly support the Raid of Ruthven, but he emerged during that period as a trusted advisor to the king and subsequently worked to bring down Arran's regime. By the time of the Armada crisis, though, Bothwell was increasingly opposed to James's policies, and in particular to those favoured by the Chancellor, John Maitland of Thirlestane. Maitland wanted to see an end to the political dominance of the nobility, and their replacement as Scotland's governing elite by a class of lower-born professional administrators – in other words, men exactly like John Maitland. James shared his vision: to a man, and wherever they stood in the quarrels of Protestant against Catholic, England against Spain, the old nobility of Scotland rejected it.[324] Bothwell summed up perfectly the aristocrats' hatred of the (relatively) low-born, jumped-up, pen-pusher John Maitland, calling him 'a puddock-stool of a [k]night'.[325]

The upshot was a febrile series of revolts, intrigues and attempted coups, with Bothwell at the heart of many of them.[326] There were endless tales of Catholic plots, of Jesuit agents galore and of Spanish armies poised to invade. Above all, there were witches. Witchcraft was everywhere, an explanation for everything and an excuse for denouncing anyone. In April 1591, for example, an anonymous writer contributed some notes on affairs in Scotland that ended up in England. The ninth Earl of Angus was said to be dying. Why? He had been bewitched. The Earl of Bothwell had been committed to prison. Why? He had been using witchcraft to try to kill the king. Many private individuals had been arrested. Why? They were witches, and they, too, were seeking to kill the king. Add a Catholic agent allegedly arranging for huge sums of foreign gold to be brought to the Earl of Huntly, and it seems clear that April 1591 was not a good month for calm reflection and mature political discourse in Scotland.[327] As far as Bothwell was concerned, he had been dragged into the mire that followed the breaking up on Halloween, 1589, of a witches' sabbat at the ruinous old kirk on the sea shore at North Berwick, the witches having arrived there by flying down the Forth in sieves. Under examination in the following year, several of the alleged witches implicated Bothwell, and claimed that he was the instrument by which the Devil would kill King James. The earl was imprisoned but managed to escape. Many of the nobility, and certainly Bothwell himself, believed that the whole affair had been contrived by Maitland. James had other ideas. North Berwick followed hard on the heels of several abortive attempts by a Danish fleet to bring his bride to Scotland: the storms forcing it back were so unnaturally great that they could only have been caused by witchcraft, and they compelled James to cross the North Sea himself to bring back his bride. Moreover, the chief purpose of the North

Berwick sabbat supposedly had been to conjure up another diabolical storm to sink the king and queen in their return voyage. Such real or imagined dramas at sea gave an entirely new and alarming gloss to the fact that Bothwell was also the Lord High Admiral of Scotland.

Suddenly, King James was a convert. Witches were real, witchcraft was endemic in Scotland, and his own cousin, Francis Stewart, Earl of Bothwell, was Satan's lieutenant on earth.[328]

****

On 23 November 1589, in the bishop's palace at Oslo, the 23-year-old James VI, King of Scots, was married to Anna, the 15-year-old sister of King Christian IV of Denmark-Norway. Christian was one of the most prodigious drinkers in Europe, and one of Anna's more unexpected traits was a lifelong love of beer.[329] The royal couple sailed to Scotland in April 1590, and on 17 May the new Queen of Scots received a spectacular coronation in the abbey church of Holyrood. The queen might have been very young, but she soon showed herself to be a determined, independent character with a political will of her own. She came to loathe Maitland with a vengeance, but she enjoyed the company of glamorous, cosmopolitan young aristocrats, including such dangerous characters as the Earl of Bothwell, who enchanted her by gossiping to her in French, and her particular friend, the staunchly Catholic Henrietta Stewart, Countess of Huntly, the Duke of Lennox's sister. Meanwhile the birth of an heir, Henry Frederick, on 19 February 1594, transformed the political situation in Scotland, burying the old hypotheses about the succession once and for all.

A Queen of Scots required her own household. Perhaps because they belonged to a family that was opposed to Maitland and supportive of Bothwell, Anna appointed two of the Ruthven girls, Barbara and Beatrix, as ladies-in-waiting. Such appointments generally precluded marriage, so Countess Dorothea had to weigh the loss of two advantageous matches for her daughters against the undoubted influence at court that the positions would bring. However, her choice might have had fatal consequences, for ultimately, the roles of Barbara and Beatrix are crucial in understanding the events of 5 August 1600 at Gowrie House and their aftermath. During the 1590s, the dowager Countess also had some important decisions to make about the destinies of her other daughters. Mary was already married to John Stewart, fifth Earl of Atholl, but on 30 August 1594, Atholl died in his town house at Perth, literally across the road from Gowrie House and its turret chamber, thus taking away the young Earl of Gowrie's brother-in-law, probable role-model and mentor in conspiracy. At the king's behest, Mary Ruthven's widowhood was brief: in March 1596 she was married to yet another John Stewart, in this case Lord Innermeath, who was thereby able to become the new Earl of Atholl. Meanwhile, a far more contentious marriage had been arranged for Margaret Ruthven. John Graham, third Earl of Montrose, had succeeded the first Earl of Gowrie as Lord Treasurer, and sat on the jury that condemned him to death. He was hated by Gowrie's friends and family, who believed that he had been 'an especial instrument and mean[s]' in the first earl's downfall. This animosity was felt particularly by the fifth Earl of Atholl, 'who married the daughter of Gowrie, and with her he entered into the feuds of her father' against Montrose. The feud was ended in 1590 thanks to Bothwell's mediation, and in December 1593 the Countess Dorothea was presumably in the congregation when her daughter Margaret married John Graham, the Master of Montrose.[330] In time, their son would become a legend: James Graham, fifth Earl and first Marquess of Montrose, the dashing, doomed leader of the Cavalier cause in Scotland during the British civil wars. Margaret Ruthven did not live to witness his destiny, for she died when he was six, and was thus spared the gruesome spectacle played out in Edinburgh one day in May 1650, when the severed head of her son was impaled on the Edinburgh tolbooth, next to the skull of her brother, the Earl of Gowrie.

Three more of the Ruthven girls got married in the 1590s. In 1598 Isabel married Sir Robert Gordon of Lochinvar. No doubt Countess Dorothea thought of this as a useful connection to the mighty Gordon dynasty, especially at a time when the chief of the Gordons was such a favourite of the king; in 1599 he was made Marquess of Huntly, jointly the first holder of that title in Scotland. In fact, the marriage was a disaster. Sir Robert Gordon turned out to be a psychopath who enjoyed randomly murdering his tenants, and Isabel swiftly divorced him. However, her son by Gordon eventually became the first Viscount Kenmure, and in 1628 he attempted to bribe the Duke of Buckingham into restoring the earldom of Gowrie to himself. Unfortunately for Kenmure, he paid the bribe the night before Buckingham was stabbed to death at Portsmouth, and the Gowrie title remained unclaimed.[331] The youngest Ruthven girl, Dorothea, had her own ideas about love and marriage. According to a local legend at Huntingtower, formerly Ruthven Castle, Dorothea was being courted by John Wemyss of Pittencrieff, 'much her inferior in rank and fortune'. Despite this, he was allowed to visit her at Ruthven and to stay overnight. The peculiar layout of the castle should have ensured propriety: Wemyss was to lodge in one tower and Dorothea in the other, and at that time, there was no connection between the two buildings. Even so, the resourceful Dorothea managed to cross to the other tower before the doors were closed for the night, and made for Wemyss's room. Someone in the family, most likely a jealous sister, told the countess, who hobbled up the one stairway, confident that she was blocking her daughter's only escape. Young Dorothea had other ideas. She ran *up* the stairs instead, got on the roof, and leapt the nine-foot gap to the battlements of the other tower, 60 feet above the ground. She dashed down to her own room, got into bed, and when her mother's frantic search finally led her back there, she found Dorothea seemingly asleep and had to apologise for unjustly suspecting her of illicit fornication. The apology was short-lived, for the next night Dorothea eloped and married Wemyss. To this day, the space between the two towers of Huntingtower Castle is known as 'the maiden's leap'.[332]

The greatest of the Ruthven marriages does not seem to have been a product of Countess Dorothea's machinations: instead, it emerged from that rarest commodity of all in aristocratic marriages, true love. In 1590 Lilias Ruthven, then in her mid-twenties, caught the eye of the most eligible bachelor in Scotland, the 16-year-old Ludovic, second Duke of Lennox.[333] The eye-catching was probably a consequence of geographical proximity: Lennox's chief seat, Methven Castle, was barely three miles from Lilias's home at Ruthven, and chance meetings and neighbourly social calls would have been inevitable. Lennox became completely obsessed with Lilias and determined to marry her. The prospect horrified whole swathes of the Scottish political elite. After all, until Prince Henry was born in 1594 Lennox was the most probable successor if James died – which was an ever-present possibility during the king's furious and unrestrained hunting trips, or during the almost equally ever-present plots of the Earls of Bothwell or Huntly. A Ruthven queen, and Countess Dorothea as mother-in-law to the king, would hardly be palatable to those who had not been the best of friends to the Ruthvens over the years. The opponents of the relationship worked frantically on the king, trying to persuade him to disallow the marriage, and even dangled a nubile young Douglas girl and several English wenches before the duke as substitute bedfellows.[334] Maitland also got the poet John Burel to write an entire book, dedicated to the duke, and filled with classical examples that proved the disastrous consequences of blind passion.[335]

Ludovic was having none of it: he wanted Lilias Ruthven. By the king's command, Lilias was shut away at Wester Wemyss, but on 19 April 1591, after riding all night, Lennox abducted her and carried her off to Dunkeld. There, safe in the heartland of her brother-in-law Atholl, the young lovers were married the next day.[336] Lilias Ruthven was the Duchess of Lennox, the only duchess in the British Isles, and not even King James could undo it: as the words of the wedding ceremony proclaim, no man could put them asunder. But God could, and just over a year later, on 11 May 1592, young Duchess Lilias died. She was buried in the great 15th century Gothic church of the Holy Trinity in Edinburgh. Perhaps she lies there to this day, although the church itself is long gone. Instead, the mortal remains of the Ruthven Duchess of Lennox probably repose beneath Platform Two of Edinburgh's Waverley railway station, near the left luggage store.[337]

****

The love affair between Ludovic and Lilias seems to be a straightforward if fated romance, but it might have been more complex than that. The Duke of Lennox's godfather was Sir William Keith of Delny in Ross-shire.[338] Keith became the king's valet in 1579, and four years later he was described as having the king's 'special favour'.[339] In the mid-1580s he was one of James's agents in London, deeply involved in the dissembling and bluff that surrounded Scotland's response to the trial and execution of Mary, Queen of Scots.[340] He became Master of the Wardrobe and joined the Privy Council in 1588.[341] Over the winter of 1589–90 he was part of the Scottish negotiating team in Denmark, and played a key role in finalising James's marriage to Anna. However, the trip also cost him his job at the Wardrobe: the king objected to the fact that Keith dressed better than he did, which was not difficult, given James's execrable dress sense. By the time that he returned from Denmark, though, Sir William had other things on his mind, namely another marriage project: his own. He intended to marry Dorothea Stewart, dowager Countess of Gowrie. Having failed to stop the Ruthven-Lennox marriage, James was determined to stop this one, and this time he had more success. Keith was summoned before the Privy Council in April 1591, but he left Edinburgh before the charge could be delivered.[342]

Although his marriage had been vetoed, Keith remained closely associated with the Ruthvens and their political allies, notably Lennox and the erratic Earl of Bothwell. On 27 December 1591 Bothwell led a raid on the Palace of Holyroodhouse itself, gaining access through the stables of the Duke of Lennox's lodgings. Contemporaries were well aware of the possible implications of this, and of the dangers inherent in an alliance of Bothwell, Lennox and the duke's new family, the Ruthvens. In January 1592 an anonymous note was attached to the door of King James's bedchamber, pointing out that 'those that the duke hath melled *[had dealings]* with hath not forgotten the death of the earl Gowrie', and naming specifically Sir William Keith, the duke's godfather, and John Colville, Bothwell's principal advisor, whose wife was the young Earl of Gowrie's aunt. Although the writer was anonymous, it was immediately assumed that the note was in support of Chancellor Maitland, whose suspicions of the duke had recently led him to wall up the door in Holyrood Palace between his chamber and Lennox's.[343]

A few weeks later, the long tradition of bloodfeud within Scottish noble society reached its shocking and bloody climax. On 7 February 1592, on the beach at Donibristle on the Fife shore of the Firth of Forth, James Stewart, Earl of Moray, was brutally murdered at the instigation of the Earl of Huntly. Moray was Bothwell's cousin, and the king's utter failure to prosecute his friend Huntly for the murder seems to have rejuvenated Francis Stewart's one-man crusade to change the direction of James VI's reign. Bothwell made another unsuccessful attempt to seize the king in June 1592, when he descended on Falkland Palace with 400 men. Not unnaturally in the circumstances, James became even more jittery than usual about his personal security. In August, therefore, Dorothea, Countess of Gowrie, paid for Bothwell's persistent plotting and the Ruthvens' apparent complicity in it by receiving a royal summons to surrender her 'very fair house' at Holyrood, the 'New-frater House' which her father-in-law had been granted in December 1564:[344] James was evidently worried that any building adjacent to the palace could be used as the point of entry in yet another attempted coup, especially if it was a building full of Ruthvens. The countess was furious, protesting that it was her own house 'which her self builded', and in the end she clung on to it.[345]

In December 1592, a sensational new political scandal erupted in Scotland. The 'affair of the Spanish blanks' began when a Catholic agent was arrested on Great Cumbrae island in the Firth of Clyde, where he was waiting for a ship to take him overseas. He was found to be carrying eight large sheets of paper addressed to King Philip of Spain. These were blank apart from the signatures, some of which were individual, some collective. The signatures were those of the Earls of Huntly, Erroll, and Angus.[346] In essence, these 'blanks' were to be proofs to Philip of the earls' good faith, for the king could fill them with whatever text he chose. In return, the earls expected to receive a massive Spanish subsidy with the promise of an army to follow it. James's reaction infuriated the Kirk, many of his nobility and Elizabeth of England. Instead of ordering the immediate arrest of the earls, James displayed astonishing leniency towards them, permitting them to remain at liberty and refusing to forfeit their lands. This merely compounded the outrage that many felt about James's abject failure to prosecute Huntly for the murder of Moray. By October 1593, the Earl of Atholl in particular had had enough. He decided to take direct action against the 'Spanish factioners' around the king, and drew in his 15-year-old brother in law, the Earl of Gowrie, along with the Earl of Montrose, who was both Atholl's half-brother and the father-in-law of Gowrie's sister. Forbidden by royal proclamation from approaching Stirling, Atholl and his allies made for nearby Doune. James pursued them, and the King of Scots' decisive action in leading his own troops in person undid the rebels' cause. Atholl and the others immediately agreed to surrender Doune to the king, rather than risk being condemned as traitors. Atholl retired to Dunkeld, leaving Montrose and Gowrie to surrender to the royal army. The brothers-in-law refused to draw their weapons, stating that they were 'the king's faithful subjects and ready to obey him'. Montrose was placed under house arrest, but because of his age, no action was taken against Gowrie.[347] James presumably realised that the young earl had been drawn into the plot because of what he represented, not for his own sake; nominally involving Gowrie would allow Atholl to call on the Ruthvens' manpower resources if he needed them.

Meanwhile, the Earl of Bothwell remained in a bizarre limbo world, technically forfeited and suspected of treasonable witchcraft, but still wandering quite freely around the streets of Edinburgh. In July 1593, the Ruthven family's close allies, Lennox, Atholl and Mar, engineered a meeting between the disgraced Bothwell and King James, hoping that Bothwell's return would diminish Maitland's influence. To get Bothwell into the palace required accomplices, namely Dorothea, Countess of Gowrie, and her daughter the Countess of Atholl, who saw to it that the necessary doors were opened at the right moments.[348] When James found Bothwell in his chamber, he panicked, screaming 'Treason! Treason!' Bothwell and his allies pleaded for mercy, but James was convinced his end was nigh: 'Strike, traitor, and make an end of thy work, for I desire not to live any longer'. He even alluded to Bothwell as the devil incarnate, and claimed that the earl had come for his soul. At that point the Earl of Mar and Countess Dorothea's old lover, Sir William Keith, arrived with more supporters of the allegedly demonic earl. James was incapable of playing the role of the courageous martyr for very long, and he quickly gave in. He accepted Bothwell's submission in return for an agreement that the earl would finally face his long-delayed trial for witchcraft. Although Bothwell was acquitted following a shambolic farce in court, James soon turned against him once more – partly due to the urging of Chancellor Maitland, who had returned to court, and partly because the king was determined to avenge the humiliation he had suffered at Bothwell's hands.

In the following spring, 1594, Bothwell organised an armed rising to coincide with the meeting of Parliament in April, when James would finally (and very reluctantly) forfeit the earls incriminated in the 'Spanish blanks' affair. On 2 April, Bothwell arrived at Leith, hoping to be reinforced there by Atholl and Gowrie. They never materialised, although they did support Bothwell in print. The three earls and their supporters issued a proclamation to the ministers of the Kirk who had assembled at Dunbar, requesting their blessing on their rebellion.[349] They attacked the 'Spanish factioners' and condemned the leniency that had been shown to them by the king. The earls claimed that they had been forced to take action both for the nation's security – for they claimed another Spanish Armada was on its way, its destination, Scotland – and for their own, against those who sought 'our blood day and night in such barbarous form as heretofore was never heard within this realm'. Supportive words were not enough for Bothwell. He fled to England, where he agreed to enter into an unholy alliance with the Catholic earls of the 'Spanish blanks'. Bothwell's new friends rose in revolt against their forfeitures, and at Glenlivet in October 1594 they defeated a makeshift royal army. James himself then took the field, the rebels refused to fight against the ordained monarch, and the earls' cause melted away. This effectively marked the end of Bothwell's political career in Scotland. Five months later he went into exile, where he remained for the rest of his life; but his relationship with the Ruthvens was by no means at an end.

****

In 1594, at the age of 16, John Ruthven, third Earl of Gowrie, had already been deeply implicated in conspiracies against the king, and he (or his mother) probably felt that a period of voluntary exile, ostensibly to further his studies, would be politic for all concerned. Gowrie had already received an impressive education, first at the local school in Perth, then at the University of Edinburgh from about 1589, where he seems to have had no difficulty in combining academic study with his fledgling career as a conspirator and rebel. On 12 August 1593 he successfully defended his thesis in the *viva voce* disputation, and was awarded the degree of Master of Arts, aged 15.[350] When he considered the prospect of further study at a foreign university, Gowrie seems at first to have considered Oxford or Cambridge, but he finally settled on Padua.[351] On 6 August 1594 the young Provost of Perth informed his town council that he was going abroad for an indeterminate period. The town continued to elect him regardless, and Gowrie appointed sheriffs depute for the county of Perthshire as a whole.[352] The earl then left for Italy, armed with letters of recommendation from James VI and accompanied by his old tutor from both Perth and Edinburgh, William Rynd.[353] His timing was either immaculate or disastrous. It meant that he left Scotland just before the two men who had dominated his young life, the Earls of Atholl and Bothwell, left the scene in their very different ways. It meant that he could not become involved in any more of their plots, but it also meant that whenever Gowrie returned to Scotland, he would find it a very different place from the one that he had left.

Dating from 1222, the University of Padua was one of the oldest and most illustrious in the world. Strictly speaking, it consisted of two separate universities specialising in different disciplines, and Gowrie apparently studied at the *Universitas Iuristratum*, covering a curriculum that included law and theology. The university's star lecturer at the time, albeit at the 'companion' *Universitas Atristarum*, was Galileo Galilei. The world's first proper anatomical theatre had just been built there when Gowrie arrived, and one of the earliest and most illustrious students to use it was William Harvey, the discoverer of the circulation of the blood, who probably arrived at Padua some months after Gowrie left. In November 1595 the earl wrote two letters from Padua: the only two that have survived from his entire life. One was to John Malcolm, minister at Perth. It was a violent denunciation of Catholicism, based on what Gowrie had seen in Italy, and contained rumours that he had heard of the brutal punishments inflicted on godly Protestants by the agents of 'Rome, that mother of all vice, and whorish synagogue of devils'.[354] The other, written on 24 November 1595, was addressed to

King James VI. Gowrie thanked him for his 'good countenance at all times', and especially for a letter that James had sent him. Reading between the lines of Gowrie's sycophantic reply, it seems possible that the king's letter to him might have been some sort of forgiveness for his previous involvement in plotting, coupled with an assurance that James was now satisfied with the earl's loyalty. 'God of his mercy grant that I see your Majesty in such a good estate as I wish, which will give me the greatest contentment of all'; Gowrie could have been a consummate courtier in the making.[355]

According to some accounts, Gowrie was so widely respected at Padua that he was elected rector, but there is no confirmation of this in the university records. The young earl left the university before November 1598. By then he was at Orleans, where he encountered his cousin, the Master of Gray, an irrepressible old schemer who was unimpressed with the young earl: 'I found fault that he was rather fashioned like a pedant then a courtier'.[356] Gowrie stayed at Orleans for several months.[357] Although the city had been a Catholic stronghold in the bitter French civil wars of religion that had just ended, there was nothing sinister in this, for Orleans, too, had a great university, one with a long tradition of welcoming Scottish students. Archibald Campbell, seventh Earl of Argyll, allegedly later claimed that he had visited the house in Orleans where Gowrie lodged and found the following prophecy there, presumably among the graffiti: Gowrie 'should have too much love, fall into melancholy, have great power and rule, and die by the sword'.[358] He was at Geneva by the end of 1599, staying for some months as a house guest of Theodore Beza, the great theologian and successor of Calvin as the spiritual leader of reformed Protestantism in Europe. He went on to Paris, where he met the English ambassador, Sir Henry Neville. In his report to London, Neville described Gowrie as a strong Protestant and anglophile, 'a nobleman of whom, for his good judgment, zeal and ability, exceeding good use could be made on his return'. Gowrie arrived in London on 3 April 1600. He waited on Elizabeth I, who received him warmly, and they had a number of meetings together.[359] He was also feted by her chief minister, Robert Cecil. Finally, Gowrie set out for his homeland, and early in May 1600, he arrived in Edinburgh.[360]

The accounts of what the Earl of Gowrie did in the next few days and weeks need to be treated with caution. Like Argyll's story about the house at Orleans, they were all written in the aftermath of the slaughter at Gowrie House, and the authors invariably looked for (or invented) omens of what was to come. For example, there are various anecdotes of the dealings between Gowrie and King James in the months of May and June. The earl was said to have been welcomed back into Edinburgh by a large crowd of his friends on horseback, prompting the king to comment caustically 'there were more with his father when he was conveyed to the scaffold'. When they met, James is said to have subjected Gowrie to 'many jests and pretty taunts' about his warm reception in England, and suggested that Gowrie must have received a large English bribe. Some weeks later, James is meant to have turned abruptly to the earl and asked 'what would make a woman part with child? The earl answered, sundry things, but especially if a woman with child get a fright. Then the king, after a scornful laughter, said "If that had been true, my lord, I had not been sitting here" ' – a reference to the murder of Rizzio in his pregnant mother's presence, at the instigation of Gowrie's grandfather. When Gowrie's sister Beatrix mocked the club foot of Dr Herries, he replied 'mistress, ere it be long, a great disaster shall befall you'. Herries became one of the key players at Gowrie House on 5 August 1600, but his words might have had other meanings, if they were ever really spoken at all. At least one of the stories has a strong ring of truth to it, though. Old Colonel William Stewart, Arran's sometime crony and the man who had arrested Gowrie's father at Dundee, who still hanging around the court as a military advisor, occasional troubleshooter, and the holder of a belated knighthood. Gowrie is said to have shunned him in public, saying 'it is not seemly he should cross my teeth'.[361] Other, more ominous, reports claim that when asked if he would be avenged on Stewart for his part in his father's death, Gowrie replied *'aquila non captat muscas'* – 'an eagle killed no flies', 'meaning that his revenge should not be so low'.[362]

Accompanied by a large retinue, the third Earl of Gowrie returned to Perth at about six in the evening of 20 May 1600. Within weeks he was presiding over the justice ayres, having resumed his family's traditional offices of provost and sheriff.[363] In June, King James summoned a convention to meet at Edinburgh. He wanted a vote of 100,000 crowns to enable him to raise an army to make good his claim to the English throne: he knew all too well that some in England were toying with the pretensions of the Infanta Isabella, King Philip II's daughter, who had a convoluted claim to the throne. When Gowrie spoke in response to the royal request, he apologised that his long absence from the country might mean he was speaking in ignorance of all the circumstances. He then opposed the vote of taxes, partly because it was so large, partly because there was no guarantee of how soon the troops would be needed – in other words, they did not know how long it would be before Elizabeth died. From other speakers, there was more than a suggestion that, if they voted for an army before it was actually needed, the king might find other ways of spending the money. James was furious.[364] Another of the (possibly apocryphal) tales of the sense of impending disaster has a courtier pointing at Gowrie after his convention speech and saying, 'yonder is an unhappy man: they are but seeking occasion of his death, which now he has given'.[365] But the alleged speaker was Sir David Murray, who would soon be the proud new owner of the Ruthvens' Scone estate, so he can hardly be rated a disinterested witness.

The high summer of 1600 in Scotland was a time of unsettling signs and portents. The tension engendered by the king's apparent ambition to invade England was heightened by the strange case of Lady Waristoun, beheaded for murdering her husband (her two accomplices were burnt alive), and a great dearth that sent prices soaring and killed children in their droves.[366] It would hardly have been surprising for the Ruthvens to wish to remove themselves from such a febrile atmosphere. At the start of July Gowrie and his heir Alexander, the Master of Ruthven, set out for Trochrie Castle, the Ruthven hunting lodge in Strathbraan. Trochrie was always small, but it is a pathetic remnant now, just a fragment of one small turret standing incongruously in the lawn of a holiday cottage. It was in good hunting country, and the Ruthven brothers presumably spent much of the month of July happily chasing the deer and renewing their sibling relationship, for Sandy Ruthven had been only 12 when Earl John left for Europe. According to the logic of the royal narrative of the 'Gowrie Conspiracy', though, the brothers were also spending time at Trochrie in plotting to kill or seize the King of Scots: a plot born of cold-blooded determination to avenge the execution of their father, 'Greysteil', Earl of Gowrie.

****

Apologists for the Ruthven brothers have invariably (and paradoxically) dismissed the idea of revenge as a motive by adopting the very lines of argument that James used to talk down Sandy Ruthven. As the king said, he had been young and not directly responsible for the execution of the first Earl of Gowrie, and he subsequently restored the Ruthven titles and estates. True; but James also restored some of the men who had been more directly responsible for 'Greysteil's' death, and he never brought to justice the chief perpetrator, the Earl of Arran. Perhaps Countess Dorothea brought up her sons to believe that the king himself was directly responsible for their father's death, and she might well have drummed into them the humiliation that she suffered at the hands of the king and his courtiers after the earl's execution, when she was virtually trampled underfoot at the opening of Parliament. (The six-year-old John Ruthven and the three-year-old Alexander might even have witnessed this scene themselves, and retained searingly painful childhood memories of the event.)

Even if the Ruthvens did seek vengeance, their actions could be regarded as part of the accepted culture of Scotland's aristocracy. Bloodfeud between noblemen was endemic, as shown by such long-running and vicious quarrels as that between the Gordons and the Stewarts that culminated in the death of the 'Bonnie Earl o'Moray'.[367] There was no statute of limitations on bloodfeud: the hacking to pieces of Arran by James Douglas avenged the Earl of Morton, Douglas's uncle, 16 years after Morton was executed at Arran's instigation, and Douglas, in turn, was killed by Arran's lackeys another 12 years later. Feuding Scottish noblemen had long memories, so there was nothing unlikely in the third Earl of Gowrie and his brother seeking to avenge their father 16 years after his death. Moreover, the young Ruthvens would have grown up not just with tales of bloodfeuds, but living proof of their reality: their early guardian, mentor, and brother-in-law, the Earl of Atholl, could easily have passed on to them his experiences of feuding with the Earls of Morton and Montrose, and their other early mentor, the Earl of Bothwell, was living proof that it was possible to feud with the king himself.

But the Ruthvens' cultural milieu of murder extended much further afield. The Earl of Gowrie had travelled widely in Europe, and he and Sandy lived in an age when assassinating European heads of state was in vogue: William of Orange and Henri III of France had already fallen victim to assassins, Henri IV would do so within 10 years, and these were only the most prominent examples. Moreover, Gowrie had clearly absorbed many Italian fashions during his time at Padua – conclusively demonstrated by the way in which he wore his two swords Italian-style on 5 August 1600. He also certainly knew his Machiavelli, so presumably he would have been familiar with the passage in Chapter VIII of *The Prince*, where Machiavelli describes the career of Oliverotto of Fermo in the 1490s. The passage has chilling echoes of the events at Gowrie House, and could even have provided Gowrie with part of the template for a murder plot, if that was what he intended. Oliverotto invited his uncle, the ruler, to a banquet, at which they started to discuss serious matters. Oliverotto suddenly got to his feet and said that such things should be discussed more privately, and led his uncle to another room. Once inside, armed men emerged and slaughtered the ruler and his friends.[368] For a young man with revenge on his mind, reading such passages in Machiavelli could easily have provided food for thought.

Plotting a hypothetical assassination is one thing; finding a willing 'lone gunman' is quite another, and one of the greatest weaknesses in the theory of a murder plot with revenge as the motive is the likely fate of the assassin. Sandy Ruthven, the would-be instrument of vengeance, must have known that if he killed the king, he was signing his own death warrant. If he did not die there and then, he would presumably have met a regicide's death on the scaffold a few weeks later, as no successor regime would have been magnanimous about the example of murdering heads of state. In that sense, his attempted assassination of James, if such it was, would have been nothing but a suicide attack. If this was so, then perhaps an explanation for Sandy's behaviour might be found in the motivation of other suicide attackers down the ages: a fanatical belief in the rightness of their cause, allied to a belief that martyrdom will bring them a glorious immortality. Sandy's alleged actions immediately on entering the turret chamber – covering his head disrespectfully, and proclaiming himself to be his father's avenger – suggest both cold premeditation and cold anger, not a hot-blooded, spur-of-the-moment killing. If he then had last-minute doubts, he would not be the last would-be murderer to do so.

This interpretation of Sandy Ruthven's actions on 5 August 1600 lacks credibility on several crucial points. His failure to overpower the much older and smaller king hardly smacks of a determined and ruthless murderer, but certainly does smack of a nervous and confused young man whose plan is going badly wrong. The fact that Sandy Ruthven chose to wear a 'pyne dowlit', a concealed shirt of chain mail, on such a hot day does not suggest a young man careless of his life; rather, it suggests that he thought he was likely to be in physical danger at some point, although that could argue equally well for his being an attacker who knew he might need to defend himself or a potential victim who feared an assault from the king and his attendants. Then again, if Sandy really was so hell-bent on assassinating the king, and so careless of his own life, he could easily have killed James that morning, when he spoke to him privately in the park at Falkland. Bringing James to Gowrie House simply to kill him was not only pointless, it risked defeating what was undoubtedly one of the key objectives of the Ruthven brothers throughout the day on 5 August: that John Ruthven, Earl of Gowrie, should be seen to be innocent of whatever transpired.

Whatever the nature of their scheme, the Ruthvens were no fools. For the wider interests of the House of Ruthven, it was vital that Sandy *alone* should bear the responsibility for the fate of the king, and be seen to bear it, particularly if the scheme went wrong. The family had already lost everything once, 16 years before, thanks to the plots of a previous Earl of Gowrie, and the Ruthven boys would have learned that lesson all too well at Dirleton Castle from his widow, their mother, Dorothea, dowager Countess of Gowrie. Therefore, the entire 'Gowrie Conspiracy' was devised around one central principle: the Earl of Gowrie himself had to be seen to be innocent of it. If his innocence was beyond question, he could not be accused of treason. If he could not be accused of treason, the Ruthven lands, castles and riches could not be forfeited, yet again. This imperative explains Sandy's insistence throughout 5 August that his brother knew nothing of what he was doing: the Master was effectively mouthing evidence for the defence in any future case against the earl. A circumstantial piece of evidence to support this argument might be the absence of William Ruthven of Freeland, head of the next most senior branch of the family, from Gowrie House on 5 August, although his younger brothers Alexander and Harry were heavily involved in the day's events. If it had been intended that the chiefs of the name of Ruthven should have cast-iron alibis for whatever transpired, the Freeland line managed the matter rather more successfully than Ruthven, himself.[369]

A determination to exculpate the earl himself explains what has always been one of the most confusing aspects of the story of the 'Gowrie House affair', the seemingly inexplicable behaviour of the two brothers towards each other, and towards the king. Why did Sandy Ruthven try so hard to convince King James that Gowrie knew nothing of the 'pot of gold', and why did he go to such elaborate lengths to get Gowrie out of the way at the dinner? Why did Gowrie seem so surprised by the king's coming, and why had he not prepared a meal for the royal guest? Why did Gowrie go through the elaborate charade of shouting for horses after Cranstoun spread the rumour that James had left Perth? After all, if Gowrie was innocent of his brother's plans and Sandy was acting entirely on his own initiative, as some have claimed, then the earl's behaviour at that time could not have done more to incriminate him in them. Above all, the earl had to have a very public alibi. According to several accounts, this was supposed to be his attendance at the Tuesday morning sermon in Perth: the Earl of Gowrie could hardly be guilty of the king's murder or disappearance if most of the prominent townspeople of Perth could bear witness to the fact that he was in church at the moment the king died or vanished.[370]

Of course, James's insistence on continuing with the hunt would have thrown the brothers' plans into disarray, delaying his arrival in Perth for several hours; and, of course, when he was finally accompanied by Lennox, Mar and the rest, rather than coming alone as Sandy had requested. The Ruthvens must have thought that the promise of treasure would have been a more than sufficient lure to bring James hotfoot to Perth, but they reckoned without the king's addiction to hunting and, perhaps, without his innate suspicion of the Ruthven family. The king's late arrival might explain why Gowrie had no dinner prepared for him: after all, according to the logic of an 'assassination plot' that was meant to be carried through in the morning, why should he have prepared a meal for a king who was meant to be already dead? According to the guests who were already in Gowrie House, the two servants who had gone with Sandy to Falkland gave Gowrie ample forewarning of the king's arrival after riding ahead of the royal party. Andrew Henderson got to the house at about ten, Andrew Ruthven some time later, but still the earl made no move to organise hospitality for the king. This inaction, and Gowrie's apparent discomfort when the king arrived, might have been born of surprise that Sandy had decided (presumably unilaterally) to go on with a plan whose moment had passed; or so the earl might have assumed when the morning dragged on with no sign of James arriving in Perth. Perhaps the earl was thrown by the news that Lennox, his erstwhile brother-in-law, and Mar, his godfather, were coming too, in case they were drawn into danger; for treachery against one's own kin, and especially between godparent and godchild, was looked upon as even more heinous than treachery to one's country.[371] In any event, Gowrie excused himself from the meeting of the town council that followed the church service, and later dismissed the Hay brothers abruptly, perhaps to give himself time to think and to modify his plans.[372] The decision to proceed after all with whatever the Ruthvens had in mind, despite the presence of the entire royal hunting party, displays either breathtaking audacity or breathtaking stupidity. In one sense, though, the presence of the courtiers, and courtiers to whom the Ruthvens were so closely related, actually made it easier for the brothers to maintain the essential element of their plan. Gowrie would still have his alibi, and by chance, it would now be even more unimpeachable than before: after all, who was likely to question the word of the Earl of Mar and the Duke of Lennox?

At very short notice, therefore, Gowrie (or someone else) conjured up a dramatic new contingency plan. The rumour that the king had already left Gowrie House and was riding out of town was desperate, but potentially plausible. As Andrew Lang pointed out over a century ago, it would have been shot to pieces immediately if anyone had bothered to check whether or not the king's horse was still in the stable,[373] but in times of crisis, common sense is often one of the first casualties. Allowing for this, and adopting the tenuous inner logic of the 'pot of gold' story (which Lennox, at least, knew by that time), then if Sandy Ruthven had taken the king away from his retinue to show him a secret in private, it was reasonably feasible for the two of them to want to slip out of town surreptitiously to view the 'treasure' at a secret location that Sandy only revealed when he was alone with James. (The notion that the 'pot of gold' and its carrier could have been concealed in Gowrie House without the Earl of Gowrie's knowledge has always been regarded as one of the greatest weaknesses in the story.) Above all, the cry for 'horses' meant that Gowrie could stay with Lennox, Mar, and the rest of the party – and if they all fell for the bait and rode out of town, so much the better, for yet again, the earl would be physically removed from the attack on the king, in the presence of a body of unchallengeable witnesses.

If this was the revised plan, and if indeed it was hatched in great haste, it explains the farcical sequence of events that wrecked it. For Gowrie to get on his horse to ride after the king, his horse needed to be available: but it was at Scone. For the king to leave surreptitiously, there had to be a convenient gate for him to leave by; but Gowrie's porter, ignorant of the new plan (and probably of any plan at all), innocently affirmed that it would have been impossible for the king to have left. Finally, there is the clinching proof that what happened that afternoon at Gowrie House was hastily conceived and calamitously executed: the fact that Lennox, Mar and the rest happened to be milling around, waiting for their horses, directly beneath the chamber where Sandy Ruthven was botching whatever he intended to do with his king. Gowrie House had other turret chambers – notably two that led off the private apartments, at the back of the courtyard and therefore much further from the street (see Plan B). It also had the detached 'Monk's Tower', in the corner of the garden and at the side of the river, which would surely have been a better location for any action against (or by) the king (see Plan A, p.24). But then, the exact location of the royal hunting party should have been academic: if there really was a murder plot, and if the Master of Ruthven had played his part properly, the King of Scots should already have been dead, long before Lennox, Mar, Gowrie and the rest of them rode off in fruitless pursuit of him from the street beneath.

****

All of this suggests that the events at Gowrie House, and the actions of the Ruthven brothers, do not fit comfortably with the theory that what happened on 5 August 1600 was a premeditated assassination plot. That theory is also directly contradicted by the only two witnesses to what was said in the turret chamber, Andrew Henderson and King James himself. According to the published narrative of the king's story, after Sandy Ruthven had locked James in the chamber, disrespectfully donned his cap, and drawn Henderson's dagger, he:

> held the point of it to the king's breast, avowing now
> that the king behoved to be in his will, and used as he
> [wished]; swearing many bloody oaths, that if the king
> cried one word, or opened a window to look out, that
> dagger should presently go to his heart; affirming, that
> he was sure that now the King's conscience was
> burdened for murdering his father.[374]

James's subsequent words to Sandy suggest that he seems to have jumped to the conclusion that Ruthven intended to kill him, but his own account of Sandy's words show that this was simply not the case. The words used are those of an abductor threatening his victim with dire consequences if he fails to cooperate; the mention of Sandy's father is not spoken as a motive for murder, but as an explanation for the young man's hostility to the king. This reading contradicts Henderson's first deposition, where he stated explicitly that Sandy said 'Remember ye my father's murder? You shall now die for it'.[375] In his second deposition, made in November, Henderson altered his

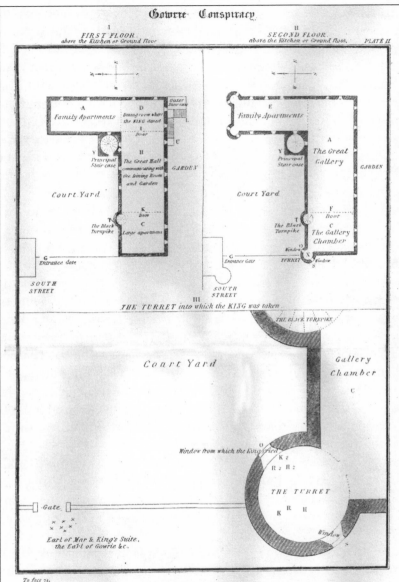

Gowrie Conspiracy

I
FIRST FLOOR.
above the Kitchen or Ground floor

II
SECOND FLOOR.
above the Kitchen or Ground floor

PLATE II

III
THE TURRET into which the KING was taken.

K, R, H—Position of the King, the Master of Gowrie, and Andrew Henderson on their entrance into the Turret and at the commencement of the struggle. K2, R2, H2—Their relative situations at the time the King cried for help. The door at U led by a flight of steps to the Garden. The greater part of the second floor (Plan II.) was occupied by a Gallery A, which extended over the whole of the front of the building. The Turret communicated with the Gallery Chamber. The King, with Ruthven, left the Room D, passed through the Hall H to the Stair Case Y, which they ascended. Sir John Ramsay and others went up the Stair Y into Gallery A. F—Door to the Gallery Chamber which was locked, and they tried to break open. Ramsay then ran up the Black Turnpike T, and entered the Gallery Chamber C. Ruthven was thrust down the Turnpike wounded.

If the King stood opposite the door and looking towards it, then when Ruthven entered and advanced towards him the situation would be nearly that of the letters K, R, H,—K being the situation of the King; R that of Ruthven; H that of Henderson. Here the situation was so far changed that Henderson H2 is now on the right of Ruthven R2 and on the left of the King K2, the two latter being between the former and the window. In this situation Ruthven took hold of the King's throat with his left hand and put his right in the King's mouth to prevent his cries. The window S looked directly to the Spy tower; this was the wrong window, and Henderson went to window O.

Plan B

testimony to something much more like the king's own. After drawing the dagger, Henderson has Sandy saying 'Sir, you [must] be my prisoner! Remember on my father's death!'; when James tried to speak, Sandy cried 'Hold your tongue, sir, or by Christ you shall die!'

Henderson's second deposition was made well after the official narrative was published, and might therefore have been brought into line, consciously or subconsciously, with the royal account. However, the suggestion that Sandy wanted to make the king his prisoner, not to kill him, concurs with one of the more inexplicable aspects of the events in the turret chamber, the production of a garter to bind the king's hands. If the Ruthvens' motive was assassination, Sandy had no need to tie James up: unlike Henderson and the Master of Ruthven, King James was wearing no armour, and in such a confined space, he could easily have been stabbed to death in an instant. Henderson's November deposition has James asking Sandy, 'What is it you crave, man, if you crave not my life?', and Sandy replying, 'Sir, it is but a promise'. It is possible that this mention of a 'promise' by Henderson was a mistake on his part, a confused conflation of Sandy getting James to promise that he would not attempt to escape while Sandy went to consult with Gowrie, or else a misremembering by Henderson of a phrase that had appeared in the published royal narrative.[376] But if Henderson was remembering the context correctly, it strengthens the proposition that what was really happening in Gowrie House that afternoon was an attempted *coup d'état*, abducting the king to force him to do something that the Ruthvens wanted.

If the Ruthvens sought to abduct or somehow constrain the king, they would have had ample precedent on their side. Taking action against an unsatisfactory monarch was not just a long-standing tradition among the Scottish nobility, it was regarded as an inalienable political right.[377] Within living memory, members of the nobility had engineered Queen Mary's abdication in 1567 and King James's abduction in 1582, with William Ruthven, first Earl of Gowrie, playing a central role in both events. In that sense, the third Earl and the Master of Ruthven would have been acting in almost respectable aristocratic and family traditions by seeking to secure, and perhaps overthrow, King James VI. Luring James into a Ruthven household and detaining him in a second 'Raid of Ruthven' lacked originality, but such a hypothesis helps to explain some of the more puzzling aspects of the 'Gowrie House affair', such as the presence of the garter and Sandy's original insistence that James should come to Perth at once, with only a minimum of (easily overpowered) attendants. If the Ruthven brothers were attempting to kidnap James and stage a coup on 5 August 1600, they had an agenda; over the centuries, noblemen who seized Scottish monarchs wanted him or her to do something that they wanted, to implement a new policy or abandon an old and unpopular one, to elevate a new favourite or destroy an old one. If all the Ruthvens wanted was a 'promise', as Henderson allegedly claimed, they faced the obvious problem that a promise obtained under duress could later be repudiated by James. But that depends on what sort of promise the Ruthvens wanted, on what sort of pressure they could exert on the king to grant it and on what happened to the king afterwards.

In 1600 the Presbyterian Kirk desperately needed a champion to fight its cause, a champion who could get the king to promise that he and Scotland would return to a more godly path. The long-running quarrel between king and Kirk had come to a head in 1596. In September the Kirk's leader, Andrew Melville, denounced James to his face as 'God's silly vassal'; in November one of Melville's lieutenants was arrested for preaching a seditious sermon, and later gaoled. This, and rumours of risings by the king's Catholic friends, sparked mass rioting in Edinburgh in mid-December. James and his ministers interpreted this as an embryonic revolution and moved out to Linlithgow, returning a few days later with an army. Seeing the way the wind was blowing, the city fathers of Edinburgh ejected the obstreperous clergymen and apologised fulsomely to the king.[378] The Kirk was defeated and divided, and largely remained so for the rest of James's reign, even having to stomach the re-introduction of bishops. It is just possible that some of the extremists refused to accept the situation, and sought to rectify it by turning once again to the family that had always been among the Kirk's strongest allies. It has been suggested that the timing of Gowrie's return to Scotland was prompted by some in the Kirk, who sent an emissary to him in France in the autumn of 1599. Perhaps significantly, this emissary was none other than Robert Bruce, the stubborn clergyman who later persistently refused to accept King James's version of the events at Gowrie House.[379] If Gowrie truly was acting on behalf of the Kirk, it might also be significant that Perth's ministers were not actually in the town on 5 August 1600; they were attending a synod in Stirling.[380]

Moreover, the Kirk certainly did not act on behalf of Gowrie. It meekly toed the royal party line in denouncing the Ruthven brothers as assassins and traitors: the only dissenting voices came from the five ministers of Edinburgh, four of whom climbed down almost immediately, leaving just the diehard Bruce. But then, in 1582 the young Ruthvens' father presented the Kirk with a *fait accompli* when he staged the 'Raid of Ruthven' without its prior knowledge or approval, so it is not impossible that his sons aimed, at least in part, to repeat the example by staging a coup that would benefit the Kirk, albeit not sanctioned by it in advance. If this was the Ruthvens' intention, it was surely far too ambitious: even if a detained James promised on 5 August 1600 to restore the Kirk's authority, it was highly unlikely that a freed James would keep his promise on the sixth. The young Ruthvens should have learned that lesson from the history of their own father, whose government's policies were overturned by the king as soon as James was free of Ruthven control. A restoration of the Kirk might have been a desirable by-product of whatever the Ruthvens planned to do in 1600, but it could hardly have been their main objective.

But as with so many aspects of the 'Gowrie House affair', it is possible to look at this evidence from entirely the opposite direction. After all, if King James sought to humble the Kirk, as he undoubtedly did, then surely he possessed a powerful motive to bring down the family that had long been regarded as among the Kirk's staunchest champions. Perhaps the King of Scots had determined that, for reasons of state, the Ruthvens had to die.

CHAPTER SIX

FOR THE GOOD OF THE STATE

'If I would have taken their lives, I had causes enough.' By his own admission, King James VI had ample motive for killing the Ruthven brothers at Perth on 5 August 1600. Contemporaries who studied the royal narrative and the other evidence saw the inconsistencies, noted the contradictions, observed the implausibities, and came to a terrible conclusion: the King of Scots was a murderer and a liar. He and his 'green coats' had gone to Gowrie House with the express and premeditated intention of slaughtering the Earl of Gowrie and his brother, to be followed by the systematic destruction of the entire House of Ruthven. This interpretation of the events of 5 August proved irresistibly attractive to some later writers, and was upheld unswervingly by the Ruthvens' descendants and apologists for generations to come. And so the alternative legend of Gowrie House was born. The innocent young Ruthven brothers had been 'entrapped by the craft of a bigoted and sensual monarch and cruelly murdered in their own house' by his perjured and amoral henchmen, 'the court parasites' who benefited from their downfall.[381] For well over two centuries, the events at Gowrie House defied proper and neutral analysis because they were a political battleground between those who believed in the king and those who believed in the Ruthvens. The history of the 'Gowrie House affair' was not written dispassionately and analytically: it was written to contribute to one side or the other of an ongoing party political battle.[382] At the heart of that battle was the posthumous reputation of King James VI and I.

At first sight, James certainly had 'causes enough' for destroying the Ruthvens. The entire history of the family over the preceding 50 or 60 years had shown them to be ambitious and a potential threat to the Stuarts. But a family's long record of conflict with the crown was no reason for that crown to attempt to obliterate it from the historical record. The relationship between the Stuarts and the Gordons had arguably been much worse, with Gordon armies going into the field against Mary and James on several occasions; but by 1600 the Gordon chief, Huntly, was the king's best friend. More immediately, John, Earl of Gowrie, had spoken out strongly in the convention of June 1600 against voting taxes to the crown for an army that could invade England if that country perversely refused to recognise James's overwhelming right to be Queen Elizabeth's successor. But Gowrie was not the only one who had spoken out against the king's pet scheme. Even more vocal opposition came from Alexander Seton, Lord Fyvie, the Lord President of the Privy Council. Far from ordering the killing of Fyvie for resisting his royal will, James made him the guardian of his second son (the future King Charles I) just five months later, and eventually made him Earl of Dunfermline. In the fall-out from the June convention, James proved to be far angrier with the burghs, which had flatly refused to vote him any money at all, than he was with the likes of Fyvie and Gowrie.[383]

Money and sex have ever provided the most common motives for murderers, and one or both of them might have driven King James to slaughter the Ruthvens. The crown still owed the family some £80,000, the vast sum that the first Earl of Gowrie had loaned to the king when he was Lord Treasurer of Scotland (and which had been inflated by the steady devaluation of the pound Scots over two decades). The third earl had returned from his European tour to find no prospect of the debt being repaid. With his own debts mounting, he had been forced to petition the king for protection against his creditors.[384] The fact that James agreed to this is surely inexplicable if he was simultaneously planning to murder Gowrie a few weeks later. Even so, Gowrie's debt to the king's saddler, Robert Abercromby, was the pretext that Sandy Ruthven apparently gave out for James's visit to Perth: the financial relationship between the king and the Earl of Gowrie was clearly somewhere at the back of both of their minds in the days leading up to 5 August. Following this line of argument through, and putting it crudely, killing the Ruthven boys not only immediately cancelled James's debt to them, it also provided a welcome windfall in the shape of the Ruthven lands. But if James had applied this logic consistently and ruthlessly, he would rapidly have decimated Scotland's (and later England's) noble and mercantile elites. The notoriously spendthrift king was always heavily in debt to individuals and institutions, many of whom waited for repayment for years on end, if not for all eternity. The

Edinburgh goldsmith 'Jinglin' Geordie' Heriot was owed vast sums by the crown on a fairly permanent basis, primarily as a result of Queen Anna's insatiable demand for new jewellery, but James seems never to have considered eliminating this debt by simply eliminating Heriot.[385]

Undoubtedly, then, the huge Ruthven debt would not have been sufficient reason for King James to risk his life in Perth on 5 August 1600; but perhaps sex, or sexual jealousy, was. James's wife, Anna of Denmark, was both young and vivacious. There had always been rumours that she found glamorous young courtiers more interesting than her shambolic husband, and it would not have been surprising if those who sought explanations for what had happened at Gowrie House deliberately made up a tale of sex and revenge, the oldest and simplest explanation for the newest and most complicated of mysteries. The most common form of the legend that grew up had Anna secretly giving Sandy Ruthven a ribbon, or a locket on a ribbon, that the king had given her.[386] Sandy wore it under his shirt, but one hot summer's day he fell asleep in the garden of Falkland Palace. King James passed by, saw the ribbon (or locket) under the open collar and stormed off towards the queen's quarters. One of her ladies–in–waiting (perhaps one of Sandy's sisters) saw what had happened, retrieved the ribbon (or locket), and rushed to the queen by a shortcut. When James arrived and demanded to be shown the ribbon (or locket), the queen innocently produced it. The king left, muttering 'Devil take me, but like is an ill mark'. The story, which markedly resembles the affair of the 'queen's jewels' in *The Three Musketeers*, was extant by the middle of the mid-18th century, but there is no contemporary corroboration of it.[387] In an alternative version, the queen fell for Gowrie himself, 'a lord of a comely visage, good stature, and of an attracting allurement', and James promptly despatched Ramsay and his other hit-men to murder his love rival.[388] Yet another version was supposedly told some time in the 1660s to the father of the historian Robert Wodrow (1679–1734) by an octogenarian former servant of Gowrie's, who claimed to have been present on the fateful 5 August. This story, too, is reminiscent of another, in this case 'Sleeping Beauty', and it is just as much of a fairy tale:

> His master, he said, was one of the handsomest, loveliest men he set his eyes upon. Some time after, the king and queen being together, he asked her whom she thought to be the handsomest man she knew. The queen replied, his Majesty. 'Well,' said the king, 'I believe you think so;

> but next to me, whom think you the properest man in
> Scotland?' The queen said she saw none more
> handsome than the young Earl of Gowrie. After that the
> king took up a jealousy.[389]

These hints of a *crime passionnel* were associated with the 'Gowrie House affair' from the very beginning: only 15 days after the slaughter, one of the English border wardens reported that the killing had been triggered by the king's jealousy of the queen's affection for Gowrie.[390]

The 18th and 19th century commentators on the 'Gowrie House affair' could barely bring themselves to discuss the other possible sexual explanation for what might have happened.[391] King James's passion for good looking men (or, as one Ruthven descendant put it, his 'infamous propensities')[392] had been apparent for years, and in later life he bestowed lavish favours on young men who caught his eye. The most famous and controversial example was George Villiers, younger son of an obscure Leicestershire knight, who attracted the king's attention when aged 22 on no better grounds than his fine pair of legs. Less than 10 years later, Villiers was England's only duke, her Lord High Admiral and effectively her chief minister. The enemies of Buckingham and James's previous favourites knew that parading a likely young man before the king might bring untold political and financial rewards to both the favourite and his promoters. After all, it was exactly this kind of factional power play that had brought the young Villiers to James's attention in the first place, beginning his inexorable rise to power. If James VI had set his eyes on Sandy Ruthven in 1600, or Sandy had set his on the king, the stakes would have been high indeed; furthermore, to this day Ruthven family tradition holds that James 'fancied the Master of Ruthven and was also cuckolded by the Earl of Gowrie'.[393]

Debate about all of this has raged since the king's own day. Was it overt homosexuality, indiscreet homoeroticism, or merely a desperate quest for love by a naturally affectionate man who had never known his parents (one of whom was blown up and throttled, the other beheaded), who had no close relations, and who had spent his entire life surrounded by avaricious and ambitious men seeking to manipulate him for their own ends? From any of these perspectives, the events at Gowrie House can be seen in an entirely different light. Sandy Ruthven was a tall 19-year-old, very much James's preferred specification. James and Sandy going up to the turret chamber alone, with doors locked behind them, might have had quite another purpose; there is a suggestion of this in the

Duke of Lennox's evidence, where the Earl of Gowrie allegedly said that 'his Majesty was gone up quietly upon some quiet errand'.[394] Of course, the 'quiet errand' could have been a call of nature, but if that was so, why go so far, and to such an inappropriate 'lavatory' as a second floor turret chamber? Continuing the logic of this theory, the 'wrestling' that John Ramsay witnessed when he burst into the chamber could also have been something else entirely. Sceptics have long poured scorn on the idea that the king could have overpowered the young, fit Master of Ruthven, but perhaps he would not have needed to if Ruthven was already literally in a delicate position. In this scheme of events, the tragedy in the turret chamber would not have been the first gay lovers' quarrel to end in murder, nor would it be the last. A recent popular history of the Stuart family makes much of the king's order to Ramsay, 'strike him [Sandy] low, he wears a pyne dowlit' (a concealed shirt of chain mail), suggesting that the only way James could have known of this item of clothing was if it had 'already been removed while they made love'.[395] However, this is hardly credible. For one thing, it was a very hot August day, so it would have been entirely plausible for the Master's shirt to be open, revealing the doublet beneath – especially as he had just ridden to Falkland and back. For another, James must have felt or seen such a garment while he was wrestling with Sandy. Moreover, if seduction had been the intention on either side, why go to such elaborate lengths to attempt it in Gowrie House, surrounded by dozens of people, rather than somewhere much less conspicuous – and why have an 'armoured man' in place to witness the *denouement*?

Other motives were produced to explain this alleged royal pogrom. Many courtiers were jealous of the Ruthvens, and were envious of their wealthy and extensive estates. Gowrie was a favourite of the Kirk and the common people, and this popularity made him a potential threat to the king. All of these whispers, these supposed justifications for the murders of the Ruthven brothers, passed into legend, handed down the generations among the Ruthvens' descendants and apologists. Eliza Gulston, an ageing, embittered half-blind spinster, was by the mid-1820s the unlikely senior surviving representative of the Ruthven bloodline, and firmly convinced that she had thus become the rightful Countess of Gowrie. Eliza believed that 'the Gowrys were a race of uncommon talent … all the nobility wished to get rid of so superior a family'.[396] Similarly, one of the many stories that circulated in Perth in the 18th century claimed that James was jealous of the earl's wealth and popularity, feared that he would eventually seek to avenge his father's death, and so ordered a pre-emptive strike against the Ruthvens.[397] Of course, this was all hearsay, hindsight and myth, but it is significant that the overwhelming majority of the myths that grew up around the 'Gowrie House affair' were vehemently hostile to King James; and myths have a habit of becoming fixed much more firmly in popular consciousness than less romantic and less dramatic truths.

Rubbishing the king's most obvious motives for murdering the Ruthvens, or at least pointing out their implausibility, does not eliminate the possibility that *something* was in James's mind on 5 August: some 'secret cause', as Robert Bruce put it, some dark and now unknown reason that drew the King of Scots to Gowrie House. For instance, James might have suspected that the Earl of Gowrie was a devil-worshipping warlock in league with the pope; but that, as they say, is another story.* We can never know with absolute certainty whether or not King James had any compelling motive to drive him to murder, and if he did, what that motive might have been. But we can know with a reasonable degree of certainty whether what actually happened at Gowrie House on 5 August 1600 was or was not a carefully stage-managed royal plot to murder the Ruthvens.

****

The whispering campaign against the king began almost immediately. As early as 11 August, just six days after the events at Gowrie House, Patrick Galloway's sermon welcoming James back to Edinburgh confronted head-on the already widely held belief that 'the king was a doer, and not a sufferer; a pursuer, and not pursued'.[398] As each piece of new evidence emerged, it was picked over, compared with the existing record, and frequently found wanting. The 'pot of gold' story was ridiculous; why should the king go to see it in person, rather than sending someone else or having the gold and the 'man in the field' brought to him? If the king was suspicious before he got to Perth, why did he still agree to go alone to the turret chamber with Sandy Ruthven? How could Sandy leave the king alone in the chamber, or else alone with Andrew Henderson, who was either a quivering wreck or the man who had just knocked a dagger from Ruthven's hand? Why take the king to a chamber with a window opening onto one of the busiest streets in Perth? How did the king overpower Sandy, and why was the Master not taken alive, as he could have been? Why did some accounts say that crucial doors were open,

* See below, pp. 190-4

others that they were locked shut?[399] Then there was the refusal of the five Edinburgh ministers to believe the substance of the king's first account. If such unimpeachable leaders of the community doubted the story, it was hardly surprising that the credulous 'rude multitude' took a lead from them. To many, King James also had 'form': even if he had not actually sanctioned the killing of the Bonny Earl o' Moray, he had certainly exculpated Huntly, who undoubtedly had sanctioned it, and James had done his level best to cover up the whole affair. To the cynical, the sceptical and the downright hostile, the holes in the official story of the 'Gowrie Conspiracy' were so gaping that only one conclusion was possible: it was all a pack of lies, and if that was the case, the King of Scots was a murderer. Again.

At the start of September, the English government got wind of a sensational new development. The royal version of events, encapsulated in the newly-published official narrative, had been challenged by a mysterious and anonymous tract that at once vindicated the Ruthven brothers and accused King James of premeditated murder. Not surprisingly, this alternative version of the events at Gowrie House was rapidly suppressed and was long thought to have been lost: a persistent 'urban myth' in Perth centred on old men who knew other old men who had supposedly seen a copy of the pamphlet years before.[400] In fact, one copy of the 'Ruthven Vindication' did survive. It was evidently smuggled out of Scotland by an English agent, and was received on 4 September 1600 by Sir John Carey, deputy governor of Berwick, the man to whom it was nominally addressed. Carey immediately forwarded it to London. After its initial perusal by Queen Elizabeth's ministers, it was filed away and forgotten amidst the voluminous chaos of the State Paper Office, avoiding scrutiny and destruction by Elizabeth's successor.[401] The torn, fragmentary and partly illegible 'Vindication' provides a fascinating alternative explanation of what might have happened on 5 August 1600, especially when it is coupled with the oral traditions that were handed down from generation to generation in the Ruthvens' home town. Typical of this process was the experience of the Lord Provost of Perth who ordered the demolition of Gowrie House 200 years later. He had heard the story of the Ruthvens' innocence 'from my father, who had it from his mother, as she heard it from her grandmother, who was alive at the time'.[402]

Much of the first paragraph of the 'Vindication' is missing, but it seems to suggest that the Earl of Gowrie returned to Perth on 31 July 1600, intending to ride on to visit his mother at Dirleton Castle. He had given his servants leave to sort out their affairs in Perth prior to going south – hardly the action of a man plotting treason, or so the author of the 'Vindication' argued. Other sources elaborate on the earl's supposed intentions. After seeing his mother, he apparently intended to ride on to Seton Palace, between Dirleton and Edinburgh, where he was to meet the 12-year-old Lady Margaret Douglas. This was no innocent social call; it would be the first stage in the process by which the young Margaret would marry John Ruthven and become the new Countess of Gowrie. Margaret Douglas was the only child, and thus heiress, of the eighth Douglas Earl of Angus, an old friend of Gowrie's father. Preventing the Angus lands, castles and titles falling into the hands of the Ruthvens might have given James another powerful motive to eliminate them, for a Gowrie-Douglas marriage would have created far and away the most powerful noble house in lowland Scotland.[403] If King James wanted to lay an elaborate trap for the Ruthven brothers, for this reason or any of the others, he would need accurate and up-to-date intelligence of the intended crime scene. According to the 'Vindication', Friday 1 August saw an unexpected visitor arrive at the door of Gowrie House: none other than Doctor Hew Herries, who would be at the centre of events four days later and who had certainly been used by James for secret missions in the recent past.[404] For reasons unknown, the club-footed doctor requested a tour of the house. He was shown round by the Earl of Gowrie, whose sister Herries had (allegedly) recently warned of a great disaster that was about to befall her. Perhaps significantly, Herries would be one of very few key players in the events of 5 August who never gave evidence. But that was for the future. In the immediate present, the first week of August 1600, the killing ground had been reconnoitred. It remained only to spring the trap.

The 'Vindication' claimed that Sandy Ruthven was summoned to Falkland by the king, not sent there by Gowrie. James had supposedly sent several earlier letters to the Ruthven brothers, demanding their attendance at the hunting.[405] According to other accounts, the incriminating letter of summons was found when the clothes of either the dead earl or the dead master were searched, and was promptly and surreptitiously destroyed by the king's men. Gowrie had allegedly ignored the earlier letters because he believed that if he joined the hunt in Falkland Park, he would be shot dead during the chase.[406] There was also said to have been a letter of the king's to another Ruthven, the young men's uncle, commanding him to meet James in Perth on 5 August. But the evidence for this is shadowy. Calderwood, the only source for the story, named the uncle as William, but there was no such person.[407] Returning to the 'Vindication', Sandy Ruthven planned only to stay overnight at Falkland before riding on to the shore of the Firth of Forth, where he would meet Gowrie on the morning of the sixth. The brothers would then make the short crossing of the Firth to join their mother at Dirleton. There is indirect confirmation of some of this. The Scotland of 1600 was nothing like as bureaucratic as England, as James soon learned. Even so, every letter sent out from the monarch was duly recorded in the Lord Treasurer's accounts, for the messenger boys who delivered them had to be paid. As the recipients' distance from the court determined how much the boys earned, recording their names was essential to deter inflated claims for expenses. The treasurer's accounts for 1600 show that towards the end of July, a messenger was sent from Edinburgh to the Earl of Gowrie, and later another was sent from Falkland to the Master of Ruthven.[408] To the supporters of the Ruthvens, these entries damn King James, the murderer who ensnared two entirely innocent young men.

However, it is only possible to read sinister connotations into these letters by deploying hindsight on the grandest scale. The King of Scots naturally and regularly sent private letters to his principal noblemen, so the July letters could have been perfectly innocent, or connected with something else entirely. The letter to Gowrie was sent at the same time as one to the Earl of Atholl, that to Sandy Ruthven at the same time as one to Drummond of Inchaffray, neither of whom died violently and mysteriously.[409] True, Drummond was at both Falkland and Gowrie House on 5 August 1600, saw Sandy Ruthven talking to the king at seven in the morning, and subsequently invited Sandy (his cousin) to breakfast, an invitation that Sandy refused on the grounds that he had been commanded to wait upon the king. Therefore, it is possible to construct a case for Drummond being at Falkland because both he and Sandy were responding to summonses sent to them in the same pair of royal letters recorded in the treasurers' accounts, but this is extremely tenuous, to say the least. Even if it could be proved that the letters to the Ruthvens were invitations to the brothers to join the royal hunting party, this in itself would not prove the existence of a royal assassination plot: it might only prove that the king thought the Ruthvens needed some exercise.

The 'Vindication' agreed with the official version that Sandy spoke to the king on the morning of 5 August 1600, but in the 'Vindication', of course, it is James who tells him that he will go to Perth that day, and Sandy sends Henderson ahead so that Gowrie can prepare for this unexpected royal visit. (Conspiracy theorists who wished to prove that Henderson never went to Falkland at all had their case severely undermined by the fact that even the Ruthvens' staunchest apologist was perfectly happy to admit that Henderson was there.) According to the 'Vindication', Gowrie was at dinner when Henderson arrived, and he hastily ordered a larger meal to be prepared for the royal party. This point is confirmed by some of the state's own evidence, unlike another tradition that lingered in Perth for centuries. According to this, Gowrie was attending the wedding feast of a young man called Lamb and his bride called Bell, when he was informed that the king was coming. Because the royal visit was entirely unexpected, and no dinner was prepared, Miss Bell's father urged Gowrie to take the wedding dinner with him, which he did.[410] But no mention of such a wedding occurs in any contemporary account, be it from the Ruthvens' friends or their enemies.

Instead, the wedding story might have been a confused crossover from another legend associated with the 'Gowrie House affair'. A number of members of the greatest Perthshire clan, the Murrays, happened to be in Perth on 5 August 1600, and several of them became involved in the events around Gowrie House. William Murray of Tullibardine struggled with the Earl of Gowrie himself, and the Murrays played a key part in eventually bringing the town back under control. But why were they in Perth at all? According to the conspiracy theorists, Sir David Murray, comptroller of the king's household, had sent a secret message to his cousin Sir John, requesting him to bring a large party to Perth on the afternoon of 5 August; and it is certainly feasible for James's route from Falkland to Perth to have taken him past Balvaird Castle, then the principal Murray seat, where further messages could have been exchanged.[411] Sir John, it was said, duly despatched his son William with some 300 horsemen; and William had hated the Ruthvens for the best part of two decades.[412] More prosaic and rather more plausible is the theory that the Murrays were in Perth simply by coincidence, attending the wedding of one of their own.[413] Nevertheless, exaggerating the size of the force available to the king was essential to the cause of the Ruthvens' apologists. The author of the 'Vindication' claimed that James had come to Perth with 60 men, regardless of any Murray presence (which, significantly, he never mentioned). However, a wide range of sources confirm fairly precisely that the royal party consisted of no more than 20 men, many of whom were unarmed, and several of whom were hardly obvious members of a 'hit squad': among these was the splendidly named John Bog, who looked after the king's beer cellar, while two other royal servants went off drinking with a townsman of Perth, hardly a likely course of action for would-be assassins.[414]

The pitiful manpower available to King James is also confirmed implicitly by the sequence of events. If there really had been 300 heavily armed Murray horsemen in the town, let alone up to sixty royal retainers, why did they do next to nothing? Only a handful of Murrays appear anywhere in the record of the day's events, and if a huge armed posse of them really existed, why did it allow the Perth mob to besiege Gowrie House unhindered for hours? One Ruthven apologist explained away this problem in splendidly surreal fashion by postulating that the 300 Murrays slipped through the gardens of Gowrie House to the Tay, where (entirely unseen) they climbed onto boats which took them downstream, so that they could form James's escort when he eventually left Perth.[415] Finally, if the king truly was leading a squad of assassins to Gowrie House, why did he leave behind at Falkland the man best qualified to lead it – Colonel Sir William Stewart, professional soldier, arch-conspirator, the nemesis of John and Sandy Ruthven's father? Stewart was supposedly living in fear of the Ruthvens, dreading the prospect of them eventually bringing the vengeance of bloodfeud against him.[416] Perhaps this very fact would have made it too dangerous to include Stewart in any royal 'death squad'.[417] The deaths of the Ruthven brothers at the hands of someone like John Ramsay could be presented to the world as self-defence or an accident with a reasonable degree of plausibility; indeed, the notion that the Ruthvens were killed by courtiers unused to wielding swords, and who panicked at seeing their king under attack, is probably the most plausible explanation for the failure to take the brothers alive. But if the Ruthvens had died at the hands of Sir William Stewart, it could have been nothing but a royally-crafted assassination, pure and simple.

The 'Vindication' continued. It said next to nothing about the royal party's dinner, bridal or otherwise, and the departure of the king and Sandy Ruthven to the turret chamber. It went on to claim that James himself sent Sandy out to call Sir Thomas Erskine and John Ramsay to follow them up to the chamber. When Erskine, Ramsay and Hew Herries reached the chamber, they slew Sandy Ruthven and threw his body down the stair. According to a different, but equally biased, account, no dagger was found on or near the body; Sandy's only weapon was a rusty sword, incapable of being drawn from its scabbard.[418] Meanwhile, the king's servants, not Gowrie's, had circulated the rumour that James was riding across the South Inch. Gowrie called for his horse, heard the king shouting from the window, and rushed up the Black Turnpike, with only Thomas Cranstoun accompanying him. The 'Vindication' claimed that Gowrie reached the top of the stairs calling out loyally to see if the king was alive, but was then attacked by the courtiers, John Ramsay striking him dead after the earl had dropped his two swords in surrender. The Kirk's historian Calderwood, who was violently hostile to James (partly, perhaps, because he had known Gowrie personally), reported the even more damaging whisper that Gowrie's death wound was really a stab in the back.[419]

The author of the 'Vindication' was quick to damn the witnesses who had provided the basis of the king's story. Christie, the porter, was said to have been in on the plot, and to have passed all the keys of Gowrie House to the courtiers. There is a plausible note here; by his own admission, Christie had worked for Gowrie for only five weeks, so presumably he would have had no strong personal loyalty to the earl. He ended up working for the new Murray owner of Scone palace. The author of the 'Vindication' also believed that Erskine, Ramsay, Herries and the rest would have given very different evidence if they had been able to talk 'straytlie'.[420] Finally, of course, there was the star witness himself: Andrew Henderson, the 'armoured man'. In the 'Vindication', and in much of the street gossip of the day, Henderson came forward and admitted to being the man in the turret chamber only after being promised a pardon. Having secured this, he then recited the story that the king wanted him to tell. According to the 'Vindication', an Andrew Henderson who was telling the truth would have admitted that he was serving dinner in the hall when Sandy Ruthven was killed. According to Calderwood, he was eating an egg.[421] According to both, he was a puppet, coached by Patrick Galloway and bribed by James to corroborate the king's story of what happened in the turret chamber, thereby proving that James and John Ramsay could not have committed murder. But if the king had devised an incredibly complex, minutely planned murder plot, why did he not have a far more credible professional perjurer trained up in advance, instead of leaving so much to weigh on the shoulders of the derided and pitiful Andrew Henderson?

****

James's critics have made much of the perceived shortcomings of the official narrative of what took place at Gowrie House. But compared to the 'Ruthven Vindication', the king's story is a masterpiece of consistency and coherence. The 'Vindication' entirely omits the inconvenient truth that the king had spent hours hunting before he rode for Perth; having ensnared Sandy Ruthven at breakfast time, why should James dawdle? The claim that Christie the porter had handed over the keys of Gowrie House was categorically denied by Christie's own evidence. The 'Vindication' has Gowrie going up the Black Turnpike supported only by Cranstoun; but Cranstoun's own evidence contradicted this, as did that of others on the Ruthven side, and crucially, Cranstoun was one of the very few witnesses to give evidence before the fully fledged royal narrative had emerged, along with any attendant pressure to conform to it. Meanwhile, the 'Vindication' put Sir Thomas Erskine in two places at once. According to this account, Erskine went up the stairs with Ramsay and helped to kill Sandy Ruthven. But ample eye-witness evidence, much of it from disinterested sources, confirmed that Erskine was in the street, and was grabbing hold of Gowrie's collar when the author of the 'Vindication' insisted that he was in the turret chamber. Erskine was known to be one of the king's closest friends, one of the most important members of the royal household and one of the small elite band that had been schooled with him. One of their other classmates had been Erskine's cousin Mar. Therefore, inventing an enhanced role for the Erskines in an 'assassination' of the Gowries was an indirect way of insinuating that James must have been responsible for their deaths, and had employed some of his oldest and most trustworthy friends to do the deed.

Equally inventive is the 'Vindication's' suggestion that James might have killed the Ruthven brothers because of their popularity in England. In truth, from the viewpoint of King James VI nothing, but nothing, could possibly have been more counter-productive. From the very beginning, the suspicion that he might have sanctioned the brothers' deaths seriously damaged the king's public image south of the border. The English were hardly likely to want a murderer as their next monarch, and James was undoubtedly shrewd enough to realise this. A cold-blooded murder of the Earl of Gowrie, who had been received so recently and favourably by Queen Elizabeth, was a sure way of jeopardising James's life-long ambition, the succession to the English throne. James later told Robert Bruce that he regretted the earl's death, and that he realised with hindsight it would have been possible to arrest Sandy Ruthven, rather than kill him. The king's enemies used these statements to try and paint him as an evil, dissembling hypocrite. Far from this, James's remarks smack of a consummate politician's common-sense realisation that actions committed in his name, in the heat of the moment, have caused him untold and deeply regrettable political damage.

The many known and undisputed facts of what happened on 5 August can only be made to concur with the 'conspiracy theory' of a royal murder plot by attributing to that plot's creator an almost psychic degree of foreknowledge and second-guessing. For James to go up alone to the turret chamber with the intention of killing both Ruthven brothers, Sandy must have done exactly what the king wanted him to do at every stage, including locking the doors behind them – with all the attendant risks for James if his scheme backfired. Alternatively, the doors could have been locked behind them by another; perhaps this had been the real purpose of John Ramsay's seemingly bizarre perambulation through the chambers of Gowrie House, complete with a bemused hawk on his hand. When the moment of crisis came, the king had to call out for help at exactly the right moment, and the courtiers had to be in exactly the right position under the turret.[422] John Ramsay had to time his dash to the turret chamber with the precision of an Olympic runner, and Olympic runners are not normally encumbered by hawks. Gowrie had be within earshot of the turret chamber at precisely the right moment. To accomplish this, he must have acted on the rumour (spread by the king's men, in this version) that James had left Perth by going at once to the stable and insisting on having his horse made ready, despite already having been told that the horse was in Scone. Gowrie then had to be released from the clutches of Erskine and the Murrays so that he could run up the Black Turnpike, rather than the main stair. Such a royal plot would have depended entirely on Gowrie coming immediately, without mobilising an overwhelming force of Ruthven manpower from the surrounding streets. Everything hinged on precise timing that would do credit to the most exact synchronisation of digital watches in an age that still relied on hourglasses and sundials. In other words, the theory of a royal plot could only have been devised by someone who studied the story of 5 August 1600 after the events took place, and read back into them a string of coincidences that would have disgraced a third-rate hack novelist.

If there really was a royal plot to eliminate the Ruthvens, the 'pot of gold' story must either have been a lie told to Lennox by the king, or a lie told by Lennox to the world. If the former, James must have invented it and attributed it to Sandy Ruthven to make it seem that the latter had invited him to Perth. But such a tale was bound to be regarded as incredible, and the remarkably intelligent King James, a man who could

IACOBVS · 6 · D · G · R ·
SCOTORVM ·
ÆTA · 29 ·
1595 ·

King James VI in 1595, aged twenty-nine, in a portrait attributed to Adrian Vanson. © *National Galleries of Scotland; licensor www.scran.ac.uk*

EARLE. OF. GOURIE

The arms of the Earls of Gowrie; from the Atholl monument at Dunkeld Cathedral. *Author's photograph*

A Victorian reconstruction of the scene in front of Gowrie House. The king calls from the window of the turret chamber; the Earl of Gowrie clashes with courtiers at the entrance to the courtyard; townspeople begin to gravitate toward the fray. In reality the west wall of the house was incorporated into the curtain wall, not set back from it. *Author's collection*

A nearly contemporary representation of the scene in the gallery chamber. John Ramsay stabs the Earl of Gowrie (armoured and carrying two swords) while treading on the corpse of Sandy Ruthven. James VI is at right; Andrew Henderson, the 'armoured man', at left, about to flee down the 'black turnpike'. The sparrowhawk previously carried by Ramsay flies free. *Author's collection*

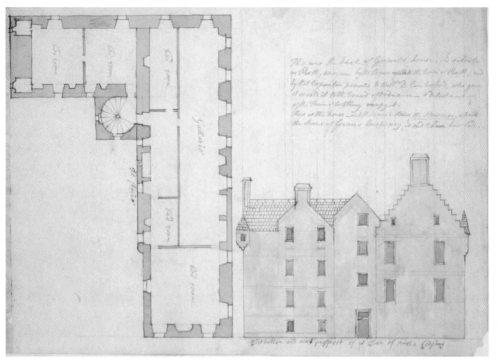

Plan of the second floor of Gowrie House, and its west elevation, drawn in c.1724-36. This clearly shows the long gallery installed by the first Earl of Gowrie in 1579 and the 'trance' alongside it, through which James VI and Sandy Ruthven would have passed to reach the gallery chamber (here called a 'bed room') at the west end of the building. © *National Library of Scotland; licensor www.scran.ac.uk*

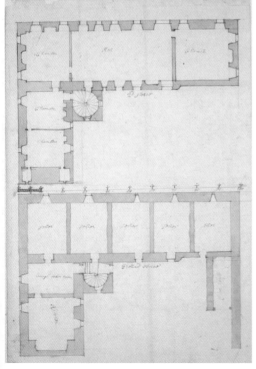

Plan of the first floor of Gowrie House, showing the ground (bottom) and first (top) floors of the building. The hall where most of the courtiers dined is clearly marked; the chamber where the king dined was to the left / east, as shown on Plan B. © *National Library of Scotland; licensor www.scran.ac.uk*

The east wing of Gowrie House, which contained the principal Ruthven apartments, and the main doorway into the building, through which James VI and the hunting party would have passed. The niche above the door would have been occupied by the Ruthven coat-of-arms and possibly by their motto, Deid Schaw (= 'Do Something'). Engraving published in 1789, originally drawn by General George Henry Hutton in 1783. *Author's collection*

The south side of Gowrie House, drawn by in 1783 and published as an engraving in 1823. This gives a sense of the first Earl of Gowrie's garden, at right, and suggests that the hall on the first floor had a large south-facing window, later largely closed up. © *National Library of Scotland; licensor www.scran.ac.uk*

Hutton's drawing of the north side of Gowrie House, 1783, showing evidence of its use as an artillery barracks (notably the sentry box and the ammunition boxes to the right of it). The 'black turnpike' rose from the site of the door at furthest right on the ground floor. © *National Library of Scotland; licensor www.scran.ac.uk*

Hutton's drawing of the south side of Gowrie House, 1783, showing the relationship of the house to the buildings on the other side of Speygate. © *National Library of Scotland; licensor www.scran.ac.uk*

An unusual view of Gowrie House from the north, showing its proximity to the River Tay and its shipping. This engraving was published in 1802, only four years before the demolition of the site commenced. *Author's collection*

Speygate today, looking north-east and showing the site of Gowrie House. The edge of the car park, and the far wall of the Victorian buildings beneath the steeple, represent the boundaries of the property. The chamber where the king struggled with Sandy Ruthven was approximately on the site of the 4x4 vehicle. *Author's photograph*

St John's Kirk, Perth. The burial place of the young second Earl of Gowrie and a number of other Ruthvens, it was also the scene of John Knox's sermon in 1559 that triggered the Scottish Reformation. *Author's photograph*

The curious augmented coat of arms of the Ruthven family, with the armoured figure apparently praying towards the crown and uttering the words 'tibi soli', 'for thee alone'. This record of the arms, from the Forman-Workman armorial at the Lyon Court in Edinburgh, was defaced following the attainder of the Ruthvens in 1600. © *Court of the Lord Lyon*

Huntingtower Castle. Originally named Ruthven Castle, or the Place of Ruthven, this was the family's chief property and the scene of the 'Raid of Ruthven', 1582. In the seventeenth century it consisted of two separate tower houses, roughly nine feet apart; it has been suggested that this arrangement reflected the complex status of two sons of the first Lord Ruthven, legitimated in 1480, or else that the second tower was intended as a dower property. The gap between the two towers was filled during the eighteenth century. *Author's photograph*

General George Henry Hutton's drawing of Scone Palace, 1775. This shows the building that was substantially built for the first Earl of Gowrie, c.1579-80, and subsequently altered by David Murray, first Lord Scone. The nineteenth–century palace on the site incorporates much of this building. © *National Library of Scotland; licensor www. scran.ac.uk*

The 'Ruthven lodging' at Dirleton Castle, East Lothian. Dirleton came to the Ruthvens by marriage in 1515 and was the favourite seat of Dorothea, Countess of Gowrie. The lodging, built from c.1579 onwards, had two floors of private chambers, all supplied with relatively new luxuries such as leaded glass in the windows, green glazed tiles on the floors and proper dry-stool closets instead of garderobes. *Author's photograph*

The last surviving fragment of Trochrie Castle, Perthshire, where the Ruthven brothers spent much of July 1600. The castle had been granted to the first Lord Ruthven in 1500; following the 'Gowrie conspiracy', it passed to the Stewarts of Grandtully. *Author's photograph*

Falkland Palace. Built between 1501 and 1541 on the site of an earlier royal castle, the palace stood at the south-east corner of a large deer park. It was here, at about 7 a.m. on 5 August 1600, that the Master of Ruthven approached King James VI with his story of a 'pot of gold' at Gowrie House. *Author's photograph*

Ludovic, second Duke of Lennox (1574-1624). The eldest son of Esmé Stuart, first Duke of Lennox (1542-83), the first great favourite of King James VI, Ludovic was brought up in France until his father's death, when James brought him to Scotland. He was briefly married to Lilias Ruthven, sister of the Earl of Gowrie and Master of Ruthven.
© *Trustees of the British Museum*

John Erskine, second Earl of Mar (c.1558-1634), was schooled with King James VI, who nicknamed him 'Jock o'the Slates'. He was the godfather of John, Earl of Gowrie, who was thus named after him. In 1600 he was effectively the king's principal minister and also served as guardian to the heir, Prince Henry, much to the fury of Queen Anna. © *Earl of Mar and Kellie; licensor www.scran.ac.uk*

Sir William Allan, The Murder of Rizzio (c. 1833). This famous painting shows the distraught Mary, Queen of Scots, being restrained as Rizzio is stabbed to death before her eyes. The terminally ill Patrick, third Lord Ruthven, is the man in armour brandishing a dagger in his left hand, directly behind the Italian. © *National Galleries of Scotland; licensor www.scran.ac.uk*

Fast Castle, on the Berwickshire coast. The fortress of Robert Logan of Restalrig, and possibly intended as the place of captivity for James VI following a successful coup on 5 August 1600. (*Author's photograph*)

Peregrine, thirteenth Lord Willoughby de Eresby: memorial at Spilsby church, Lincolnshire. Willoughby was a friend of the third Earl of Gowrie and governor of Berwick at the time of the 'conspiracy'. (*Author's photograph*)

Vox Dei, title page of a book published in 1623 in praise of James VI and I. At the bottom right, John Ramsay, with sword raised, tramples 'Treason' (i.e. the Earl of Gowrie) underfoot. The explanatory frontispiece begins with the couplet 'Truth-telling Ramsy, Treason doth withstand / And for the Kinges life liftes his happie hand'. This was one of many allegorical representations of the 'Gowrie House affair': reference to it can also be seen in the Rubens ceiling of the Banqueting House, Whitehall. (© *Trustees of the British Museum*)

Anna of Denmark, Queen of Scots: an engraving made in 1595, when the queen was twenty-one. Her first child Henry, then Duke of Rothesay and later Prince of Wales, had been born in the previous year. (© *Trustees of the British Museum*)

Sir Roger Aston, the English expatriate who was at once a trusted servant of James VI and an English agent, shown on his funerary monument at Cranford church, Middlesex. *Author's photograph*

Sir George Home, later first Earl of Dunbar (d. 1611). In 1600 a member of the 'Chamber faction' opposed to the Earl of Mar, Home later became James's de facto viceroy of Scotland and took charge of the George Sprot case in 1608. *National Galleries of Scotland*

Mary Ruthven (1623-44), daughter of Patrick Ruthven, last surviving brother of the third Earl of Gowrie. She married Sir Anthony Van Dyck, and the descendants of their daughter, Justina, became the senior representatives of the Ruthven bloodline. © *Trustees of the British Museum*)

Robert Cecil (1563-1612), chief minister during the last years of Elizabeth I's reign and the first nine years of James VI and I's English reign, although Cecil did not initially favour James's claim to the English throne. He was alleged to be the lover of Barbara Ruthven, sister of the last Earl of Gowrie.
© *Trustees of the British Museum*

The assassination of Henri IV of France by Francois Ravaillac, together with scenes from Ravaillac's punishment and execution, as illustrated in a near contemporary print of c.1610. (© *Trustees of the British Museum*)

The old Tolbooth, Edinburgh. Built in the 14th century and demolished in 1817, the building was the venue for the parliament of November 1600 that condemned the Ruthvens as traitors. The heads of John, Earl of Gowrie, and Alexander, Master of Ruthven, were subsequently affixed to iron pins on the roof of the building. (*Engraving by J Storer, 1818; Author's collection*)

defeat English bishops and Kirk moderators alike in theological debate, would surely have been able to concoct a better excuse for paying a visit to Gowrie House – especially as the outcome of that visit wrecked the king's plans, already made public, for an important conference at Linlithgow on 11 August to resolve pressing security issues in the Borders.[423] If the Duke of Lennox was lying, he was in good company, for virtually all of the other witnesses must have been lying too. To be successful, perjury must be consistent and precisely detailed. But the witnesses had an alarming habit of contradicting each other, admitting ignorance of events or actions when pretending to knowledge would have helped the king's case, or simply providing evidence that unhelpfully contradicted the king's story. If the king's men succeeded as assassins, they failed miserably as perjurers; and the greatest failure must have been that of James VI himself. Those who want to find King James guilty of the murder of the Ruthvens at Gowrie House have to prove that he lied about what happened, consistently and systematically, from the evening of 5 August 1600 until his dying day. He certainly told some lies about the events at Gowrie House; for instance, he told his brother-in-law, King Christian of Denmark, that the Ruthvens had been killed by unarmed men.[424] Perhaps this was just the start of an entire quarter century of systematic lying. But if that was so, James did not lie merely to the whole world: he also lied to his own son. *Basilicon Doron* was a book that the king had begun to write in 1598. It contained his thoughts on government, religion, and much else besides, and was intended as a training manual in kingship for his son and heir Prince Henry, then aged four. It was never intended for publication, and at first only seven copies were produced. James regularly scribbled additional notes and comments, and sometime after 5 August 1600 he returned to his statement that 'virtue or vice will oftentimes, with the heritage, be transferred from the parents to the posterity'. To this, James added 'witness the experience of the late house of Gowrie'.[425] If the king really had killed the Ruthvens, he lied about it in a private document that its intended recipient, his own young son, would not be able to read for years to come.

****

Ultimately, the greatest weakness in the argument of the Ruthvens' apologists was pointed out by James himself at the end of his statement to Robert Bruce: 'If I would have taken their lives, I had causes enough: *I needed not to hazard myself so*'. Even if one accepts a sinister explanation for the presence of the Murrays in Perth, the king would still have been taking a quite astonishing risk to ride into the Ruthvens' own house, in their own town, in order merely to kill two young men. The French ambassador in London recognised this simple truth immediately, even though, as he reported, it was not what people wanted to believe.[426] As it was, James came within a hair's breadth of losing his life when, firstly, he wrestled with Sandy Ruthven; secondly, when the Earl of Gowrie and his men stormed the gallery chamber; and thirdly, when the Perth mob besieged Gowrie House. Perhaps no other monarch in British history has been as careful of his personal safety as King James VI and I, so if he really did go to Perth intending personally to oversee murder, he was behaving in a spectacularly and uniquely uncharacteristic way. It was a perverse way, too, for if James wanted to bring down the House of Ruthven, why did he seemingly target the wrong brother – the heir, Sandy, and not the head, the earl? If the king simply wanted Gowrie dead, an ambush or hunting 'accident' – the very fate that Gowrie allegedly feared – would have been neater and quieter; and if the earl refused to come to Falkland, no doubt something could have been arranged in his own hunting grounds of Strathbraan. Alternatively, a conveniently deniable death at the hands of some amenable nobleman at feud with the Ruthvens would have echoed the Bonnie Earl o' Moray's death at Huntly's hands eight years before. Even on 5 August, Gowrie could easily have been killed in his own garden by one or more of the hunting party, the deed hidden from public view by the surrounding wall and the fruit trees that Gowrie's father had planted.[427] But none of these solutions would have made Gowrie a traitor. It is this, and this alone, that gives the 'Ruthven Vindication' what little inner logic it has. If the primary object of James and those around him was not just to kill Gowrie, but to ensure that his estates could be forfeited for treason, then somehow they had to manufacture a situation in which Gowrie attacked the king in person, with all the risks attending such a strategy. The decisive evidence that they did not do this is provided by James's treatment of the remaining Ruthven brothers, William and Patrick.

If the king wanted to destroy the entire House of Ruthven, not just the head and the immediate heir, he would surely have ensured that the two youngest boys – the next heirs, the potential future earls – were secured at exactly the same time that he acted against the two eldest. As it was, no serious attempt was made to arrest William and

Patrick Ruthven until well into the next day, the sixth, miserably. Failing to secure the younger boys caused im. for James in the months and years that followed. It force the exiled heir, William, in absentia, in order for the forfe. Ruthven estates to take place. It soured his relations with where the boys were favourably received. The survival of m... ...irs of the House of Ruthven also raised a terrible prospect for the future. If the younger brothers believed that the king had killed their siblings, they might at any time revive the Ruthven bloodfeud against the Stuarts – the very reason that Sandy Ruthven had given for wanting to kill James, according to the official version of events. Far from doing so, the last brother, Patrick, was quite content to accept a pension from the king, who was equally content not to find a pretext for executing a dangerous potential regicide. Even when he was set free from the Tower, Patrick Ruthven did not hunt down the murderer of his brothers and avenge them with James's blood: instead, he pottered contentedly among his potions and chemicals. There is only one plausible explanation for all of this. James did not simultaneously arrest the younger Ruthvens simply because he had never planned in advance to kill their elder brothers. Patrick and the rest of the Ruthvens did not seek to avenge themselves on James because once the heat of the moment had passed and passions had cooled, they all knew perfectly well that the king had not been responsible for the deaths of John and Sandy.

****

The persistence of the notion that King James Stuart could have been responsible for the deaths of the Ruthvens owes more to 19th-century prejudices than it does to 16th-century facts. Most educated Victorians saw their own past from the perspective of 'the whig interpretation of history': the notion that British history had been an inevitable progression towards constitutional monarchy, parliamentary democracy, economic progress and enlightened imperialism (in other words, Victorian Britain, at least in their own eyes). Those who seemed to stand against this inevitable process were damned as blinkered reactionaries at best, irredeemably evil bigots at worst. Deluded by their entirely irrational belief in the 'divine right of kings', the monarchs of the royal House of Stuart occupied a prominent place in this pantheon. The unreasonable refusal of Kings James I and Charles I to yield power to an enlightened Parliament, the driving force of the future, was condemned vehemently

.y the great Whig historians, as were the personal habits of the Stuart kings. Relying too much on the near-contemporary jibes of embittered English courtiers with grudges, the historians presented a colourful and abiding picture of King James as an incoherent Scottish buffoon who dribbled, fiddled embarrassingly with his codpiece, slobbered over pretty young men and treated his enemies with cynical brutality. From this mindset, it was all too easy for many to convince themselves that what happened on 5 August 1600 must have been a vicious, premeditated royal plot to butcher two innocent and heroic young men. To Victorian minds, many with classical or legal training, at once forensic and ordered, the haphazard way in which the evidence had been assembled and the royal story presented to the world, with all its internal inconsistencies and contradictions, screamed of perjury and deliberate falsification.[428]

Even with the 'Whig interpretation' firmly dead and buried, recent history has if anything reinforced deep-seated scepticism about the words and deeds of governments. Suspecting rulers and politicians of spin, lies, conspiracies and cover-ups seems somehow more natural than accepting that, with obvious exceptions, they generally tell the truth and do a reasonably competent job. The same gap between perception and reality applies to King James VI and I. Modern historians have long seen him as a highly intelligent, tolerant, lenient monarch, determined to reconcile opposing factions in church, state, and Europe as a whole; not exactly the obvious personality traits one would expect from a man who committed murder at Gowrie House on 5 August 1600.[429] But among the rapidly dwindling percentage of the general population who know anything at all about him, perceptions of King James remain rooted in the school of dribbling, fiddling, slobbering and that lazy old soundbite, 'the wisest fool in Christendom'. The only recent major portrayals of James on British television departed from this norm – only to replace it with a vision of the king as a devious bisexual psychopath.[430] This King James could certainly have been the villain of the piece at Gowrie House on 5 August 1600. But the real King James could not have been, and was not.

CHAPTER SEVEN

WOLF'S CRAG

George Sprot was a nobody. He scraped a living as a notary in Eyemouth, an isolated Berwickshire port where fishing and smuggling vied to be the main employer. He was the legal factotum for Robert Logan of Restalrig, drunkard, bandit, pirate, inveterate plotter, and one of the inner circle of conspirators around both the Earl of Bothwell and another devious arch-schemer, Patrick, Master of Gray, who was his first cousin. In 1586 Logan went to England in the entourage of Gray, James's somewhat unlikely choice as an ambassador to plead for the life of his mother, Mary, Queen of Scots. Logan took the opportunity to approach Queen Elizabeth's spymaster, Sir Francis Walsingham, suggesting that he sell all Gray's secrets to the English government.[431] No wonder he was once described as 'a vain, loose man [and] a great favourer of thieves'; even so, on balance the same writer thought him 'a good fellow'.[432] Logan owned Fast Castle, perched fantastically on the Berwickshire cliffs near Eyemouth, which he used as a safe-house for some of Scotland's most wanted. Logan allegedly sheltered Bothwell there while King James's authorities hunted high and low for the satanic earl, and in 1598 Logan hosted his wife's kinsman, George Ker, one of the chief emissaries between Scottish Catholics and the pope. Even today, the few remaining sea-girt stones of Fast Castle are well worth the steep and breathless cliff walk from the heights above. Dizzying, precarious and seemingly impregnable, Fast was an ideal base for Logan's nefarious activities, and in due course Sir Walter Scott immortalised it as 'Wolf's Crag' in *The Bride of Lammermuir*.

Fast Castle was just the sort of place to inspire tales of treasure and black magic. In July 1594 Logan entered into a contract with John Napier of Merchiston, later the inventor of logarithms, who was to employ magic to unearth an unnamed and mysterious treasure buried somewhere in the sea-caves under Fast. Napier was to get a third of the haul, but he insisted on writing into the contract a clause guaranteeing him free passage out of Fast after the treasure was found. Nothing came of Napier's treasure hunt, apart from a falling out between the two contractors; Napier subsequently forbade the letting of any of his property to anyone named Logan.[433] In the early 1600s, Robert Logan abruptly sold off Fast and all his other property. Having thus turned all his worldly wealth into liquid assets, the seventh Laird of Restalrig promptly caught a fever and died at Edinburgh in July 1606, aged 51. George Sprot's main source of income died with him, and the notary took to forgery, producing documents to order for those willing to pay. He also took to the bottle, propping up the bars of Eyemouth and rambling drunkenly about the important men and important secrets that he had got to know through his dead employer.

In April 1608, Sprot finally went too far. One night, when in his cups, he blurted out that Logan of Restalrig had been directly involved in the Gowrie conspiracy, that Logan had written letters to and received them from both the Earl of Gowrie and Sandy Ruthven, and that he, Sprot, had copies of some of the incriminating documents.[434] Sprot was promptly arrested and turned over to the authorities in Edinburgh. Logan's alleged letters were found in Sprot's pockets, and under interrogation before the Privy Council, the notary abandoned his original story and testified that he had forged the letters. There the matter rested, with the notary languishing in prison, until in June a new urgency was injected into the case. In 1600 Sir George Home was a bit-part player in the Gowrie House affair, one of the royal councillors who attempted to manage the king's version of events. By 1608 he was a far grander figure: the Earl of Dunbar, Lord Treasurer of Scotland and Privy Councillor of England – the man on whom King James relied to get things done in his homeland. Dunbar had come north to manage the latest in a series of conferences at which royal control of the Kirk would be extended still further. By coincidence, Dunbar brought with him a disinterested English observer with quite impeccable credentials. George Abbot, Dean of Winchester and Master of University College, Oxford, accompanied Dunbar to Scotland to advise on his attempts to implement James's plans for the Church. Within three years, and thanks in part to Dunbar's posthumous recommendation, Abbot would be Archbishop of Canterbury.

With Abbot at his side, Dunbar now took charge of the Sprot case. His first act was to release the notary from strict confinement, and to treat the severe leg wounds that he had suffered during torture.

Dunbar's kindness had an astonishing effect on Sprot's testimony, which suddenly changed, diametrically and mysteriously, into essentially a combination of his two previous stories. On 5 July 1608 the notary testified that although he had forged all the letters to blackmail Logan's son, Logan senior did indeed know of the Gowrie conspiracy in advance. Sprot now claimed that he had seen one original letter of Logan's to Gowrie, which he had been shown by Logan's vicious old right-hand man, Laird Bower. (At that time, recipients returned particularly important or incriminating correspondence directly to the sender, and Bower was allegedly the go-between for Logan and the Ruthvens.) According to one of the 'Sprot/Logan' letters, Logan trusted Bower with all his darkest secrets, and in return, Bower 'would not spare to ride to Hell's Gate to pleasure me'.[435] The notary was re-examined on a number of occasions and stuck to the new version of the story, though not without introducing a number of new contradictions and circumstantial details.[436] On 15 July, Sprot stated that he wrote the letters during harvest time in 1606, which would have been only a matter of weeks after Logan's death. In the statement that he made on the following day, 16 July, the Eyemouth notary recalled the bitter winter of 1602. Logan had been about to leave Fast Castle, which he had recently sold, when he got Bower to bring him all his correspondence with the Ruthven brothers, and threw it on the fire. A few weeks later, Logan and his entourage gathered at another of his properties, the house of Gunsgreen overlooking Eyemouth harbour, to celebrate Yule. This turned out to be a fraught festive season, with Logan's wife acting in a peevish and nervous manner, blaming all and sundry for her husband's inexplicable actions in selling off all his lands. Sprot claimed that at some point during this Yule holiday, Logan let on that he knew that Bower had shown Sprot the original Ruthven letters, and got the forger to swear that he would never reveal anything of Logan's involvement with Gowrie.[437]

On 9 August 1608 Sprot was told that his death was imminent, and that he would see the lords of the Privy Council no more. But the doomed notary had one more surprise to spring. The next day, a Wednesday, Dunbar and the rest of them unexpectedly faced George Sprot once again. Belatedly, and suspiciously, the prisoner claimed to have just remembered the existence of *another letter*, the most important of them all. He claimed to have left this behind in his chest when he was arrested, and he now proceeded to recite large tracts of it from memory, albeit imperfectly. The authorities made a hasty search of Sprot's house and found two letters which were brought back to Edinburgh either on the evening before Sprot died, or on the very day that he was executed.[438] One was the document that became known as 'Letter I' (of five); the other, much longer, letter was the one that Sprot had been reciting from memory. This was the letter that became known as 'Letter IV', supposedly from Logan to Gowrie, and both taken and returned by Bower. Sprot claimed that Logan began writing this letter at Fast Castle in July 1600, though it was eventually finished at Gunsgreen, whence it was addressed. Sprot supposedly noticed the letter lying on Logan's table after the old reprobate left the room. He read it, then put it back. Later, Logan ordered Laird Bower to bring him the original of 'Letter IV' so that he could burn it. Bower, who could not read, asked Sprot to help him find it, only to be told that it was not to be found. In fact, Sprot had found the letter and kept it. According to this version of events, then, when George Sprot sat down in the summer of 1606 to forge letters implicating Robert Logan in the 'Gowrie Conspiracy', he was basing them on a genuine original – the model for 'Letter IV'. One of the very last acts of George Sprot's pathetic life was to scribble an endorsement on the backs of the two letters: 'this is copied of the principal *[= the original]*, likewise the note written upon the back is written by me, George Sprot'. A few hours later, the Eyemouth notary was hanging from a rope.[439] When his body was taken down, it was quartered and the head set up next to that of John Ruthven, Earl of Gowrie.[440]

****

The Sprot case provides a suitably baffling sequel to the labyrinthine complexities of the 'Gowrie House affair'. Firstly, George Sprot's behaviour throughout seems utterly incredible. In effect, he changed his testimony from one that gave him a chance of escaping with his life to one that guaranteed his execution on the scaffold. In no fewer than nine depositions made from 5 July onwards, Sprot consistently adhered to a story that made him (as well as the dead Logan) guilty of treasonable foreknowledge and concealment of the 'Gowrie Conspiracy'. Modern mindsets fail entirely to explain why the notary should seemingly have chosen, quite deliberately, to act out this very public death wish. Cynical contemporaries, looking for any evidence with which to damn King James, suggested that Sprot was promised that his family would benefit if he continued to toe a particular party line up to the moment of his death.[441] Perhaps Sprot had been set up as a classic 'patsy', the means by which James could finally eliminate the lingering doubts about his version of the events at Gowrie House. His unexpected appearance was certainly highly convenient for the king. As one English courtier put it, 'the king is somewhat pleased with a late accident [= *the arrest of Sprot*] ... touching Gowrie's conspiracy that makes it hang more handsomely together'.[442]

Ultimately, perhaps the only even vaguely satisfactory explanation is the one that Sprot himself gave, however uncomfortable secular mentalities might find it: he knew he had sinned mightily against his God, and the only way of expiating that sin was for him to die on the scaffold.[443] His speech to the Edinburgh mob that had come to see him die was entirely consistent with his behaviour in prison over the previous weeks: 'if he had a thousand lives to render, and were able to suffer ten thousand deaths, it is not sufficient satisfaction and recompense for his so foul and horrible offence'. Sprot asked for his words to be recounted by ministers from every pulpit in Scotland, to warn their congregations of the dangers of consorting with irreligious men like Logan and Bower. He then started to sing the sixth psalm 'loud and tunably', and exhorted the audience of 500 to join in. At the end, he reaffirmed the truth of his confessions one last time. According to George Abbot, who was there, Sprot was then pushed from the ladder, but as the rope throttled the life out of him, he clapped his hands several times – a traditional way of reaffirming that his last words from the scaffold were the truth, and not something extorted from him for public consumption.[444]

Ultimately, though, Sprot's motives for dying, and even for forging the letters, are relatively unimportant: the 'how' of the letters' creation is far more important than the 'why', for if even only a tiny part of one or more of them is original – or based on an otherwise lost original – then the letters provide the best evidence of all that there truly was a 'Gowrie Conspiracy' in 1600. However, the evidence seems to stack up overwhelmingly against such a conclusion. Having seemingly elected to die, Sprot concealed the most vital piece of evidence of all, the existence of 'Letter IV', until the last moment, producing it like a rabbit from a hat when he was under the very shadow of the noose. The fact that 'Letter IV' supposedly lay undisturbed in Sprot's chest in Eyemouth for about four months, and was overlooked in the searches that turned up the other 'Logan letters', almost beggars belief. The internal contradictions in Sprot's evidence are also highly suspicious, to say the least: for example, he placed Logan in both Dundee and Edinburgh on

5 August 1600, and also assumed that the illiterate Laird Bower who could not recognise 'Letter IV' in 1602 would have been able to show him the correct letter two years earlier.[445]

During his examination on 10 August, after making his explosive revelation about the existence of 'Letter IV', Sprot expanded on the context in which the letter was allegedly written. He claimed that he had overheard a conversation between Logan and Laird Bower, during which Bower criticised Logan's intention to sell off his lands. Logan replied that 'he should spend all that he had in the world, and hazard his life with his Lordship [Gowrie]'. When Sprot asked Bower what it was all about, Bower replied 'that he believed that the Laird should get Dirleton, without either gold or silver ... they had another pie in hand, [rather than] the selling of any land'.[446] Bower gloomily warned Sprot not to interfere in Logan's business, because within a few days 'the Laird would either be landless or lifeless'. The idea that Logan was to get Dirleton Castle in return for helping Gowrie found its way into Sprot's 'Letter II', where 'Logan' wrote to 'Bower' that 'I care not for all the land I have in this kingdom, in case I get a grip of Dirleton, for I esteem it the pleasantest dwelling in Scotland'.[447] The Earl of Gowrie handing Logan of Restalrig his parents' favourite home, his own mother's dower property, is only marginally less incredible than Logan mentioning it in a letter to the illiterate Bower, who would have had to get someone to read it out to him. On the other hand the dowager Countess was nearly 60, a good age for the time, and it would have been entirely feasible for Gowrie to promise Logan the reversion of the estate. In fact, this is essentially what actually happened to Dirleton after the Ruthven lands were forfeited: the countess lived there until her death, when the castle passed to Sir Thomas Erskine. Moreover, in 1599 there had actually been some discussion of a possible exchange of properties, including Dirleton, involving Alexander, Lord Home, whose connections to the Ruthvens ran deep. Home was at once Logan of Restalrig's half-brother and Sandy Ruthven's godfather; he had succeeded to his title at the age of 12, and during his minority, his guardian was Sandy's father, the first Earl of Gowrie.[448] Indeed, he had almost become John and Sandy's brother-in-law, too: in 1582 he was offered a choice between Dorothea and Lilias Ruthven, 'virgins undefamed and of lawful age to marry', but the proposed marriage fell through.[449]

Sprot's letters became the chief exhibits for the prosecution in the posthumous treason trial of Robert Logan, which proceeded in Edinburgh in June 1609. The accused was in an even worse state than the dead Ruthven brothers had been at their trial back in 1600, for what was left of Robert Logan literally had to be dug up from a three-year-old grave so that he could appear before his judges. The whole affair was a breathtaking piece of self-interested illegality on the part of the Earl of Dunbar, who stood to benefit directly if Logan's son and heir lost his inheritance. Dunbar had bought much of Robert Logan's property while the Laird of Restalrig was still alive, but never paid the family fully for it; forfeiting the estate on the grounds of Logan's alleged treason conveniently cancelled Dunbar's debt to his son. Inevitably, cynics found it easy to conclude that Dunbar had arranged the entire matter to benefit himself. Despite the fact that Sprot had confessed to forging four of the letters, a string of witnesses came forward in 1609 to testify that they were definitely in Logan's hand, and the court accepted this evidence.[450] The five 'Logan letters' had never been produced as evidence at Sprot's own trial: the notary was condemned solely by his own confession, and the indictment against him was based on mangled abstracts of his verbal recollection of two of the forged letters, not on the text of the letters themselves. The letters were kept back, presumably to serve Dunbar's private purposes at the eventual trial of the dead Logan.[451]

Sprot's very helpful change of story in July 1608, to implicate Logan again rather than just himself alone, also furthered Dunbar's cause. But if that was so, why had Sprot originally testified to Logan's involvement in the 'Gowrie Conspiracy', and then changed his testimony, following torture, to incriminate himself? Logic would suggest that the two stories are the wrong way round: many criminals on the road to a full confession admit to a lesser charge first, only revealing their more guilty secrets after lengthy interrogation. This raises the suspicion that Sprot's original testimony was close to the truth – and for some in Scotland's government, far too close to that truth. On 6 August Sprot withdrew one of the depositions that he had made before the start of July, in which he accused Sir Harry Lindsay, Laird of Kinfauns, and Sir James Scrymgeour, Provost and Constable of Dundee, of complicity in the 'Gowrie Conspiracy' (Lindsay was meant to have been the mysterious, un-named third recipient of Logan letters).[452] Torture persuaded Sprot to retract this highly inconvenient notion that the Earl of Gowrie had powerful accomplices who had never been traced, but when Dunbar returned to Scotland, it suited his own purposes for Sprot to revert to something more like his original story – as long as that story named no embarrassing names, and regardless of the fact that by testifying to both his and Logan's foreknowledge of a 'Gowrie Conspiracy', George Sprot effectively signed his own death warrant. It might also be significant that none of the papers containing Sprot's statements between April and 5 July have survived. Voluminous paperwork relating to the case from 5 July onwards exists in the archives of the then Lord Advocate, Thomas Hamilton; but he should also have been in charge of the case before that date.[453] Perhaps he and Dunbar took the executive decision to consign all of Sprot's more inconvenient testimony to the flames.

Finally, there is the '64,000 dollar question' of the Sprot affair: is 'Letter IV' genuine, in any shape or form? In 1902, an extensive and detailed expert analysis of Sprot's and Logan's handwriting concluded that *all* of the letters produced at Logan's trial were forgeries by Sprot, and no subsequent analysis has diverged from that verdict.[454] Therefore, 'Letter IV' is just as much of a fake as the other four, which are clearly modelled upon it. But the fact that Sprot wrote the 'Letter IV' that existed in 1608–9 does not preclude the possibility that in 1606 he had copied it from an original, subsequently destroyed, or that he could have written it down from his recollection of an original that he had seen in July 1600, or December 1602, or both. If the latter, it could explain some of the more unconvincing elements of 'Letter IV'. Logan's emphasis on security, and his insistence that the letter would be burned after Bower returned it to him, is contradicted by the fact that according to Sprot, the letter plainly continued to exist. In the letter itself, 'Logan' warns 'Gowrie' that if the plot misfired, they could expect 'the utter wrecking of our lands and houses, and extirpating of our names'.[455] This smacks of hindsight, for it describes the exact fate which befell the House of Ruthven in 1600. The same could be said of 'Logan's' hope that 'the king's buck-hunting at Falkland, this year, shall prepare some dainty cheer for us', and 'his' suggestion that 'Gowrie' should ensure that 'his old pedagogue' William Rynd knew nothing of their dealings.[456] This conveniently matched Rynd's testimony in 1600, which was public knowledge and which claimed that Gowrie had deliberately kept Rynd ignorant of his plans. Such comments are probably all embellishments by Sprot, perhaps to make the letter's content clearer to those who would read it. Indeed, Sprot admitted quite openly that this was what he did. When he first confessed to forging the letters, Sprot stated explicitly that he had set out 'to make the matter more clear by the arguments and circumstances' in comparison with the original letter that Laird Bower had let him see.[457] In other words, Sprot never claimed that he had made a verbatim copy of 'Letter IV': he had deliberately modified the wording 'to make the matter more clear'.

****

Several passages in 'Letter IV' smack of the truth. The first gives one motive for taking action against King James: '[by] God's grace, we shall bring our matter to a finish, which shall bring contentment to us all that ever wished for the revenge of the Machiavellian massacring of our dearest friends.' There is an echo of this in the undoubted forgery, 'Letter V', where 'Logan' talks of their scheme bringing 'revenge of Grey Steil's death'.[458] 'Grey Steil' was the nickname of the first Earl of Gowrie; Logan of Restalrig had been one of his fellow 'Ruthven Raiders', and had briefly lost Fast Castle when the earl's government fell. Of course, revenge for the first earl's execution was put forward by King James himself as the Ruthven brothers' motive, and this line was taken in all the published accounts of what had happened at Gowrie House; so this, too, could have been an interpolation by Sprot. On the other hand, the insertion of the word 'Machiavellian' in 'Letter IV' is completely unnecessary, and entirely unexpected from a provincial notary whose education was presumably fairly rudimentary. It was also spectacularly mis-spelled ('Maschevalent'), suggesting that it could have been an unusual word which Sprot recalled from the original but simply did not understand.[459] Even if Robert Logan had not travelled in Europe, he certainly had many contacts with the Continent, not all of them necessarily legal. He also knew that the Earl of Gowrie had been in Padua, and Gowrie certainly came into contact with the works of Machiavelli there.

When it comes to revealing how the 'Gowrie Conspiracy' would be carried out, 'Letter IV' is vague. It refers only to Logan telling Sandy Ruthven his plan 'to bring all your lordship's associates to my house of Fast Castle be sea … making as it were but a manner of passing time, in a boat on the sea, in this fair summer tide'. Gowrie and Logan would meet beforehand to finalise the details. Sprot here provides another detail that seems too elaborate and irrelevant for a forger to include: the meeting of Logan and Gowrie would be accompanied by a pleasant repast of 'hattit kit' (syllabub), sugar, 'comfeitis' (sweetmeats) and wine. 'Letter I', to an anonymous recipient, similarly has 'Logan' suggesting 'that we meet all at my house of Fast Castle, for I have concluded with Master Alexander Ruthven how I think it shall be meetest to be conveyed quietly in a boat, by sea'. There is more detail in 'Letter V', also to the unnamed recipient, who is to be one of four men coming to Fast in 'one of the great fishing boats, by sea to my house, where you shall land as safely as on Leith shore'.[460] The castle would be quiet, but they were to signal once they were within half a mile, and they would be brought safely ashore. On one reading, none of this necessarily means that the kidnapped king was to be taken to Fast Castle by sea: the passages could simply refer to a meeting of the conspirators that was to take place after the plot succeeded. But 'Logan' would hardly have been likely to specify that he was referring to the king, and a reasonably competent forger like Sprot could be expected to avoid making such an elementary blunder. Of course, it is equally possible to read the letters from precisely the opposite direction. Surely the information that Sprot included was far too incriminating for Logan or Gowrie to commit to paper, particularly when they had already met to finalise the issues mentioned in the letters, *and when the letters themselves contain injunctions to burn them?*

Perhaps the key passage in 'Letter IV' that rings true is when 'Logan' describes how he had given shelter to the Earl of Bothwell, and how he hopes that both Gowrie and Bothwell will be present with him at a dinner on 5 August 1601 to celebrate the first anniversary of their success.[461] Implicitly, then, 'Logan' hints here at a second motive for the 'Gowrie Conspiracy': the restoration of Francis Stewart, Earl of Bothwell, to his rank and dignity in Scotland. In the days immediately after the slaughter at Gowrie House, James and the Scottish government believed that some greater, unseen power lay behind the actions of the two young Ruthven brothers. On 15 August, they were enquiring into 'from what fountain this matter has sprung; it is to be thought those two young men would never have enterprised so great a treason as to lead a king to the shambles [= slaughter] like a lamb'.[462] Two weeks later, Patrick Galloway in his Glasgow sermon dealt with the widespread suspicion that the Ruthvens could not have acted alone, and concluded 'I doubt not but he had a backe[r]: the Lord discover it … '.[463] Who better than the Earl of Bothwell?

The king's disgraced cousin would have had very obvious motives for initiating, or participating in, a plot by the Ruthvens and their friends like Robert Logan. By 1600, the once mighty Francis Stewart was a desperate man. The earl was drawn increasingly to magic and necromancy, perhaps evidence of an increasingly frantic search for any means that might restore his fortune.[464] It would have been very clear to him that he would never return to Scotland while James continued with his present policies and advisors, for the king's personal animosity towards him was abundantly clear and just as abundantly immutable. Bothwell might have picked up news that those who had taken over his lands wanted to strengthen their legal title to the estates.[465] Bothwell's only hopes of preserving his inheritance and returning to Scotland, albeit slim and desperate hopes, were for the king either to promise him a pardon or for the king to be overthrown. Thus the 'promise' that Sandy Ruthven sought to extract from James might have been a guarantee of Bothwell's pardon; this, after all, had been Bothwell's own objective in every attempt he made to seize the king during the 1590s.[466] But if that strategy failed, the removal of King James – perhaps temporarily, perhaps permanently – might bring in a the new regime that would allow him to return. This scenario became far more plausible if he was one of the key players in that new regime, the instigator of a *coup d'état* that seized the person of the king, ousted his existing ministers and dramatically changed the direction of Scottish state policy.

But if the Earl of Bothwell was either behind Gowrie's plot, or had foreknowledge of it and expected to benefit from its successful outcome, he did not act as he might have been expected to. Rather than getting as near to Scotland as possible, he left the Netherlands and proceeded via Paris to Spain, ending up there by July 1600. He promptly fell ill, and would have been in no position to return to Scotland as a restored favourite if James lived after 5 August, or perhaps as regent if he died.[467] In the years to come, Bothwell lived off a meagre Spanish pension and continued to plot against James, submitting increasingly ambitious and elaborate invasion schemes to the Spanish authorities. He might have sponsored further schemes against the king, his cousin: in 1602 Francis Mowbray, a long-time Bothwell supporter, attempted to poison James, and there was a rumour in the following year that Bothwell's old friend Lord Ochiltree had pledged to kill the king.[468] After James ascended the English throne, Bothwell simply became an irrelevance and, to the Spanish, an embarrassment with a licentious lifestyle that attracted the interest of the Inquisition. He became an increasingly sad and pathetic expatriate, drifting deeper into poverty and sickness. Francis Stewart, Earl of Bothwell and Lord High Admiral of Scotland, a man who had once ruled the nation,[469] eventually died at Naples in 1612, almost forgotten, having spent his last years earning whatever he could by telling fortunes and taking part in displays of skill-at-arms. If the 'Gowrie Conspiracy' was really undertaken partly or wholly on his behalf, he was one of its last casualties. But the most direct connection between Bothwell and the 'conspiracy' has been overlooked by those who have written on the subject.

For on 5 August 1600, Bothwell might have had his own man inside Gowrie House.

****

One of the most inexplicable episodes of the 'Gowrie House' affair is Sandy Ruthven's abrupt exit from the turret chamber, having lost his nerve in the face of the king's censures and promises. It is astonishing that Ruthven took such a risk, but perhaps he assumed that James would keep his word (which, to a considerable extent, he did), and that Andrew Henderson would do nothing to assist him (and, but for the half-opening of a window, and the wrong window at that, he was right in this, too). It has always been assumed that Sandy went to consult his brother, the earl. But it would have been virtually impossible for them to have met: John Ruthven was outside Gowrie House with Lennox, Mar and the rest all the time. The only time he left them was when he went back into the building to check on the truth of the rumour that the king had left, but he could hardly have known then that Sandy would have second thoughts and leave the chamber when he did, so it is difficult to see how Gowrie could have deliberately intended this as a ploy to meet his brother and shore up his fragile confidence. By mid-October 1600, the English agents in Scotland, who were assiduously analysing in minute detail the various stories of the Gowrie House affair, were convinced that Gowrie and his brother could not have met at this point.[470] However, the Master of Ruthven could easily have met with someone else, a man who, by his own confession, certainly was inside the building at the right time. This individual has generally been overlooked in accounts of the 'conspiracy', or else consigned a part among the insignificant 'servants and retainers' who made up the numbers on the day. This was Thomas Cranstoun, the man who passed on to Gowrie the rumour that James had already left Perth.

Cranstoun's actual words to Gowrie – 'his Majesty has gone to the South Inch' – could have been a coded message to let him know that Sandy had either already secured (or murdered) the king or was about to do so, and that Gowrie therefore needed to reinforce his alibi by getting well away from Gowrie House with as many eye witnesses as possible. Indeed, one account of 5 August states explicitly that this was so; the name 'South Inch' was rumoured to be the conspirators' secret signal.[471] Secondly, Cranstoun himself could have been the man who hardened Sandy Ruthven's resolve after the Master left the turret chamber in a panic, and reiterated the order that they had to go on with the attempt on the king. Cranstoun was also the only witness to the supposed fact that Gowrie went back into Gowrie House to find the boy that he wanted to send to Scone for his horses, but met no one.[472] If Cranstoun was telling the truth, Gowrie could not have met Sandy Ruthven, for the depositions of other witnesses establish where the earl was at all other times. If Cranstoun was lying, either 'South Inch' could have been some sort of signal from Sandy to his brother, or else Cranstoun and Gowrie together could have met Sandy inside the house. In either event, Thomas Cranstoun plainly knew rather more about what was happening than he revealed in his deposition. Thirdly, Cranstoun's deposition is important more for what it omits than for what it includes. Cranstoun makes no mention at all of what he had been doing, or where he had been, before he allegedly heard the 'Chinese whispers' that the king had left Gowrie House. Even his own defence, his one chance of saving himself from a traitor's death, has him appearing virtually out of thin air at the end of the fateful dinner.[473]

All of this suggests that Thomas Cranstoun was rather more than the humble stabler to the Earl of Gowrie that he claimed to be, and certainly rather more than the innocent man that he claimed to be on the scaffold. In fact, he was a younger brother of Sir John Cranstoun of That Ilk, and thus distantly related to the Ruthven brothers: the mother of the first Lord Ruthven had been a Cranstoun. He was also a distant relation of the 'other' Thomas Cranstoun, the Earl of Bothwell's right-hand man.[474] As recently as June 1600, Sir John Cranstoun had been accused of harbouring the 'other' Thomas and his brother, who had been lurking on the English side of the border for several years. For some unknown reason, they chose that particular moment to return to Scotland and make contact with the senior branch of their family. By 'our' Thomas Cranstoun's own deposition, he was out of Scotland between 1589 and 1597, a period that coincided almost exactly with the last and most bitter of the great religious civil wars in France – a war that provided ample opportunities for foreign mercenaries, and the younger sons of Scottish nobility and gentry were always willing candidates for such employment. Although there is no direct evidence to confirm whether or not Cranstoun was a veteran mercenary (he would have been in his fifties or sixties in 1600), his prominence and competence in the vicious sword fight in the gallery seems to add weight to the suggestion that he was. His command to Gowrie's steward George Craigengelt to 'keep the gate' has a soldierly ring to it, and Craigengelt's interrogators clearly seem to have sensed that the steward was following Cranstoun's orders in a pre-arranged strategy to 'secure the perimeter' of Gowrie House.[475] This would explain why the eminently qualified Thomas Cranstoun did not become the 'armoured man' in the turret chamber. If he really was an experienced soldier, he was simply more useful elsewhere.

Thomas Cranstoun swore that he had not talked to Gowrie or the Master of Ruthven during the fortnight before 5 August. So his own evidence begs a crucial question: where, exactly, was Thomas Cranstoun during that time? Naturally, he could have been at one of the Ruthvens' other residences, engaged in innocent servile tasks. On the other hand, he could certainly have got to the English border and back, or to Cranstoun and back, well within a fortnight, so it was perfectly feasible for the one Thomas Cranstoun to have met with the other and plotted the murder or kidnapping of a king. On the same principle, it would have been easy for any of the Cranstouns to have got to Fast Castle, or to any other Border rendezvous where they could have met with Robert Logan of Restalrig; and Logan was distant kin to the Cranstouns. Sprot's 'Letter I' refers to an earlier meeting to discuss the plot between 'Logan' and the letter's unnamed recipient at 'Cap.h.', perhaps Capheaton, in Northumberland, far enough from the Scottish border to avoid detection by King James's men, close enough to Fast Castle for Logan to get there easily, and possibly a convenient hideout for assorted Cranstouns and their associates.[476]

****

Returning to the pathetic Eyemouth notary, there is a final element of Sprot's 'Letter IV' that has a ring of truth about it. In a postscript, 'Logan' wrote to 'Gowrie': 'I will never forget the good sport that Mr A[lexander] your brother told me of a noble man of Padua, it comes so oft to my memory. And indeed it is [apropos] to this purpose we have in hand'.[477] Sprot evidently found the 'Padua' detail so important that he inserted it, with embellishments, in some of his other forgeries. 'Letter I' was supposedly written by Logan on 18 July 1600 to an anonymous third party, suggesting that the recipient, Logan and Sandy Ruthven should meet in Edinburgh. 'Logan' warned the recipient to be wary of Sandy, 'because he is somewhat consety *[= full of conceits]*, for God's sake be very wary with his reckless toys of Padua; for he told me one of the strangest tales of a nobleman of Padua that ever I heard in my life, resembling the like purpose'.[478] The Padua story also turned up in another form in 'Letter V', supposedly penned by Logan to the same unknown recipient on 31 July 1600, where 'Logan' urged him to remind Sandy Ruthven of 'the sport he told me of Padua'.[479] The mysterious references to Padua are hardly the sorts of details that a third-rate provincial clerk would be expected to know, or to invent. Moreover, Sprot betrays himself by seeming to imply that Sandy Ruthven, with '*his* reckless toys', had been a student at Padua, rather than his elder brother Gowrie. All in all, the 'Padua' story seems most likely to be Sprot's half-remembered distortion of something written or said by Logan, inserted by Sprot into his forgeries to give them a ring of authenticity. It might also provide a clue to one of the most important and mysterious aspects of the 'Gowrie House affair': the suggestion that England, and her ageing, magnificent queen, lay behind what happened that day. For during 1600, a certain 'nobleman of Padua' was living his life no more than a dozen miles from where Robert Logan and George Sprot were living theirs. He was also no ordinary nobleman. He was one of England's greatest living war heroes. He also happened to be a personal friend of John Ruthven, Earl of Gowrie.

CHAPTER EIGHT

SOLDIERS OF THE QUEEN

When the third Earl of Gowrie arrived at Padua late in 1594 or early in 1595, he became part of a small but growing British presence in the student body. Gowrie spent an unusually long time there, perhaps almost four years, and presumably got to know the other British students well. If so, he would quickly have realised that many of his English contemporaries shared one fateful, stellar connection : they were friends of the would-be political colossus, military genius and kingmaker of his day, Queen Elizabeth's glamorous but fatally flawed favourite, Robert Devereux, second Earl of Essex. When, just six months after the 'Gowrie House affair', Essex launched a feeble rebellion in a last, desperate attempt to regain the favour and dominance that he had lost, several of those who stood alongside him were alumni of the University of Padua and Gowrie's contemporaries. Essex's secretary, Henry Cuffe, matriculated at Padua in 1597, and was executed with his master in 1601. Francis Davison entered the university at much the same time, combining his studies with his role as Essex's chief agent for European intelligence. Roger Manners, fifth Earl of Rutland, was at Padua in 1596 and was later implicated in Essex's rebellion. Thomas, fifteenth Lord Grey of Wilton, whose grandfather had sparred with Patrick, Lord Ruthven, back in the 1540s, was at Padua from 1594, and although he later fought alongside Essex in Ireland, he ultimately helped to put down his rebellion and sat as one of Essex's judges. But Grey was 'touchy, irascible, somewhat unstable' and virulently anti-Scottish. Having avoided Essex's treason, he was drawn into the Catholic 'Bye plot' of 1603, an early attempt to overthrow England's new Scottish king. He spent the last decade of his life in the Tower of London, keeping company with Gowrie's brother Patrick. All in all, the University of Padua in the 1590s was a remarkably fertile breeding ground for future conspirators.[480] Whether Gowrie knew any of the future English plotters, or discussed political 'what ifs?'

with any of them, will never be known. But Gowrie certainly did get to know one of his English contemporaries at Padua: the most famous of them all, and the one who in 1600 was the best placed to assist any 'Gowrie Conspiracy'.

****

Peregrine Bertie, thirteenth Baron Willoughby de Eresby, held one of England's oldest titles. He owed his then unusual Christian name to the peregrinations of his parents, Protestant exiles in the reign of the Catholic Mary Tudor. He became one of the greatest English generals of his day, serving as commander-in-chief successively in the Netherlands and Normandy. His bravery was a byword: he commanded the heroic English cavalry charge at the Battle of Zutphen in 1586. 'Testy and choleric' in his own words, but also witty and intellectual, Peregrine Bertie was hugely respected by his enemy, the Duke of Parma, his ally, King Henri IV of France, and his queen, Elizabeth I.[481] The popular balladeers adored him, just as they idolised his much younger friend and political ally, the Earl of Essex. But a combination of ill health and consistent lack of ambition wrecked Lord Willoughby's career. He spent much of the 1590s travelling around various European resorts, attempting to mend his health. In 1596 he arrived in Padua and promptly matriculated at the university (this was a legal ploy; matriculated students of Padua were exempt from the attentions of the Inquisition).[482] Although Lord Willoughby would then have been a 41-year-old 'mature student', and stayed in Padua for no more than a few months at most, the fact remains that he was an undergraduate contemporary of the 18-year-old Earl of Gowrie. Given Gowrie's fascination with the art of war, it would have been highly unlikely for him not to have sought out one of Europe's most famous generals.

After he returned to England, Willoughby was appointed governor of Berwick-upon-Tweed, a position for which he had been soliciting for years. Although this could have become a comfortable sinecure for a sick, old, semi-retired warhorse, Willoughby threw himself into the job with gusto, reorganising the garrison, eliminating corruption and inefficiency, and taking very seriously the defence of a border that would soon simply disappear off the map. Quite apart from making many enemies among the corrupt and inefficient of Berwick, not to mention among Scotsmen who detested his arrogant bravado, the new governor was soon in the middle of a serious international incident, and one that was largely of his own making. In June 1599, partly on his own initiative, and partly with discreet sanction from London, Lord Willoughby authorised an extraordinary covert operation into an independent country. This was to seize Edmund Ashfield, a Buckinghamshire gentleman acting as an intermediary between English Catholics and King James. Willoughby entrusted the mission to his cousin John Guevara, the grandson of a Spanish mercenary who had settled in England. Guevara and his 'snatch squad' of half a dozen horsemen caught up with Ashfield on Leith links, northeast of Edinburgh. Posing as friendly compatriots, Guevara and his men plied Ashfield with wine and persuaded him into their coach, which promptly made for the border and the vast new walls of Berwick. James VI sent Willoughby a stinging letter of protest, but the old general had dealt with enough monarchs in his day not to be fazed by criticism from this one, and Ashfield stayed in an English prison.[483]

The most remarkable aspect of the whole Ashfield affair is that Willoughby had an elaborate contingency plan in place in case Guevara found the road to Berwick blocked. Willoughby owned his own fast pinnace, and he stationed her off Prestonpans, east of Leith, in case Guevara needed to get Ashfield away by sea.[484] This was by no means the last of Willougby's maritime activities. Over the winter of 1600–01 he either built or (more likely) converted a ship at Berwick for service against the Dunkirk privateers, which regularly raided shipping all along the coasts of northern England and Scotland. Willoughby's private warship was of 140 tons, manned by 100 men and mounting 16 guns. In the spring of 1601 he operated her mainly in the Forth, but running such a large ship entirely at his own expense proved crippling even for such a relatively wealthy man as Peregrine, Lord Willoughby.[485] He needed new money to keep the ship at sea, and in the summer of 1601 Willoughby found a new partner. John Guevara drew up the indenture of agreement, which ostensibly committed the partners to sending the ship on a voyage to the Indies, the Canary Islands, and into the Mediterranean.[486] There was nothing remarkable in any of this, for the exploits of Drake, Hawkins and Raleigh had made the sea the very height of *de rigueur* for the Elizabethan great and good. What was remarkable was the identity of Lord Willoughby's partner. The new half-owner of the most powerful warship on the east coast of Britain was none other than Robert Logan, Laird of Restalrig.

On the day that Logan signed the agreement with Willoughby, his kinsman and retainer Matthew Logan allegedly said to the forger, George Sprot,

Woe's me that ever I should see this day, that the Laird
show grow a seaman! ... It is true that I have oft thought
that the Laird would pass away, for he is minded to sell
all that he has, and would to God that he had never been
born ... He might have lived well enough at home.
I find he has ever been [excited], and his mind has ever
been set on passing out of the country this year past -

– in other words, since the time of the Gowrie House affair.[487]
Although Matthew Logan denied every word that Sprot attributed to
him, the passage rings true. Logan did indeed sell off all his lands
before he died, despite the fact that he had never discernibly been in
financial trouble – quite the opposite. In an age when land ownership
was the be-all and end-all for many well-born Scots, Logan's actions
seem incredible. Investing a large amount in a ship intended for
distant parts, presumably carrying the sometime Laird of Restalrig
aboard her, is only marginally less fantastic. The most plausible
explanation for Logan's actions is also the most sinister. If he was
overseas, he could not be tried for treason; if he had no lands, they
could not be forfeited even if he was so charged. Robert Logan was
behaving suspiciously like a man with something to hide.

Meanwhile, Lord Willoughby had not forgotten his old Padua
contemporary and Logan's alleged fellow-plotter, the Earl of Gowrie.
Two of Willoughby's sons met Gowrie at Paris in 1599, and sent his
respects to their father.[488] When Gowrie left England in April 1600,
after his meeting with Queen Elizabeth, his passport specified that he
should enter Scotland at Berwick, where he was entertained lavishly by
the governor.[489] At the time of the 'Gowrie House affair' itself, though,
Willoughby was on extended leave in Lincolnshire, trying to shake off
yet another bout of serious illness. He had less than a year to live.
Willoughby spent his last months under two huge clouds of suspicion,
which came upon him in quick succession. His connections with
Gowrie made some (including the Earl of Mar) suspect that he was
privy to the 'conspiracy', and as the whispers continued through the
shortening winter days, Willoughby fell into a fit of seasonal
depression.[490] No sooner had this talk of his involvement in the Gowrie
affair started to fade than the second body blow struck Lord
Willoughby. On Sunday 8 February 1601 his old friend, Essex, ran
through the streets of London with some 300 companions, attempting
to rouse the City – to defend Essex against his enemies, as his apologists

and most historians have claimed, or to overthrow the Queen and set himself up as England's ruler, as the earl's enemies counter-claimed. Essex went to the block 17 days later, by which time a new whispering campaign had begun at court and among Willoughby's many enemies in Berwick. There had been two great conspiracies in Great Britain within the space of six months, and Lord Willoughby de Eresby had been a personal friend of both of the chief plotters; surely some coincidence? But Queen Elizabeth wrote in person one last time to her 'good Peregrine', assuring him that she, at least, regarded him as loyal.[491] Willoughby had little time in which to concern himself with the dark rumours that stuck to his name. He caught a chill on the deck of his and Logan's warship, and within days, he was on his deathbed. On 21 June 1601 he wrote to Cecil, recounting the deaths of a cousin and a former servant, and adding that 'I shall follow them ere long, being now very sick. I beseech you be a father to my eldest son when I am dead'.[492] Willoughby died at Berwick four days later, and with him died Logan of Restalrig's dreams of a new life overseas, safe from awkward revelations about the 'Gowrie Conspiracy'. Peregrine Bertie's ship made one last voyage, carrying his body down the coast to Lincolnshire, where the thirteenth Lord Willoughby de Eresby was laid to rest beneath a spectacular monument in Spilsby church.[493]

Regardless of the fact that Queen Elizabeth herself discounted the rumours about Peregrine, Lord Willoughby, his unexpected relationships with both Gowrie and Robert Logan helped to give rise to the most elaborate of all the conspiracy theories that have been constructed around the events of 5 August 1600. In this version of events, the Ruthven brothers sought to smuggle King James out of Gowrie House and Perth. Perhaps their destination was their own castle at Dirleton, or else (if one believes Sprot's 'Letter IV') it might have been either Logan's Fast Castle, or somewhere altogether further afield. Both Dirleton and Fast would have been within easy range of Berwick and its sympathetic governor. Moreover, that same governor would have provided the means by which the king could be brought, quickly and securely, to his final destination. Willoughby had shown that abduction by sea was in his thoughts when he ordered his pinnace to lie offshore in case it was needed to transport Ashfield to England. In August 1600, the target would have been far greater than a drunken Catholic gentleman – but so would the means of transportation. Lord Willoughby's pinnace, lurking somewhere off the mouths of Forth or Tay, would carry King James into captivity. Perhaps this was the vessel referred to in Sprot's 'Letter IV', rather than the fishing boat mentioned in 'Letter V'; although Sprot could just as easily have based on his mysterious vessel on the contemporary rumours of an English ship lying offshore on 5 August, or on the warship owned by Willoughby and his old master, Logan of Restalrig.

The abduction of a king was the stuff that brought about wars, and was hardly likely to be entered into lightly, or sanctioned by mere earls of Scotland and barons of England, no matter how illustrious. Therefore, proponents of the 'English kidnap' theory have argued, the abduction of James VI must have been sanctioned by one of three people, or by a combination of one of them with the third. One was the man who would be king, or at least Lord Protector, of England. The second was the man who was determined to stop him. The other was the Queen of England herself.

****

The rumour that the 'Gowrie Conspiracy' had been hatched in England, and promoted by the chief authorities there, began to circulate within days of the events in Perth.[494] Within a month, Edinburgh street gossip had it as gospel that a mysterious English ship had been lying off the coast, ready to play its part in events. King James himself even raised the matter with Nicolson, the English agent, who denied that any such ship existed.[495] It was no secret that in 1600, relations between Scotland and England were particularly strained. James was bitter about Elizabeth's persistent refusal to acknowledge him as her heir. On the English side, there was suspicion of James's apparently increasing sympathy towards Catholics. On both sides, there was a huge litany of lesser grievances and complaints, both real and imagined. The upshot of all this was the convention of June 1600, when James demanded heavy new taxes to pay for an army intended to invade England if his right to the succession was denied.[496] Matters were clearly going too far, and the very day before he rode to Gowrie House, James VI wrote to Queen Elizabeth to tell her that he was sending an ambassador to clear up the misunderstandings between them.[497] Events overtook him, and the ambassador spent most of his time explaining to the queen why she should believe her cousin James's version of the events at Gowrie House, rather than the gossip that made James out to be a cold-blooded killer.

The English response to the events of 5 August, at least in official circles, was shaped not only by distrust of James, but by respect for the young men who had died in Perth and what they stood for. For over half a century, the Ruthvens had been one of the most pro-English families in Scotland, and in that respect John, Earl of Gowrie, seemed to be cast from the same mould as his father and grandfather before him. The English envoy at Paris believed that England could make 'exceeding good use' of him.[498] In London, he was liberally entertained by Queen Elizabeth and her ministers. Consequently, it was entirely plausible for Gowrie to have been an agent of England, and it has been suggested that the Ruthvens really lured James to Perth by claiming that they had a message for him from England about the English succession.[499] The problem with this interpretation of events is that in political terms, there was more than one 'England'. There was the glamorous, militarist England of the queen's favourite, Robert Devereux, the 34-year-old Earl of Essex. Despite being adored by the public and surrounded by a stellar entourage of poets, playwrights, and military men like Lord Willoughby, Essex was in disgrace with the queen following a succession of disastrous campaigns in Spain and Ireland. Then there was the methodical, bureaucratic England of Robert Cecil, the hunchbacked 37-year-old son of William, Lord Burghley, Elizabeth's chief minister for 40 years, who had trained up his younger son to succeed him. Although he would never win any charisma competitions with the Earl of Essex, Cecil was witty, shrewd and highly competent. Finally, there was the once-glorious but fading England of Queen Elizabeth herself. The memories of triumph over the Armada had given way to the realities of endless war, unsuccessful battles, famine, plague and mass beggary. The Ruthvens might well have been serving one of these Englands on 5 August 1600 – but which one?

'Gloriana' herself was highly unlikely to have sanctioned any form of action against her cousin James. True, he infuriatingly refused to listen to her advice, but that had been the case for over 20 years. Deep down, the queen probably knew that he was almost bound to succeed her, even if she did not declare it publicly. Elizabeth had burned her fingers in her dealings with his mother, Mary, Queen of Scots, who had been both an embarrassment and an ongoing security nightmare during her 20-year captivity in England. Elizabeth would hardly have been keen to see history repeat itself by kidnapping Mary's successor and bringing him to captivity in England, even if she had the remotest justification for doing so. Elizabeth was also perhaps the last monarch in Europe who would have considered authorising an assassination or kidnapping of a fellow monarch. She had been the target of more plots than perhaps any other contemporary ruler, and besides, sovereigns chosen and anointed by God had to stick together. This was why she had refused to take action against Mary for so long, and why for two decades she refused overtly to help the Dutch (Protestant, but rebels) against Philip II of Spain (Catholic, but the Lord's anointed). Such sensibilities might have dictated Queen Elizabeth's thinking, but they would not have bound Essex and Cecil. Unlike the queen, they had to think the unthinkable, to imagine what would happen when Gloriana died.

When the unthinkable finally happened, in March 1603, King James VI was Robert Cecil's favoured candidate for the English throne, thanks to two years of delicate and surreptitious correspondence. But in August 1600 James was very much Essex's candidate, and James reciprocated: he detested the Cecils for the part they had played in his mother's execution. No one could have known then that Essex would destroy himself spectacularly only six months later. True, he was out of favour, but he had been out of favour before and had returned to it; the queen was old, crotchety and fickle, and had always possessed a fatal soft-heartedness toward Robin Devereux. While the old queen lived, she kept the charismatic but unstable earl and the methodical, devious Cecil in balance. Cecil's greatest fear must have been that her death would trigger the unchallenged ascendancy of Essex the Kingmaker, and oblivion (or worse) for Robert Cecil. But if James VI was removed from the scene, or fatally discredited, Cecil might be able to place on the English throne the Infanta Isabella, the King of Spain's sister, or any of the other contenders.

If Cecil was a worried man during the second half of 1600, his concerns were as nothing to his rival's. The Earl of Essex was becoming an increasingly desperate man. On Christmas Day he wrote what became his last letter to James VI, suggesting that the king send an ambassador to Elizabeth to persuade her finally to proclaim him her successor. Essex damned Cecil and all his other enemies as 'men so base, so cowardly, and that know themselves to be so odious'. He accused them explicitly of plotting to make the Infanta Isabella England's sovereign after Elizabeth, and implicitly of having sanctioned the Gowrie conspiracy, 'their devilish plots with your Majesty's own subjects against your person and life'.[500] Essex's letter seems to have panicked James, who agreed to send an ambassador. He also sent Essex a private note of seven lines, which the earl placed in a little bag and wore around his neck. The ambassador – none other than the ubiquitous Earl of Mar, whom Essex himself proposed for the job – did not come south in time to save the fallen favourite, and as his rebellion collapsed around him and he hastily burned his papers as royal troops neared his house, Essex threw the bag containing James's note into the fire.[501]

Essex had accused Cecil of being behind the 'Gowrie Conspiracy', but in August 1600 Essex was desperate enough, and hated Cecil enough, to accuse his rival of anything. As it was, Cecil seemed to be as surprised as anyone else in England by the events of 5 August 1600 in Perth. Publicly, at least, during the early days of August 1600 Cecil and the English government were obsessed with the ongoing war in Ireland, not with events in Scotland.[502] But Cecil was a master of dissembling and the art of 'deniability', as his masterful manipulation of the Gunpowder Plot later demonstrated. Essex had an obvious vested interest in denigrating Cecil, but on the other hand, Essex also still had many friends at court and in government who might have picked up some sort of proof, or else just an incriminating whisper, of Cecil's complicity in the 'Gowrie Conspiracy'. Cecil did give a tantalising and characteristically ambiguous clue to his thinking about the 'Gowrie House affair', when he wrote in October 1600 that 'on my conscience there was some purpose in Gowrie to have made a welter in that kingdom [Scotland]'. Cecil does not say whether he first had this thought before or after 5 August; whether, for example, Gowrie said something suspicious to Cecil back in April.[503]

****

If the Ruthvens wanted to abduct James VI, be it on England's behalf or anyone else's, and if they wanted to get him to a 'safe house' like Fast Castle, then somehow they had to get the king out of Perth during the afternoon of 5 August 1600. In fact this need not have been as problematic as it sounds, even after James turned up unexpectedly with an entire hunting party. The kidnappers would have been aided greatly by the geography of Gowrie House in relation to the rest of Perth. It would have taken only one or two men to bundle a tied and captive king out of the house and through its gardens. The wall surrounding Gowrie House and grounds would have made the abduction largely invisible to the outside world, especially if James's attendants were either in the street and yard at the front or, better still, riding out of Perth across the South Inch. The only place from which the kidnappers could be observed would have been the upper stories of the houses across Speygate, but on an August day the first Earl of Gowrie's apple trees would probably have obscured most of those views, even if anyone happened to be at the windows concerned at the wrong time. The king could then have been put into a boat on the Tay, either directly from the grounds of Gowrie House or (more publicly, and thus more riskily) from the dock that adjoined the grounds, directly outside the town wall.[504] A sailing craft would have been at the mercy of wind and tide, so it is just possible that Sandy Ruthven's insistence at Falkland that the king should come to Perth immediately, and his and Gowrie's disquiet when James did not get there until the afternoon, might have been due to a realisation that they had missed the tide. Some sort of oared vessel would have been a much better option, but depending on its size, this might have entailed a larger crew, and such accomplices never came to light in the weeks after 5 August. Even so, it would have been theoretically possible for the Ruthvens to get King James out of Perth by boat.

Getting him out of town would have been the easy part; getting him to his destination would have been rather more problematic. The Ruthven crew could have landed him somewhere downstream of Perth and taken him overland through Fife, then by sea again across the Firth of Forth to Dirleton or Fast Castles. But this route was bound to take them close to Falkland Palace, and to the search parties of frantic courtiers who were bound to have been scouring Fife and Perthshire after their monarch disappeared. It would have been better for the hypothetical Ruthven boat to take James downstream and all the way out to sea, but doing so would have meant overcoming wind, tide, and – most problematic of all – Dundee. Dominating the mouth of the Tay, where the great firth narrowed to an entrance less than a mile wide, Dundee was traditionally and often violently hostile to Perth and the Ruthvens. After all, the first Earl of Gowrie's fate had been sealed when he was betrayed and arrested there. But two of the curious aspects of the 'Gowrie House affair' are the presence of possible Ruthven accomplices at Dundee on 5 August 1600, and the mysterious activities of members of the Lamb family. John Lamb was accused of making 'filthy and unnatural speeches' against James that day in Dundee, presumably after the news of the Ruthvens' deaths reached the town; he subsequently vanished. George Lamb was in Dundee on the fourth, and testified that he saw John Lamb going down to the harbour there at about four in the morning of the fifth; George claimed that he then returned to Perth, and knew nothing else. Patrick Lamb was the man accused of carrying a wooden beam to try and batter down the gates of Gowrie House. James Lamb was unloading coals at the dock on the South Inch, perfectly placed to assist any boat setting off down the river.[505] One of the legends that grew up around the 'Gowrie House affair' had the earl attending the wedding of one of the Lambs; perhaps this was a distorted memory of the family's involvement in the events of 5 August. Meanwhile Gowrie's servant Younger, one of those initially suspected of being the 'armoured man', was eliminated from that enquiry only *because he was in Dundee on the fifth.*

The final Dundee connections were provided by the many dubious confessions of George Sprot. In one of his earlier depositions, before the Earl of Dunbar returned to Scotland, Sprot named Sir James Scrymgeour and Sir Harry Lindsay as accomplices in the 'Gowrie Conspiracy'.[506] Sprot later withdrew the accusations, but this begs the question of why he had named these particular individuals in the first place, rather than anyone else. Lindsay was Laird of Kinfauns, and Kinfauns Castle stood on the north bank of the Tay; its adherence or neutrality would have been very useful to a Ruthven boat carrying a kidnapped king down the river. Scrymgeour was the Provost and Constable of Dundee, and his 'blind eye' could have permitted that boat to win out to the open sea. According to another of Sprot's statements, although admittedly one that he later contradicted, another of the chief suspects in the plot against the king was in Dundee on or around the time of the 'Gowrie House affair': Logan of Restalrig himself, accompanied by his right-hand man, James 'Laird' Bower. Some or all of these connections are fantasy, and as fantasists go, George Sprot takes some equalling. But bearing with his story for a little longer , and with the whole unlikely theory of a trussed-up King of Scots sailing down the Tay, getting past Dundee would have brought the Ruthven boat near to its destination, as identified by the Edinburgh mob and various conspiracy theorists ever since: Lord Willoughby's pinnace, lying off the mouth of Tay or Forth, ready to receive its unwilling royal guest before sailing south to Dirleton, Fast, or the coast of England. But in the life-or-death factional struggle that was tearing English politics apart in 1600, Lord Willoughby was very much the Earl of Essex's man, and Essex, of all people, had very good cause to keep James VI firmly alive and firmly on his throne.

****

Like his father before him, John Ruthven lived and died a hero of the Presbyterian kirk, and was regarded as a martyr in its cause for generations thereafter. It was even claimed that 18th-century Presbyterians drew a grim satisfaction from the fact that King George I was proclaimed in Edinburgh on 5 August 1714, the anniversary of the

'Gowrie House affair': the rule of the Stuarts had finally ended, in a belated posthumous justification of the dead Ruthven brothers.[507] But almost immediately after his death, two 'black legends' began to circulate, blackening the last Earl of Gowrie's name. One made him out to be a dabbler in the dark arts, but the other was perhaps even more damning to his reputation as a bulwark of the Kirk. According to this story, Gowrie's time at Padua had caused him secretly to abandon his faith and convert to Rome.

Less than 10 days after the events at Gowrie House, King James was saying publicly that the Earl of Gowrie had often tried to convince him to negotiate with the pope.[508] This seemed to corroborate a letter of the year before from the English agent in Scotland, Nicholson, who had picked up the news that Gowrie had converted to Catholicism while he was in Italy.[509] This charge was presented by Patrick Galloway in his sermon on 11 August 1600 and blended with the apparently incontrovertible evidence of the earl's interest in magic to create the most damning accusation that could possibly be brought against such a darling of the Kirk, namely that Gowrie was at once a papist and a satanist. It was a line swiftly taken up by others, such as John Dykes, a Presbyterian minister, who penned lines that allied these charges to the Ruthven brothers' alleged desire to avenge their father:

> Beelzebub, proud rebel, brewed this breasche [discharge];
>
> His Romish court conspired, right well acquent [acquainted]
>
> To play such pageants, princes to dispeasch [dispatch],
>
> Syne all the mischief magic could comment [recommend]
>
> And falset, feighing fiend to seem a saint,
>
> With bold revenge in bloody breast's upblown ...[510]

This was all propaganda, a natural and inevitable part of the process of tarnishing Gowrie's image *post mortem*. On the other hand, some of the people to whom the earl was talking in 1600 were hardly Bible-reading, sermon-attending bulwarks of the Kirk. While he was in Paris during February and March 1600, Gowrie might have met the Earl of Bothwell, his old conspiratorial ally, but by that time a Catholic convert and effectively an agent of Spain. Gowrie certainly met with that other veteran schemer with moveable religious principles, Logan of Restalrig's cousin, the Master of Gray. In Brussels at around the same time,

Bothwell was meeting with the Catholic Alexander, Lord Home, one of his bitterest enemies from former days, to attempt a reconciliation aimed at furthering the Catholic cause in Scotland.[511] It was whispered that Home's innocuous European tour in 1599 was really a cover for a secret mission to the Vatican on James's behalf, and by the end of that year he was overtly James's ambassador to Henry IV of France. Gowrie, Home and Bothwell could all easily have met together in Paris in the first months of 1600. Any other agendas inspiring all this frantic conversation between expatriate Scottish noblemen are lost now, and unlikely ever to come to light. In terms of the 'Gowrie Conspiracy', it could mean everything or nothing: depending on one's preference, Gowrie was hatching a plot with the papistical agents of the Antichrist, or he was catching up on the news over some French wine with old friends who just happened to be Catholics.

Lord Home's closeness to Gowrie and Logan of Restalrig, and his attempted reconciliation with Bothwell, might suggest that he was a potential conspirator, and if the 'Sprot/Logan' letters are believed to any degree, the plotters had at least considered recruiting him. If the plan was to bring the king to Fast Castle, Home's support would have been invaluable: his extensive border estates, powerful castles at Hume and Dunglass, and considerable manpower, could have formed a buffer zone between Fast and any liberating army, assuming that James's ministers had any idea where their king had been taken.[512] According to one of the 'Sprot/Logan' letters, though, 'Logan' condemned his half-brother Home as a man who 'will never help his friend nor harm his foe'. In 'Letter II', 'Logan' warned 'Laird Bower' to keep Home ignorant of their plans, for he would rather be 'eirdit quik' [buried alive] than have Home know of them.[513] This phrase seems to have come from a conversation of Logan and Sprot in 1602, as reported by the notary. Logan had met with Lady Home, who said 'she knew that I had been in some dealing with the Earl of Gowrie about Dirleton'. Logan told Sprot not to have any dealings with her, 'for I had rather be *eirdit quick* than either my Lord or she knew anything of it'.[514] If 'Logan' was right, Home's neutrality and caution paid off: within five years he was the first Earl of Home. Nevertheless, the connections between the Ruthvens and the Homes survived the apocalypse of 5 August 1600. In 1608 John and Sandy Ruthven's sister Beatrix, once Queen Anna's favourite lady-in-waiting, married Sir John Home of Cowdenknowes, who was Lord Home's heir at the time of the 'Gowrie House affair', and whose grandson eventually inherited the Home earldom.

Some time in 1601, the Earl of Bothwell handed the Spanish government a list of sympathisers who would support an invasion of Scotland. The list included the names of Robert Logan of Restalrig and the Earl of Gowrie.[515] If Bothwell was correct, so, too, was his cousin James VI – the Earl of Gowrie was a secret convert to Rome, and thus a double-dealing hypocrite. The obvious difficulty with Bothwell's list is that in 1601, the last Earl of Gowrie was dead. It is possible that the famously meticulous Spanish bureaucrats got the date wrong when they filed the paper away, or that Bothwell was exaggerating the extent of his support, or that he submitted an older document and simply forgot to delete Gowrie's name. A fourth possibility exonerates all parties. Bothwell might not have been referring to the dead John Ruthven at all, but to his fugitive brother William, to many the rightful fourth Earl of Gowrie. Bothwell would have had every reason to ignore the act of Parliament that obliterated the Gowrie title. A similar act in 1593 had rescinded his own, and legally reduced him to plain Frank Stewart; but he still referred to himself as Bothwell, as did almost everyone else, and also grandiloquently signed himself 'Admiral of Scotland' in all his dealings with the Spanish government, even though that hereditary title was just as dead to him as the earldom of Gowrie was to the Ruthvens. The shadowy William Ruthven would have had every reason to support a Spanish invasion that might restore him to his rightful inheritance, even if he did not actually convert to Catholicism. His much better known younger brother Patrick certainly did convert at some point in his life, but there is strong evidence to suggest that John Ruthven never did. John Colville, the invariably well informed English agent and sometime husband of the Earl of Gowrie's great-aunt, told Cecil in 1599 that Gowrie was one of the very few Scots noblemen not to convert to Rome while visiting Europe.[516] Gowrie had also corresponded with Theodore Beza, Calvin's successor, and stayed with him for several weeks while returning from Padua – hardly the actions of a Catholic convert, even one who was trying to conceal his conversion.

The legend of Gowrie's conversion to Catholicism was deliberate disinformation, put about by King James and his ministers to denigrate the dead earl's reputation and to convince the Kirk that its idol had feet of clay, if not cloven hooves. Moreover, attacking the dead Gowrie in this way was not only disingenuous, it was breathtakingly hypocritical. Arguably the king's closest friend was George Gordon, whom James had just made the first Marquess of Huntly; and although Gordon had nominally converted to the Kirk, few from the king downwards believed in his sincerity. Only a few months before, James had signed a letter to the pope, requesting that the Scots-born William Chisholm, Bishop of Vaison in France, be made a Cardinal to promote James's claim to the English throne at the Vatican. James signed the letter using the respectful forms of address to the pope required by Catholic etiquette. A copy quickly reached Queen Elizabeth, who demanded an explanation: both James and his secretary, Elphinstone, swore that the document must be a forgery. When the story was leaked more publicly by the Vatican itself years later, the king claimed that Elphinstone, by then Lord Balmerino, had slipped the document into a pile of others so that James would sign it unknowingly, and the secretary was promptly and unjustly sentenced to death for treason.[517] In the summer of 1600, though, James's most immediate concern relating to the Catholic faith was none of this. It was the fact that the newest and most important Catholic convert in Scotland was certainly not the Earl of Gowrie, even if there had been any truth at all in the rumours that circulated after his death. It was James's own wife, the Queen of Scots.

CHAPTER NINE

TIBI SOLI

One of the most puzzling aspects of the 'Gowrie House affair' is that neither side had any obvious cause for acting against the other at that precise moment. By his own admission, King James had ample motives for humbling the Ruthvens, but none of them were particularly new, and it was foolish – if not literally suicidal – for him to take action against the family in their own house and town. Similarly, there was little cause for the Ruthvens to move against James when they did. If they sought to repeat their father's 'Raid of Ruthven', they lacked the urgency of his motivation, the need to bring down a hated favourite who might have restored Scotland to Rome. There was no Esmé Stewart monopolising power in 1600; as Catholic favourites went, the Marquess of Huntly was not in the same league. If the Ruthvens sought to restore the Kirk to power following its humiliating defeat in 1596, their apparent failure to recruit any Kirk leaders to their cause might have defeated the object. The Ruthvens opposed James's policy on the English succession, but so did many others, and in broader terms the succession issue was no more urgent in 1600 than it was 10 years earlier, given Queen Elizabeth's perverse refusal to die. And so on. No motive seems quite urgent enough or important enough to demand action on 5 August 1600, and the consequent blood sacrifice that took place at Gowrie House. None of the men involved seem to have had such a motive; but a woman did.

In 1600 Anna of Denmark, Queen Consort of Scots, was 26 years old, and had been married to her curious husband for 11 years. Tall, blond, graceful and vivacious, Anna was far from being the vacuous air-headed blonde portrayed by Victorian and later writers, despite her insatiable craving for jewellery and expensive gowns.[518] She was both politically astute and politically involved, as her early intrigues against Maitland of Thirlestane, James's Chancellor, clearly demonstrated. Anna also had a powerful motive for wanting to see some form of action taken against her royal spouse. For a mother, it was perhaps the most powerful motive of all: she wanted to get her child back. Prince Henry Frederick, Duke of Rothesay and later Prince of Wales, was born in 1594, but he was immediately taken away from the queen and placed in the care of James's old school friend, John Erskine, Earl of Mar. This was normal practice for 16th century royal children, and, indeed, for Scottish aristocratic offspring in general.[519] James himself had been brought up by Mar's mother, and his daughter Elizabeth, born in 1596, was fostered out to Lord Livingstone. Even so, Anna railed incessantly against the fostering of her eldest child, which was totally contrary to Danish practice. Her protests were at least as much political as maternal, for control of the heir to the throne and his upbringing could hardly have been a more important political issue, but Anna was clearly not being disingenuous in demanding control of Henry. She also made several attempts to get Princess Elizabeth back, even though she liked Lord Livingstone and his wife (who also gained custody of Anna's second daughter, Margaret).[520] But she detested Mar, and worked constantly against his control of her son. Before 1600 she had instigated several failed plots to free Henry from Mar's control, but all had come to nothing. The prince was growing up in Stirling Castle, and Anna might have started to contemplate extreme measures to liberate him.

The summer of 1600 was a particularly traumatic time for the queen. She was pregnant with her fifth child, the future King Charles I, who would be born in November. The fourth child, little Princess Margaret, was dying; she fell ill in December 1599 but lingered until August, dying aged 20 months just a week or two after the events at Gowrie House.[521] The queen's mood cannot have been helped by a serious misunderstanding between James and herself over the very issue that mattered to her most, the custody of Prince Henry. In June, Anna was either told by James, or convinced herself that James had told her, that Henry was to be taken away from Mar and given back to her. At the end of the month, the king told her that he had not meant any such thing, only that the prince could come and visit her briefly before returning to Mar's custody.[522] As if these emotional traumas were not enough, Anna was also in the process of embracing a new faith, with all the mental turmoil that might have entailed. Her conversion to Roman Catholicism was a lengthy process. She began to attend Catholic services from about 1593, and increasingly avoided both Presbyterian and her native Lutheran ceremonies. In 1596 the Kirk publicly censured her lifestyle, particularly her uncontrollable extravagance and her liking for parties and dancing. The ministers' strictures probably served only to encourage the queen along the road to Rome. Her closest friend, Henrietta, Marchioness of Huntly (the Duke of Lennox's sister), was a lifelong Catholic, and undoubtedly encouraged Anna.[523] In 1599 a veteran Jesuit priest, Robert Abercromby, was allowed access to court and eventually received the queen into the Catholic Church.

Anna's conversion, her pregnancy, her grief for her dying daughter and her bitterness at her husband's apparent duplicity, all might have strengthened her conviction that she had to wrest her son from Mar's grip. It would have been natural for her to turn to the Ruthvens, a family that she plainly liked and trusted, even though they now belonged to different faiths. Even if the legends of a romance between Anna and Sandy Ruthven (or the Earl of Gowrie, or both) are discounted, Sandy's sisters Barbara and Beatrix were two of her ladies-in-waiting, and both were among Anna's most intimate friends and confidantes. The Ruthvens were also linked to one of the two powerful groupings at the Scottish court, the 'Chamber faction' that centred on the queen, Sir George Home, the Earl of Montrose and Sir James Elphinstone, the secretary. There was a strong rumour to the effect that the 'Chamber', not the Kirk, had been truly responsible for bringing Gowrie back from Europe to strengthen it against its enemies, the faction headed by Sir Thomas Erskine, Sir Edward Bruce – and the Earl of Mar, who by the summer of 1600 was regarded as the king's closest advisor.[524] A plot on the queen's behalf could have grown out of this bitter faction-fight, and could just as easily have been the brainchild of the Ruthvens or the queen herself.

Quite apart from her obvious links with the Ruthven family, Anna was also closely connected to others whose names cropped up on the fringes of the 'Gowrie House affair', or were otherwise connected in some way to the doomed Earl of Gowrie. George Sprot named Sir Harry Lindsay of Kinfauns as one of Gowrie's accomplices in a confession that he later retracted. Lindsay was Anna's Master of the Household, and was married to one of three Chisholm sisters. Another of them was married to James Drummond, Abbot of Inchaffray, the key witness to the conversation between Sandy Ruthven and King James in Falkland Park at breakfast time on 5 August 1600. The third sister was married to John Napier, alchemist, mathematician and former business partner of Robert Logan of Restalrig. The Chisholm girls had a brother, William Chisholm, Catholic bishop of Vaison, the man on whose behalf James had written secretly to the pope. The man who became the scapegoat in that affair, the Catholic Secretary Elphinstone, was a leader of the 'Chamber faction', and was also the man to whom the distraught Countess of

Gowrie turned for support after her sons' deaths. Elphinstone was evidently given, or else somehow obtained, a few of the Ruthven family papers, which still survive in his family's manuscripts.[525] Additionally, Logan's half-brother and Sandy Ruthven's godfather, Alexander, Lord Home, had assisted Anna in a previous attempt to win Prince Henry out of the Earl of Mar's control, back in 1595. The queen's secretary, William Fowler, was also a poet and author whose long-time literary patron was Francis, Earl of Bothwell. Fowler spent much time at Padua in the 1590s, and as there were few Scots at the university, he would almost certainly have known the Earl of Gowrie there.[526] Another figure on the fringes of the queen's household was a Captain John Ruthven, the procurer of Rhenish wine for both her cellars and the king's, whom she had recommended to her brother King Christian for service in the Danish army. On the weekend before the tragedy at Gowrie House, the Earl of Gowrie met a mysterious 'Captain Ruthven' at the ferry across the Tay at Dunkeld, and John seems to have been the only Ruthven holding that rank at that time.[527] Finally, the nurse to Queen Anna and all her children was Margaret Stewart, Lady Ochiltree; and Margaret was the elder sister of Dorothea, Countess of Gowrie.

****

The composition of Queen Anna's household also provides tantalising insights into one of the most mysterious of all the many dimensions of the 'Gowrie House affair'. During the 1590s, one of the queen's closest Catholic friends was William Schaw, her husband's Master of Works. Schaw largely rebuilt Dunfermline Palace for her and included a Catholic chapel within the new extension. However, Schaw's rather greater claim to fame is also a highly controversial one: many regard him as the founding father of modern freemasonry. In 1598 and 1599 he promulgated what became known as the two sets of 'Schaw statutes', which laid down rules for the organisation of Masonic lodges and for the regulation of the craft throughout Scotland.[528]

A few enigmatic hints of Masonic activity lurk at the very edges of the Gowrie story. Making due allowance for the questionable nature of much of the evidence surrounding George Sprot's conviction, it includes a report of a conversation between Robert Logan of Restalrig and his factotum, Laird Bower. Justifying the sale of all his lands, Logan allegedly said, 'I am for no land, I have told you before and will tell you again', before enigmatically adding, '*You have not learned the art of memory*'.[529] The 'art of memory' was at the heart of early freemasonry, and was alluded to in the second set of Schaw statutes. Originating in Classical times, the art was essentially a technique for improving the capacity of an individual's memory, and had been an essential skill for the ancient orators and poets. The key to the 'art of memory' was conjuring up the thought of a great building, and placing ideas and images in different 'rooms' within it; hence the original link between the art and masonry. But by the 16th century the art was regarded as something occult, part of the movement known as Hermeticism (derived from the Greek Hermes, the messenger of the gods). This was based on a quest for spiritual truth born out of a fanciful interpretation of Ancient Egypt, its rituals, hieroglyphics, and fascination with astrology. Inevitably, Hermeticism and the 'art of memory' became bound up inextricably with alchemy too. John Napier and his son Robert were leading practitioners; the alchemical commonplace book of Patrick Ruthven, the last of the tragic Ruthven brothers, is full of Hermetic symbols and references.[530]

There were at least two experts in the 'art of memory' at the Scottish court in the 1590s, and both had strong ties to the queen. William Fowler, Anna's secretary, worked closely with Schaw, her chamberlain as well as being Master of Works. Fowler's manuscripts suggest that he taught the queen 'the art of memory'. This would not be surprising: Anna was intelligent and intellectually curious, and both of her parents had been passionately interested in science, particularly astronomy. The other expert, Alexander Dickson, served as secretary to the Catholic Earl of Erroll, whose wife was one of the queen's closest friends. Therefore, William Schaw was bound to have been influenced by Hermeticism and the 'art of memory'.[531] Certainly, the second Schaw statutes specified that members had to be tested annually in the 'art of memory', so if Logan of Restalrig's mention of the art to Laird Bower actually took place, and was not one of Sprot's inventions, then Robert Logan was clearly a man well versed in Hermeticism, or Masonry, or both. So, too, was King James VI, 'Great Britain's Solomon' – the builder of the Temple – who had an abiding interest in Masonic theory. In April 1601 he went back to Perth to absolve the town of any involvement in the Ruthven brothers' treason. There, he was admitted as a *freeman, mason and fellowcraft of the Lodge of Scoon*', and six dozen glasses were smashed to celebrate his installation.[532]

****

In the immediate aftermath of the tragedy on 5 August, Queen Anna was said at first to be happy that James was safe, but a very different story soon started to emerge.[533] She was furious at James's dismissal of the Ruthven sisters from her service, almost his first act after he got back to Falkland on the evening of 5 August. She effectively went on strike, refusing to leave her bed or get dressed for two days.[534] James tried to placate her by spending an inordinate amount on a French tightrope dancer to entertain her, but Anna was not won over so easily. Two months later, Sir John Carey, the sick Lord Willoughby's deputy and thus the acting governor of Berwick, reported that Anna was 'very narrowly looked unto, and a strait watch kept about her'; Carey claimed that after the birth of her child she was to be kept as a prisoner for speaking out against those who had been in the royal party at Gowrie House. In reality, by the end of the month James and Anna were going out of their way to show their affection for each other. The queen was displaying great kindness to the new knights of Gowrie House, Ramsay, Erskine and Herries; James was proclaiming to all within earshot that he had the best wife in the whole world. The English ambassador was probably not alone in finding this behaviour bizarre, and wondering whether it was not all a show being staged for public consumption.[535] At much the same time, the Master of Gray heard a very different story. Gray was in England, mistrusted by everyone and with a known penchant for exaggeration; but he also had his own sources of information in Scotland, so his evidence should not be dismissed out of hand. According to Gray, James and Anna were in 'very evil menage'. The queen had said publicly that James wished to imprison her, but warned him to beware, 'for she was not the Earl of Gowrie'. The king said he believed she was mad, but Anna replied furiously that he would find she was neither mad nor beside herself if he tried to move against her.[536]

A third account of Anna's words and deeds at this time comes from Roger Aston, who wrote a long letter to Robert Cecil on 1 November. An illegitimate son from a middling Cheshire family, Aston had been domiciled in Scotland for decades, serving first the Regent Lennox and his son Lord Darnley, then King James VI. He simultaneously fed intelligence back to his homeland and served as one of the king's most trusted personal servants. These roles were not as incompatible as they might seem: Aston provided James with a reliable channel of communication to the English authorities. The king heaped him with rewards, giving him over £5,000 in gifts in the decade before 1600. At court, he always dined on the same table as the Duke of Lennox and Sir George Home. In due course, Aston became a knight and James's Master of the Wardrobe in England. He married a sister of

Andrew Stewart, third Lord Ochiltree, and thus became the brother-in-law of Andrew Kerr, one of the king's gentlemen of the bedchamber and the son-in-law of Queen Anna's nurse, the Countess of Gowrie's sister. Therefore, Aston was very well connected at court, and was well placed to obtain particularly revealing information about the actions of the key players.[537] According to him, Sir George Home, the future Earl of Dunbar, spoke plainly to James about the queen's role in the 'Gowrie House affair': 'what the queen's part in the matter [was], God knows', Aston added.

> The presumptions were great both by letters and tokens,* as also by her own behaviour after the deed was done. All which was laid open before the king [by Home] and yet he could not be persuaded to take up the matter right, but has and does seek by all means to cover her folly. She has now won so far in to the king by her behaviour towards him as no man dare deal in that matter further. She does daily keep the preaching and entertains the king in a more kind and more loving sort than ever she did before. She now will obey the king in whatsoever, and his will shall be obeyed.[538]

If Aston was correct, Home clearly possessed secret knowledge of the backdrop to the 'Gowrie House affair'. In later years, it was alleged that he had been heaped with honours to ensure that he kept his mouth shut,[539] and his role in the 'Sprot/Logan' affair looks suspiciously like an attempt at a cover-up, ensuring that no inconvenient names were named by the Eyemouth forger. The same agenda can be detected eight years earlier. Up until about 14 or 15 August 1600, the government seemed keen to pursue the anonymous but undoubtedly powerful accomplices who were presumed to have been behind Gowrie, stated loudly that this was what it was doing, and seemed to consider Bothwell the most likely candidate for the role. Within days, though, this policy was quietly dropped and replaced by an apparent need to obliterate any suggestion of a broader conspiracy. This abrupt change of direction coincided exactly with the third week of August, and a possible explanation can be found in the death during that week of little Princess Margaret. Already consumed

---

* ie, between Anna and the Ruthvens, before 5 August.

by grief for the deaths of her Ruthven friends and anger at the expulsion of her Ruthven servants, the death of her daughter made Queen Anna hysterical and inconsolable, and perhaps some uncomfortable and unguarded truths emerged from the grieving queen.

In the immediate aftermath of 5 August, the interrogation of witnesses and the pursuit of alleged accomplices was organised by Home and the Chancellor, the Earl of Montrose. Only a few weeks earlier, Gowrie had been said to be politically inseparable from Montrose, his sister's father-in-law, but perhaps the Countess of Gowrie's vitriolic insult directed at the Earl of Montrose on 6 August, 'Ah, ah! False traitor! Thief!' was really an oblique hint that Montrose had betrayed her sons.[540] Montrose feared that he was about to be dismissed from the chancellorship and replaced by Mar, so he and his friends might have been prepared to contemplate a bold counter-stroke.[541] Therefore, it is just possible that, along with the queen herself, the 'Chamber faction' also knew of, and tacitly sponsored, Gowrie's plot. None of its leaders rode to Gowrie House, unlike Mar, whose decision to ride to Perth with James could have unexpectedly played into the hands of the 'Chamber', the queen, and the executors of their projected coup, the Ruthven brothers. If the king had disappeared in the afternoon of 5 August, the 'Chamber' would automatically have assumed control at both Falkland and Edinburgh (which, to some extent, is what actually happened). If he had reappeared, even if under duress, to order the release of Prince Henry to the queen, the 'Chamber' would have implemented those orders, because Mar, crucially, would not have been at Stirling Castle to resist them. If there is any substance to this reading of events, the likes of Montrose and Home would have had every reason immediately to cover their tracks. Home's apparent attempt to blame the queen for the conspiracy ensured his immediate survival and his future indispensability to the crown, but it begs an obvious question: how, exactly, did Home come to know so much about the queen's role in the plot, unless he had been involved in it himself in some way? Faced with such evidence of rampant disloyalty throughout his palace and government, King James had every cause to connive in a cover-up, if only to ensure that his wife's name was kept out of the inquest into the events at Gowrie House and that his own weakness as a monarch was not exposed to the world.

Thus it undoubtedly came to suit all concerned to concur with the proposition that the Ruthven brothers, acting alone, tried to kill the king at Gowrie House on 5 August 1600. This need to cover tracks might explain why the government was so keen to reverse its previous policy of pursuing accomplices by promulgating the deposition made by Gowrie's tutor, William Rynd, on 22 August 1600. Rynd testified to a panel chaired by Montrose that the Earl of Gowrie had been convinced of the truth of one of Machiavelli's dictums, that 'he was not a wise man, that having intended the execution of a high and dangerous purpose, communicate the same to any but himself; because keeping it to himself, it could not be discovered nor disappointed'.[542] Rynd's story was corroborated by the Minister of Perth, so it seems likely that Gowrie was influenced by Machiavelli's opinion; but that does not preclude the possibility that Gowrie was part of a wider conspiracy, with anonymous accomplices in high places, and that he deliberately kept the plans for executing the plot from his confederates (with the debatable exception of Logan of Restalrig). Drawing more and more conspirators into a plot, and entrusting them with its details, is usually a sure path to betrayal by the 'weakest link', and hence to the failure of the whole scheme – a lesson that was lost on the Gunpowder Plotters five years later, who made precisely that simple mistake. Conversely, if the Ruthvens' scheme backfired, they alone would take the blame, and their accomplices could (almost) legitimately deny all knowledge of any conspiracy.

On 19 November, just over a fortnight after Aston wrote his letter about the queen's role, and on the very day that saw the dismembering of the Ruthven brothers' bodies, Queen Anna was delivered of her child, Prince Charles. The king rode to be with her at Dunfermline, and Nicolson reported that 'they never loved better'. But James also brought with him the Earl of Mar, and effected a nominal reconciliation between the queen and her son's guardian.[543] For a few months, at least, James and Anna remained on reasonably good terms. Sometime in the spring of 1601 they conceived another child, Robert, Duke of Kintyre, who lived for just three months in 1602. But the shadow of the 'Gowrie Conspiracy', and Anna's lingering resentment over her enforced separation from her eldest son, continued to fester in the background of their relationship. She made Henry's return to her one of the key conditions of her forgiveness to those who had been her enemies, such as Ramsay and Erskine.[544] By the spring of 1601 she was working against Mar once more and refusing to attend the sermons of Patrick Galloway, whom she detested for his key role in the propaganda campaign against the Ruthvens.[545] In June 1601 Galloway was dismissed from court at the queen's instigation.[546] By the end of 1602, Anna's determination to avenge or restore the Ruthvens was said to be common knowledge, and the English agent described her as 'that violent woman'. In January 1603 Beatrix Ruthven was secretly admitted to the queen's quarters, and had a long conversation with her.[547] James was predictably furious: he immediately brought in workmen to block up some of the passages between the queen's quarters and his, and made all of Anna's servants swear on oath that they would prevent any further contact with the Ruthvens.[548] At the end of January, some two months before James' and Anna's lives were transformed by the death of Queen Elizabeth of England, Roger Aston had a long conversation with the Queen of Scots, during which Anna admitted freely that she still loved the members of the 'House of Gowrie'.[549]

The queen's determination to right the perceived wrong done to her Ruthven friends was clearly consistent and abiding. So, too, was her other unshakeable objective: to get Henry back. Her husband's departure to claim the English throne gave her perhaps her best opportunity since August 1600. James had arranged for Anna and the children to follow him south in May 1603, but on 4 May she turned up at Stirling Castle with a party of supporters and demanded that Henry be handed over to her. The Earl of Mar was in England with the king, but his wife steadfastly refused to accede to the queen's demand: Mary Stuart, Countess of Mar, was the Duke of Lennox's sister, King James's cousin, and thus of the blood royal, so she was hardly likely to be intimidated by a queen's peremptory commands. An awkward standoff developed. The stress of it all proved too much for the queen, who was four months pregnant and miscarried of a son on 10 May – a self-induced act, according to one report. Anna was put to bed to recover in the hostile surroundings of Stirling Castle. While she lay there, the Earl of Mar returned, having hurried back north to deal with the crisis. James had ordered him to bring both the queen and Prince Henry to England, but Anna refused to travel with Mar, who in turn refused to travel without the prince. In the circumstances, James had few options. He gave in to his implacably strong-willed wife, effectively dismissed Mar from his role as Henry's guardian, and sent north the one man whom all parties trusted and who could be relied on to sort out the mess: Ludovic Stuart, Duke of Lennox.[550] Having got what she wanted, Anna left Stirling on 27 May and entered England on 1 June. On 25 July, she was crowned Queen of England during James's coronation service. In due course, she got Barbara Ruthven back, but she also lost her cherished son: Henry, Prince of Wales, died on 6 November 1612, three months short of his nineteenth birthday.

****

Queen Anna's regard for the Ruthvens was shared by Britain's other crowned female. For the last 30 months of her life, Queen Elizabeth I sheltered and subsidised the surviving members of the family.[551] However, her death in March 1603 put paid to their security. As James VI and I made his leisurely progress south through his new kingdom, he continued to pursue the Ruthvens. At Belvoir Castle on St George's Day 1603, James wrote a letter to the English Privy Council. Above all, he wanted a proclamation for the arrest of the brothers of 'the traitor, the Earl of Gowrie'. He reserved most of his venom for one of their sisters. Barbara Ruthven, 'a woman of lewd behaviour of body' and 'ill minded toward us', was to be summoned before the Council and then exiled from the British Isles.[552] The proclamation to arrest William and Patrick was duly issued, signed by James at Burghley House on 27 April – one of his first official executive actions as King of England. According to the proclamation, the Ruthvens had 'crept into this kingdom with malicious hearts against him, disguising themselves in secret places, where he is informed that they not only utter cankered speeches against him but are practising and contriving dangerous plots and desperate attempts against his royal person'.[553] But despite the subsequent arrest of Patrick Ruthven at Kirkby Malzeard, James's attitude towards the family then softened rapidly and mysteriously. On 30 May, he wrote from Greenwich to Countess Dorothea, ordering her to keep Barbara under house arrest; within a month, forlornly wandering the globe had been downgraded to strolling through the gardens of Dirleton. Even this demand was soon relaxed. On 19 June, Barbara wrote to the English Privy Council to thank the king for commiserating with her 'unhappy and hard estate', and for showing her clemency. By his command, she was about to retire into the country.[554] In September 1603 she was granted a pension of £200 a year 'in commiseration of her distress'; although her family was 'hateful on account of the abominable attempt against the king, she has shown no malicious disposition'.[555] Within the space of just five months, something or someone had clearly brought about a dramatic sea change in King James's attitude towards at least one of the Ruthven family. That someone was almost certainly Robert Cecil, the king's chief minister in England and the man to whom he effectively owed his throne. The something was probably the fact that Cecil was sleeping with Barbara Ruthven.

Early in 1604, the Earl of Mar returned to Scotland and wrote a bizarre letter to Cecil:

> Amongst many other news I found before me here at my first coming one was most frequent, that my Lord Cecil should marry Barbara Ruthven. In truth this has been enquired of me by twenty sundry since my homecoming, and I cannot conceive what should move any man to imagine this, except perhaps some who think you would be even with Sir Thomas Kennedy, and take his mistress over his head as he has done yours.[556]

There seems to be no other reference to these intricate and intriguing sexual shenanigans. Sir 'Thomas' Kennedy must be an error for Sir John, who was one of the king's Scottish attendants; in 1622 Lady Barbara Ruthven acted as administratrix for the deceased Sir John Kennedy. Sir John had an illegitimate daughter, Dorothy, his sole heiress and intended executrix. The fact that she had the same name as Barbara's mother, King James's reference to Barbara's 'lewd behaviour of body', and Barbara's intervention in the probate process, all point to Dorothy being the child of Sir John Kennedy and Barbara Ruthven.[557] In the light of this, it is more than likely that Sir John was the mysterious 'Kennedy' who hastily sent word to Dirleton Castle of the attempt to arrest Barbara's brothers, and thereby probably saved their lives. As for the reference to Robert Cecil's previous mistress, this must be an allusion to the fact that in 1603 Sir John Kennedy married Elizabeth Brydges, the glamorous and very rich heiress of Sudeley Castle in Gloucestershire, who had previously been wooed by Cecil's bitter rival, the Earl of Essex. Kennedy's marriage to Elizabeth ended violently in 1609, when Lady Kennedy turned up at a neighbour's house 'bare legged, in her petticoat, old cloak and night gear', having been thrown out by her husband.[558] Thanks to Queen Anna's continued friendship and patronage – and perhaps to the influence of her alleged lover, Robert Cecil – Barbara Ruthven gradually returned to court and in 1617 even became the queen's chief lady-in-waiting. But Anna died just two years later and her court was broken up, forcing Barbara into debt so serious that she contemplated marriage, retirement to Scotland, or both.[559] Barbara chose marriage, namely to one Gilbert Seaton, but this proved short-lived; she was buried at Greenwich on 29 December 1625, aged about 50.[560]

Meanwhile, her last surviving brother, Patrick Ruthven was finally released from the Tower in August 1622. From 1616 Patrick had been paid an annual pension of £200 from the Exchequer, a sum intended to fund 'apparel, books, physic, and such other necessities'.[561] Securing payment of the pension was a constant battle: earlier in 1622 he tried to bribe the Lord Treasurer's secretary to secure the payment of almost two years' arrears.[562] However, on his release the sum was increased to £500, and the royal grant described him as 'our well-beloved Patrick Ruthven, esquire'.[563] With this income, the freed Patrick could maintain something like a gentleman's estate, if not that of an Earl of Gowrie. His release was conditional on his staying exclusively in the Cambridge area: Patrick seems to have lodged at Haslingfield, presumably with the local lord of the manor, Sir William Wendy, whose ancestor had been the royal physician to Henry VIII, Edward VI and Queen Mary.[564] For someone with Ruthven's scientific and medical interests, there could hardly have been more suitable 'student digs'. However, he did not stay there for very long, as in February 1624 he was granted royal permission to live in Somerset.[565]

Patrick's release was naturally of more than a little interest to those two ageing survivors of the Gowrie House affair, the Earls of Kellie and Mar. On 13 August 1622 Kellie (the erstwhile Sir Thomas Erskine) wrote to his cousin Mar about the possible explanations:

> Your lordship may perhaps hear that Holdernesse is the
> doer of it, but it is not he that has done it, though he
> was long about it. My niece, the Lady Gerard, is the
> doer of it, and by the moyen [= *mediation*] of my Lord of
> Buckingham. It is thought that he should marry her, and
> if so be I wish that it may be for both their goods.[566]

'Lady Gerard' had been born Elizabeth Woodford; she was the widow of Thomas, Lord Gerard, Lord President of Wales, who died early in 1618, and was thus a remarkably prestigious match for a man who was still technically a state prisoner. She and Patrick were probably married by 1623, when their daughter Mary was born. William followed in 1625 but died young; Patrick was born on 16 April 1628, followed by Robert in 1629 and Elizabeth in 1633.[567] Nothing more is known of Lady Gerard, who was evidently dead before 1639, but 'my lord of Buckingham', George Villiers, was the favourite of both the king and the Prince of Wales. James had been seriously ill in 1619, and thereafter power passed increasingly into the hands of Buckingham and Charles. The prince evidently never believed that there had been a plot against his father at Gowrie House; at least, that was the story passed down to Patrick Ruthven's descendants. Charles apparently presided over the Privy Council meeting in 1622 that gave the order to set Patrick free, and presumably also authorised the more than doubling of his pension.[568] Patrick's cause might also have been aided indirectly by the death of Queen Anna in March 1619. If the queen had been implicated in the 'Gowrie House affair' in any way, then there could no longer be any danger to her from Patrick or any of the Ruthvens.[569]

The Earl of Kellie's letter suggests that even if he was not directly responsible for Patrick Ruthven's release, the Earl of Holdernesse clearly supported the move and had been working towards it for some time;[570] and 22 years earlier the Earl of Holdernesse had been John Ramsay, the man who killed Patrick's brothers. The Earl of Kellie's own niece was to marry Patrick; and 22 years earlier the Earl of Kellie had been Sir Thomas Erskine, the man who had denounced the last Earl of Gowrie as a traitor to his face, moments before his death. Moreover, both Kellie and the Earl of Mar, the same Earl of Mar to whom the king had cried for help from the turret chamber window in Gowrie House, plainly welcomed this marriage. Perhaps with the queen dead and the king clearly not long for the world, those most directly responsible for the outcome of events on 5 August 1600 simply decided that it was time to forgive and forget.

The comparative and increasing leniency shown towards Patrick and Barbara Ruthven during James's reign mirrored the treatment of the family as a whole.[571] A few changed their names to comply with the law, but very many did not. Throughout the king's reign, the name of Ruthven recurs time and again in Scottish wills and parish registers. The Ruthven who was most closely under his control, Patrick, was generally referred to as 'Ruthen' and signed himself as such: a 'name change' so feeble as truly to make an ass of the law. In reality, James I's injunction against the very name of Ruthven was a dead letter almost from the start. William Ruthven of Freeland used his own surname on a charter as early as 1607, his son Thomas was knighted under it in 1633. It remained only to formalise the situation. On 12 and 17 November 1640 a Scots Parliament dominated by the crown's opponents, the Covenanters, ratified two measures that effectively rehabilitated the Ruthvens. The Ballindean line of the family was legally permitted to bear their old surname again; not that, in practice, any of them had ever abandoned it. Patrick Ruthven, too, was given back his surname and the right to own property.[572] Crucially, though, he was not given back the titles and lands that were rightfully his, although at some point before 1631 he had drawn up a detailed 'to do' list of the steps necessary for the restoration of the titles to himself.[573] As it was, the Covenanter leadership desperately needed the support of powerful landowners in their struggle against the king, and were hardly likely to take lands off them to restore the earldom of Gowrie to Patrick Ruthven. Moreover, Ruthven was far away in London, out of sight and out of mind. He was also tainted by two traits that made him anathema to the Covenanters: he had converted to Catholicism, and he had become a client of the man whose father his brothers had allegedly tried to kill.

****

During the 1630s Patrick Ruthven became something of a figure at the court of King Charles I and Queen Henrietta Maria. His medical 'career' no doubt opened doors for him, but his curious past must also have helped him to acquire patients from among the voyeuristic. He also seems to have acted informally as the London agent for at least one Scottish aristocrat: in June 1639 he informed an anonymous 'my lord' that he had discussed his 'matter of Galloway' with the Earls of Argyll and Stirling, and enquired if there was anything else he could do for the recipient 'in this country'.[574] Ruthven's contacts paved the way for his daughter's stellar but all too brief career. By the late 1630s, Mary Ruthven was one of the ladies-in-waiting to the queen. Although she had no fortune to bring to any marriage, her status, high birth, and obvious friendship with the queen made her an attractive proposition for the eligible bachelors who thronged the court. Better still, Mary was undoubtedly very beautiful. That much is certain from her portrait, painted by the man who won the contest for her hand; and few would dispute her new husband's ability to record a face on canvas.

Mary Ruthven, aged about 17, married Sir Anthony Van Dyck, aged 40, in Queen Henrietta Maria's private Catholic chapel at Somerset House on the frosty morning of 27 February 1640. On that day, Patrick Ruthven, 'of St Martin's in the Fields', assigned £120 of his pension to

Mary, perhaps in lieu of the dowry that he could not afford. Mary Ruthven had a small dowry all the same; it was provided, not by her father, but by King Charles himself.[575] The days when the Ruthvens had been seen as a threat to the monarchy and as the standard-bearers of Presbyterianism were long gone. Sir Anthony was a devout Catholic, the queen's chapel was the only legal Catholic place of worship in England, and the glorious portrait that he painted of his young wife shows her delicately fingering her rosary.[576] At some point Van Dyck also painted a double portrait of himself with his new father-in-law; this was seen at Knole in Kent in about 1785 by Joseph Gulston, who married one of Patrick's great-great-great-great-granddaughters. Gulston described 'the Earl of Gowry': 'hand very fine, glove on the other. Full front breastplate. Melancholy. Long hair hid and white slash'd habit. Leans on his sword. Green sash, buff apron'.[577] The painting has disappeared long since, as has the extraordinary and unprecedented group painting that Van Dyck made of himself, his new wife, and their closest friends: the King and Queen of Great Britain.[578]

On 1 December 1640 Mary gave birth to the Van Dycks' child, a healthy daughter. But the artist's health had failed. On 9 December, Sir Anthony Van Dyck died in his home at Blackfriars, surrounded by unsold and unfinished artwork; an inventory of his possessions apparently totalled some £13,000-worth of jewels, paintings, and 'rich household stuff'.[579] But that same day a christening ceremony took place at St Ann's church, south of Ludgate, now just a few forlorn stones hidden in an alley near St Paul's Cathedral, where Sir Anthony would be laid to rest. Thus, as her father's life entered its final hours, the tiny girl was christened Justina Mariana Van Dyck. Perhaps her grandfather Patrick Ruthven was present, and he seems immediately to have become the protector of his infant granddaughter's interests. After all, under the terms of Van Dyck's will little Justina was the co-heiress with her mother of Sir Anthony's very substantial fortune,[580] and in due course, she would also become the heiress of the Ruthvens, Earls of Gowrie.

In July or August 1642, as England and Wales slid inexorably into civil war, Mary Ruthven married again, this time to Sir Richard Pryse of Gogerddan, a few miles outside Aberystwyth in Cardiganshire. When the new Lady Pryse went down to Wales, her inherited wealth caused much Cymric jaw-dropping: she brought with her the likes of a £400 pearl necklace, a rich Arras hanging and a damask bed. But before the end of 1644 Mary, Lady Pryse, formerly Lady Van Dyck, née Ruthven, was dead, aged no more than 21. An orphan at the age of three, Justina was left in the care of her stepfather, miles behind Royalist lines, while most of the fortune to which she was now sole heiress was still in her father's house in Parliamentarian London. But she still had one person who could speak out for her in the capital: her grandfather. In March 1645 Patrick petitioned the House of Lords on behalf of his 'fatherless and motherless' granddaughter Justina.[581] He claimed that one Richard Andrews had been removing Van Dyck's paintings from his house at Blackfriars, under-valuing them to pay off Sir Richard Pryse's creditors, and then sending them abroad, where he sold them on at huge profits. Other of Pryse's creditors were simply wandering into the Blackfriars property and taking what they wanted.[582] Ruthven asked the Lords to order a halt to further exports, which they seem to have done, but in February 1647 he had to go back to them, complaining that Andrews had flouted their order and was continuing to send Van Dyck's possessions abroad.[583]

There is evidence suggesting that Sir Richard Pryse was not quite the innocent party in all of this that he initially seems to be. Years later, a former employee of his testified that, although the story of the Blackfriars paintings was correct as far as it went, it was also true that Pryse was systematically siphoning off for his own and his son's use that part of Van Dyck's inheritance that he and Lady Mary had managed to get out of London before travel between the capital and Cardiganshire became well-nigh impossible because of the war. The civil war and its aftermath made it virtually impossible to prevent Andrews and Pryse doing what they liked. Patrick probably never saw his grand-daughter again, for she was brought up by her stepfather in Cardiganshire. A witness later testified that Sir Richard Pryse could not have spent very much on her education, 'for he only gave her diet and clothes as a gentlewoman ordinarily [has] in the country ... [but] that she had a maid for most of the time to wait on her'.[584] Intriguingly, though, Pryse evidently complied with the wishes of Justina's dead parents in one crucial respect: she was brought up as a Catholic.

In 1648 Justina's grandfather Patrick Ruthven drew up a power of attorney to Lettice Ellinsworth of Westminster, giving her powers over his pension of £500 per annum. The civil war was over, the king was defeated, and perhaps Patrick felt it was time to be bold: at first, he signed the document as 'Earl of Gowrie', proof positive that his brother William was dead and that, at least in his own mind, he was now the fifth earl by right. But then he had second thoughts, and discretion got the better of him: he struck out 'Gowrie' and replaced it with 'Ruthven'. In April 1651 he issued another power of attorney, signing as 'Patrick, Lord Ruthven'.[585] At much the same time, a scurrilous history of James I's court outlined Patrick's earlier life, and then described his present circumstances: 'now failing, he walks the streets, poor, but well experienced also in chemical physic, and in other parts of learning, which he got, whilst he lost his liberty'.[586] On 24 May 1652, Patrick Ruthven died in poverty, aged 68, in the King's Bench prison. The last of the tragic children of the first Earl of Gowrie and Countess Dorothea was buried at St George's, Southwark.[587]

****

Patrick Ruthven's eponymous son, born in London in April 1628, married Sarah Head on 14 July 1656 at St Martin-in-the-Fields and in November of that year submitted a petition to the Lord Protector, Oliver Cromwell.[588] The petition is an astonishing mixture of errors and downright untruths: either young Patrick had been seriously misled about his family's history, or he was deliberately distorting the record. Firstly, he claimed that he was the grandson of John, Earl of Gowrie, 'whose life, honour and estate were sacrificed to the court pretence of a conspiracy'. Even if he had confused his uncle John with his grandfather William, this was an astonishingly crass mistake to make. Patrick junior then recounted his father's 19-year imprisonment in the Tower accurately enough, but claimed that the main Ruthven barony had been restored by the Scots Parliament, rather than just the cadet branch of Ballindean. He claimed that he was entitled to his father's pension of £500 per annum, by then in arrears of some £5,000. He claimed that payment had been forgotten due to 'the distractions of these times' (the civil war), leading his father into debt 'which cast him into prison, where he died, leaving the petitioner and another son [Robert] in a very poor and lamentable condition'.[589] Patrick finished pitifully: 'that your Highness would be pleased, if not to restore him to his family's former splendour, yet to such a subsistence as may not altogether misbecome the quality of a gentleman, honour with beggary being an unsupportable affliction'. Cromwell referred the petition to his council, recommending a 'tender and speedy consideration' of it; instead, they seem to have buried it. Perhaps someone had unearthed the notes someone else in the regime had made on Patrick six years before. These described him as 'a most violent and bitter fellow against the Parliament', who had lived for some time in Sweden and had solicited unspecified rewards from the exiled King Charles II – presumably the same sorts of rewards that he now sought from Charles's bitterest enemy, the Lord Protector.[590]

In September 1667 Patrick took a second wife. As 'Ruthven, Patrick, Lord ... widower, 39', then residing at the Little Almonry, Westminster, he married Jane MacDannell of Ross-shire, a widow of 42. After that, Patrick disappears entirely from the record. Jane's age at marriage, and the absence of any christening records for children of his first marriage, presumably means that he died without issue. There is no other reference to his 'very poor and lamentable' brother Robert after the mention in the 1656 petition, and certainly no record of his marriage, so he, too, almost certainly died in poverty and obscurity, without any legitimate heirs to carry on the Ruthven name. At any rate, no descendants of Patrick or Robert Ruthven ever came forward, and Justina became the sole claimant to the family's lost titles and estates. In the early 1650s, when she was in her early teens, she married John Stepney, the nephew and heir of Sir John Stepney, third baronet of Prendergast in Pembrokeshire. The claim to the lost Ruthven titles passed to their descendants. One, the last Prendergast baronet, was groom to the 'grand old Duke of York' and was promised the earldom of Gowrie if the duke became king, but both men died in the 1820s before the promise could be effected.[591] In 1863–4 another of the family got as far as framing a petition to Queen Victoria, requesting the restoration of the Ruthven titles,[592] and even in the 1990s, with the Earldom of Gowrie itself in the hands of a 'famously charming' scion of the Freeland line, the heirs of Justina, of Patrick Ruthven and the original earls were still investigating a restoration of the lesser Ruthven titles.[593]

****

Tibi soli: for thee alone; but not quite alone. On 5 August 1600 the Ruthvens acted in whatever they regarded as being in their own best interests; in the history of the Ruthven family, unadulterated altruism tended to be in short supply. Whatever else they hoped to achieve during that sultry afternoon in Perth, or perhaps in the following days at Fast or Dirleton castles, John and Sandy Ruthven might have been acting directly or indirectly on behalf of one or more of several people. One was Francis Stewart, Earl of Bothwell, Gowrie's old friend, who would be restored to his lands and honours. One was Robert Cecil, whose struggle to the death with the Earl of Essex hinged on the attitude and fate of James, King of Scots. One was Queen Anna of Denmark, James's wife. Then there was the shadowy 'Chamber', the faction of Lord Chancellor Montrose, Secretary Elphinstone and Sir

George Home, which might have sought to win their vicious power struggle with the Earl of Mar by doing what Scottish factions had often done to Scottish monarchs.

These are the obvious candidates for the role of the mysterious, powerful 'backer' of the 'Gowrie Conspiracy', and the candidacies of several of them, Bothwell and Queen Anna on one hand, Anna and the 'Chamber' on the other, are not necessarily mutually exclusive. After all, Anna had always liked Bothwell, whom she found glamorous and fascinating; in 1595 she even faced an accusation that 'Bothwell went commonly to bed with her'.[594] Coupling Bothwell's restoration to the demand to liberate her son from Mar and Stirling Castle might not have been too high a price for her to pay for Ruthven support. Moreover, if Prince Henry was to be pried from the grip of her husband and the Earl of Mar, Anna would need powerful allies to ensure that the *status quo ante* was not restored. If such a secret alliance between the queen and the earl really existed, it might have been initiated by the emotionally overwrought Anna; but it is much more likely to have been initiated by the calculating old schemer, Bothwell, and his young lieutenant Gowrie, with his direct access to the queen through his sisters. The members of the 'Chamber' might have considered that bringing back the erratic Bothwell was a price worth paying for unchallenged political power. A little later, in 1602, it was confidently reported to the English court that the 'Chamber' wanted to bring Bothwell back to Scotland for precisely that reason, and after all, the Earl of Montrose had been Bothwell's ally in the early 1590s, along with the tragic Earl of Gowrie.

When set against all the other possible motives for their actions, the theory that the Ruthven brothers sought somehow to persuade King James to release Prince Henry into his mother's custody appears to be the most credible. If Sandy Ruthven really did seek only to extract a promise from the king, as Andrew Henderson claimed, then this is probably the only promise obtained under duress that could have remained binding after the brothers released James: after all, it is essentially what happened in 1603, when Anna tested her will against her husband's and won. Killing the king would not have achieved Anna's aim in 1600 or 1603, as James's instructions to Mar specified that Henry should remain with the earl until the age of 18, and should not be given to the queen even if James himself died.[595] If compelling James to release the prince and restore Bothwell really was the basis of the Ruthven brothers' scheme, then their ideal outcome would probably have seen James acceding immediately to their entirely reasonable and just demands when presented with them by Sandy Ruthven in the turret chamber. If he perversely refused to do so, the king would be removed from Gowrie House and detained – perhaps at Fast Castle if there is any truth in the 'Sprot/Logan' letters, perhaps at Dirleton – until he conceded, just as he had done when abducted by their father 18 years earlier. Perhaps the brothers had it in mind that if he did not agree to their demands, they would force him to abdicate – just as his mother had done when detained by their father 33 years earlier.

The abdication of James VI seems inconceivable as an outcome, as it would surely have been to Queen Anna's detriment; but in fact, the opposite is the case. With her son installed on the throne of Scotland as King Henry I, Anna undoubtedly would have been the strongest candidate to be regent. After all, there was the powerful and relatively recent precedent of Queen Marie de Guise, both Queen Mother and Regent of Scotland. An abdication would have transformed Anna at a stroke from a decorative but largely impotent consort into the ruler of Scotland, and she would have remained so for anything up to 15 years. From this new position of strength, Anna would hardly have been too harsh on the Ruthven family, given the prominence of Beatrix and Barbara Ruthven in her own household, her apparent affection for Gowrie and Sandy, and the tense relationship between herself and a husband thankfully removed from the scene by one means or another. All in all, if the 'Gowrie Conspiracy' had succeeded, there was a chance that Queen Anna would have emerged from the events of 5 August 1600 as the new ruler of Scotland, supported by her trusty friends the Earls of Gowrie and Bothwell. Failing that, at the very least she would have been a mother who had got back her child.

CHAPTER TEN

THE TRUTHS LONG CONCEALED

The truth of what happened in the turret chamber at Gowrie House on 5 August 1600 died with King James VI and I at Theobalds in Hertfordshire on 27 March 1625, and it can probably never now be established for certain. To hazard even a guess at what happened in that tiny confined space, and why it happened, is fraught with difficulties. The sources available to historians today are largely the same as those that were available to our predecessors a century or two ago, and those sources, many of which were originally compiled by violent partisans for or against the Ruthvens and King James, are full of contradictions and inconsistencies.[596] Even so, the sources suggest that, on the balance of probabilities, the Ruthven brothers sought in time-honoured fashion to constrain or abduct the king and to force on him a new set of policies. The same balance of probabilities suggests that the Ruthvens did not act alone, and that at least in its inception their scheme involved the tacit support of high-ranking accomplices in Scotland, and perhaps in England too, their principal objective being to restore the custody of Prince Henry to Queen Anna. Nevertheless, 'balance of probabilities', resting on evidence that is inevitably largely circumstantial, will always permit doubt, disagreement and argument. No doubt some will have read the evidence for and against the theories set out in the preceding chapters and will have come to entirely different conclusions of their own, regardless of the conclusions put forward here. If that is true of the Ruthvens' motives, it is doubly so when considering the events of 5 August 1600 themselves. Whatever the brothers had planned to do, their scheme backfired horribly within the walls of Gowrie House, particularly after King James and Sandy Ruthven left a room full of eye-witnesses and went upstairs alone, and especially in those fateful few minutes in the turret chamber. If what happened there can be reconstructed, it would explain why the elaborate plot to secure the king failed. It might also provide pointers towards what could be the last and darkest secrets of the House of Ruthven.

****

It did not take long after 5 August 1600 for the people who have difficulty with the human obsession with conspiracy theories to make themselves heard. Less than a month after the drama at Gowrie House, Sir William Bowes wrote to one of Queen Elizabeth's courtiers to report a story he had picked up from John Preston, one of James's ambassadors to England. According to this second-hand account, James and Sandy were passing a picture of the first Earl of Gowrie when the king said angrily that he had been a traitor. Sandy protested and swore at him, James panicked, and shouted 'Treason! Treason!' from the window. Now it was Sandy's turn to panic. The youngster manhandled the king to try to persuade him to stop, then fell to his knees before him. But Ramsay and the rest were already on their way, high on adrenaline as they raced to save their king, and through no fault of their own, the Ruthven brothers were doomed.[597] The story of the Earl of Gowrie's picture soon surfaced elsewhere, for example in a derivative History of Scotland produced close to the time and in the report of the French ambassador in London.[598] According to another account, Sandy might have wanted to speak to James privately to discuss his desire to persuade his brother, the earl, to grant him the lucrative estate of Scone Abbey. John Ruthven had been granted it at the age of two, when he was still merely a younger son, and Sandy had been arguing that he should now succeed the earl as Abbot of Scone.[599] Alternatively, perhaps Sandy sought James's guarantee that he would be granted the place as gentleman of the bedchamber that he had long sought.[600] To some writers, these hints have provided the basis of a theory which sees Sandy acting alone against the king while keeping Gowrie entirely ignorant of his intentions; to others, it provides an innocent explanation for Sandy wanting to take James to one side, an action that the king misinterpreted, thereby triggering a series of events that led ultimately to two violent deaths.

The idea of a misunderstanding, an accidental brawl, and a horrific escalation, is a deeply attractive one in many ways. It avoids many of the difficulties with other readings of the 'turret chamber' story, and with all the various 'conspiracy theories'. It also accords well with the long-standing perception of King James's character: that of a coward who might have panicked needlessly in a tense and awkward situation. There are examples of James doing exactly that. In 1593, the Earl of Bothwell was admitted to Holyrood Palace by a combination of conspirators that included the Countess of Gowrie and her daughter, the Countess of Atholl. According to one account, Bothwell surprised the half-naked James as he was coming out of his toilet. The king fled to the queen's chamber door and started hammering on it, screaming 'Annie! Annie! Open the door! Let me in! Annie!'[601] The king's nervousness did not diminish as he got older. In 1617 James visited Sir George Bruce's coal mines at Culross. These were the first mines to extend out under the sea, and were regarded as one of the wonders of the age. Bruce took the king and his party along a mine that came out at a small island, where the coal was loaded directly onto ships. Emerging from the shaft and unexpectedly seeing waves, James panicked and cried 'Treason!' Bruce escaped the fate of the Ruthven brothers by hastily pointing out the pinnace that would take James ashore if he did not wish to return through the mine.[602]

In this light, it is perfectly feasible to look on what happened in the upper rooms of Gowrie House as some sort of hideous accident. James and Sandy Ruthven would have had to get to the turret chamber by going through the first Earl of Gowrie's impressive new gallery, and we know from David Hume and John Ramsay that this gallery contained paintings. It would have been highly unlikely for a portrait of the gallery's creator not to have had pride of place, so it is conceivable that James and Sandy stopped before the image of the first Earl of Gowrie, and that some sort of inappropriate comment was made on one side or the other. It is equally conceivable that *both* of the participants panicked: James because of his nature, and perhaps a sudden realisation of the implications of being alone with a Ruthven; Sandy, struck by the enormity of what he was doing and fast running out of options when his would-be assistant Henderson lost his nerve.[603] If it had all been an accident caused by the king's nervousness and cowardice, his ministers and propagandists would have had cause to invent a conspiracy to explain away the deaths of the Ruthvens (and to justify the subsequent forfeiture of their estates) and to present the king as the gallant hero of the hour. This is a highly attractive proposition, but it simply does not fit the facts. Above all, those who favour the idea of an accidental brawl have to explain away the fact that either Sandy Ruthven deliberately wanted King James to come to Perth, or King James deliberately wanted Sandy Ruthven to take him there.

*****

For those who regard the Ruthvens as guilty men, and equally for those who damn James VI, one of the aspects of the story that has always caused most difficulty is the 'pot of gold'. Why did the brothers invent such a patently ludicrous tale, and why did James fall for it (or else, why did such an intelligent man concoct a 'cover story' so feeble)? Surely, as sceptics said at the time, a pot small enough to be carried by one man was hardly going to be worth the king's attention. In any case, surely the investigation could have been delegated to any of the king's subordinates.[604] Even if the pot-carrier really was a Jesuit, this was hardly cause enough for the king to ride to Perth; Jesuits turned up in Scotland regularly, and James did not go out of his way to chase any of the others. But the 'pot of gold' story is much more credible than it has usually been acknowledged to be. Throughout the 1580s and 1590s there were persistent rumours that a vast Spanish treasure, intended to finance the reconversion of Scotland to Catholicism, had vanished somewhere in the country; in 1588 it was confidently reported to be at Callander, less than 40 miles from Perth, and even in the 1960s, such rumours could launch a full-scale treasure hunt at Logan of Restalrig's old haunt, Fast Castle.[605] Indeed, on the very day of the drama at Gowrie House one of the Douglases wrote a letter to his uncle, telling of a huge Spanish payment that James had refused because he considered the price – the restoration of Bothwell – to be too high.[606] There was also a new urgency to the pursuit of the old chimera of Spanish gold: James knew that England and Spain had begun preliminary peace negotiations at Boulogne in May, but did not know on 5 August that these had broken down a few days earlier.[607] If there was Spanish treasure to be had in Perth, the King of Scots needed to get his hands on it as quickly as possible, for there was unlikely ever to be any more.

Tellingly, there is also a previously unknown account of the 'Gowrie Conspiracy' that provides substantive corroboration of the royal version of the events in Perth and which adds one crucial detail to the long-discredited story of the 'pot of gold'. The author of this newly discovered account was the highly knowledgeable and well connected Roger Aston. The timing, nature and purpose of Aston's account of the 'Gowrie House affair' all help to establish its credibility. On 15 August 1600 he wrote a long letter from Edinburgh to his 'good brother', an Englishman seeking employment at, and receiving a pension from, the Scottish court.[608] The importance of Aston's account is that he wrote it over a fortnight before the official narrative of the events of 5 August was published, and only four days after James's return to Edinburgh and Patrick Galloway's dramatic sermon that first named Andrew Henderson as the man in armour. It clearly reflects the substance of the story as it was circulating at that moment at court and in the capital; Aston makes it clear that he had been talking to the likes of Sir William Stewart, the king's old military troubleshooter. It is not impossible that Aston had also seen James's original letter from Falkland to the Privy Council, and that at least some of his account is a more detailed and accurate synopsis of that long-lost source than the second- or third-hand summary sent by Nicolson to the English court on 6 August. Aston claimed that his account was a 'very true discourse as you shall see shortly in print': in other words, it was based on essentially the same material that would soon form the official published narrative, and forms a crucial link between the first accounts that emerged in the week after the incident at Gowrie House, and those that emerged a few weeks later.

According to Aston, after Sandy Ruthven described to King James the capture of the strange man in the field, he 'assured the king the man he had taken was newly landed from other parts and had that treasure with letters of credit to sundry of the nobility here, assuring the king it would discover great matters'. This is perfectly compatible with the suggestion that the mystery man was a Jesuit, or some other agent in the pay of the Catholic powers. However, the statement about letters of credit immediately elevates the 'pot of gold' story even further into the realms of the credible. It has echoes of genuine conspiracies in previous times, notably the 'Spanish blanks' affair, and the possibility of examining evidence of disloyalty against named noblemen of his kingdom was something that James simply could not pass up, even if he harboured doubts about Sandy Ruthven's story. But if making public the point about the letters of credit would have strengthened the king's story, why was it not mentioned in the published narrative or the subsequent depositions of the key witnesses? Perhaps James took the view that even mentioning the possibility of disloyalty among his nobility opened too many cans of worms at a time when he desperately needed national unity to bolster his quest for the English throne. His favourite, the Marquess of Huntly, was a Catholic, and his wife, Queen Anna, had recently converted to Rome. If there was a chance, even the slimmest chance, that Sandy Ruthven's story was true, and the letters of credit implicated some of those closest to him, James would have had good cause to ride to Perth, and then to take the apparently astonishing risk of going alone with the Master of Ruthven to view the 'evidence'. Afterwards, James could hardly have admitted that such thoughts were in his mind, so any suspicions of his Catholic spouse and subjects that he might have harboured during the morning of 5 August 1600 were comprehensively hushed up before that day ended. The king and his ministers did not want *any* great names being connected with the Gowrie conspiracy in any shape or form.

Aston's account provides important new information about several other aspects of the events of 5 August. Aston went on to describe the departure of the hunting party for Perth, but again, he provides valuable extra detail, not found in the other accounts. For instance, Aston lists the royal party, and explains why others turned up in Perth in haphazard fashion:

> The whole number that was with his Majesty was not
> above ten persons. Because you shall know all I set-down
> their names: the duke, the Earl of Mar, Sir Thomas
> Askew [*sic* for Erskine] and his brother James, my lord of
> Lindores, William Stewart, the Laird of Orkell,
> Monggogrime's [*sic*; = Montgomery's] son, John Ramsay,
> Doctor Herries and John Moor, page of the chamber as
> Ramsay was. Some of the officers followed, but not so
> soon as the king by a good while.

Aston recorded their reception by the Earl of Gowrie on the South Inch of Perth, and the beginning of the dinner at Gowrie House. Most of the detail of the meal, and Gowrie's toasting of the hunting party, corroborates other accounts, but once again, Aston provides important clarification.

> When his Majesty had almost dined the earl came to the
> duke and the Earl of Mar and desired them with the rest
> of the gentlemen to go to their dinners which they did,
> except Sir Thomas and William Stewart who remained
> still with the king, but the earl being desirous to be quit
> of them as well as the rest pressed his Majesty to
> command them to go to dinner, which he did and they
> obeyed, leaving none in the chamber but the carver and
> Mr Alexander his brother, whom I may call cruel butcher.
> The earl placed them to dinner but would not sit down
> himself, for other matters [were] in his head then.

Aston's account effectively corroborates the deposition of Craigengelt, the carver, *which was taken the day after Aston wrote his letter*, but his information about Erskine and William Stewart is found in no other account of the affair.

Again according to Aston, Sandy Ruthven then quietly urged the king to send his brother away, 'for you must know by the way that Alexander would in no ways have his brother to know of the purpose that was between him and the king'. Then Aston repeats the usual elements of the royal story: the walk through the second floor rooms, with Sandy securing the doors behind them (four doors, in this account), and the arrival at the 'little chamber, where there was a man standing prepared for the purpose'. His account of the actions of James and Sandy in the chamber, and the conversation between them, adds nothing new to the other accounts, but corroborates such details as Henderson's opening of the wrong window, and Sandy's bringing a garter to bind the king. In Aston's version of events, James then cried:

> 'I am a free prince and I will die before I be bound', and with that leapt to his neck and got him [Sandy] by the throat; he got the king by the cheekblade [*sic*], having two fingers in his mouth. They struggled a long time, the king having the better of him [so] that he was constrained to cry upon the other [man] for help, who answered 'I have no power to help, my power is taken from me'. Contending thus a good while, his Majesty being sore fought on, and it was no [small] marvel, for he dealt with a very able man as was to be found of his years. His Majesty drew himself towards the window which by good fortune was half open[ed] by the man as you heard before, his hands being occupied with his elbow he cast it open, and looking out, the first man he saw was the Earl of Mar, to whom he cried 'Fie! Treason! My Lord of Mar, I am murdered!'

Aston then recounted the rumour of the king's departure, and the coincidence that had brought them directly under the turret chamber while they waited for their horses to arrive. 'The Earl of Gowrie was with the rest as though he knew nothing of the purpose'. Aston describes how Lennox, Mar and the rest raced up the main staircase and through the second floor rooms, finding three of the four doors unlocked, but the final one was still bolted against them, and so strong that it withstood all attempts to break it down.

Aston's account of Ramsay's frantic race up the Black Turnpike, the king's cry to him 'Fie, Ramsay, strike the traitor!', his discarding of his inconvenient sparrowhawk, and his stabbing of the Master of Ruthven, corroborates the other accounts, although Aston added one evocative detail: Ramsay 'drew his dagger and struck Alexander four strokes low because he had a secret *[doublet]* upon him, the blood sprang out and bled *[onto]* the king'. According to Aston, Sir Thomas Erskine, Dr Herries, 'and a young boy called Wilson, James Erskine's page' then arrived at the top of the turnpike. 'His Majesty having these four which I have named thought himself in safety, but now came on the greatest danger.' Aston recounts Gowrie's arrival with his armed retinue:

> finding his brother lying upon the stair, [Gowrie] came
> forward with Mr Thomas Cranstoun before him came
> to the chamber where his Majesty was, crying 'they shall
> all die!'. Cranstoun fell to Sir Thomas very hotly; the
> earl having two rapiers delivered sharply. Herries
> defended the door and fought very well.

Ramsay cried out that the king was slain, which confused Gowrie, and gave Ramsay the opportunity to run him through. Cranstoun was wounded, 'and shall die on a scaffold': Erskine and Herries were both wounded in the right hand, and Ramsay had been run through the thigh. (Aston's account of the wounds received on both sides is more substantial than that found in any other version of the story.) Aston then recounted the threat posed by the townspeople, until 'gentlemen of the country [presumably the Murrays] came in, and so his Majesty got a sufficient part of the magistrates of the town, who [when] they understood the truth they came upon their knees and craved his Majesty's pardon'.

****

If Roger Aston's account of the 'letters of credit' is true (and it has to be said that no other source even hints at their existence), then it is possible that by omitting any suggestion of disloyalty on the part of his Catholic nobles, King James VI deliberately undermined the credibility of his own version of the events of 5 August for the sake of political and religious stability in Scotland, and for the cause of his succession to the crown of England. It might have been the first of many sins of omission that were committed when King James and his ministers sat down at Falkland, and then at Edinburgh, to consider what had just happened, and what Scotland and the world should be told of it. If there truly had been any plotting by the queen or by senior ministers allied to Gowrie, the truth was kept successfully from the public, from posterity, and perhaps even from James himself: between them, the Earl of Montrose, Sir George Home and the rest managed to bury all the bad news with an adroitness that ought to be the envy of their successors. Similarly, Home's cunning politicking when the 'Sprot/Logan' forgeries unexpectedly emerged eight years later was at once astonishingly cynical and incredibly successful: simultaneously ensuring that no important names became implicated in the Gowrie affair whilst making oneself many thousands of pounds richer is, by the standards of any age, a feat of sheer political genius.

An almost equal measure of cynicism can be detected in one of the other factors that rapidly came to dominate how the story of the 'Gowrie House affair' was assembled and put across to the world. The prospect of forfeiting the lucrative Ruthven estates rapidly took on an unstoppable momentum of its own. Within days of 5 August, it was common knowledge that a parliament would meet in November to forfeit the Ruthven estates for the brothers' treason.[609] To achieve that end, the Earl of Gowrie had to be guilty of treason. Any evidence to the contrary had to be quietly forgotten: Sir William Bowes was undoubtedly correct in suggesting that even if there had never been a 'Gowrie Conspiracy' at all, it rapidly became politically expedient to invent one and to reinforce the story through all available political, spiritual and legal channels.[610] Subsequently, the distribution of the Ruthven lands to so many great men both bound them permanently to the king's version of events and kept them silent about any contradictions inconveniently lodged in their memories. It also ensured that a large and powerful party of beneficiaries would block any subsequent attempts to restore the Ruthvens to their rightful inheritance.[611] Naturally, all of these developments looked suspicious to contemporaries, especially those who already detested the king and his ministers. They looked even more suspicious to later writers, accustomed to supposedly more correct ways of dealing with such fluid concepts as justice and the truth. But in 1600 the royal government of Scotland was constructing a treason prosecution, not breaking a news story or thinking of the reactions of future authors. In terms of their own, very limited, aims, they achieved their objectives completely. In terms of History's judgement upon them, they failed utterly.

King James's ministers were evidently masters of the art of omission, but when it came to informing the world and posterity of their version of events, they managed the affair incompetently from the very outset – at least, when judged by modern standards. The haphazard way in which different versions of the king's story seeped out inevitably led to the charge that witnesses had been suborned and evidence 'modified' to fit the official line; but to be fair to them, James and his ministers were not thinking like 'spin doctors'. Throughout, they were reactive, not proactive: a published narrative emerged only a month after the events at Gowrie House, and only because it was apparent that the versions of the story circulating during that month, through sermons and other channels, had not been sufficient to quell the profound scepticism in Scotland and beyond. The witness statements from the Duke of Lennox and the others who had actually been at Gowrie House were not taken until November, two months after the published narrative emerged, so naturally it seemed to some contemporaries (and even more so to later writers) that those witness statements were compromised by a perceived need to concur with the king's account. But those statements were not actually intended to shore up the king's account at all: they were intended to provide the conclusive proof that the Earl of Gowrie was guilty of high treason, thereby enabling Parliament to forfeit his estates, so the statements simply did not need to be taken until just before the parliament met. True, there were many apparent contradictions and inconsistencies between the various accounts, but James and his advisers explicitly recognised this, and frankly admitted as much to the public. In the final analysis, they explained this apparent problem in a way that accords far better with human nature than some of the more far-fetched conspiracy theories that circulated in the 18th and 19th centuries.

The fifth of August, 1600, was a day of high drama and, for the individuals concerned, a day of the greatest stress imaginable. Those who have experienced such days directly or indirectly know all too well that details become blurred and exaggerated, even within minutes and hours of the events happening. Accounts produced several weeks or months later, following cold reflection, can introduce greater accuracy about some details, but are equally likely to confuse or omit others. Moreover, the evidence of the 'Gowrie Conspiracy' is often secondhand, with all the innate problems of such evidence. The very first piece of written evidence about the events of 5 August, James's letter from Falkland, has disappeared, and only secondhand summaries of it exist. Patrick Galloway's sermon on 11 August was a secondhand version of what James had previously said to him. And so on. In such circumstances, it is not surprising that there were inconsistencies: it would only have been surprising if there had been none.

****

Central to the disbelief that greeted the king's story from the very beginning is the almost supernatural figure of the man in armour. If he was actually present in the turret chamber, and played the part described by James and the other accounts, then he must surely rank as the most pathetic assassin's accomplice in history. That case is strengthened if one accepts that Andrew Henderson was the armoured man: a man who (by his own admission) spent the entire episode paralysed with fear, whose one and only action, the opening of the window, was blighted by the fact that he initially *opened the wrong window*, and whose tale that he had disarmed the Master of Ruthven was almost certainly a lie manufactured to ensure his pardon. If there was no man in armour, then Henderson was just a stooge, parroting the king's script for the promise of a pardon and a pension; and if there was no man in armour, King James VI was at best a liar, at worst a murderer. But the cynics' proposition that James needed a 'third man' in the turret room, to provide corroboration of his story, can cut another way, too. If there never was an armoured man, why did James need to invent one? He had Ramsay's account, and Ramsay had seen him wrestling with the Master of Ruthven in the turret chamber: that evidence alone, added to the word of a king, might have explained the death of Sandy Ruthven more neatly than the unnecessary addition of the man in armour. The king's account would still have been greeted with scepticism, but it would hardly have been greeted with any more than it actually was. By mentioning the armoured man, James created a massive problem for himself. He had to find the man, and the man had to agree with his version of events. Enter Andrew Henderson.

Of all Gowrie's servants who had not actually taken up arms on the afternoon of 5 August, Henderson alone went into hiding, suggesting that he, alone, had something to hide. From that point on, his account of events is actually far more plausible than the Ruthvens' apologists allow. Henderson desperately needed to dig himself out a very deep hole, and to do that, he urgently needed to find a powerful and sympathetic friend. In that context, writing to Patrick Galloway made perfect sense. Although later generations have condemned Galloway as a sycophantic royal puppet, Henderson would have known him as the respected former minister of Perth, who came back to the town soon after 5

August to assist the enquiry into that day's events. Galloway said that Henderson was 'a man that fears God and dealt uprightly with all men', but cynics could easily respond to the effect that he would say that, wouldn't he? Nevertheless, it would have been quite natural for Henderson to approach Galloway as a man that he trusted, and equally natural for Galloway to act as the go-between who eventually secured Henderson's pardon, knowing that the production of the 'armoured man' would strengthen his, Galloway's, place in the king's esteem.

Despite Patrick Galloway's overly theatrical revelation of Henderson's existence during his Edinburgh sermon on 11 August, this interpretation of his sudden reappearance is more likely than the alternative, the conspiracy theory which has the devious Galloway casting around for a suitable stooge and settling on Andrew Henderson. After all, why was the stooge already in hiding, unless he had always been something more than a stooge? No one saw him in Falkland, although it would plainly have strengthened the king's story if a courtier with a flexible conscience had conveniently recalled seeing him there. Later that day, no one claimed to see Henderson anywhere other than in the main body of Gowrie House. Two witnesses, John Ramsay and Robertson the notary, saw him in or near the turret chamber, although their identifications were uncertain.[612] So was the king's, if the story of James claiming to have recognised Henderson's 'smaick' well enough is true. But this was reported only by Calderwood, a staunch partisan of the Kirk and opponent of James, writing long after the event, and in any case, in the turret chamber Henderson's face was probably obscured by a helmet. Not only was there virtually no evidence against Henderson, the king himself sent out virtually a personal signal to the frightened chamberlain in the letter that he dictated at Falkland overnight on 5–6 August: 'the Master [of Ruthven] called to the man there present to kill the king. That the man answered, he had neither heart nor hand; *and yet is a very courageous man* [my emphasis].' The King of Scots himself had stated unequivocally that the man in the chamber was not guilty of treason, and yet Henderson behaved like a terrified little man, caught up in great events beyond his comprehension, and fearful of the interpretation that could be placed on his actions.

Partial corroboration of Henderson's story was provided by Robert Oliphant, a retainer or companion of the Earl of Gowrie. Oliphant, a 'black, grim man', was identified as the 'armoured man' in early accounts of the Gowrie House affair, but then discounted. Late in 1600, though, Oliphant was reported to the Scottish Privy Council for saying that both in Paris and Scotland, Gowrie had tried to recruit him for the role of the 'armoured man'. Oliphant refused, so Gowrie recruited Henderson instead, who lost his nerve when he found himself alone with the King of Scots. If Oliphant was speaking the truth, or anything like it, Henderson therefore had foreknowledge of the plot and lied about it under oath to make himself seem like an innocent dupe. On the other hand, Oliphant's statement dramatically corroborated Henderson's evidence: there really had been an 'armoured man', and Henderson's incompetence in the role can be partly explained by the fact that he was merely a substitute. Oliphant's testimony also raises the possibility that Gowrie mapped out his conspiracy, both in outline and in detail, long before he returned to Scotland in April 1600; if true, this would suggest that John Ruthven had determined upon action against the king long before the queen or his sisters gave him the immediate cause for so doing. Robert Oliphant vanished before he could be arrested for his treasonable words.[613] He turned up again in England in June 1608, at precisely the same time that George Sprot was about to change his testimony yet again. Oliphant was arrested at Canterbury before he could take ship for France and spent nine months in prison, but in the spring of 1609 James ordered his release, yet another example of the much more lenient attitude that he adopted after ascending the English throne towards anyone connected with the 'Gowrie Conspiracy'. The name of Oliphant had come up in one other context on 5 August 1600. When James set off for Perth, his courtiers and attendants set off haphazardly after him. None of them save the Duke of Lennox knew of the 'pot of gold': they thought that James was riding in pursuit of the Master of Oliphant, who had been misbehaving himself in Angus.[614]

****

Many have been suspicious of the discrepancies between Henderson's different accounts. However, James Hudson, one of the English agents in Scotland, managed to speak privately with Henderson in mid-October, and found that he was easily able to reconcile the supposed differences between Henderson's August testimonies and the king's.[615] The same principle can be applied to the differences between the August and November depositions. Apart from the possibility that Henderson naturally recollected events slightly differently three months after his first deposition, it is certainly true that his two depositions were made when his own circumstances were very different. In August, Henderson was desperate to clear himself of any involvement in the Ruthven brothers' conspiracy. Only by doing so could he save his own life, so he blackened Sandy Ruthven's reputation ferociously, emphasising the most horrific interpretation of his actions, and stating baldly that Sandy had sought to assassinate the king. By November, Henderson's pardon was certain, so he no longer needed to prove his own innocence (except to wider public opinion, of course, but that was unlikely to be convinced by anything he said). By then, too, Sandy Ruthven's guilt was taken as read, so the critical imperative was now to condemn the Earl of Gowrie for treason, thereby permitting the forfeiture of the Ruthven lands. For the purposes of King James and his ministers, Henderson's testimony about what Gowrie said on the evening of 4 August and the morning of 5 August was now considerably more important than his evidence of what Sandy Ruthven said and did in the turret chamber.

Even if we accept Henderson as the armoured man, the critical question remains: why did he do nothing in the turret? He claimed to have snatched the dagger that Sandy Ruthven was using to threaten the king, but James himself recalled nothing of this. But if Henderson really did do nothing, the simplest explanation is also probably the most plausible of all: he did nothing because, all along, it had been intended that he should do nothing, or next to nothing. King James VI might not have needed a 'third man' in the turret chamber: but the Ruthven brothers certainly did. Firstly, they needed a witness to the fact that Sandy Ruthven had acted alone against the king. If the plan went wrong, Andrew Henderson's testimony would have added to the considerable weight of evidence exonerating the Earl of Gowrie from any responsibility for the king's kidnapping or death, and thus from any charge of treason against the House of Ruthven. It could be argued that Henderson would have been just a feeble and easily discredited witness for the Ruthvens' story as he turned out to be for the king's; but his evidence became one of the main foundations of the latter, and would have been only a relatively secondary part of the former. Secondly, if the plan was to bundle the king out of Gowrie House to a waiting boat, or to any alternative location by any alternative means, then Sandy Ruthven would have needed an extra pair of hands. Perhaps Thomas Cranstoun or Andrew Ruthven could have joined the kidnappers on the lower floors of Gowrie House, providing the sword-wielding escort that would take King James VI out of Perth, to a place and a fate to be decided by the third Earl of Gowrie and his brother. Thirdly, Henderson's very presence in armour might have been intended to unsettle the king, creating an unbearable psychological pressure that would compel James to agree to whatever the Ruthvens demanded. Not long before the tragedy unfolded at Gowrie House, James was reported to have reminded John, Earl of Gowrie, of the part that his grandfather had played in the murder of David Rizzio, very nearly causing Mary, Queen of Scots to miscarry; and when Patrick, Lord Ruthven, burst into the fateful supper party at Holyrood Palace in 1566, he had been an armoured man. Perhaps John and Sandy Ruthven hoped to convince James that the ghost of their grandfather had returned. If so, Andrew Henderson must rank as one of the least convincing spectres in the history of both play-acting and the paranormal.

Henderson lived to tell yet more tales. He was quietly freed soon after the parliament of November 1600, as was William Rynd, Gowrie's old tutor. Henderson returned to his post as chamberlain of Scone, albeit for its new Murray owner, and was rewarded with a remarkably (and, to many, suspiciously) generous pension from James.[616] In 1603 he became a bailie of Perth and a member of its town council, but he held office for only a year. This was said to have been because he was universally hated in the town, where he was seen as a stooge, coached by the likes of Patrick Galloway to provide an alibi for the tyrant who had murdered Perth's beloved provost.[617] In the next century, he was remembered as not having 'the courage to look a man in the face, but always had the appearance of a crestfallen creature, whose countenance seemed to confess the justice of the general contempt under which he was fallen'.[618] Official records provide some confirmation of the way in which the Gowrie House affair haunted Andrew Henderson for the rest of his life. Barely seven months later, in March 1601, he and Sir Hew Herries argued openly in the street. The prurient licked their lips and looked forward to the truth about the affair emerging at last, but nothing more was heard of it.[619] Henderson bought a fine estate at Lawton, but he quarrelled constantly with his new neighbours, who assumed that his wealth had been obtained through perjury and complicity in murder.[620] In the winter of 1605–6 Henderson was attacked by Agnes Ramsay, the wife of a Perth glass-maker, who threatened to shoot him dead.[621] Two years later he fell out with his new master, Lord Scone. He accused Scone of disloyalty and of taking away the pension James had granted him, but Scone suggested to the king that Henderson was simply being manipulated by others, 'for he was never very wise, and he has lost a good part of the wit which he had'. This certainly seems to be confirmed by a remarkably frank letter that Henderson wrote to the king at this time, which also coincided with the unfolding of the Sprot case; he complained of 'the infamous libels' that were circulating in Perth, namely that 'your Majesty is called a murderer, and my part a manesworne [= *perjured*] knave'. The quarrel between Henderson and Lord Scone smouldered on, and in 1612 Henderson attempted to exploit his 'special relationship' with the king by going in person to the court at Whitehall to complain of Scone's behaviour. Henderson rapidly exhausted any remaining credit he had with the monarch by refusing to accept his verdict that Scone was innocent. He carried on grumbling to James 'of things which were more impertinent and did no way [pertain to] him, so that it appeared clearly that it was not matter, but a conceived malice, that bred in him this idleness'.[622] The king placed him under house arrest. Plainly, Andrew Henderson would be able to extort no more rewards for his knowledge of the Gowrie House affair, and the king was apparently no longer worried about Henderson broadcasting that knowledge in a fit of pique. If Henderson really had been a royal stooge, lying to conceal the truth of what truly happened at Gowrie House, the king's offhand treatment of him makes almost no sense; but if Henderson was telling the truth all along, his capacity to make mischief was negligible. The 'armoured man' had finally been exposed as a man of straw.[623]

****

It has been said that James pursued the Ruthvens with 'extraordinary vindictiveness', and that 'even in the pages of Scottish history … there are few instances of so pitiless and prolonged a vendetta against a noble house'.[624] In fact, nothing could be further from the truth. The comparative and surprising leniency that James showed over the years towards Patrick and Barbara Ruthven, and the part played by John Ramsay in Patrick's release from the Tower, reflected a peculiar ambivalence towards the events of 5 August 1600 on the part of some of the participants in them. Indeed, once tempers cooled and there had been time for reflection, even some of the key players started to doubt what had actually occurred that day. By the middle of October, King James himself was said to be unsure whether the Ruthven brothers really had acted treasonably.[625] The Duke of Lennox allegedly said privately that he did not know whether the events of 5 August had been instigated by Gowrie or the king.[626] This apparent uncertainty, so different to the vehement denunciations of the Ruthvens contained in the official narrative, is reflected in the treatment of some of the 'supporting cast' at Gowrie House, namely those who had been Gowrie's dinner guests before the king arrived in Perth, who were surely the likeliest candidates to have been the earl's chief accomplices. Yet John Moncreiff, the man who had shown John Ramsay around Gowrie House, was granted a pension in 1601 and was knighted in 1604. His brother Hew, who had drawn his sword on Gowrie's behalf and been indicted for treason before Parliament, was restored to his property less than a year later; King James's personal insistence on this led to a bitter quarrel with his Lord Treasurer, who resigned in protest.[627] Almost all the others who had been charged with treason escaped equally lightly. Patrick Eviot was soon pardoned, only to be murdered in bed by his wife a few years later. Harry Ruthven of Freeland also quickly obtained pardon. He was alive in 1610, when he was arrested for uttering treasonable words about the conspiracy. He was arrested, but freed again in April 1611.[628] The one exception to this seemingly inexplicable royal generosity was Harry's brother Alexander, the man who had called for and stolen gunpowder on 5 August 1600, who had been probably the most active leader of the Perth mob that day, and who had allegedly been the man publicly to query the king's paternity. He disappeared from the record, but according to one tradition, he fled to Durham, married, and adopted his wife's surname of Trotter for safety. A few decades later, one of his descendants moved to Downpatrick in Ulster, and this line eventually produced Edward Southwell Trotter, who changed his name back to Ruthven. And so a Ruthven became a thorn in the side of the crown once more, for Edward was one of the most prominent Irish nationalist politicians of the early 19th century.[629]

The treatment of the 'accomplices', and of the surviving Ruthvens themselves, suggests that James and his ministers soon knew that what happened at Gowrie House was not all it had seemed to be; nor, indeed, what it had been made out to be in sermons and the printed word. The abrupt switch from seeking out accomplices of the Ruthvens to the very clear position that they had acted alone suggests that at some point around the third week of August 1600, James learned the truth of what the brothers had intended to do, and the names of those who might have tacitly supported them. It then became imperative to conceal all evidence of this broader plot, especially as the official story of attempted regicide had taken on a momentum of its own and could not be contradicted without the king becoming a laughing stock among his own subjects and his fellow monarchs. The mysterious affair at Gowrie House had been a hellish conspiracy against the Lord's anointed, and its story was known throughout the British Isles and all of Europe. For the sake of King James's public reputation, that story had to be maintained at all costs, even if deep down, many of the inhabitants of Scotland, and England, and perhaps even James Stuart himself, had never really believed in it.

However, the government's desperation to dismiss any talk of accomplices in high places was undoubtedly aided by the pains the Ruthvens had taken to ensure precisely the same end. As well as providing John and Sandy Ruthven with ample precedent for plotting against Scotland's monarchs, their father and grandfather had always made their political moves within, and supported by, extensive kin, neighbourhood and friendship alliances. The last Earl of Gowrie seems deliberately to have gone against this strategy. Instead he favoured secrecy and a reliance on as few immediate accomplices as possible, even if he might have previously sounded others – the queen, or Bothwell, or 'the Chamber faction' – or been sounded by them, together with what seems to have been an unduly elaborate attempt to ensure that he possessed an alibi for whatever his brother was undertaking within Gowrie House. This tight, secretive, overly complex conspiracy might have been a new generation's instinctive rejection of the ways of its predecessors, but it was also almost certainly a by-product of Gowrie's own life and times. By 5 August 1600, he had been in Scotland for just four months in the previous six years. He had spent most of that time in Italy, where he had learned Italian habits: James allegedly chided him with this during Gowrie's last meal on earth, when he referred to the rude foreign manners that he now seemed to prefer to good honest Scots hospitality.[630] Gowrie also picked up the Italian style of sword-fighting, and might also have picked up Italian fashions in conspiracy. By definition, he was far removed from events at home, and the Scotland of 1600 was a very different place from the Scotland that he had left in 1594, already a veteran plotter against James Stuart at the age of just 16. In 1600 the king was more powerful than when Gowrie left for the Continent, and bloodfeud was in decline. Gowrie's prolonged absence from Scotland, and his consequent reliance on deputies to run Perth and Perthshire for him, might have made his neighbours cast covetous eyes over the lands and offices of a family feared for its long-standing interest in the black arts: a euphemism, at least in part, for being highly educated and intellectually curious, not common conditions among a Scottish aristocracy that might have been jealous of such attainment.

John Ruthven could hardly have identified all of the changes in Scotland during the four months that he was back in the country, even if he had wanted to. Instead, he relied on a youthful over-confidence and arrogance, born perhaps of the enthusiastic, head-turning reception he received from everyone from Queen Elizabeth downwards. Perhaps he also believed too much in the protection of his magical charms and in the predictions of astrologers. He certainly depended too much on books, and on one author in particular. The teaching of Machiavelli warned him against recruiting accomplices, unless it was done at the very last minute – which is precisely what he seems to have done in the case of Andrew Henderson, with disastrous consequences. Gowrie was allegedly called home from Europe by two immensely powerful interests that sought his support, the Presbyterian Kirk and the Chamber faction at court. Misinterpreting the political situation, and perhaps misunderstanding the grumbles and hints of his sisters or members of the 'Chamber', John Ruthven decided on precipitate and independent action. He seems to have acted entirely on his own initiative in devising the time, place and method for the attempt on the king. Abstract Italian theory won out over generations of Ruthven family experience; and Machiavelli had not legislated for an elaborate conspiracy being wrecked by the doubts, nerves and inadequate wrestling abilities of a 19-year-old youth, and by the panic-stricken ineptitude of his terrified and unprepared accomplice.

What all of this meant was that, quite literally, the Ruthvens no longer had any friends, or at least not enough that mattered. Their friends were dead, or in exile, or else the last Earl of Gowrie had decided quite deliberately to shun them. Perhaps Gowrie had at least the tacit understanding of some in England, notably Lord Willoughby or Robert Cecil; but it is more likely that the strength of Gowrie's English connections convinced him that the realm south of the Tweed would applaud his coup and gave him a false sense of his own importance. It is possible that Gowrie entered into an unholy alliance with Logan of Restalrig, who might have been intended to provide a place to hold the king if he had to be got away from Gowrie House: Logan's precipitate sale of all his lands certainly suggests that he had something profoundly important to hide, but this assumption hinges on the shaky evidence of George Sprot, a self-confessed forger and perjurer. It is equally possible that Gowrie had sounded his old ally the Earl of Bothwell, that Bothwell made available some of his agents in Scotland (notably Logan and Thomas Cranstoun), and that one of

Gowrie's intentions on 5 August was to extract from the king a promise to pardon the exiled earl; but Bothwell's movements in the summer of 1600 suggest that he was not privy to the timing of any move against the king by the Ruthvens. Then again, if Gowrie was acting on behalf of the queen, perhaps at the behest of his two formidable elder sisters who served her, he seems to have taken none of the queen's other allies in 'the Chamber' into his entire confidence; even if he did, they were naturally quick to deny it. Gowrie rejected his potential allies, and in death, they rejected him. If the Earl of Cromarty, that rabid old apologist for James VI, got anything right at all about the 'Gowrie Conspiracy', it was that the court which tried the dead Ruthvens was made up chiefly of their relations and neighbours.[631] Not only were they anticipating rich pickings from the Ruthven lands; they were condemning two young men born at the wrong time, who had tried to employ the methods of contemporary Italy and of an older, more brutal Scotland in a greatly changed land.

****

King James VI and I returned to his native realm only once after 1603. On 5 July 1617, he made a grand triumphal entrance into Perth. Once again he went into Gowrie House, now rechristened the King's Lodging, and there he met all the surviving witnesses of the events of 5 August 1600. Sir Hew Herries was long dead, but all the rest stepped forward in turn to confirm once more the royal story of what had happened 17 years before. James embraced them all, with one notable exception: Andrew Henderson was allowed only to kiss hands. The king is said to have gone up to the turret chamber one last time. There, he knelt down on the floor and wept copiously. The blood of the slaughtered Ruthven brothers was reportedly still visible; but then, their 'blood' was still being shown off as a gruesome (and exceptionally implausible) tourist attraction 200 years later.[632] Both symbolically and in reality, King James VI and I found it almost impossible to be rid of Ruthven blood.

EPILOGUE:

THE DEATH OF KINGS (II)

An old Scots woman is alleged to have said that one of the few satisfactions to be expected on the Day of Judgment will be to learn the truth about what really happened at Gowrie House on 5 August 1600.[633] But when all the rational explanations and likely hypotheses that could explain the 'Gowrie House affair' are exhausted, there remain the strangest and perhaps most important aspects of all.[634] The first connects the Ruthven family directly to the legitimacy, or otherwise, of King James VI and I. If James Stuart was not the son of Mary Queen of Scots and Henry, Lord Darnley, then he was illegitimate; and if he was illegitimate, every monarch of Scotland since 1567, of England since 1603 and of Britain since 1707, including the present incumbent, has been a usurper. If the Ruthvens knew of this, or suspected it, there could hardly have been a more potent motive for the slaughter at Gowrie House. However, it is still not necessarily the last and darkest secret associated with the 'Gowrie Conspiracy': that drama was played out in Paris in May 1610, and perhaps only the unravelling of this last mystery will finally satisfy that impatient old woman.

****

During the fateful afternoon of 5 August 1600, a Ruthven – Alexander of Freeland, cousin to the last Earl of Gowrie and his brother – allegedly shouted angrily towards the turret chamber at Gowrie House, 'Come down, thou son of Seigneur Davie, come down!' explicitly damning the king as the bastard son of a long-dead Italian musician. King James's own testimony suggests that Sandy Ruthven's attack on him was connected in some way with the crown of Scotland: James told Sandy that even if he killed his king, he would not succeed to the throne. But John, Earl of Gowrie, and Alexander, Master of Ruthven, were not descendants of Queen Margaret Tudor and the English royal line.* However, there is also another possible connection between the events at Gowrie House and the destiny of the British crowns, a connection that might explain the apparent harking-back in the Perth of 1600 to the murder of Rizzio in the Edinburgh of 1566.

When the dying third Lord Ruthven made his dramatic, pain-wracked entrance into the supper chamber of Mary, Queen of Scots, the first charge that he laid against David Rizzio was that 'he has offended your [Majesty's] honour, which I dare not be so bold to speak of'.[635] Ruthven's statement is unequivocal: he believed that Rizzio had enjoyed improper sexual relations with the queen. Darnley effectively repeated the charge, and although Mary defended herself vigorously against her husband, she never actually responded to Lord Ruthven's accusation. Ruthven was soon to make another categorical and seemingly inexplicable reference to Mary's body. During the discussions about the fate of the queen that followed Rizzio's murder, he stated that 'I feel certain, and I will stake my life on it, that the baby is only a girl, and there will be no danger'. Ruthven's remark might have been a manifestation of his family's supposed predilection for sorcery and foretelling the future, but it might have been something much more. It is generally accepted that the future King James VI and I was conceived on or about 19 September 1565.[636] On that date, and for the two preceding nights, Mary, Queen of Scots, and her new husband Lord Darnley, were the guests of Patrick, Lord Ruthven; so it is probable that James was conceived within the walls of Ruthven Castle. The peculiar architectural arrangement of the castle, with its two separate tower-houses, was ideal for illicit sexual relationships, as the story of Dorothea Ruthven and the 'maiden's leap' demonstrates. Therefore, it is just possible that the Ruthven family knew, or suspected, that something untoward had happened at Ruthven Castle in September 1565.

Six months later, Lord Ruthven or anyone else with a basic grasp of female anatomy would have been able to make a reasonable guess at the date of conception. But even if Patrick Ruthven and his family had doubts about the paternity of the foetus that became James Stuart, they had a very strong vested interest in keeping those doubts firmly to themselves. James's legal father, Lord Darnley, was the champion of the Lennox Stewarts, who were close kin to the Ruthvens and also

* See Appendix B.

their closest political allies. After Darnley's death and the coronation of James, it would have been even more imperative for the Ruthvens to stifle their suspicions. They owed everything, including ultimately an earldom and one of the greatest offices of state, to a succession of regimes that acted in the name of the young king; the only alternatives, the restoration of Mary, Queen of Scots, or the coronation of a Hamilton, would have been unutterable disasters for their prospects. It was vital for the members of the House of Ruthven to pay lip service to the notion that James VI was the legitimate son of Darnley and Mary, even if they had reason to believe that he was not. This does not rule out the possibility that in the meantime, the story of the king's illegitimacy went down the generations as the greatest family secret of the Ruthvens, and that the secret was both revealed and destroyed during the afternoon of 5 August 1600. Perhaps by donning his cap in the king's presence, Alexander, Master of Ruthven, was not simply showing disrespect to his sovereign, but proclaiming that as far as he, Sandy Ruthven, was concerned, James VI was not actually his sovereign at all, and never had been.

****

Whispered doubts about the legitimacy of James Stuart were doing the rounds within hours of the child's birth at Edinburgh Castle, if not before. Lord Ruthven's accusations against Rizzio could easily be interpreted as a veiled suggestion that the Italian was really the father of the queen's child. Mary was clearly all too aware of such rumours, and their potentially damaging political consequences. Hence the embarrassing farce on the day of James's birth, 19 June 1566, when Mary's despised and drunken husband was virtually dragged to her bedchamber and made to declare that he was undoubtedly the father of the infant prince.[637] Hence, too, the spectacular (and cripplingly expensive) Renaissance extravaganza, the first in British history, that was laid on at little James's christening at Stirling on 17 December 1566, and in two subsequent days of exuberant partying designed to impress representatives from France, England and Savoy, despite being held in the depths of a Scottish winter.[638] None of it did the queen much good, and when she subsequently blasted what little was left of her reputation by appearing to connive in the murder of her husband, Darnley, and then in short order marrying his suspected murderer, Bothwell, all the whispered suspicions could finally be shouted out loud. Edinburgh graffiti portrayed the queen as a mermaid, a common euphemism for a whore, and a barb from Ovid mysteriously appeared on her wedding night, fastened to the gate of Holyrood Palace:

As the common people say,

Only harlots marry in May.[639]

If the notion of David Rizzio as James's true father was common currency from the very beginning, it took far longer for an even darker suspicion to emerge. In 1830 some workmen were supposedly repairing the wall of Mary's chamber in Edinburgh Castle, where James had been born. Inside, they found a small oak coffin containing the mummified remains of a male child, covered in silk and cloth-of-gold embroidered with the initial 'J'.[640] This tale was most likely a deliberately damaging 'urban myth' circulated at a time when the popularity and credibility of the British monarchy was at an all-time low; moreover, Queen Mary never intended her son to be called 'James', as she apparently always intended his primary Christian name to be 'Charles'.[641] But bearing with the legend for a while, the story goes that Mary's child was either stillborn, or died immediately after birth, and – perhaps unknown to the mother – was substituted by the new-born son of John Erskine, Earl of Mar, whose elder son and successor King James closely resembled. There is no reason why Mar's wife could not have had a child at the right time (their two known children were born in 1558 and 1562), and such a switch would readily explain the ferocious loyalty that Mar and his son later displayed towards James, and the trust that the king, in turn, placed in the Earls of Mar. For instance, his decision to entrust the upbringing of his son, Prince Henry, to the younger Mar, against all the entreaties of his own wife, would be far more explicable if James and Mar were actually brothers, secretly committed to the preservation of a royal bloodline that was really and secretly Erskine, not Stuart. Conversely, if the last Earl of Gowrie and his brother somehow learned of this secret, and threatened to expose it, another dimension could be added to the mystery of Gowrie House.

There was hardly anything particularly novel in suspicions of royal bastardy, and James would certainly not be the last prince to have his paternity challenged. As with all political leaders, all kings had their critics, and unpopular monarchs who proclaimed rather too loudly that they ruled through divine authority were particularly vulnerable to charges that their hereditary right came not from God but from the gutter. Moreover, the rumour mill was fuelled by the fact that politically convenient births of heirs to controversial monarchs in distinctly questionable circumstances were relatively common occurrences among European royalty. In France, the birth of the future King Louis XIV in 1638, after his parents' marriage had been barren for 20 years, eventually inspired an entire genre in both literature and film – the legend of the 'man in the iron mask'. In 1688 the apparently miraculous birth of a son to James VI's 55-year-old Catholic grandson James VII and II seemed a mite too convenient for England's Protestant elite, who held that James's son died and was replaced by a healthy baby smuggled into the royal bedchamber in a warming pan. Compared with some of these rumours and legends, the evidence to suggest that King James VI was not really the legitimate son of King Henry Stewart, Lord Darnley, is certainly circumstantial, but perhaps rather more substantial than most.

Like the birth of Prince James Francis Edward Stuart in the summer of 1688, it was politically imperative that the child born to Mary, Queen of Scots, in 1566 should be a healthy son. In the fraught political and religious situation of the day, any alternative – a still birth or a girl – would have been an unmitigated disaster. The legality of female succession was still not entirely clear-cut; as John Knox's tirade against the 'monstrous regiment of women' had demonstrated, many Scots remained deeply uncomfortable about the notion of a female monarch, and certainly had no desire to repeat the experiment. In 1566, anything other than a healthy son would at the very least have triggered speculation about a new husband for the queen, given the obvious precariousness of her marriage to the alcoholic Darnley. At worst, the resultant succession crisis could have triggered a bloody civil war – and although such a war eventually broke out, it only followed Mary's abdication, and a highly unlikely chain of events that no one could possibly have foreseen in the spring and summer of 1566. Therefore, despite all the implausibilities inherent in the two legends, there is a powerful inner logic underpinning the theory of a conspiracy by Mary and certain of her key advisors to pass off a son who might not have been Darnley's as the legitimate son of the King and Queen of Scots.

The notion that King James Stuart was actually Davey Rizzio's son was certainly not the exclusive preserve of the Ruthven family. Henri IV, King of France, once contemplated James's nickname of 'Great Britain's Solomon' and remarked cynically that it was entirely apposite, for, like

Solomon, James was the son of David. An English diplomat in Scotland wrote gloomily to Queen Elizabeth's favourite Robert Dudley, Earl of Leicester, even before James was born: 'Woe is me for you when Davy's son shall be King of England'.[642] James himself was well aware of the whispers about his parentage. When the king and his agent, the Earl of Arran, launched an all-out attack on the power of the Presbyterian Kirk in 1584, the ministers countered by spreading the rumour that Rizzio was the king's true father, a slander that drove the sensitive 18-year-old monarch to tears.[643] Even James's legal father, 'King Henry' Darnley, had expressed his doubts about the paternity of Mary's child – although it has to be said that by the time of James's birth, Darnley was bitter, insanely jealous and not a particularly credible witness. On the night that Rizzio was killed, according to Lord Ruthven's own account, Darnley snapped at Mary that she had not come to his bedchamber since Rizzio 'fell into familiarity' with her, 'within these six months', a statement that dated the 'familiarity' to about the time they had all been at Ruthven Castle.[644]

These dark rumours about King James's true paternity persisted for years. If anything they acquired ever more currency, for as James got older, it became increasingly apparent that he bore little resemblance in personality or physique to either of his supposed parents, Darnley and Queen Mary. In the 1590s, John Colville, who implausibly juggled the twin careers of Presbyterian minister and English spy, wrote a pamphlet arguing that James was illegitimate, although he subsequently retracted the charge in a flagrant attempt to regain royal favour.[645] Colville was part of the conspiratorial clique around the Earls of Bothwell and Gowrie, and his cousin and fellow-plotter James Colville had been married to Lilias Ruthven, the first Earl of Gowrie's sister. Lilias might well have been present as a teenager in Ruthven Castle at the time of the royal visit in September 1565, and so in a position to supply Colville with some grounds for his charges. It is even more likely that one of the key players in the 'Gowrie House affair' was in the castle when the king, the queen and the Italian fatefully came to stay. Dorothea Stewart, later Countess of Gowrie but then Mistress of Ruthven, would have been in her mid-twenties, and unlike Mary, already the mother of at least two children. Dorothea would almost certainly have played a prominent part in the entertainment of the royal party, and as a woman of almost exactly the same age as the queen – and a Stewart to boot, so distant kin to Mary – Dorothea was perfectly qualified to be the queen's guide and confidante inside the peculiarly arranged walls of Ruthven Castle.

David Rizzio's most recent biographer concludes that it is highly unlikely for him to have been the father of King James, and this is certainly the most sensible reading of the evidence.[646] The sheer amount of gossip about the kings paternity was probably just that, and no more – malicious gossip, engendered by the peculiar circumstances of James's birth, the astonishingly dysfunctional nature of his family and the chaotic Scottish political scene throughout the first 20 or 30 years of his life. It would only have been surprising if King James Stuart had *not* been accused of being an Italian singer's bastard, or else an Erskine changeling. On the other hand, and if, despite all of the weight of logic and probability, David Rizzio really was the true father of King James, and thus the ancestor of the entire modern royal family, it would theoretically be possible to prove it. After his initial, hasty burial, Rizzio was later reburied in the royal vault of Holyrood Abbey. Even allowing for the depth and sincerity of Mary's grief over the death of a favourite servant, this in itself was a remarkable posthumous dignity for an Italian commoner, and caused howls of protest from the Protestant establishment.[647] It might be more explicable if Mary knew, or suspected, that Rizzio was the true father of the heir to the Scottish throne. The vault in Holyrood Abbey must be the most basic and anonymous royal mausoleum in the world: today, it resembles a somewhat neglected coal bunker, and could easily be mistaken as such were it not for an understated interpretative plaque bearing the royal arms of Scotland. The vault was desecrated at the Glorious Revolution, but Rizzio's remains were gone from it long before then. They were reportedly removed after Mary's abdication and reburied in the Canongate cemetery, where a grave reputed to be his is still clearly identified as such.[648] Therefore, Rizzio's DNA might be recoverable, and able to be compared with that of the modern royal family.[649] There are descendants galore of the Erskines of Mar, so it would be easier still to test the theory that James VI was a changeling. Of course, it might be a different matter to find a member of the royal family willing to undergo a DNA comparison that might effectively bastardise his or her entire bloodline, and to find politicians willing to sanction a test that might conceivably end the days of monarchy in Britain.

****

If the illegitimacy of King James VI and I really was secret knowledge possessed by the Ruthvens, it might be connected somehow to the undoubted fact that the first Earl of Gowrie was the last certain owner of the Casket Letters, which were passed to him by the Regent Morton's illegitimate son in 1581 or 1582. These were the mysterious, lost documents that implicated Mary, Queen of Scots, in the murder of her husband Henry, Lord Darnley, King James's legal father. Copies were produced at Mary's first trial in England, shortly after she sought sanctuary there, and their incriminating nature provided some of the justification for shutting her away in a succession of gloomy English castles for 20 years. But copies, as the case of George Sprot proves, do not necessarily give the whole story, certainly not the true story, and the extant copies of the Casket Letters do not prove that King James was illegitimate.[650] Argument rages to this day over whether or not the surviving letters are genuine, or clever forgeries produced by Moray's government and based on the manipulation of real letters written by Mary. As far as the paternity of King James is concerned, though, this point is academic. The 'casket' originally contained rather more documents than were presented in public – 10 more, to be precise. Although the contents of a couple of the missing documents can be surmised, the rest are lost. There *might* have been documents that proved or hinted at James's illegitimacy, but if such had existed, the Regent Moray and his sidekicks would have had good reason to conceal or destroy them. They wanted documents that proved Mary's foreknowledge of the death of Darnley, and might have been perfectly prepared to manufacture them if they could not find suitable proof in her own hand. But they owed their authority and all they possessed to the simple fact that they served James VI, undoubted King of Scots by hereditary right, and any evidence to suggest that the infant to whom they bowed the knee was actually not undoubted king by heredity would at once have threatened their power, if not their very lives.

Regardless of whether or not any evidence of his illegitimacy in the Casket Letters had been destroyed before they came into the first Earl of Gowrie's possession, King James – who presumably only knew the contents of the copies – could not have known this for certain. After all, the Regent Moray, the man most likely to have seen and destroyed the evidence, died when the child-king was just four, and Moray would not necessarily have confided in any one else. On the other hand, if Moray had *not* destroyed such evidence, and it had come intact into Gowrie's hands, James faced the potential nightmare of having documentary proof of his illegitimacy in the hands of a man whose family could possibly corroborate it from their memories of what might have happened when the king was conceived at Ruthven Castle in September 1565. In this context, the grant of the earldom of Gowrie, which could have happened just after William Ruthven became the owner of the Casket Letters, might be seen as a blatant bribe to ensure that he did not broadcast their contents to the world. For his part, Gowrie might subsequently have surrendered the originals to the king as part of the price for returning to favour after the 'Raid of Ruthven', but equally, his continuing possession of them could have compelled James to deal leniently with him. It is certainly the case that Gowrie refused to sell the Casket Letters to Queen Elizabeth, who was desperate to get hold of them. He might have taken the documents with him when he tried to flee the country by ship from Dundee in 1584: legend has it that when an old house in the town was pulled down, a bundle of old letters in French was found hidden in a chimney.[651]

The Casket Letters are highly unlikely to have been the 'treasure' that drew King James to Gowrie House on 5 August 1600: he would hardly have gone hunting in Falkland Park for four hours if he had even the slightest inkling that the most important documents his mother ever wrote, or else the proofs that he was not the rightful legitimate King of Scots, were within his grasp. But it is just conceivable that at Gowrie House, the Ruthvens sought to blackmail him into agreeing to their demands by threatening to produce the originals of the Casket Letters; an urn containing ashes, found within a hidden closet of the house when it was demolished in 1807, was inevitably identified as the final repository of the lost documents.[652] Alternatively, the letters could have been produced after James's abduction, or abdication, or murder, to justify the Ruthven coup. King James, denounced and discredited as an illegitimate usurper: perhaps that was what the events of 5 August 1600 were really all about.

****

If Henry Stewart, Lord Darnley, King of Scots, was not the father of King James VI and I, and if James was not an Erskine changeling, then the next most likely candidate for paternity is undoubtedly David Rizzio. His candidacy would be supported by the sheer weight of scurrilous gossip about his intimacy with Mary Queen of Scots, much of which was already circulating during his lifetime. The next most likely candidate would be Mary's eventual third husband, James Hepburn, Earl of Bothwell, even though their relationship apparently did not begin until months after

Rizzio's death. But there is a third candidate, too. There was no such gossip connecting his name to the queen's, either at the time or later; there is only the very flimsiest amount of feeble circumstantial evidence. Identifying him as a possible candidate at all on the basis of such 'evidence' would normally be considered laughable. But in the many-layered mystery that is the 'Gowrie Conspiracy', even such wildly implausible ideas need to be aired, if only for future writers on the subject to dismiss them out of hand.

'I feel certain, and I will stake my life on it, that the baby is only a girl, and there will be no danger.' Why, exactly, would Patrick, Lord Ruthven, have staked his life on the sex of Mary's unborn child? The obvious answer is that he did so out of arrogant aristocratic bravado; the fanciful answer is that the alleged warlock was basing his statement on astrology.[653] There is an even more unlikely answer, however. David Rizzio had no children: certainly none in Scotland that the likes of Lord Ruthven would have known of. But Patrick Ruthven knew a young man who had already fathered a succession of girls, probably three by the time of Rizzio's death. The same young man certainly paid court to Mary, Queen of Scots, albeit almost two years after James was conceived. He was William, the Master of Ruthven, the future first Earl of Gowrie. William was the same age as the queen. Like her, he was married; but their marriages need not have precluded the briefest of encounters at Ruthven Castle in September 1565. If this most unlikely of couplings ever took place, both sides would have had powerful reasons for concealing the fact that it had. Mary could not permit any challenge to the legitimacy of her child: hence Darnley's embarrassing public acknowledgement of paternity on the day of James's birth. Moreover, the Ruthvens could hardly publicly brand their kinsman and ally Darnley, the King of Scots, as a cuckold, and then denounce the child-king James VI as a bastard, *even if he was a Ruthven bastard.* Hence, perhaps, the third Lord Ruthven's keenness to hint at improper conduct between the queen and Rizzio, as a way of diverting attention from any other candidates for the paternity. Ruthven's subsequent and appallingly casual attitude to the life of the queen and her unborn child seems incredible if that child was his grandson, but perhaps it is a little less incredible if Mary's child was actually a grandson who should never have been conceived, let alone born; for revealing the truth about its father's identity would have destroyed everything that the House of Ruthven had ever stood for.

For all of this to have happened, though, Queen Mary Stuart would have had to have sex with William, then the Master of Ruthven, at Ruthven Castle sometime between the 17th and 19th of September,

1565. It is sometimes said that it was virtually impossible for female monarchs to enjoy illicit sexual relationships; for example, those who contend that Elizabeth I of England always remained a 'virgin queen' use the notion of ever-present ladies-in-waiting to dismiss the idea that she could have slept with Robert Dudley, Earl of Leicester. But Renaissance court etiquette was not necessarily quite that restrictive – or at least, it was as restrictive as a king or queen wanted it to be. Maria Theresa, wife of King Louis XIV of France, probably took this principle to extremes when her chosen illicit bedfellow was allegedly not only a mere page, but a page who was, to boot, a black dwarf; the existence of the little black baby that resulted was kept from *le roi soleil* only with the greatest difficulty.[654] Mary's own career suggests that it would not have been impossible for a determined suitor to sleep with the queen, whether the queen was a willing participant or not. A young French poet, Pierre de Chastelard, fell madly in love with her, and Mary responded by flirting outrageously with him. One night in 1563 Chastelard got in to her chamber at Holyrood and hid himself under her bed. Although he was discovered, the very fact that he had got under the royal bed so easily suggests that his intentions were not entirely over-ambitious. Chastelard escaped with a ticking-off, but failed to learn his lesson. When Mary set off on a journey to St Andrews a couple of days later, he followed her, and burst into her room at Rossend Castle in Burntisland as she was undressing. Once was unrequited puppy love; twice was high treason. Chastelard was executed, declaiming just before his death, 'Adieu, toi si belle et si cruelle, qui me tues et que je ne puis cesser d'aimer' (Adieu, the most beautiful and most cruel princess in the world!).[655]

Potentially, overnight stays at castles like Rossend (or Ruthven) presented better opportunities for royal sexual misadventures than the royal palaces, with their formal layout of apartments and serried ranks of inquisitive flunkies. Castles were smaller, more intimate and less formal. If further proof were needed, Mary's controversial 'abduction and rape' at the hands of the Earl of Bothwell provides it. On 24 April 1567 Bothwell seized the queen and carried her off to his sea-girt castle at Dunbar, where (according to Mary) he 'ravished' her. Writers have spilt much ink in sterile debates over the extent of Mary's complicity, if any, in these events. What is certain is that she stayed at Dunbar for 12 days, probably not against her will for at least the final part of that period, that she probably became pregnant there (she miscarried of Bothwell's twins in July), and that she married Bothwell less than a month later. Even if Mary had initially gone unwillingly to Dunbar, circumstances within the castle's walls quickly turned her into an enthusiastic lover and fiancée.

Despite this, the proposition that William, Earl of Gowrie, fathered King James VI, seems patently absurd. However, some distinctly slender circumstantial evidence can be advanced to support it. By 1567 William Ruthven was the fourth Lord Ruthven, and he made what appears superficially to have been a completely uncharacteristic attempt to woo Mary, Queen of Scots, during her captivity at Lochleven Castle. Perhaps Ruthven viewed himself as a potential fourth husband for the queen, assuming that her marriage to Bothwell and his to Dorothea Stewart could be ended conveniently (and by that time he still had no son and heir by Dorothea, only more daughters). Such an unlikely match becomes less far-fetched if William believed that he was the father of the King of Scots: marrying Mary would have regularised the dysfunctional family group by making him notionally the stepfather to his natural son. By 1584, William was the first Earl of Gowrie, and on trial for high treason. One of the charges brought against him centred on his alleged claims to close kinship with the king; it foreshadows James's strange comment to Sandy Ruthven about him never being likely to succeed as King of Scots. The Ruthvens were indeed closely related to James: William Ruthven was his first cousin, albeit via a female and illegitimate line. But there were many others, notably the likes of the Lennox Stewarts and the vast illegitimate progeny of King James V, who were closer in blood, or at least in the 'blood of kings'. Perhaps, then, their hints at a 'special relationship' referred to an entirely different kind of kinship, one that could never be made public, for to do so would have guaranteed the destruction of the House of Ruthven. Whether King James VI himself knew all of this, or suspected it, can only be guessed at. If he did suspect, it would immediately strengthen the highly implausible argument that James himself instigated the events at Gowrie House on 5 August 1600, with the added twist that the young Ruthvens who died that day might have been his own brothers.

****

Paris, 14 May 1610

Henri IV, King of France and Navarre, was in a great coach, en route from the Louvre for an afternoon conference at the Arsenal de France with his ailing chief minister, the Duke of Sully, who was too ill to follow protocol and attend on his monarch. They had much to discuss. French armies were massing in Champagne and Dauphiné, preparing to march against the Habsburg forces of the Emperor Rudolf II and

King Philip III of Spain. Only the day before, Henri's wife, Marie de Medicis, had undergone a special service of consecration at Saint-Denis cathedral, giving her full authority as regent of France while her husband led his armies into Germany. A great European war was imminent, one that would be triggered by France and her highly experienced, much-loved monarch.*

The king wished to inspect the decorations erected to mark his wife's imminent ceremonial entry into the city, so he drew back the curtains. As the coach turned from the rue Saint-Honoré into the rue de la Ferronerie, the narrow street ahead was blocked by a Parisian traffic jam, in the shape of wine and hay carts that could not get past each other. The coach came to a halt outside the premises of Pontrain, a notary, and the coachman tried to pass the obstruction by pulling in sharply to the left, leaving the great coach leaning in the gutter. As the king's coach halted, a tall, muscular young man with red hair jumped onto the wheel and, through the open window, stabbed the king twice with a long dagger. The Duke of Épernon, the ambitious colonel-general of infantry who was attending the king that day, threw a cloak over the monarch and ordered the coach to turn back to the Louvre. By the time it arrived there, King Henri IV was dead.[656]

His assassin, François Ravaillac, made no attempt to resist arrest. The royal guards managed to prevent his being lynched on the spot and took him to the nearby Hotel de Retz, where he was interrogated. He was unrepentant, indeed almost philosophical, about the deed that he had committed: 'I know very well he is dead: I saw the blood on my knife and the place where I hit him ... I've done what I came to do'.[657] Ravaillac, the unemployed and unmarried son of a dysfunctional Angouleme family, was a religious fanatic, much given to mysticism and visions. He saw himself as God's chosen defender of the pope and the true faith, on whom the king was treacherously preparing to declare war. For years he had seen himself as a man with a mission: initially the mission manifested itself as an urge to meet the king personally and convince him of the error of ways, but after a series of rebuffs, Ravaillac's mission had hardened into assassination.[658] His judges in the *parlement* of Paris were not persuaded of his higher motives. The young man was condemned to death as a regicide, and on 27 May 1610 he received his

---

* The 400th anniversary of Henri's assassination in 2010 has been commemorated fulsomely in republican France, whereas the 350th anniversary of the Restoration of his grandson King Charles II has been virtually ignored in monarchical Britain.

punishment. At the place of execution, the Place de Grève, his right hand, which he had used to strike the fatal blow, was plunged into a cauldron of fire and brimstone. Ravaillac screamed to God, and cried 'Jesus Maria'. The flesh was pulled from his chest, arms, thighs and legs with red-hot pincers. Boiling oil, resin, wax, sulphur and brimstone were poured upon the wounds, and molten lead upon his navel. By now, perhaps an hour had passed. Then four horses were fastened to his limbs and set off in different directions. Ravaillac withstood over an hour of this before finally dying. His judges had intended to have the body burned and the ashes scattered, but the furious Paris mob now intervened. They hurled themselves onto the body and literally tore it apart, ripping limbs away from the executioner's grasp. It was said that one woman even ate some of the assassin's flesh. The remaining body parts were either stamped underfoot or burned.[659]

In a final act reminiscent of (and perhaps inspired by) the fate of the Ruthvens, on whose behalf Henri IV had intervened barely two years earlier,[660] Ravaillac's immediate family were banished from France under pain of death and his wider kin were forbidden to use the reviled name of Ravaillac ever again. Even his birthplace was ordered to be demolished, and for all eternity, nothing else was to be erected on its site.

Like other assassins, before and since, Ravaillac consistently claimed that he had acted alone and that he was not part of a wider conspiracy. Indeed, in the past there had been several similar but unsuccessful attempts to kill Henri IV. Although he had brought to an end over 30 years of violent religious conflict in France, old hatreds died hard, and many on both sides of the religious divide continued to hate a monarch who had been a Protestant, only to convert to Catholicism with the apparently cynical ease epitomised in one of history's most famous throwaway lines, 'Paris is worth a mass'.[661] It was thus perfectly feasible for a lone fanatic, of either faith, to have been responsible for the death of such a controversial king; but the particular circumstances that existed at the time of Henri's death, and the sequel to it, inevitably caused much speculation.[662] For despite the fate that befell him, François Ravaillac had achieved his objective. The king was dead, the invasion of Germany was aborted, and it was these facts that triggered the inevitable conspiracy theories – these facts, that is, and the belief that a king, the lord's anointed, could not possibly have been killed by such a worthless, low-born creature. Circumstantial evidence of a conspiracy could certainly be assembled by those minded to do so. In the days immediately following the king's death the Duke of Épernon acted as one of the key power-brokers, effectively arranging the palace coup that established Queen Marie as regent for the infant King Louis XIII, thereby overthrowing Sully and Henri's other ministers. Yet Épernon's mistress, Catherine du Tillet, had provided the penniless Ravaillac with money, only Épernon and his confidantes had access to the assassin in the crucial hours immediately after the murder, and Épernon was governor of Angoulême, Ravaillac's home province.[663] Even so, most writers now accept Ravaillac's claim of sole responsibility, a claim that he repeated over and over again to his interrogators, and for the last time as the horses began to pull his bones apart: 'it was I, I alone, who did it'.[664]

The new government of France quickly reversed Henri IV's policy of war on behalf of the German Protestants, and the great conflict between France and the Hapsburgs was delayed for a quarter of a century. By that time France was arguably far stronger than she had been in 1610, and her enemies far weaker. From that conflict France emerged triumphant: the victorious, imperious France of Henry's grandson King Louis XIV, *le roi soleil*.

The 'Ravaillac dagger' had therefore changed the course of the history of France, and probably that of Europe too. As such, to this day it possesses an almost mythic status in France; but it also provides the last, extraordinary, aspect of the story of the Ruthvens.[665] The dagger itself was seized by the future Marechal de la Force, a member of the king's guard on that fatal day in May 1610. Under interrogation, Ravaillac claimed that he stole the weapon from a stranger who had left it lying on the table of a tavern on the rue Saint-Honoré. He claimed that he had been struggling for months to reconcile the murder of the king with his conscience, but the fortuitous appearance of this dagger decided him. He stole it, he said, 'with the intention of killing the king ... because it seemed to him the appropriate knife to carry out his purpose'.[666] Even then, Ravaillac prevaricated for another fortnight and even left Paris. Finally, he resolved to act, returned to the capital, sharpened the stolen knife on a stone, and followed the king's coach when it set off from the Louvre. When the coach ground to a halt in the Parisian traffic, Ravaillac realised that his moment had come. From being just an anonymous stolen blade, the 'Ravaillac dagger' instantly became perhaps the most influential single weapon in European history.

If Ravaillac's confession to the random theft of the weapon that he used to kill the king is true, then it must represent one of the most astonishing coincidences in history. If it is not true, then perhaps there is yet another secret, sinister and still unknown dimension to the story of the 'Gowrie Conspiracy'.

For the 'Ravaillac dagger' had been used before.

The dagger bore the heraldic emblems of its original owner, tell-tale proofs that were used 366 years later by the Marechal de la Force's descendants, and the expert whom they consulted, to identify the weapon's provenance.

The stranger from whom Ravaillac 'stole' the dagger had to have been Sir John Ramsay, Viscount Haddington, later Earl of Holdernesse.

The 'Ravaillac dagger' was the same weapon that Ramsay used at Gowrie House on 5 August 1600 to kill Alexander, Master of Ruthven, and John, Earl of Gowrie.

APPENDIX A

THE RISE OF
THE HOUSE OF RUTHVEN

The Ruthvens, a family of Norse descent, were settled in Perthshire by the 1190s. Walter Ruthven was knighted by King Alexander II (1214–46), and his son William was heavily involved in the succession crises, English occupation, and wars of independence that followed the sudden death of Alexander III in 1286. William Ruthven twice paid homage to King Edward I, the 'Hammer of the Scots', but in July 1297 he also led 30 men to support William Wallace at the siege of the then English-held town of Perth. Camping out at night beneath Kinnoull Hill, across the Tay from Perth, Ruthven's men ambushed six English hay carts that blundered past their hiding place. Concealing five men under the hay in each cart, he and Wallace donned captured armour and tricked their way past the town's guards. Two thousand Englishmen were slaughtered when the rampant Scots followed them into Perth, and Ruthven's reward was to be appointed Sheriff of Perthshire by 'The Wallace'.[667] In 1313 Robert the Bruce, as King Robert I, confirmed the Ruthvens' right to be hereditary sheriffs of that county if the head of the family was of age.[668]

For much of the 14th and 15th centuries the Ruthvens played little part in national politics, but they finally returned to national prominence with Sir William Ruthven's eponymous great-grandson. By the 1480s William Ruthven was one of the staunchest supporters of the increasingly unpopular James III; on 29 January 1488 the king made him Lord Ruthven.[669] Six months later, the king's army fought the battle of Sauchieburn against a rebel force nominally commanded by James's own son and heir, James, Duke of Rothesay.[670] The royal army was routed and the king killed. William, first Lord Ruthven, seems rapidly to have reached an accommodation with the new King James IV and received many grants of land from him. His son and heir, William, Master of Ruthven, was killed at the disastrous Battle of Flodden in 1513, but the family's prospects were amply repaired two years later by the marriage of the new heir, Lord Ruthven's grandson, another William, to Janet Haliburton. She was the daughter and eldest co-heiress of Patrick, fifth Lord Haliburton of Dirleton, and thus brought to the marriage the estate and castle of Dirleton, near the coast of East Lothian. The Haliburton title could descend through female heirs, meaning that Janet was already a baroness in her own right when she married William Ruthven, so her title descended to their son and his successors.[671]

The first Lord Ruthven, one of relatively few senior Scottish lords not to fall at Flodden, was rapidly promoted by James IV's widow Queen Margaret Tudor, the *de facto* ruler of Scotland. Before the end of 1513, William, Lord Ruthven, was a privy councillor, one of four appointed to attend continually on the queen. In the following year he was one of the ambassadors sent by Margaret to her brother, King Henry VIII of England, and in 1515 he was appointed one of the guardians of the infant King, James V. This period probably marked the beginning of the Ruthven family's consistently anglophile stance, and during the years that followed, both Lord Ruthven and his grandson displayed unswerving loyalty to James while Queen Margaret and her second husband, the Earl of Angus, competed for control of the young king. The second Lord Ruthven succeeded his grandfather to the title in 1528. James V appointed him to the Privy Council in 1541 and made him one of four commissioners tasked with ending the endemic violence in the Borders. Following the king's unexpected death in 1542 at the age of 30, Lord Ruthven became one of the four 'keepers' of the infant Mary, Queen of Scots. During the English invasions that followed during the 'Rough Wooing', Henry VIII's attempt to impose the marriage of Mary to his son Edward, Ruthven usually took a pro-English stance. This was shaped in part by his adherence to Matthew Stewart, thirteenth Earl of Lennox, one of the two strongest candidates for the position of heir to the infant Queen Mary's throne. Lennox was strongly pro-English, and in April 1544 he left Scotland for 20 years of exile in England. He damned himself in the eyes of many Scots by signing an agreement acknowledging Henry VIII's supremacy over Scotland and surrendering his claim to the throne to the English king.[672] Nevertheless, Lord Ruthven and Lennox remained friendly and politically close. Within a couple of years, too, Lennox and the Master of Ruthven were married to half-sisters: Ruthven to Janet Douglas, the Earl of Angus's illegitimate daughter by Janet Stewart of Traquair, Lennox to Margaret Douglas, Angus's legitimate daughter by Queen Margaret, who was thus a plausible candidate for the succession to the English throne as well.

By the 1540s, William, Lord Ruthven, and his eldest son Patrick were firm adherents of the new faith, Protestantism.[673] At the 1543 parliament, Lord Ruthven, 'a stout and discreet man in the cause of God', lobbied strongly for the adoption of a vernacular Bible, then a sure sign of Protestant leanings.[674] Thus Ruthven inevitably clashed with the most powerful churchman in a Scotland that was still officially Catholic, Cardinal David Beaton, Archbishop of St Andrew's, who was said to hate Ruthven's 'knowledge of God's Word'.[675] Beaton tried to remove Lord Ruthven from his post of provost of Perth, replacing him with John Charteris, Laird of Kinfauns, a relation of Beaton's ally Patrick, fourth Lord Gray. The Ruthvens and the Charterises had been rivals in and around Perth for years; the latter were provosts of the town of Perth for almost half of the previous 60 years, and had inevitably clashed with the Ruthvens, hereditary sheriffs of the county of Perthshire. As for the Lords Gray, they controlled Dundee in the same way that the Ruthvens controlled Perth, and the two towns were ever rivals for the command of the River Tay and its hinterland.[676] Just as the Ruthvens were invariably sheriffs of Perthshire, so the Grays were invariably sheriffs of adjacent Forfarshire.

In July 1545 the Ruthvens seemed in firm control of Perth, with Patrick, the 25-year-old Master of Ruthven, taking up residence in the town itself to try and pre-empt any moves by the Cardinal's supporters. Presumably he would have stayed in the large, L-shaped riverside town house that later became known as 'Gowrie House'. Faced with the Ruthvens' possession of such a strategically sited headquarters, and of the town as a whole, Charteris and Gray were left with little option other than to launch a full-scale attack on Perth. They planned a two-pronged assault: the main force under Gray and Charteris would storm the bridge, while at the same time their ally the Master of Rothes and his men were to come up the Tay by boat and attack the South Port (which actually stood on the west side of the town walls). News of the planned assault filtered into Perth, and with Patrick Ruthven at their head, the townsmen took up positions in the closes around the two Ports in the early morning of St Mary Magdalene's Day, 22 July. At the Bridge Port the drawbridge was up but deliberately left unguarded so that, lulled by the apparent lack of defences within the town, Lord Gray and his forces decided to attack before the other force appeared. The drawbridge was let down and Gray's men advanced. Suddenly, Ruthven and his supporters poured out of buildings and yards on all sides. A fierce fight followed, but the advantage of surprise was with Ruthven and the people of Perth. Some 60 of Charteris's followers perished on or around the Perth bridge, although the leaders were able to escape.[677] The two parties subsequently went before the Privy Council to resolve their differences, but the feud was only ended definitively when the Master of Ruthven killed John Charteris in an Edinburgh street in 1552.[678] For his part, Cardinal Beaton made no further moves against the Ruthvens, and there is no evidence that the family played any part in his brutal murder at St Andrews on 29 May 1546.

In the summer of 1546 the second Lord Ruthven became Lord Privy Seal of Scotland.[679] He served in this office until his death six years later, and became a particularly staunch supporter of the queen dowager, Marie de Guise, despite holding religious views that were diametrically opposed to hers; Marie's favour to the Ruthvens in their dispute with Gray and Charteris might have been decisive in shaping this unlikely alliance.[680] Despite his relatively new political stature, the second Lord Ruthven was no longer a young man by 1546, and as the battle on Perth Bridge had shown, his heir was becoming increasingly prominent in the affairs of Perth and Scotland. The Duke of Somerset's crushing victory at Pinkie in September 1547 made it seem very likely that England would finally achieve its centuries-old objective of conquering its northern neighbour, and in the circumstances, it is hardly surprising that many Scots decided to collaborate. Some did so out of defeatism, some out of fear, some out of an ideological sympathy with Protestant England. Like many others, though, Patrick Ruthven's collaboration was sealed by English gold.[681] Late in the evening of 19 December 1547, Patrick Ruthven called on Sir Andrew Dudley, admiral of the northern seas, then commanding English forces in the Tay. He made him an offer: he would deliver the town of Perth to the English, along with the allegiance of both his father and Lord Drummond. 'He will take money I perceive', Dudley observed.[682] For the English, Perth should have been a prize well worth the having. Remarkably, though, Somerset seemed underwhelmed by the Master of Ruthven's offer. England's Lord Protector simply made no reply, so on 23 January 1548 Ruthven went again to Dudley and repeated it.[683] Over the next six weeks, Ruthven wrote repeatedly to Dudley to find out if he had heard from Somerset, but still the Protector prevaricated.[684] Perhaps Ruthven had somehow got wind of the fact that his great rival Patrick, fourth Lord Gray, had signed a formal agreement with the English to deliver to them his castle of Broughty, and to assist them in capturing Perth, in the process ejecting from it his enemies (unnamed, but obviously the Ruthvens).[685] In June, Somerset finally took action and employed Lord Grey of Wilton to sound Ruthven's loyalty. Grey found Ruthven to be 'so addict[ed]' to the English cause that he knew of no one else in Scotland who was so committed to it. The offer to betray Perth was made once again, and at last, at the end of June 1548, the English finally authorised Patrick Ruthven's plan.[686]

But by then, it was already far too late. In extremis, Scotland's rulers fell back once again on their 'auld alliance' with France: King Henri II's price included a marriage between Mary, Queen of Scots, and his own son, the Dauphin Francis. Consequently, a French army arrived at Leith on 17 June, the Treaty of Haddington between France and Scotland was signed on 7 July, and a string of Scottish and French military successes characterised much of the year 1548.[687] Perhaps sensibly recognising the way the wind was blowing, Patrick Ruthven made himself scarce in the Lammermuir hills, attending to seemingly unavoidable and pressing business.[688] When he eventually wrote again to Lord Grey at the start of August, Ruthven hoped Grey would excuse him for not having acted sooner, but he had good cause, which he would reveal when he eventually met Grey. The earls of Erroll and Marischal had put him out of his 'mayrshippe' of Perth, but he had won it back, and once he knew exactly what they were doing, he would show himself openly. 'Give thanks to the Lord', Ruthven wrote portentously, 'and He will bring all your affairs well to pass, as He did to the bairns of Israel, when they kept His commandments ... Read this writing and rive [tear] it'.[689] By now, the Duke of Somerset had Patrick Ruthven's measure. He seems to have summoned the Master to London, to arrive on 'Holy Rood Day' (14 September), but when he failed to appear, the Lord Protector ordered his arrest. 'We find fault at his failure,' Somerset wrote, 'and seeing there is no trust in men who promise, not caring to perform'.[690]

In March 1552, William, second Lord Ruthven, attended his last meeting of the Scottish Privy Council.[691] By October he was dead, and Patrick became the third Lord Ruthven. As the 1550s went on, Marie de Guise successfully prised the House of Ruthven away from its Anglophile inclinations by judiciously bribing it with large amounts of French gold, while that other potential focus for the Ruthvens' loyalty, the Earl of Lennox, remained in exile in England. Consequently, there was little to prevent the third Lord Ruthven reinventing himself as a key player in the new regent's government. In 1552–3 Patrick Ruthven even served briefly as 'coronet of footmen' in a unit of Scots troops raised to fight in Europe for the French army. His very brief service brought even more 'gifts' his way, though typically, he was dissatisfied with having been 'ane futtman lang aneuch' and sought a cavalry command instead.[692] He was appointed a Privy Councillor in 1553 and Lieutenant of the Middle March in 1558, a position which entailed the defence of a key part of the border at a time when England was still at war with Scotland's traditional ally, France. Lord Ruthven also served as provost of Perth from 1553, building up a strong body of support among the craft guilds of the town, whose members were staunchly Protestant, and vigorously promoted their rights.[693] At Easter 1559 Queen Regent Marie de Guise demanded that Ruthven should suppress Protestantism in Perth. Ruthven refused, allegedly telling her that:

> he avowed, he could make their bodies to come to her
> Grace, and to prostrate themselves before her, till she
> was satiate of their blood; but to cause them [to]
> do anything against their conscience, he could not
> undertake.[694]

Instead, Patrick Ruthven allowed John Knox to come to Perth; and the rest, as the saying goes, is history.

****

Patrick, third Lord Ruthven, was married twice. His first wife, Janet Douglas, was the illegitimate daughter of Queen Margaret Tudor's second husband, Archibald Douglas, Earl of Angus. Patrick Ruthven and Janet Douglas had at least eight children, but the heir, Patrick, Master of Ruthven, was dead by 1561. In 1557 Patrick senior married Janet Stewart, Countess of Sutherland and dowager Lady Methven, whose fourth (but still not last) husband he thus became. The marriage between Lord Ruthven and the Countess of Sutherland was then reinforced by an intricate interweaving of the Ruthven and Methven genealogies. Patrick Ruthven's daughter Jean married Janet's son, the second Lord Methven, and on 17 August 1561, Patrick's second son William, later the first Earl of Gowrie, was married to Dorothea Stewart, Janet's daughter by the first Lord Methven. These elaborate matrimonial arrangements were entirely overshadowed by the fact that two days after the Ruthven wedding, Mary, Queen of Scots, returned to her native land.

APPENDIX B

THE RUTHVEN 'CLAIM TO THE THRONE' AND THEIR 'LOST HEIR'

One of the more puzzling aspects of the 'Gowrie House affair' is the suggestion that the Ruthvens somehow had a claim to the throne of Scotland, and perhaps to that of England also. There were King James's strange words to Sandy Ruthven in the turret chamber of Gowrie House: 'suppose you take my life, neither you nor your brother will be king after me; yea, the subjects of Scotland will root you out, and all your name!' Why say this at all, unless the Ruthvens somehow had a claim on the throne? Then there was the charge brought against the Ruthvens' father, the first Earl of Gowrie, of claiming to be of royal blood; and after all, the only previous holder of the title had become King of Scots.[695] These obscure allusions were given more weight by Bishop Gilbert Burnet, Bishop of Salisbury, confidante of King William of Orange and author of the *History of My Own Time*. Born in Edinburgh and raised largely in Aberdeenshire, Burnet took a natural interest in Scottish history, even if it fell outside 'his own time', and when he considered the 'Gowrie Conspiracy', he produced a breathtaking theory to explain what had happened on 5 August 1600. Burnet's father, a strong Presbyterian who knew many of those who had been implicated in the events of that day, had concluded that the Ruthven brothers really did hatch a conspiracy against the king, and his son duly provided the reason for their actions. Quite simply, John Ruthven, Earl of Gowrie, was the next heir to the crown of England.

Burnet provided chapter and verse for his astonishing claim.[696] Queen Margaret Tudor, widow of James IV of Scots and sister of Henry VIII of England, married Archibald Douglas, Earl of Angus, as her second husband. Their child was Lady Margaret Douglas, the mother of Lord Darnley, James VI's father. James thus had a double line of descent from Margaret and the House of Tudor, giving him far and away the strongest hereditary claim to succeed the childless Elizabeth I. So far, Burnet was on firm ground. But he went on to claim that Margaret's third marriage, to Lord Methven, produced a legitimate son, whose daughter was the mother of John, Earl of Gowrie. If Burnet's descent was correct, Gowrie would have been the next heir to the English throne, after James himself. Burnet's authoritative statement sent those interested in the 'Gowrie House affair' off on a wild goose chase that lasted for some 150 years, especially because there seemed to be circumstantial evidence to support it. There was a persistent legend that England itself acknowledged that claim. When Gowrie spent a month at Elizabeth's court in the spring of 1600, en route from the Continent back to Scotland, it was said that he was entertained with all the honours due to a Prince of Wales, and that an honour guard was provided especially for him.[697] This was pure fiction. Gowrie was lavishly entertained at the English court, but to no greater extent than his status as a visiting foreign nobleman from a traditionally pro-English family demanded. Then there was the peculiar clue that Francis, Earl of Bothwell, let slip to Toby Matthew, Dean of Durham (and later Archbishop of York), in 1593, when he turned up in England demanding sanctuary after yet another abortive attempt to abduct his cousin, King James. According to Bothwell, there was a secret candidate for the Scottish crown, on whose behalf Bothwell expected to be lieutenant or regent.[698] No monarch of full age or full wits needs a regent; but John, Earl of Gowrie, was just 15 at the time.

Then again, there was the mysterious addition to the Ruthven coat of arms that Gowrie supposedly adopted while in Italy: an armoured man, praying in supplication to an imperial crown above his head, with the motto *Tibi Soli*, for thee alone. To be fair to Burnet, much was made of this in King James's own day. In 1609 James's agent in Venice, Sir Henry Wotton, sent him a 'strange relic' that had been found in a dancing school in Padua, namely the *Tibi Soli* emblem. Unfortunately for the conspiracy theorists, the addition to the coat of arms had a much longer history. It had been adopted by William, first Earl of Gowrie, in the early 1580s, and had appeared on a fireplace installed at Ruthven Castle.[699] During his treason trial, the first earl had been accused of 'challenging that honour to be of his Highness' blood', but this hardly constituted a claim to the throne. Gowrie, through his

Douglas mother a first cousin once removed of King James, had probably been stressing the closeness of his blood relationship to the king in a court thronged by Stewarts, who arrogantly assumed that their surname alone gave them a special relationship with the monarch. In its original meaning, *Tibi soli* could have been a proclamation of the Ruthvens' loyalty to the crown, and specifically to King James, at a time when that loyalty was being questioned. Perhaps John, Earl of Gowrie, put a different and altogether more ambitious construction on the motto: it was said that the armed man on the design in the dancing school was reaching for the crown with his sword. But there is a rather greater likelihood that his much-vaunted Paduan graffito was simply the idle doodling of a bored undergraduate, not proof positive of a determination to be the next King of England.[700]

Gilbert Burnet's spectacularly false 'red herring' was finally and comprehensively demolished early in the 19th century, when painstaking research brought to light key documents that established the truth about the Ruthvens' family tree. Henry, Lord Methven's eldest son, the Master of Methven, of whom so much was made by Burnet, belonged to a short-lived first marriage to a shadowy 'Lady Leslie', not to his second marriage to the Queen dowager. The Master died in battle on the field of Pinkie, in 1547, having never married. His father, Lord Methven, had a further four children by his third wife, Janet Stewart, Countess of Sutherland. However, they were all born while he was still married to his second wife, Queen Margaret Tudor, so in 1551 Methven obtained papers of legitimation for all four children – including Dorothea, who would marry the future first Earl of Gowrie 10 years later.[701] Confirmation came from a 1567 court case in which Janet Stewart herself made it abundantly clear that Dorothea was her daughter, and no one else's.[702]

****

John, Earl of Gowrie, would not have become the next King of England, much less the next King of Scots, by somehow disposing of James Stuart on 5 August; but there was more than one way for a man to get a throne. The earl undoubtedly would have known that if James VI of Scotland did not succeed to the English throne, then the two next most likely candidates were both women. The Infanta Isabella of Habsburg was Philip II's daughter, and so, unsurprisingly, she was the favoured candidate of her brother, the new King of Spain, and of many

English Catholics. However, Isabella finally wed in 1599. That left the Lady Arbella Stuart, who undoubtedly possessed the bloodline of a potential Queen of England. Her grandmother, Lady Margaret Douglas, was Queen Margaret Tudor's only daughter. By her marriage to the Earl of Lennox, sometime Regent of Scotland, Lady Margaret produced two sons. The elder was Henry, Lord Darnley, but Darnley also had a brother who was some 10 years younger. Charles Stuart, who became Earl of Lennox in 1571, stayed well clear of Scotland and duly found himself a wife in England. Elizabeth Cavendish was 20, Lennox 19, when they married in November 1574 after a lightning romance that was almost certainly engineered by Elizabeth's formidable mother, the Countess of Shrewsbury, better known to history as 'Bess of Hardwick'. Charles barely had time to witness the birth of his daughter, Arbella, in 1575; he died of tuberculosis in April 1576, aged just 21, and Arbella's mother followed him to the grave in 1582. An orphan at the age of seven, Arbella was brought up by Bess of Hardwick. Bess was just as fiercely independent as her crowned namesake, and equally astute politically. She carefully groomed the young Arbella as a potential future queen of England, knowing full well that Arbella's English birth would make many prefer her to the leading contender for the throne, her first cousin, King James VI. Bess ensured that Arbella had a broad education to rival Queen Elizabeth's, but not even the mighty Countess of Shrewsbury could overcome the character traits that Arbella shared with her long-dead uncle, Lord Darnley. Like 'King Henry', Arbella Stuart was vapid, impulsive, and completely lacking in sound political sense. She did not even possess Darnley's great saving grace. He had been stunningly handsome; instead, Arbella Stuart inherited the long nose and plain features of the Tudors.

Romantic legend had it that John, Earl of Gowrie, met Arbella Stuart during a stay in England, that the two were attracted to each other, and that Gowrie determined to marry her. If there is any truth in this story, it would have provided a classic motive for the events of 5 August 1600. If King James perished, or else was somehow removed from contention for the English succession, Queen Arbella might reign in Whitehall after Queen Elizabeth. At her side, guiding her in a restoration of the natural order of things, would be her husband, King John. Of course, this proposition would serve equally well to support the alternative explanation of the 'Gowrie House affair', a deliberate royal strike against the House of Ruthven: King James would hardly have been magnanimous about the prospect of his nearest rival for the English throne marrying one of his most detested and powerful lords. However, the story of a romance between Gowrie and Arbella is unlikely, to say the least. John Ruthven was only three years younger than Arbella, but on the other hand, he probably visited England only once or twice in his life. He certainly spent a month there in 1600, when he was on his way back from his long sojourn in Europe. He probably also passed through in 1594, on his way to the Continent. The likeliest place for him to have met Arbella would have been the English court, but she was not there on either occasion: she was living on her grandmother's estates in Derbyshire. Even so, there is a remote possibility that they could have met. The Ruthvens had always been closely allied to the Lennox Stewarts, and Gowrie might have decided to pay a social call on one of the few survivors of that line – and his second cousin, to boot – if he happened to be passing her home. Hardwick Hall, the astonishing glass spectacle that Bess built in the 1590s and where Arbella lived for much of the time, still towers over the valley that contains the M1, one of the main routes from the south of England to Scotland and vice-versa. If the Earl of Gowrie had followed roughly the same route, it is not inconceivable that he could have met and courted the Lady Arbella Stuart.

Gowrie's death put paid to whatever matrimonial ambitions he might have harboured, and her cousin James's accession to the English throne put paid to the prospects of a crown for Arbella. At first she was well received at the court of the new King of England, but in 1610 she committed political suicide by marrying William Seymour, the grandson of Lady Catherine Grey. Catherine's elder sister Jane was Queen of England for nine days, and their grandmother the Princess Mary, briefly Queen of France, was the younger sister of both King Henry VIII and Queen Margaret Tudor. One of the many succession laws that Henry enacted deliberately ruled out Margaret and her Scottish descendants in favour of Mary and her English ones, the Greys. By marrying William Seymour, therefore, Arbella was uniting two potential rival claims to the English throne. Arbella was placed under house arrest, managed to escape, was recaptured at sea, and confined to the Tower. The woman who might have become Queen of England shared her confinement with Patrick Ruthven, the youngest brother of the man who might have become her husband.

At some date unknown, Patrick sent an enigmatic letter to Henry Percy, ninth Earl of Northumberland, who was his fellow prisoner in the Tower from 1605 until 1621.[703] Their correspondence provides another link between the two great threats against King James Stuart: Northumberland was widely presumed to have been the Gunpowder Plotters' choice as Lord Protector of Catholic England if they had succeeded in blowing the Protestant establishment sky-high. Patrick's letter began by referring to his own condition:

> It may be interpreted discretion some times to wink at private wrongs, especially for such a one as my self, that have [sic] a long time wrestled with a hard fortune, and whose actions, words, and behaviour are continually subject to the censure of a whole state ...

Nevertheless, he could not overlook the fact that Northumberland had circulated 'certain infamous verses ... to disgrace my country and myself, and to wrong and stain by me the honour of a worthy and virtuous gentlewoman':

> If the repulse of your lewd desire at the gentlewoman's hands hath inflamed and exasperated your choler against her, it was never known that to refuse Northumberland's unlawful lust was a crime for a gentlewoman deserving to have her honour called in question ... If these words sound harshly in your lordship's ear, blame yourself, since yourself forgetting yourself hath taught others how to dishonour you; and remember, that though nobility makes a difference of persons, yet injury acknowledgeth none.

The name of the 'gentlewoman', and the effect (if any) of Ruthven's letter, are unknown. Perhaps Northumberland's scurrilous poem referred to Patrick's sister, Barbara Ruthven. But if it was written at the time of the furious quarrel that took place between Patrick and Northumberland in the Tower Garden in July 1613,[704] then it could well refer to Lady Arbella Stuart. It would have been entirely natural for Patrick Ruthven to defend the honour of the woman who could so easily have been his sister-in-law, or the Queen of England, or both.[705] Patrick might have gone even further and plotted Arbella's escape. In November 1613 he was placed in closer confinement following the discovery of a potential escape route beneath his study. His servant,

James Wade, was examined, and revealed that his master was visited regularly by two physicians, an astrologer and an alchemist. Wade had heard loud hammering from the study, but took this to be part of their experimenting. A few months later, evidence emerged that Ruthven had acted as a go-between in the sale of some of Arbella's jewellery to a goldsmith and a shadowy Dr Palmer – a sale that might have been intended to finance the escape attempt. The failure of the plot was perhaps the last straw for the already fragile Lady Arbella, whose mind and body both gave way. She died in the Tower in September 1615, leaving her sometime defender Patrick Ruthven to mourn her.[706]

****

A bronze plaque on the north-east wall of St John's Kirk in Perth is surmounted by the old Ruthven coat of arms, and bears the inscription:

> *In the northeast corner in a vault close to this spot along with*
> *William Earl of Gowrie, put to death May 4 1584, and*
> *James 2d Earl, d. 1588, are the martyred remains of John,*
> *3d and last Earl of Gowrie, and Lord Provost of the Royal*
> *Burgh of Perth, and his brother Alexander Ruthven,*
> *assassinated, Aug. 5 1600.*
>
> *'The gentle and peaceable disposition of the two brothers made*
> *them to be idolised by all who knew them.'*
>
> *This monument is placed here by a lineal descendant of John*
> *3d Earl of Gowrie, Janet Ruthven-Stuart, as an act of justice*
> *and a tribute to the memory of brave, loyal and innocent men.*
> *August 5 1913.*
>
> *Post tenebras lux.*

If there is any truth at all in the inscription on the church wall, then one day or night in the 17th century, those who still loved the Ruthvens brought down their mortal remains from the stakes on which they were impaled on the walls of Perth and secretly gave them Christian burial.[707] Perhaps those who did so included the ancestor of Janet Ruthven-Stuart – and according to her family's tradition, that ancestor was none other than the son of John, the last Earl of Gowrie.

The family story goes that in the confusion at Gowrie House on 5 August 1600, Gowrie's nurse was able to slip away with the dead earl's infant son. She eventually approached a sympathetic captain and persuaded him to protect the child, who was brought up in the captain's own family and later married one of his relatives. The lad, probably named John Ruthven, grew up with 'an exceedingly amiable temperament' and became an accomplished musician, as did his son, and their line continued down to the Ruthven-Stuart family.[708] The story of the lost heir of Gowrie is deeply improbable on many counts, not the least being that such a child must have been conceived, if not born, when the earl was in France in 1599. It is just possible that Gowrie, like many a Scottish lord before him, fathered a by-blow on a French girl, but the scrupulously bureaucratic English summary of his entourage, made for the purposes of his passport back to Scotland, mentions no child and no nurse.[709] Moreover, if any child of Gowrie's had been in Perth on 5 August 1600, the fact would certainly have been known to at least some of the witnesses to the events at Gowrie House. The rewards for reporting the existence of such a child, a boy who might grow up seeking one day to avenge his father and uncle, would presumably have been substantial, and surely irresistible to desperate men like George Craigengelt or Andrew Henderson, who needed any shred of evidence to absolve themselves of imputations of treason. Thus the tale of the Earl of Gowrie's son, like so much else that surrounded the events at Gowrie House on 5 August 1600, remains lost forever in the mist-shrouded land between legend and history.

TABLE A: THE RUTHVENS AND THE TUDOR AND STUART ROYAL LINES

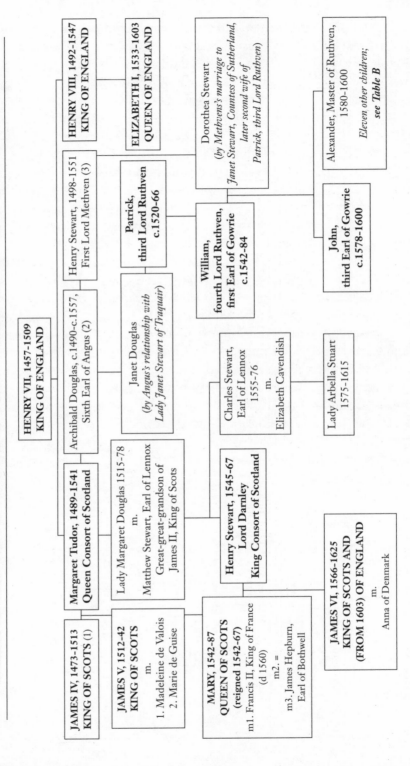

Table B: THE RUTHVEN FAMILY IN THE 16th & 17th CENTURIES: The Senior Lines

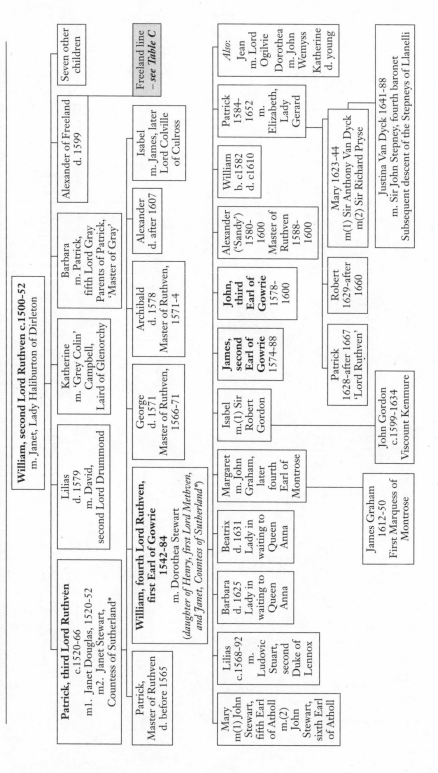

William, second Lord Ruthven c.1500-52
m. Janet, Lady Haliburton of Dirleton

Seven other children

Alexander of Freeland d. 1599

Freeland line – *see Table C*

Patrick, third Lord Ruthven c.1520-66
m1. Janet Douglas, 1520-52
m2. Janet Stewart, Countess of Sutherland*

Lilias d. 1579 m. David, second Lord Drummond

Katherine m. 'Grey Colin' Campbell, Laird of Glenorchy

Barbara m. Patrick, fifth Lord Gray, Parents of Patrick, 'Master of Gray'

Isabel m. James, later Lord Colville of Culross

William, fourth Lord Ruthven, first Earl of Gowrie 1542-84
m. Dorothea Stewart *(daughter of Henry, first Lord Methven, and Janet, Countess of Sutherland*)*

George d. 1571 Master of Ruthven, 1566-71

Archibald d. 1578 Master of Ruthven, 1571-4

Alexander d. after 1607

Patrick, Master of Ruthven d. before 1565

William b. c1582 d. c1610

Alexander ('Sandy') 1580-1600 Master of Ruthven 1588-1600

Patrick 1584-1652 m. Elizabeth, Lady Gerard

Also:
Jean m. Lord Ogilvie
Dorothea m. John Wemyss
Katherine d. young

Mary m(1) John Stewart, fifth Earl of Atholl m.(2) John Stewart, sixth Earl of Atholl

Lilias c.1568-92 m. Ludovic Stuart, second Duke of Lennox

Barbara d. 1625 Lady in waiting to Queen Anna

Beatrix d. 1631 Lady in waiting to Queen Anna

Margaret m. John Graham, later fourth Earl of Montrose

Isabel m. (1) Sir Robert Gordon

James, second Earl of Gowrie 1574-88

John, third Earl of Gowrie 1578-1600

Robert 1629-after 1660

Patrick 1628-after 1667 'Lord Ruthven'

Mary 1623-44 m(1) Sir Anthony Van Dyck m(2) Sir Richard Pryse

John Gordon c.1599-1634 Viscount Kenmure

James Graham 1612-50 First Marquess of Montrose

Justina Van Dyck 1641-88 m. Sir John Stepney, fourth baronet Subsequent descent of the Stepneys of Llanelli

Table C:
THE RUTHVEN FAMILY
IN THE 16th & 17th CENTURIES:
The Junior Lines

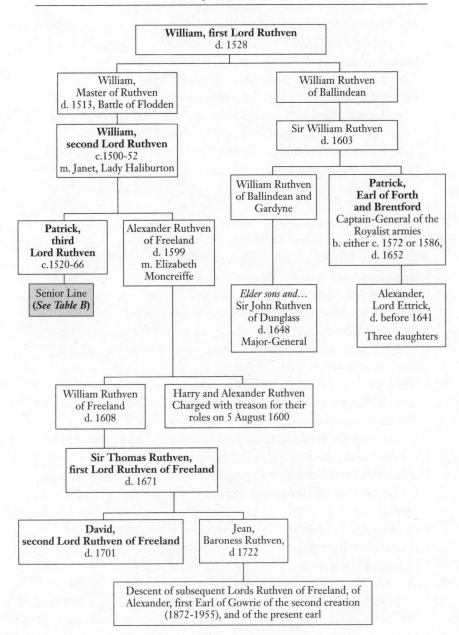

William, first Lord Ruthven
d. 1528

William,
Master of Ruthven
d. 1513, Battle of Flodden

William Ruthven
of Ballindean

**William,
second Lord Ruthven**
c.1500-52
m. Janet, Lady Haliburton

Sir William Ruthven
d. 1603

William Ruthven
of Ballindean and
Gardyne

**Patrick,
Earl of Forth
and Brentford**
Captain-General of the
Royalist armies
b. either c. 1572 or 1586,
d. 1652

**Patrick,
third
Lord Ruthven**
c.1520-66

Alexander Ruthven
of Freeland
d. 1599
m. Elizabeth
Moncreiffe

Senior Line
(*See Table B*)

Elder sons and...
Sir John Ruthven
of Dunglass
d. 1648
Major-General

Alexander,
Lord Ettrick,
d. before 1641

Three daughters

William Ruthven
of Freeland
d. 1608

Harry and Alexander Ruthven
Charged with treason for their
roles on 5 August 1600

**Sir Thomas Ruthven,
first Lord Ruthven of Freeland**
d. 1671

**David,
second Lord Ruthven of Freeland**
d. 1701

Jean,
Baroness Ruthven,
d 1722

Descent of subsequent Lords Ruthven of Freeland, of
Alexander, first Earl of Gowrie of the second creation
(1872-1955), and of the present earl

Endnotes

1   *His Majesty's Speech in the Last Session of Parliament Concerning the Gunpowder Plot* (1605), printed in *The Harleian Miscellany*, iii (1813), 6–7.

2   There are no known portraits of Gowrie, but James VI once expressed alarm that Gowrie's contemporary, the seventh Earl of Argyll, resembled him remarkably, and this description fits the extant portraits of Argyll: *CSPS, 1597–1603*, 961.

3   The following account of the events at Gowrie House is based primarily on the materials in Pitcairn, Lang and Arbuckle, unless stated otherwise, with individual incidents cited in subsequent chapters.

4   M. Nicholls, 'Strategy and Motivation in the Gunpowder Plot', *The Historical Journal*, 50 (2007), 792–6.

5   There are several recent studies of the late Elizabethan succession issue, but all emphasise the uncertainty of the outcome. See the essays in J. C. Mayer, ed., *The Struggle for the Succession in Late Elizabethan England* (Montpellier, 2004), especially those by Doran, Myers and Vignaux; and S. Doran, 'James VI and the English Succession', *James VI and I: Ideas, Authority, and Government*, ed. R. Houlbrooke (Aldershot, 2006), 25–42.

6   This was true on my most recent visit, in November 2009, and on several previous occasions, but when I first visited the museum in 2002 a temporary exhibition contained one small Victorian painting of the scene in the turret chamber. The permanent exhibition on the history of Perth makes no mention of the event, and it does not feature in the agenda of the conference planned for September 2010 to mark Perth's 800th anniversary of borough status.

7   eg, M. Lynch, *Scotland: A New History* (1992 edn), 234. A particularly popular recent history contains no mention of it at all: N. Oliver, *A History of Scotland* (2009).

8   Technically, Sandy was entitled to be called the Master of Gowrie. Although some witness depositions call him this, I have retained the more usual style.

9   Pitcairn, 157.

10   Trying the dead for treason in order to facilitate the confiscation of their property was a relatively recent innovation in Scottish law. It is said to date from an Act of 1540, but the evidence for this is unclear. It was done at the posthumous trial of the Earl of Huntly in 1563. (I am grateful to Dr Julian Goodare for this information.)

11   *Acts of the Parliaments of Scotland* (1818), iv. 213.

12   S. Reid, 'Ruthven, Patrick, earl of Forth and earl of Brentford (d.1651), royalist army officer', *ODNB*; *Ruthven correspondence: letters and papers of Patrick Ruthven, Earl of Forth and Brentford, and of his Family, AD 1615 – AD 1662*, ed. W. D. Macray (Roxburghe Club, Edinburgh, 1869); J. Barratt, *Cavalier Generals: King Charles I and his Commanders in the English Civil War, 1642–6* (Barnsley, 2004).

13   J. Blanch, *Gowrie, V.C.* (Hawthorn, Victoria, 1998).

14   TNA, HO 45/19822, papers on creation of earldom of Gowrie, 1945.

15   National Library of Australia, Gowrie Papers: (Reel 44), p1 of typescript draft of Gowrie's autobiography.

16   David, Lord Hailes, *Discourse of the Unnatural and Vile Conspiracy* (1755), 26n.

17   AKB, MS book by R. S. Fittis (catalogued at 941.32); W. Marshall, *Historic Scenes in Perthshire* (1880), 33.

18   D. Peacock, *Perth: Its Annals and its Archives* (Perth, 1849), 337–51; D. Munro, *A Vision of Perth* (Perth, 2000), 18.

19   *The Perthshire Courier*, 24 Sept. 1829, p. 3, col. 3.

20   PKA, MS B59/32/142, papers on release of Gowrie House by the army; *Memorabilia of the City of Perth* (Perth, 1806), 27–9; AKB, 'Miscellanies' (handwritten MS by D. Buist, early 19th century), p. 734. The north wall of Gowrie House, flanking the still extant Water Vennel, survived until 1865: *Perthshire Courier*, 5 Jan. 1864, p. 3, col. 1; CA, Derwydd MS H30, 'A Ramble in the Streets of Perth' (1865).

21   *CSPD, 1603–10*, 5.

22   *Extracts from the Records of the Burgh of Edinburgh, AD 1589 to 1603* (Edinburgh, 1927), 373.

23 For example, in 1636 the English traveller William Brereton saw the earl's head, still stuck on the Edinburgh tolbooth, and it remained there in 1650: P. Hume Brown, *Early Travellers in Scotland* (Edinburgh, 1891), 142; A. Bisset, *Essays upon Historical Truth* (1871), 301.

24 M. Todd, *The Culture of Protestantism in Early Modern Scotland* (New Haven, 2002), 225–6.

25 F. C. Eeles, 'The English Thanksgiving Service for King James' Delivery from the Gowrie Conspiracy', *Scottish Historical Review*, 8 (1911), 366–76; M. Morrissey, 'Preaching James VI to the Public: Preaching on Political Anniversaries at Paul's Cross', *James VI and I: Ideas, Authority, and Government*, ed. R. Houlbrooke (Aldershot, 2006), 109–10; Turner, 190–209.

26 Accuracy seems to have become a slightly moveable feast by then, as 1 August, not the 5th, was stated to be 'the day of Gowrie's conspiracy'; HMC, *Mar and Kellie*, I. 212. Cf D. Cressy, *Bonfires and Bells: National Memory and the Protestant Calendar in Elizabethan and Stuart England* (2004 edn), 57–8, 59. Restoration of the custom: J. Nicoll, *A Diary of Public Transactions and Other Occurrences, Chiefly in Scotland, from January 1650 to June 1667*, ed. D. Laing (Bannatyne Club, 1836), 374–5, 449

27 Calderwood, vi. 72.

28 National Library of Australia, Gowrie Papers: (Reel 18) Walter Montagu-Douglas-Scott *(probably the brother of the eighth Duke of Buccleuch)* to Gowrie, 5 March 1944, and latter's reply, 10 May; draft of Gowrie's letter to the BBC; reply from Lord Inman, 4 February 1947; (Reel 6) Transcript of BBC programme 'The Gowrie Conspiracy', broadcast 15 January 1947; (Reel 44) letters and papers on the 'Gowrie conspiracy' from 1943–4. The programme provided the first professional engagement for the much-loved Scottish comedian Rikki Fulton: obituary, *The Scotsman*, 29 Jan 2004.

29 Conversation of Lord Macaulay with Colonel John Stepney Cowell (later Sir John Cowell Stepney, Bart.), 29 July 1851, recorded in Cowell's commonplace book: CA, Stepney MSS, F233.

30 *Skotlands Rímur: Icelandic Ballads on the Gowrie Conspiracy*, ed. W. A. Craigie (Oxford, 1908). The most recent manifestation is the novel by Alanna Knight, *The Gowrie Conspiracy* (2003), which sees the unexpected arrival of a Time Lord in the Perth of 1600.

31 S. J. Kozikowski, 'The Gowrie Conspiracy against James VI:
    A New Source for Shakespeare's *Macbeth*', *Shakespeare Studies*, 13
    (1980), 197–212; A. M. Clark, *Murder under Trust: The Topical
    Macbeth and other Jacobean Matters* (Edinburgh, 1981), 109–26. I
    owe the suggestion that Shakespeare might have written *Gowrie*,
    and played the part of King James, to Dr Gustavo Turner, whose
    thesis provides the most detailed study of the lost play: Turner,
    257–61, 271–2, 281–3 and passim. It might be added that Lord
    Hunsdon, patron of Shakespeare's company when it was the 'Lord
    Chamberlain's Men' from 1597 to 1603, had known the first Earl
    of Gowrie well: Berkeley Castle muniments, Select Letters vol II,
    26 and 34, Gowrie to Sir George Carey (later second Lord
    Hunsdon), 28 Dec. 1582 and 23 Apr. 1583.

32 F. Moncreiff and W. Moncreiffe, *The Moncreiffs and the Moncreiffes*
    (Edinburgh, 1929), i. 119–20. This is almost identical to a
    contemporary French reaction, so the one might be a conflation
    of the other: Turner, 143.

33 Calderwood, vi. 45–6.

34 Arbuckle, 11; Pitcairn, 232, 245; Calderwood, vi. 46.

35 *CSPS, 1597–1603*, 678–80; Turner, 51–3.

36 Pitcairn, 313–14.

37 Pitcairn, 156–7.

38 Pitcairn, 233.

39 Pitcairn, 218–19.

40 Calderwood, vi. 50; A. L. Juhala, 'An Advantageous Alliance:
    Edinburgh and the Court of James VI', *Sixteenth Century Scotland:
    Essays in Honour of Michael Lynch*, ed. J. Goodare and
    A. A. MacDonald (Leiden, 2008), 347.

41 Pitcairn, 248–51.

42 Pitcairn, 249.

43 Sandy graduated from Edinburgh in July 1598; it is therefore
    unlikely that he went on to join John at Padua, as some writers
    have claimed. *A Catalogue of the Graduates in the Faculties of Arts,
    Divinity and Law of the University of Edinburgh since its Foundation*
    (Edinburgh, 1858), 16.

44 Pitcairn, 250.

45 Turner, 69.

46 Pitcairn, 250.

47 Turner, 81–2.

48 Pitcairn, 250.

49   Calderwood, vi. 73–4.
50   *CSPS, 1597–1603*, 681.
51   Pitcairn, 250.
52   Calderwood, vi. 49, 56; *CSPS, 1597–1603*, 684. Since 1588, Galloway had written many prefaces on James's behalf: J. Rickard, *Authorship and Authority: The Writings of James VI and I* (Manchester, 2007), 73–4, 76–7, 79–80, 81, 94, 146–7.
53   Calderwood, vi. 49.
54   Calderwood, vi. 56–9.
55   Pitcairn, 158. Cf Arbuckle, 104–5.
56   Pitcairn, 148–55.
57   Calderwood, vi. 75.
58   *CSPS 1597–1603*, 690.
59   Pitcairn, 219–21.
60   Pitcairn, 221–3.
61   *CSPS, 1597–1603*, 704.
62   Pitcairn, 223.
63   Pitcairn, 221.
64   Calderwood, vi. 59; *CSPS 1597–1603*, 690.
65   For the bibliographical history of this item, and the dissemination of the official narrative overseas, see Turner, 101–2, 136–46. It is printed in Pitcairn, 208–23.
66   Turner, 49. The pamphlet was apparently written by Thomas Hamilton, the king's advocate, and David Murray, his comptroller: NLS, Adv. MS 31.6.20, p. 144.
67   Pitcairn, 210–13.
68   Pitcairn, 214–15.
69   Pitcairn, 217.
70   Pitcairn, 218.
71   TNA, PRO 31/3/31 (Baschet's transcripts of French despatches), fos. 262, 267, 270, 277.
72   Pitcairn, 192–208.
73   Pitcairn, 193–4.
74   Pitcairn, 200.
75   Perth was a town noted for its multiplicity of bells, even after the Reformation: M. Todd, 'What's in a Name? Language, Image, and Urban Identity in Early Modern Perth', *Dutch Review of Church History*, 85 (2005), 384–6.
76   Pitcairn, 194–207.
77   Pitcairn, 196.

78   Pitcairn, 197.
79   Pitcairn, 196.
80   Pitcairn, 198.
81   M. Verschuur, *Politics or Religion? The Reformation in Perth 1540–70* (Edinburgh, 2006), 47–50, 63–4, 113, 119–20, 139–41.
82   *The Chronicle of Perth* (Edinburgh, The Maitland Club, 1831), 8.
83   Scott, 262.
84   *CSPS, 1597–1603,* 736.
85   Pitcairn, 171–2.
86   Pitcairn, 172–3.
87   Pitcairn, 173.
88   Pitcairn, 174.
89   Pitcairn, 174.
90   Pitcairn, 184.
91   Pitcairn, 184.
92   Pitcairn, 180–1.
93   Pitcairn, 181.
94   Pitcairn, 188.
95   Pitcairn, 181.
96   Pitcairn, 182.
97   Pitcairn, 182.
98   Pitcairn, 182.
99   Pitcairn, 183.
100 Pitcairn, 183.
101 Pitcairn, 184.
102 Pitcairn, 175.
103 Pitcairn, 177.
104 Pitcairn, 178.
105 Pitcairn, 179.
106 Pitcairn, 197.
107 *CSPS, 1597–1603,* 731
108 Pitcairn, 191–2.
109 Pitcairn, 191.
110 NLS, Adv. MS 31.6.20, pp. 178–9.
111 Pitcairn, 182.
112 *Acts of the Parliaments of* Scotland, iv (1816), 193–215; CSPS, *1597–1603,* 733–6.
113 PKA, Fittis Papers, MS 2/2, file 18, p. 77.
114 Calderwood, vi. 99–100.
115 *CSPS, 1597–1603,* 714–15, 719–20, 725.

116 W. Panton, *A Dissertation on that Portion of Scottish History Termed The Gowry Conspiracy*, (Perth 1812), 87.

117 *RGS, 1593–1608*, 373.

118 F. Osborne, *Traditionall Memoyres of the Reigne of King James* (1658), 93.

119 *The Diaries of Lady Anne Clifford*, ed. D. J. H. Clifford (2003 edn), 22; *ODNB*.

120 P. Drummond-Mackay, 'The Gowrie Conspiracy', *The Double Tressure: Journal of the Heraldry Society of Scotland*, 19 (1997), 37.

121 Turner, 332–7.

122 Calderwood, vi. 56–8.

123 Calderwood, vi. 85; my emphasis.

124 Calderwood, vi. 146–8.

125 Pitcairn, 302–8.

126 Calderwood, vi. 216–19.

127 Calderwood, vi. 46. Moreover, Montrose's wife was a first cousin of the countess's husband.

128 HMC, *Ninth Report, Appendix*, 196.

129 NAS, GD 6/250, 20/1/411, 220/6/628; *RPCS, 1604–7*, 597.

130 *Border Papers*, 677.

131 *Border Papers*, 682.

132 *Border Papers*, 684.

133 *Border Papers*, 684, 688.

134 *CSPS, 1597–1603*, 704, 799, 806, 817, 818.

135 *CSPS, 1597–1603*, 907; *RPCS, 1599–1604*, 511.

136 NAS, RH 1/2/436.

137 HMC, *Cecil* xv. 127–8.

138 HMC, *Cecil* xv. 376–7. Francis Wandesford was probably the 22-year-old younger son of Sir Christopher Wandesford of Kirklington.

139 *Border Papers*, 682.

140 BL, Add. MSS 72,446.

141 BL, Add. MSS 38,139, fo. 50; HMC, *Cecil*, xv. 215.

142 NAS, GD 246/75, 'A Memorandum of Such Things as are Necessary to be tried Concerning the House of Gowrie' (original document by Patrick Ruthven). Cf NLS, MS Acc. 7,400 and MS Adv. 34.6.24, fo. 190v, which corroborate the fate of William Ruthven.

143 A. Bisset, *Essays Upon Historical Truth* (1871), 268–9. However, in 1610 one Nicholas Douglas spent 10 months in prison because he was wrongly identified as William: *CSPD 1603–10*, 623.

144 Dinah Maria Craik (1826–87), the author of *John Halifax, Gentleman*, wrote a novella of that title, based on Patrick's life.

145 Pitcairn, 249.

146 David, Lord Hailes, *Discourse of the Unnatural and Vile Conspiracy* (1755), 34–6.

147 W. Sanderson, *A Compleat History of the Lives and Reigns of Mary Queen of Scots and of Her Son and Successor James the Sixth, King of Scotland* (1656), 228; *CSPS, 1597–1603*, 682.

148 *CSPS, 1597–1603*, 684.

149 Pitcairn, 218–19.

150 These items were apparently taken from the body by Sir Thomas Erskine, who passed them to his brother George, a prominent authority on the esoteric. They eventually passed to George's grandson George Mackenzie, Earl of Cromarty: *An Historical Account of the Conspiracies by the Earls of Gowry, and Robert Logan of Restalrig, Against King James VI* (Edinburgh, 1713), xiii-xiv.

151 E. Cowan, 'The Darker Vision of the Scottish Renaissance: The Devil and Francis Stewart', *The Renaissance and Reformation in Scotland*, ed. I. B. Cowan and D. Shaw (Edinburgh, 1983), 138–9; Cowan, 'Witch Persecution and Folk Belief in Lowland Scotland', *Witchcraft and Belief in Early Modern Scotland* (Basingstoke, 2008), 90 and n.40.

152 A. Bisset, *Essays upon Historical Truth* (1871), 268–9.

153 HMC, *Cecil*, xvii. 387–8; *Acts of the Privy Council of England, 1613–14*, 447; Bruce, *Papers*, 61.

154 *CSPD, 1611–18*, 212.

155 For the intellectual 'academy' in the Tower at this time, see R. I. McCallum, 'Patrick Ruthven, Alchemist and Physician', *Proceedings of the Society of Antiquaries of Scotland*, 134 (2004), 475–6.

156 Edinburgh University Library, MS D.C.I.30. The book is described by McCallum, 'Patrick Ruthven', 481–6.

157 Cf Bodleian Library, Oxford, Rawlinson MS C515, p. 54–5.

158 BL, Thomason Tracts E1528(1); McCallum, 'Patrick Ruthven', 487–8.

159 Isle of Wight Record Office, Oglander MS OG/CC/3, Patrick Ruthven to Sir John Oglander, '17 January'.

160 'Sketches of Later Scottish Alchemists', *Proceedings of the Society of Antiquaries of Scotland*, 11 (1876), 425. Cf L. Hutchinson, *Memoirs of the Life of Colonel Hutchinson* (1995 edn, ed. N. H. Keeble), 13.

161 There is much evidence to suggest that Catholicism was actually *increasing* in strength in Scotland in the 1550s and 1560s, not declining: Lynch, 'Introduction', 8–9, 18–21; J. Goodare, 'Queen Mary's Catholic Interlude', 159–68; both in *Innes Review*, 38 (1987).

162 Cowan, 49–50.

163 J. Goodare, *The Government of Scotland 1560–1625* (Oxford, 2004), 128–48.

164 *RPCS, 1545–69*, 236, 250, 277, 280–420.

165 Keith, iii. 271.

166 Knox, ii. 373.

167 Knox, ii. 406; Guy, 187.

168 S. Macauley, 'The Lennox Crisis, 1558–63', *Northern History*, XLI (2004), 276–87.

169 *CSPS, 1563–9*, 119, 154, 174; G. Donaldson, *All the Queen's Men: Power and Politics in Mary Stewart's Scotland* (London, 1983), 72, 75.

170 *CSPS, 1563–9*, 169.

171 S. Adams, 'The Release of Lord Darnley', *Innes Review*, 38, (1987), 123-53. .

172 *CSPS, 1563–9*, 172–3.

173 Weir, 71–2.

174 Weir, 81; Fraser, 240.

175 *Clan Campbell Letters*, ed. J. E. A. Dawson (Edinburgh, 1997), 122, 129–31; *RPCS, 1545–69*, 420.

176 Keith, iii. 260.

177 *CSPS, 1563–9*, 166, 168, although in the latter the messenger is named as Lord Justice Clerk Bellenden, the husband of Ruthven's stepdaughter; Guy, 211.

178 *CSPS, 1563–9*, 225.

179 Guy, 211.

180 Guy, 245–7.

181 Fraser, 247.

182 BL, Add. MSS 48,043 fos. 101–2.

183 W. Scott, *The Fair Maid of Perth* ('Border edition', ed. A. Lang, 1904), 10.

184 The account that follows of Rizzio's murder and the subsequent events of 9–11 March is largely Ruthven's own (Keith, iii. 260–78), unless stated otherwise. It has been checked against one of the original English copies (BL, Add. MSS 48,043, fos. 97–117), then supplemented by Mary's account in her letter to the Archbishop of Glasgow (Keith, ii. 411–23), and by the following secondary accounts: Fraser, 250–7; Weir, 105–17; Guy, 248–62; D. Tweedie, *David Rizzio and Mary, Queen of Scots* (2008), 139–52.

185 Guy, 252.

186 John Maxwell, Lord Herries, *Historical Memoirs of the Reign of Mary Queen of Scots and a Portion of the Reign of King James VI* (Edinburgh, Abbotsford Club, 1836), 77.

187 Nau, 4.

188 Nau, 4; Herries, *Historical Memoirs*, 77.

189 Fraser, 256.

190 *CSPS, 1563–9*, 269.

191 *CSPS, 1563–9*, 270–4.

192 Nau, 22–3.

193 *CSPS, 1563–9*, 278.

194 http://www.baronage.co.uk/bphtm-02/moa-05.html, accessed 27 November 2009.

195 J. Dow, *Ruthven's Army in Sweden and Esthonia* (Stockholm, 1965).

196 *A Diurnal of Remarkable Occurrents that have passed within the Country of Scotland since the death of King James IV till the Year 1575* (Edinburgh, 1833), 196, 292.

197 L. A. Yeoman, 'North Berwick Witches', *ODNB*.

198 Scott, 310–12. The book is now NAS, GD 51/17/13.

199 R. S. Fittis, *Ecclesiastical Annals of Perth* (Edinburgh, 1885), 132.

200 J. Cant, *The Muse's Threnodie: Or Mirthful Mournings on the Death of Mr Gall* (Perth, 1774), vi, 11, 131–3, 147–8, 167

201 J. Goodare and J. Miller, 'Introduction', *Witchcraft and Belief in Early Modern Scotland*, ed. Goodare and Miller (Basingstoke, 2008), 5.

202 D. Lloyd, *The States-men and Favourites of England since the Reformation...* (1665), 561

203 *CSPS, 1563–9*, 308. The events leading up to the pardon are described by Weir, 171–2; Guy, 282–9.

204 *RSS, v, 1556–67*, 309–10.

205 *RPCS, 1545–69*, 505.

206 Donaldson, *Queen's Men*, 81–2, 85.

207 Keith, ii. 646.
208 *CSPS, 1563–9*, 350; Fraser, 335.
209 Calderwood, ii. 374; Nau, 59–61.
210 *CSPS, 1569–71*, 84.
211 Donaldson, *Queen's Men*, 118–19.
212 Donaldson, *Queen's Men*, 119–20.
213 *CSPS, 1569–71*, 680.
214 Calderwood, ii. 419; iii. 8, 155; Herries, *Historical Memoirs*, 129–30; *Clan Campbell Letters*, 168, 174; Spottiswood, 261; *CSPS, 1563–9*, 193–200; *1569–71*, 112, 134, 145.
215 Hewitt, *Morton*, 171–3.
216 Knox, vi. 640; Calderwood, iii. 235.
217 *CSPS, 1574–81*, 197.
218 Personal observations, Dirleton Castle, 2001–9; D. Grove, *Dirleton Castle* (Historic Scotland, Edinburgh, 2003).
219 Scott, 170–1.
220 D. Howard, *The Architectural History of Scotland: Scottish Architecture from the Reformation to the Restoration, 1560–1660* (Edinburgh, 1995), 58, 60.
221 J. Gifford, *Perth and Kinross* (The Buildings of Scotland series; New Haven, 2007), 689–92.
222 A. Hay, 'The Scottish Nobilitie in An. Dom. 1577', *Estimate of the Scottish Nobility in the Reign of James VI*, ed. C. Rogers (1873), 18–19.
223 *RSS, vi, 1567–74*, 314–15.
224 Hewitt, *Morton*, 36.
225 *Accounts of the Lord High Treasurer of Scotland*, 13, ed. C. T. McInnes (Edinburgh, 1978), xxx-xxxi; J. Goodare, 'The Debts of James VI of Scotland', *Economic History Review*, 62 (2009), 935–6.
226 *CSPS, 1571–4*, 681.
227 *CSPS, 1574–81*, 1–2.
228 Hewitt, *Morton*, 44–5.
229 Donaldson, *Queen's Men*, 128–9.
230 Spottiswood, 283.
231 HMC, *Cecil MSS*, ii. 285.
232 Hewitt, *Morton*, 75–6.
233 Calderwood, iii. 556.
234 Brown, *Noble Society*, 10.
235 E. Cust, *Some Account of the Stuarts of Aubigny (1422–1672)* (1891), 89.

236 Donaldson, *Queen's Men*, 132–3.

237 A. L. Juhala, 'The Household and Court of King James VI of Scotland, 1567–1603) (Edinburgh University PhD thesis, 2000), 32–3.

238 Juhala, 'Household', 103.

239 *Memoirs of the Affairs of Scotland by David Moysie, 1577–1603* (Maitland Club, Edinburgh, 1830), 34.

240 J. Fergusson, *The Man Behind MacBeth and Other Studies* (1969), 22–87; R. Grant, 'Politicking Jacobean Women: Lady Ferniehirst, The Countess of Arran and the Countess of Huntly, c1580–1603', *Women in Scotland c1100-c1750*, ed. E. Ewan and M. M. Meikle (East Linton, 1998), 98–100.

241 Donaldson, *Queen's Men*, 137–8. For these discussions see *CSPS, 1581–3*, passim, and especially 269–85.

242 J. Goodare and M. Lynch, 'James VI: Universal King', *The Reign of James VI*, ed. Goodare and Lynch (East Linton, 2000), 16–17.

243 *Memoirs of Sir James Melville of Halhill*, ed. G. Donaldson (1969), 275, 281; Donaldson, *Queen's Men*, 138–40.

244 See eg, *CSPS, 1581–3*, 60–2.

245 *CSPS, 1574–81*, 515.

246 *CSPS, 1574–81*, 522, 527.

247 *CSPS, 1581–3*, 144–5.

248 Melville, *Memoirs*, 276–7.

249 D. Hume of Godscroft, *The History of the House of Angus*, ed. D. Reid (Woodbridge, 2005), ii. 285; Calderwood, iii. 632.

250 *CSPS, 1574-81*, 575, 623, 624; *CSPS, 1581–3*, 127.

251 *CSPS, 1581–3*, 240, 527.

252 J. Goodare and M. Lynch, 'James VI: Universal King', *The Reign of James VI*, ed. Goodare and Lynch (East Linton, 2000), 16; Lynch, 'Court Ceremony and Ritual', ibid, 79–81; Donaldson, *Queen's Men*, 140.

253 Calderwood, iii. 649; *CSPS, 1581–3*, 149.

254 Calderwood, iii. 671.

255 Calderwood, iii. 692. The head was duly taken down and buried on 10 December 1582.

256 J. Goodare, *The Government of Scotland, 1560–1625* (Oxford, 2004), 197.

257 *Further Papers Relating to the Ruthven Family*, ed. J. Bruce (1867), 4–5; *The Chronicle of Perth* (Edinburgh, Maitland Club, 1831), 4.

258 Calderwood, iii. 637.

259 Calderwood, iii. 637; Spottiswood, 320.

260 Hume of Godscroft, *History of Angus*, ii. 286.

261 *CSPS, 1581–3*, 162, 168, 192.

262 H. Dunthorne, 'Stewart, Sir William, d. 1602x4, soldier and diplomat', *ODNB*.

263 Calderwood, iii. 651–65.

264 NLS, MS 2208, fo. 5, Gowrie, Mar, Glencairn et al to John Erskine of Dun, 31 Aug. 1582.

265 *RPCS, 1578–85*, 508–9.

266 Melville, *Memoirs*, 282–3.

267 *CSPS, 1581–3*, 149–55, 170–5.

268 *CSPS, 1581–3*, 172.

269 Calderwood, iii. 691–3.

270 Spottiswood, 324.

271 Spottiswood, 328.

272 BL, MS Sloane 3199, fo. 124, Gowrie to Burghley, 29 Dec. 1582; *CSPS, 1581–3*, 232–3.

273 J. Goodare, 'James VI's English Subsidy', Goodare and Lynch, *Reign of James VI*, 112.

274 Donaldson, *Queen's Men*, 143–4; K. M. Brown, 'The Price of Friendship: The "Well Affected" and English Economic Clientage in Scotland Before 1603', *Scotland and England 1286–1815*, ed. R. A. Mason (Edinburgh, 1987), 142–3.

275 *CSPS, 1581–3*, 300–1.

276 Calderwood, iii. 715; Melville, *Memoirs*, 283–4; *CSPS, 1581–3*, 519–20.

277 Calderwood, iii. 715–16; Spottiswood, 325.

278 *CSPS, 1581–3*, 312, 326, 336–8, 348, 353, 400, 405, 447.

279 *CSPS, 1581–3*, 559; Spottiswood, 326.

280 *CSPS, 1581–3*, 567; Hume of Godscroft, *History of Angus*, ii. 290–1, 304.

281 *CSPS, 1581–3*, 538, 542, 552–3.

282 *RPCS, 1578–85*, 590.

283 *CSPS, 1581–3*, 578.

284 *CSPS, 1581–3*, 587.

285 Melville, *Memoirs*, 300; *CSPS, 1581–3*, 677, 688.

286 *CSPS, 1581–3*, 629, 660; http://ads.ahds.ac.uk/catalogue/adsdata/PSAS_2002/pdf/vol_054/54_204_210.pdf, accessed 8 June 2009.

287 NAS, MS GD 90/2/25, notes by Gowrie.

288 Calderwood, iv. 21.

289 Hume of Godscroft, *History of Angus*, ii. 304.

290 NAS, MS GC 115/112. instrument of sasine, 11 Apr. 1584; *CSPS, 1584–5*, 35, 40, 55.

291 Hume of Godscroft, *History of Angus*, ii. 305–6.

292 Calderwood, iv. 22.

293 Melville, *Memoirs*, 124

294 M. Lee, *John Maitland of Thirlestane & the Foundation of the Stuart Despotism in Scotland* (Princeton, 1959), 52.

295 Calderwood, iv. 31–4.

296 *CSPS, 1584–5*, 60, 66; Melville, *Memoirs*, 325.

297 *CSPS, 1584–5*, 65–7; Calderwood, iv. 23–5.

298 *CSPS, 1584–5*, 157–9.

299 Unless stated otherwise, the account of the trial and last speeches of the Earl of Gowrie are drawn from 'The Manner and Form of Examination and Death of William, Earl of Gowrie…', and 'The Declaration made by the Earl of Gowrie upon the Scaffold…', both published in *The Bannatyne Miscellany*, ed. Sir Walter Scott et al (Bannatyne Club, Edinburgh, 1827), 91–105.

300 Gowrie hastily scribbled some notes for his defence on an old letter requesting a loan: NAS, GD 90/2/19.

301 *Memoirs of Sir James Melville of Halhill*, ed. G. Donaldson (1969), 124.

302 *CSPS, 1584–5*, 124.

303 Patrick Ruthven, his fifth son and later the claimant to his titles.

304 C. Innes, *Sketches of Early Scottish History and Social Progress* (1861), 347. Innes claims that Gowrie was particularly fond of Spanish chestnut and walnut trees.

305 Pitcairn, 116–18.

306 Melville, *Memoirs*, 326–7.

307 K. M. Brown, *Noble Society in Scotland: Wealth, Family and Culture from Reformation to Revolution* (Edinburgh, 2004 edn), 255, 260.

308 *CSPS, 1584–5*, 118.

309 *The Acts of the Parliament of Scotland*, iii (1814). 301–2.

310 *RGS*, vi, 1580–93, 238; *CSPS, 1584–5*, 185.

311 Calderwood, iv. 200.

312 Calderwood, iv. 197–8. A slightly different version of the story was told by Hume of Godscroft, *History of Angus*, ii. 322.

313 *CSPS, 1584–5*, 290–1.

314 *CSPS, 1584–5*, 137. Mary had always expressed her hatred of William Ruthven, and her disquiet at the prominence he obtained in her son's government: *CSPS, 1581–3*, 99, 397, 422.

315 'Overtures for Queen Elizabeth her Request to the King for the House of Gowrie, in December 1584', *The Bannatyne Miscellany*, I, ed. Sir Walter Scott et al (Bannatyne Club, Edinburgh, 1827), 106.

316 *CSPS, 1583–5*, 404–5.

317 K. M. Brown, *Bloodfeud in Scotland, 1573–1625: Violence, Justice and Politics in an Early Modern Society* (Edinburgh, 2003 edn), 114.

318 Fergusson, *Man Behind Macbeth*, 74.

319 *RPCS, 1585–92*, 36; R. Grant, 'The Making of the Anglo-Scottish Alliance of 1586', *Sixteenth Century Scotland: Essays in Honour of Michael Lynch*, ed. J. Goodare and A. A. MacDonald (Leiden, 2008), 219–21.

320 *The Acts of the Parliaments of Scotland*, iii (1814), 472.

321 *CSPS, 1589–93*, 152.

322 L. Normand and G. Roberts, *Witchcraft in Early Modern Scotland: James VI's Demonology and the North Berwick Witches* (Exeter, 2000), 39.

323 R. G. MacPherson, 'Francis Stewart, fifth Earl Bothwell, c1562–1612: Lordship and Politics in Jacobean Scotland' (Edinburgh University PhD thesis, 1998), 19.

324 Lee, *Maitland of Thirlestane*, 142–3.

325 Calderwood, v. 156.

326 R. Grant, 'The Brig o'Dee Affair', Goodare and Lynch, *Reign of James VI*, 93–109.

327 *CSPS, 1589–93*, 613.

328 Normand and Roberts, *Witchcraft*, 39–40; E. Cowan, 'Darker Vision', 125–131.

329 M. M. Meikle, ' "Holde her at the Oeconomicke rule of the House": Anna of Denmark and Scottish court finances, 1589–1603', *Women in Scotland c1100 – c1750*, ed. E. Ewan and M. M. Meikle (East Linton, 1998), 107.

330 *CSPS, 1589–93*, 276; G. E. Cokayne et al, *The Complete Peerage*, ix. 149.

331 *The Scots Peerage*, ed. J. B. Paul (Edinburgh, 1904–14), v. 118.

332 D. Pringle, *Huntingtower* (Historic Scotland, Edinburgh, 1996), 23–4.

333 The girl's name appears as Sophia in many sources, but a recent analysis proves conclusively that Lilias was the object of Lennox's affections: J. Reid-Baxter, 'Politics, Passion and Poetry in the Court of James VI: John Burel and his Surviving Works', *A Palace in the Wild: Essays on Vernacular Culture and Humanism in Late Medieval and Renaissance Scotland*, ed. L A. J. R. Houwen, A. A. MacDonald and S. L. Mapstone (Leuven, 2000), 210–13, 244–8.

334 *CSPS, 1589–93*, 410.

335 J. Reid-Baxter, 'Burel, John (1565x8–1603), merchant and poet', *ODNB*.

336 *CSPS, 1589–93*, 410, 613; Calderwood, v. 128. The suggestion that Bothwell was in violent pursuit of one of the Ruthven girls at this precise time is probably a misreporting of Lennox: *Border Papers, 1560–94*, 379.

337 Alternatively, it is possible that she was reburied at Holyrood: Reid-Baxter, 'Politics, Passion and Poetry', 244–5n.

338 Presumably Keith must have been his 'godfather' at a service to receive him into the Kirk; he would probably have been either too young, or too unknown to the Aubigny Stewarts, to have been at Ludovic's original (and Catholic) christening.

339 *RSS, 1575–80*, 332; *CSPS, 1581–3*, 495

340 *Letters of King James VI & I*, ed. G. P. V. Akrigg (Berkeley, Ca., 1984), 70, 74–5, 78, 79, 81, 479; *RPCS, 1585–92*, 130n, 144.

341 *RPCS, 1585–92*, xxvii, 200.

342 *CSPS, 1589–93*, 371, 547.

343 *CSPS, 1589–93*, 622–3; Lee, *Maitland of Thirlestane*, 234–6.

344 This building is described in detail by D. B. Gallagher, 'Holyrood Abbey: The Disappearance of a Monastery', *Proceedings of the Society of Antiquaries of Scotland*, 128 (1998), 1088–90. It adjoined the great hall of the palace.

345 *CSPS, 1593–5*, 190. Original grant of the house: *RGS*, v (1546–80), 363.

346 William Douglas, tenth Earl of Angus, had succeeded to the title in 1591; his conversion to Rome horrified his family. For the affair as a whole, see F. Shearman, 'The Spanish Blanks', *Innes Review*, 3 (1952), 81–103, although Shearman's overall interpretation is unconvincing.

347 *CSPS, 1593–5*, 193.

348 Spottiswood, 394.

349 *CSPS, 1593–5*, 304–5, 327–8.

350 *A Catalogue of the Graduates in the Faculties of Arts, Divinity and Law of the University of Edinburgh since its Foundation* (Edinburgh, 1858), 11; Cowan, 149.

351 *CSPS, 1593–5*, 177.

352 Cowan, 150–1.

353 James's letters: NAS, GD 121/2/3/2.

354 Bruce, *Further Papers*, 7–9.

355 Bruce, *Further Papers*, 5–6.

356 HMC, *Salisbury*, xiv. 189.

357 HMC, *Ancaster*, 345, 347.

358 W. Sanderson, *A Compleat History of the Lives and Reigns of Mary Queen of Scots and of her Son and Successor James the Sixth, King of Scotland* (1656), 226.

359 HMC, *Cecil*, x. 133; *CSPS 1597–1603*, 630.

360 Calderwood, vi. 27.

361 Calderwood, vi. 70–1; *Border Papers, 1595–1603*, 659.

362 Pitcairn, 293, 297.

363 *The Chronicle of Perth* (Edinburgh, The Maitland Club, 1831), 7.

364 *CSPS, 1597–1603*, 663, 670.

365 Calderwood, vi. 71.

366 Calderwood, vi. 27.

367 K. M. Brown, *Bloodfeud in Scotland, 1573–1625: Violence, Justice and Politics in an Early Modern Society* (Edinburgh, 2003 edn); H. Potter, *Bloodfeud: The Stewarts and Gordons at War in the Age of Mary Queen of Scots* (Stroud, 2002); J. Wormald, 'Bloodfeud, Kindred and Government in Early Modern Scotland', *Past and Present*, 87 (1980), 54–97.

368 N. Machiavelli, *The Prince* (trans. G. Bull; 1999 Penguin edition), 29–31.

369 Similarly William, Laird of Moncreiff, was absent from the gathering at Gowrie House, unlike his younger brothers John and Hew.

370 NLS, Adv. MS 13.1.4 (1), p. 276; Centre for Kentish Studies, Maidstone: Dering manuscripts, U275/C1/17; *CSPS, 1597–1603*, 694. This suggested timing would also have kept most of the population of Perth well out of the way: Arbuckle, 104.

371 J. E. A. Dawson, '"There is Nothing like a Good Gossip": Baptism, Kinship and Alliance in Early Modern Scotland', *Perspectives on the Older Scottish Tongue: A Celebration of DOST*, ed. C. J. Kay and M. A. Mackay (Edinburgh, 2005), 41.

372 Arbuckle, 104; Pitcairn, 188.

373 Lang, 22.

374 Pitcairn, 215.

375 Pitcairn, 222.

376 Lang, 68.

377 E. J. Cowan, 'The Political Idea of a Covenanting Leader: Archibald Campbell, Marquis of Argyll 1607–1661' in Roger Mason, ed. *Scots and Britons: Scottish Political Thought and the Union of 1707* (Cambridge, 1992), 244–8.

378 J. Goodare, 'The Attempted Scottish Coup of 1596', *Sixteenth Century Scotland: Essays in Honour of Michael Lynch*, ed. Goodare and A. A. MacDonald (Leiden, 2008), 311–36.

379 Arbuckle, 2; Lang, 110. However, it is also possible that the timing of Gowrie's return was connected to the death on 9 October 1599 of his great-uncle, Alexander Ruthven of Freeland, who seems to have been the most important administrator of his estate during his absence.

380 NLS, Adv. MS 13.1.4(1), pp. 225–6.

381 CA, Derwydd MS H18, note in pencil by James Maidment (1793–1879) at back of copy of Scott's *History of John, Earl of Gowrie* (1818) presented by Maidment to Alan James Gulston.

382 This was still the case as recently as 1982, when Major & Mrs A. Ruthven-Finlayson's *Alexander Ruthven and the Gowrie Mystery: A Chronicle of Events* was published in Bognor Regis.

383 *CSPS, 1597–1603*, 661–3, 670.

384 Arbuckle, 3.

385 Arbuckle, 96; J. Goodare, 'The Debts of James VI of Scotland', *Economic History Review*, 62 (2009), 926–52, especially pp. 935–6, 949.

386 Scott, 141–3.

387 Lang, 132–3. A related legend cast Sandy as the father of the future King Charles I: E. Peyton, *The Divine Catastrophe of the Kingly Family of the House of Stuarts* (1652), 339.

388 Peyton, *Divine Catastrophe*, 337–9.

389 Glasgow University Library, GB 0247 MS Gen 12006.

390 *Border Papers, 1595–1603*, 678.

391 eg, G. P. R. James, *An Investigation of the Circumstances Attending the Murder of John Earl of Gowrie* (1849), p. l, n. – 'A suspicion most horrible always crosses my mind…I cannot venture to allude to it more distinctly, but those who have most studied the character, habits and propensities of this monarch may perhaps comprehend its nature'.

392 CA, Stepney MS F233, in John Cowell Stepney's notes on 'Gowrie'.

393 Grey, Earl of Gowrie, letter to the author, 2 Aug. 2006.

394 Pitcairn, 172.

395 Allan Massie, *The Royal Stuarts: A History of the Family That Shaped Britain* (2010), 155–9, based on researches undertaken by Christian, Lady Hesketh (1929–2006). Massie and Hesketh seem greatly to exaggerate John Ramsay's alleged status as a royal favourite, and his keenness to eliminate Sandy Ruthven as a potential threat to his position; they also entirely ignore the existence of the 'armoured man' and exaggerate the amount of time that Sandy and James spent 'alone' together.

396 CA, Derwydd MS H38, diary of Eliza Gulston, 11 May 1823. In reality, the earldom could not pass through female heirs.

397 BL, Add. MSS 35,625, fo. 110.

398 Pitcairn, 251.

399 Calderwood, vi. 70; Lang, 51–4.

400 Scott, 4–5.

401 TNA, SP 52/56/52, printed in *CSPS, 1597–1603*, 698–700, and Lang, 252–6.

402 *The Spottiswoode Miscellany*, ed. J. Maidment, ii (Edinburgh, 1845), 320.

403 Scott, 150–1.

404 *CSPS, 1597–1603*, 642, 644.

405 Cf Scott, 153.

406 Scott, 206; PKA, Fittis MS 2/2/18, p.55; Calderwood, vi. 71.

407 Calderwood, vi. 71.

408 Pitcairn, 237–8.

409 Pitcairn, 237; Lang, 134–5.

410 BL, Add. MSS 35,625, fo. 110v; Scott, 146.

411 Scott, 145. James would probably have skirted the northern slopes of the Lomond hills before cutting through the Ochils down to Glenfarg and thence to Bridge of Earn; the author has retraced several of the possible routes.

412 PKA, Fittis Papers, MS 2/2, file 17, p. 16.

413 Scott, 146.

414 Pitcairn, 207.

415 NLS, Adv. MS 31.6.20, 'Dissertation Concerning the Family of Ruthven, Earls of Gowrie', p. 150.

416 Lang, 140.

417 A William Stewart was present at Gowrie House on 5 August, but it was a different man.

418 Calderwood, vi. 73.

419 Calderwood, vi. 73. Gowrie and Calderwood were exact contemporaries at Edinburgh University: *A Catalogue of the Graduates in the Faculties of Arts, Divinity and Law of the University of Edinburgh since its Foundation* (Edinburgh, 1858), 11.

420 Lang, 254.

421 Calderwood, vi. 72–3. It was also claimed that he was at Scone all day: Lang, 115.

422 NLS, Adv. MS 31.6.20, 'Dissertation Concerning the Family of Ruthven, Earls of Gowrie', p. 152.

423 *CSPS, 1597–1603*, 674.

424 Arbuckle, 91n.

425 *King James VI and I: Political Writings*, ed. J. P. Somerville (Cambridge, 1994), p. 275 n. 215.

426 TNA, PRO 31/3/31, fo. 277.

427 Fruit trees: PKA, Fittis Papers, MS 2/2, file 17, p. 15.

428 Notably in Andrew Bisset's treatment of the story in his *Essays upon Historical Truth* (1871), 190–302.

429 For changing perceptions of James over the centuries, see R. Houlbrooke, 'James's Reputation, 1625–2005' in *James VI and I: Ideas, Authority, and Government*, ed. Houlbrooke (Aldershot, 2006), 169–190.

430 See Robert Carlyle's astonishing portrayal of James in the risibly unhistorical BBC film, *Gunpowder, Treason and Plot* (2004). The other recent portrayal came in a Channel 4 drama-documentary with the same title (Wall to Wall productions, 2001).

431 Lang, 156–7.

432 *Border Papers, 1595–1603*, 583.

433 G. J. N. Logan Home, *History of the Logan Family* (Edinburgh, 1934), 99–100; M. Kennaway, *Fast Castle: The Early Years* (Edinburgh 1992), 102–12.

434 Unless stated otherwise, this chapter is based on *The Gowrie Conspiracy: Confessions of George Sprot*, ed. A. Lang (Roxburghe Club, Edinburgh, 1902).

435 Lang, 262.

436 Full detail in Lang, 182–231.

437 *Sprot Confessions*, 7–13.

438 *Sprot Confessions*, xxxviii, 45–51.

439 Lang, 223–4.

440 Pitcairn, 276.

441 Lang, 163–4.

442 *CSPD, 1603–10*, 467.

443 See Abbot's detailed account of Sprot's confession: Lambeth Palace Library, MS 3471, fo. 136.

444 *Spottiswoode*, iii. 200.

445 *Sprot Confessions*, 5, 7, 11.

446 Pitcairn, 273.

447 Lang, 258–9.

448 HMC, *Cecil*, ix. 353.

449 *CSPS, 1574–81*, 372; K. M. Brown, *Noble Society in Scotland* (Edinburgh, 2004 edn), 126.

450 *Sprot Confessions*, xlii–xliii.

451 Lang, 174–81.

452 Lang, 217.

453 W. Fraser, *Memorials of the Earls of Haddington* (1889), i. 102.

454 *Sprot Confessions*, 70–87.

455 Lang, 260.

456 Lang, 261.

457 *Sprot Confessions*, 6.

458 Lang, 263–4.

459 Lang, 261.

460 Lang, 257–64.

461 Lang, 261.

462 Centre for Kentish Studies, Maidstone: Dering manuscripts, U275/C1/17.

463 Pitcairn, 253.

464 E. Cowan, 'The Darker Vision of the Scottish Renaissance: The Devil and Francis Stewart', *The Renaissance and Reformation in Scotland*, ed. I. B. Cowan and D. Shaw (Edinburgh, 1983), 138–9.

465 *CSPS, 1597–1603*, 691, 715

466 R. G. MacPherson, 'Francis Stewart, fifth Earl Bothwell, c1562–1612: Lordship and Politics in Jacobean Scotland' (Edinburgh University PhD thesis, 1998), 451.
467 *CSPS. Spanish, 1587–1603*, 667–8, 715.
468 MacPherson, 'Bothwell', 422–3.
469 When James went to Denmark-Norway for his marriage in 1589–90.
470 *CSPS, 1597–1603*, 712.
471 Pitcairn, 250.
472 Pitcairn, 156.
473 Pitcairn, 156–7.
474 Meikle, 'Oeconomicke Rule', 34.
475 Pitcairn, 158–9.
476 Lang, 257.
477 Lang, 262–3.
478 Lang, 257.
479 Lang, 264.
480 J. Woolfson, *Padua and the Tudors: English Students in Italy, 1485–1603* (Toronto, 1998), 90, 132, 229–30, 241, 245, 255, 259, 260, 269, 287.
481 J. West, *The Brave Lord Willoughby: An Elizabethan Soldier* (Bishop Auckland, 1998), 71 and passim.
482 West, *Brave Lord Willoughby*, 62.
483 *Border Papers*, ii., *1595–1603*, 607–18.
484 *CSPS, 1597–1603*, 538.
485 *Border Papers, 1595*–1603, 743; Lincolnshire Archives, MS 2ANC14/17, John Guevara to Robert, Lord Willoughby, c1601.
486 Logan Home, *History of the Logan Family*, 101–2.
487 *Sprot Confessions*, 39–40.
488 HMC, *Ancaster*, 345, 347.
489 BL, Add. MSS 32,092, fo. 149.
490 *Border Papers, 1597–1603*, 718; Turner, 148.
491 *Border Papers, 1595–1603*, 737.
492 HMC, *Cecil*, xi. 242.
493 A vivid account of Willoughby's last voyage was provided by John Guevara: Lincolnshire Archives, MS 2ANC14/15. For Lord Willoughby's last months as a whole, see J. West, *The Brave Lord Willoughby* (1998), 75–9.
494 *CSPS, 1597–1603*, 691.
495 *CSPS, 1597–1603*, 704.

496 S. Doran, 'Loving and Affectionate Neighbours?', *Tudor England and its Neighbours*, ed. Doran and G. Richardson (Basingstoke, 2005), 203–34 (especially pp. 224–6).

497 *CSPS, 1597–1603*, 674–5.

498 HMC, *Cecil*, x. 133

499 M. Lee, 'The Gowrie Conspiracy Revisited', *The 'Inevitable' Union and Other Essays on Early Modern Scotland* (East Linton, 2004), 106–10.

500 BL, Add. MSS 31,022, fo. 107.

501 R. Lacey, *Robert, Earl of Essex, an Elizabethan Icarus* (2001), 264, 295.

502 *Acts of the Privy Council, 1599–1600*, 555–72.

503 HMC, *Cecil*, x. 365.

504 D. Bowler and R. Cachart, 'Tay Street, Perth: The Excavation of an Early Harbour Site', *Proceedings of the Society of Antiquaries of Scotland*, 124 (1994), 467–89.

505 Pitcairn, 194–208.

506 W. Fraser, *Memorials of the Earls of Haddington* (1889), i. 104.

507 NLS, Adv. MS 31.6.20, p. 158.

508 *CSPS, 1597–1603*, 685.

509 *CSPS, 1597–1603*, 363.

510 J. Reid-Baxter, '*The Nyne Muses*, An Unknown Renaissance Sonnet Sequence: John Dykes and the Gowrie Conspiracy', *Rhetoric, Royalty and Reality: Essays on the Literary Culture of Medieval and Modern Scotland*, ed. A. MacDonald and K. Dekker (Paris, 2005), 212.

511 Lang, 130, 147n; F. Douglas, *Gold at Wolf's Crag? An Inquiry into the Treasure of Fast Castle* (Edinburgh, 1971), 135–43.

512 The Homes also had a strong interest in Fast Castle, the legal title to which was not entirely clear: M. Meikle, 'The Homes and the East March', *Lordship and Architecture in Medieval and Renaisssance Scotland*, ed. R. Oram and G. Stell (Edinburgh, 2005), 231–49.

513 Lang, 259.

514 Lang, 207–8.

515 *Calendar of State Papers, Spanish, 1587–1603*, 680.

516 HMC, *Cecil*, ix. 252.

517 R. R. Zulager, 'Elphinstone, James, first Lord Balmerino (1557–1612), administrator and judge', *ODNB*.

518 Meikle, 'Oeconomicke Rule', 105–10; M. B. Young, 'Queen Anna Bites Back: Protest, Effeminacy and Manliness at the Jacobean Court', *Gender, Power and Privilege in Early Modern Europe* (2003), 108–22.

519 J. E. A. Dawson, '"There is Nothing like a Good Gossip": Baptism, Kinship and Alliance in Early Modern Scotland', *Perspectives on the Older Scottish Tongue: A Celebration of DOST*, ed. C. J. Kay and M. A. Mackay (Edinburgh, 2005), 42.

520 Juhala, 'Household', 62.

521 Juhala, 'Household', 85.

522 *CSPS, 1597–1603*, 640–1, 661, 667.

523 R. Grant, 'Politicking Jacobean Women: Lady Ferniehirst, The Countess of Arran and the Countess of Huntly, c1580–1603', *Women in Scotland c1100-c1750*, ed. E. Ewan and M. M. Meikle (East Linton, 1998), 101–2; L. Barroll, *Anna of Denmark, Queen of England: A Cultural Biography* (Philadelphia, 2001), 176 n. 10.

524 *CSPS, 1597–1603*, 633, 639, 661; Arbuckle, 106–7.

525 HMC, *Ninth Report, Appendix*, 194–6; the papers are now in NAS, GD 156/6. Additionally, Elphinstone purchased the Restalrig estate from Robert Logan.

526 S. M. Dunnigan, 'Fowler, William (1560/61–1612), writer and courtier', *ODNB*.

527 Pitcairn, 157; Juhala, 'Household', 318; Database, 'Scotland, Scandinavia and Northern Europe, 1580–1707', http://www.st-andrews.ac.uk/history/ssne/

528 D. Stevenson, *The Origins of Freemasonry: Scotland's Century, 1590–1710* (Cambridge, 1988), 26–51.

529 Lang, 205.

530 Edinburgh University Library, MS D.C.I.30.

531 Stevenson, 82–96; M. K. Schuchard, *Restoring the Temple of Vision: Cabalistic Freemasonry and Stuart Culture* (Leiden, 2002), 201–7, 223–7, 232–3.

532 D. Crawford Smith, *History of the Ancient Masonic Lodge of Scoon and Perth No. 3* (Perth, 1898), 49–51; Schuchard, *Temple of Vision*, 177–239.

533 *CSPS, 1597–1603*, 682.

534 Young, 'Queen Anna Bites Back', 115.

535 *CSPS, 1597–1603*, 719.

536 *CSPS, 1597–1603*, 721.

537 Juhala, 'Household', 34–5, 65–6, 112–14, 351.

538 *CSPS, 1597–1603,* 723.
539 Scott, 195.
540 Calderwood, vi. 46.
541 *CSPS, 1597–1603,* 716.
542 Pitcairn, 221; Arbuckle, 102–5.
543 *CSPS, 1597–1603,* 737.
544 L. Barroll, *Anna of Denmark, Queen of England: A Cultural Biography* (Philadelphia, 2001), 27.
545 Barroll, *Anna,* 26.
546 Scott, 231.
547 Barroll, *Anna,* 27.
548 *CSPS, 1597–1603,* 1096; Barroll, *Anna,* 27.
549 *CSPS, 1597–1603,* 1110.
550 Barroll, *Anna,* 28–33.
551 *CSPS, 1597–1603,* 1110.
552 Bodleian Library, Oxford, MS Ashmole 1729, fo. 84. Cf *CSPD, 1603–10,* 9.
553 Cowan, 227–8.
554 HMC, *Cecil* xv. 139.
555 *CSPD, 1603–10,* 43.
556 HMC, *Cecil,* xvi. 29–30.
557 TNA, Prob. 11/139, fo. 264; House of Lords Record Office, MS HL/PO/JO/10/1/26, petition of Lady Barbara Ruthven.
558 *CSPD, 1603–10,* 541.
559 L. L. Peck, *Court Patronage and Corruption in Early Stuart England* (1990), 69–70; *Scots Peerage,* sv Gowrie, 266.
560 CA, SE1129, copy of assignment by Seaton and Barbara, 20 Dec. 1624. Seaton is an obscure figure, but he was a witness in the case between Lord Reay and David Ramsay (a relation of the 'hero' of Gowrie House) before the Court of Chivalry in 1631, the last time that an English court sentenced the protagonists to duel with each other.
561 *CSPD, 1611–18,* 387.
562 HMC, *Fourth Report,* 312.
563 *CSPD, 1619–23,* 443.
564 *Acts of the Privy Council of England, 1621–3,* 306; *CSPD, 1619–23,* 434, 439, 440; HMC, *Fourth Report,* appendix, 312.
565 *Acts of the Privy Council of England, 1623–5,* 177.
566 HMC, *Mar and Kellie,* ii. 131.
567 NLS, MS Acc. 7,400.

568 CA, SE1500, paper by Sir John Cowell Stepney.

569 King Gustavus Adolphus of Sweden also intervened on Patrick's behalf in 1626–7, thanks to the prompting of his friend and Patrick's eponymous cousin Colonel Patrick Ruthven (later the Earl of Forth and Brentford): Bruce, *Papers*, 105–7.

570 In August 1619, a premature report of Patrick's release had named Holdernesse (then Viscount Haddington) as the man responsible for it: *CSPD, 1619–23*, 71.

571 And in any case James's treatment of the Ruthvens was more lenient than that of the MacGregors, who had not allegedly struck against him personally: J. Goodare, *The Government of Scotland 1560–1625* (Oxford, 2004), 236.

572 *The Acts of the Parliament of Scotland*, v (1818), 460, 487.

573 NAS, GD 246/75, 'A Memorandum of Such Things as Are Necessary to be Tried Concerning the House of Gowrie'. The end date of 1631 is established by Patrick's reference to his sister Beatrix, Lady Cowdenknowes, as being still alive; her letter of 1622, pleading that some of her lands should not be taken from her, might be a response to her younger brother's enquiries, in which case Patrick embarked on a campaign to regain the peerage almost as soon as he was released: NLS, Adv. MS 33.1.1, vol 10/106.

574 Bruce, *Papers*, 107–8. Ironically, as a young man Stirling had written a vigorous defence of the king's narrative of the Gowrie House affair.

575 Cowan, 232.

576 Van Dyck, *Mary Ruthven*, c1639; oil on canvas, the Prado, Madrid.

577 CA, Derwydd MS H1, booklet entitled 'Who's Afraid'.

578 R. Blake, *Anthony Van Dyck: A Life, 1599–1641* (1999), 328.

579 CA, SE1129, deposition of Thomas Evans, 1674.

580 TNA, Prob. 11/187, fo. 383.

581 HMC, *Sixth Report*, 51.

582 C. Brown, *Van Dyck* (1982), 221.

583 HMC, *Sixth Report*, 160.

584 CA, SE1129, depositions of 1674.

585 HMC, *Laing*, i. 259–60.

586 W. Sanderson, *A Compleat History of the Lives and Reigns of Mary Queen of Scots and of her son and Successor James the Sixth, King of Scotland* (1656), 230.

587 CA, Derwydd MS H17, notebook of Alan Stepney Gulston.

588 *Notes and Queries*, third series, iii (1863), 3, 50–1.

589 Bruce, *Papers*, 110–11 (also published in Cowan, 243–5).

590 Bruce, *Papers*, 111; *The Scots Peerage*, iv. 265.

591 National Library of Wales, Cilymaenllwyd MS 123, 'Traditions and Reasonings Thereon of the Alleged Gowrie Conspiracy'. The chief family seat moved to Llanelli, Carmarthenshire, in c1705.

592 CA, Derwydd MS H17, draft petition.

593 Quotation: A. Lambert, 'Grey by Name, Passionate by Nature', *The Independent*, 5 Oct. 1993; N. Howard, correspondence and email exchanges with the author, 2004.

594 R. G. MacPherson, 'Francis Stewart, fifth Earl Bothwell, c1562–1612: Lordship and Politics in Jacobean Scotland' (Edinburgh University, PhD thesis, 1998), 388.

595 Goodare, *Government of Scotland*, 98.

596 For example, David Calderwood has been cited frequently throughout this book, but only because he is often the only source for particular 'facts'. However, Calderwood was a staunch partisan of the Kirk and faithfully recorded any piece of innuendo, no matter how unsubstantiated, that might blacken the name of King James: V. T. Wells, 'Calderwood, David (c1575–1650), Church of Scotland minister and historian', *ODNB*.

597 *CSPS, 1597–1603*, 702.

598 Pitcairn, 295.

599 *CSPS, 1597–1603*, 694; Lang, 48–9.

600 Lang, 13.

601 M. Meikle, 'A Meddlesome Princess: Anna of Denmark and Scottish Court Politics, 1589–1603', Goodare and Lynch, *Reign of James VI*, 133.

602 R. W. Cochran-Patrick, ed., *Early Records Relating to Mining in Scotland* (Edinburgh, 1878), xlix. Jenny Wormald has attempted valiantly, but not entirely convincingly, to overturn James's reputation for cowardice: 'O Brave New World? The Union of England and Scotland in 1603', joint British Academy / Royal Society of Edinburgh lecture, 24 Mar. 2003; 'Royal Dunfermline to Royal Whitehall: The Stresses of Moving House', *Royal Dunfermline*, ed. R. Fawcett (Edinburgh, 2005), 199.

603 Arbuckle, 105.

604 Calderwood, vi. 67.

605 *Memoirs of the Affairs of Scotland, by David Moysie, 1577–1603* (Maitland Club, 1830), 72; C. Saenz-Cambra, *Scotland and Philip II 1580–98* (Sevenoaks, 2005), 117, 136–7, 151, 167; Saenz-Cambra, 'James VI's *Ius Suum Conservare:* His Intrigues with Spain, 1580–1603', *International Review of Scottish Studies*, 30 (2005), 86–107; F. Douglas, *Gold at Wolf's Crag?: An Inquiry into the Treasure of Fast Castle* (Edinburgh, 1971), 1–7, 209–22.

606 HMC, *Cecil*, x. 267.

607 M. Lee, 'The Gowrie Conspiracy Revisited', *The Inevitable Union and Other Essays on Early Modern Scotland* (East Linton, 2003), 106–7, 113.

608 Centre for Kentish Studies, Maidstone: Dering manuscripts, U275/C1/17. Unless stated otherwise, the remainder of this chapter is based on this source. The recipient was possibly a Peyton of Knowlton.

609 *CSPS, 1597–1603*, 682, 684–5.

610 *CSPS, 1597–1603*, 719. Cf Turner, 68.

611 *Historical Notices of Scottish Affairs, Selected from the Manuscripts of Mr John Lauder of Fountainhall* (Bannatyne Club, 1848), ii. 547.

612 Lang, 23, 43–7. Others were said to have seen Henderson in the vicinity, but never testified formally to that effect: Arbuckle, 21–2.

613 *CSPS, 1597–1603*, 748–9; Lang, 72–7.

614 Lang, 49.

615 *CSPS, 1597–1603*, 711–12.

616 Arbuckle, 101.

617 PKA, Fittis Papers, MS 2/2, file 19, p. 82.

618 BL, Add. MSS 35,625, fo. 111; *Spottiswoode*, iii. 88.

619 *CSPS, 1597–1603*, 778.

620 Arbuckle, 101.

621 *RPCS, 1604–7*, 159–60.

622 NLS, Adv. MS 33.1.1, vol 2/55, vol 5/112; *RPCS, 1610–13*, 367–8; Arbuckle, 101.

623 Henderson apparently left Perth shortly after 1617, and died in the 1640s or 1650s: PKA, Fittis Papers, MS 2/2, file 19, pp. 109–10.

624 G. M. Thomson, *A Kind of Justice: Two Studies in Treason* (1970), 74.

625 *CSPS, 1597–1603*, 712.

626 *CSPS, 1597–1603*, 721. Only six years later, Lennox was content to appoint a Ruthven – William of Freeland – as one of the administrators of his Scottish estates: NAS, GD 220/1/F/8/4/3.

627 F. Moncreiff and W. Moncreiffe, *The Moncreiffs and the Moncreiffes* (Edinburgh, 1929), i. 106–7; ii. 543–7.

628 *RPCS, 1607–10*, 385, 406, 413, 451, 623, 844; *1610–13*, 601.

629 J. Magee, 'The Gowrie Conspiracy and the Trotters of Down', *Familia: Ulster Genealogical Review* (vol 2, no. 7, 1991), 31–9; A. F. Pollard, rev. P. Gray, 'Ruthven [formerly Trotter], Edward Southwell, 1772?-1836, politician', *ODNB*. However, it has also been suggested that Alexander returned to Scotland in c1609–11: Perth & Kinross Archive, Fittis Papers, MS 2/2, file 19, pp. 98–9.

630 Pitcairn, 214.

631 George, Earl of Cromarty, *An Historical Account of the Conspiracies by the Earl of Gowry, and Robert Logan of Restalrig, against King James VI* (Edinburgh, 1713), 12–13.

632 D. Lloyd, *The States-men and Favourites of England since the Reformation…* (1665), 561; *The Diary of Joseph Farington*, ed. K. Garlick and A. Macintyre, v (Yale, 1979), 1639 (Farington was shown the 'blood' when he visited Gowrie House in 1801). Cf *Journal of Sir John Lauder, Lord Fountainhall*, ed. D. Crawford (Scottish Historical Society, 1900), 199–200.

633 The legend is recorded in *inter alia* Lang, vii.

634 That is, other than some of the more esoteric theories that have become attached to the Gowrie House affair over the years: these include the notion that Logan of Restalrig was a secret Knight Templar whose remains, buried at South Leith church, were desecrated in a Masonic and Templar ritual (http://johnarthur.tripod.com/leithhistory/templar1.htm, accessed 8 December 2009); and the theory that the Casket Letters, or even the Holy Grail itself, were secreted at Fast Castle: F. Douglas, *Gold at Wolf's Crag? An Historical Investigation* (Edinburgh, 1971), 175, 209–22 and passim.

635 Keith, iii. 266.

636 Fraser, 240n; but see Guy, 265–6, for the sketchy nature of understanding of pregnancy at the time.

637 Weir, 136–8.

638 M. Lynch, 'Queen Mary's Triumph: The Baptismal Celebrations in Stirling in December 1566', *SHR* 69 (1990), 1–21.

639 Guy, 335.

640 The legend is explored in detail, and categorically dismissed, by Fraser, 267n.
641 The name 'James' was actually chosen by Elizabeth I: R. Allinson, 'Queen Elizabeth and the "Nomination" of the Young Prince of Scotland', *Notes and Queries*, 251 (2006), 425–7.
642 R. K. Marshall, 'Riccio, David (*c*1533–1566)', *ODNB*.
643 D. H. Willson, *King James VI and I* (1956), 50.
644 Keith, iii. 268.
645 R. MacPherson, 'Colville, John (1542?-1605), conspirator and Church of Scotland minister', *ODNB*.
646 Tweedie, David, *David Rizzio and Mary Queen of Scots: Murder at Holyrood* (Sutton Publishing Ltd., Gloucestershire, UK, 2006), 170–3.
647 Tweedie, *Rizzio*, 170.
648 Tweedie, *Rizzio*, 178.
649 *Pace* Tweedie, *Rizzio*, 172.
650 A. E. MacRobert, *Mary, Queen of Scots and the Casket Letters* (2002); A. Weir, *Mary, Queen of Scots, and the Murder of Lord Darnley* (2003), 465–74.
651 Lang, 241.
652 NAS, GD 246/75, notebook entitled 'A History of Gowrie House in Perth', pp. 25–6.
653 Moreover, the only source for Ruthven's statement is the memoir of Mary ghost-written by Claude Nau, begging the questions of how the Queen of Scots learned of the remark or whether she or Nau invented it.
654 The story is mentioned by Saint-Simon: see http://sgulland.googlepages.com/thequeen's mysterydaughter, accessed 5 March 2009.
655 Fraser, 203–6.^
656 The best and most accessible modern account of the assassination is that by R. Mousnier, *The Assassination of Henry IV: The Tyrannicide Problem and the Consolidation of the French Absolute Monarchy in the Seventeenth Century*, trans. Joan Spencer (1973), 24–7.
657 A. M. Walker and E. H. Dickerman, 'Mind of an Assassin: Ravaillac and the Murder of Henry IV of France', *Canadian Journal of History*, XXX (1995), 202.
658 Ibid, 201–29 passim, for the most recent analysis of Ravaillac's motivation.

659 Mousnier, *Assassination*, 50–2.

660 A. Bisset, *Essays Upon Historical Truth* (1871), 268–9

661 L. Bély, 'Murder and Monarchy in France', in R von Friedeburg, ed., *Murder and Monarchy: Regicide in European History, 1300–1800* (Basingstoke, 2004), 204–6.

662 Mousnier, *Assassination*, 43–9, 52–7, 105.

663 Mousnier, *Assassination*, 196, 199, 231–7.

664 'Walker and Dickerman, 'Mind of an Assassin', 228–9.

665 Sir Ian Moncrieffe of that Ilk, 'The Ravaillac Dagger and the Gowrie House Affair', *Family History: The Journal of the Institute of Heraldic and Genealogical Studies*, 11, nos. 77/78 (New Series nos. 53/54; August 1980), 135–8. A version of this paper was printed in *Lord of the Dance: A Moncreiffe Miscellany*, ed. H. Montgomery-Massingberd (1986), 168–71.

666 Walker and Dickerman, 'Mind of an Assassin', 225.

667 Cowan, 11–43.

668 *Further Papers Relating to the Ruthven Family*, ed. J. Bruce (1867), 4–5; *The Chronicle of Perth* (Edinburgh, Maitland Club, 1831), 24.

669 N. MacDougall, *James III: A Political Study* (Edinburgh, 1982), 214, 237.

670 M. A. Penman, 'Ruthven, William, of that Ilk, first Lord Ruthven', *ODNB*.

671 CA, Derwydd MS CA3, James Maidment to Alan Gulston, 12 February 1864; W. O. Hewlett, *Notes on Dignities in the Peerage of Scotland Which are Dormant or Which Have Been Forfeited* (1882), 134–8.

672 W. Fraser, *The Lennox* (Edinburgh, 1874), i. 367–88.

673 For their activities, and the rise of Protestantism in Perth, see M. Verschuur, *Politics or Religion? The Reformation in Perth 1540–70* (Edinburgh, 2006).

674 Calderwood, i. 158.

675 Knox, i. 52; M. Sanderson, *Cardinal of Scotland* (Edinburgh, 1986), 188, 190, 192, 211.

676 PKA, MS B59/26/1/9.

677 John Maxwell, Lord Herries, *Historical Memoirs of the Reign of Mary Queen of Scots and a Portion of the Reign of King James VI* (Edinburgh, Abbotsford Club, 1836), 15.

678 *The Works of John Knox*, ed. D. Laing (reprint, New York, 1966), i. 112–13; *RPCS*, I. 64.

679 *RPCS*, I. 35.

680 A. J. Cameron, ed., *The Scottish Correspondence of Mary of Lorraine* (Scottish Historical Society, third series, x, Edinburgh, 1927), 159–60, 177–9, 317–18; J. Wormald, *Lords and Men in Scotland: Bonds of Manrent 1442–1603* (Edinburgh, 1985), 149.

681 M. H. Merriman, 'The Assured Scots: Scottish Collaborators with England during the Rough Wooing', *SHR*, 47 (1968), 10–35.

682 *CSPS, 1547-63*, 50.

683 *CSPS, 1547-63*, 64.

684 *CSPS, 1547-63*, 92.

685 Merriman, 'Rough Wooing', 226.

686 *CSPS, 1547-63*, 117; *CSPD, 1547–53*, 46.

687 Merriman, 'Rough Wooing', 303–10.

688 *CSPS, 1547-63*, 152.

689 *CSPS, 1547-63*, 155. For further evidence of English doubts about Ruthven's sincerity by this time, see A. J. Cameron, ed., *The Scottish Correspondence of Mary of Lorraine* (Scottish Historical Society, third series, x, Edinburgh, 1927), 266.

690 *CSPS, 1547-63*, 165.

691 *RPCS*, I. 120.

692 *RPCS*, I. 135–6; A. J. Cameron, ed., *The Scottish Correspondence of Mary of Lorraine* (Scottish Historical Society, third series, x, Edinburgh, 1927), 345–7; P. E. Ritchie, *Mary of Guise in Scotland, 1548–60: A Political Career* (East Linton, 2002), 82, 105, 266.

693 M. B. Verschuur, 'The Outbreak of the Scottish Reformation at Perth, 11 May 1559: Knox's *History* Re-examined', *Scotia: American-Canadian Journal of Scottish Studies*, xi (1987), 47–51.

694 Knox, i. 159; Calderwood, i. 438–9; Keith, i. 186.

695 Donald III, 1093–4 and 1094–7; Donalbain in Shakespeare's *Macbeth*.

696 G. Burnet, *The History of My Own Time*, ed. O. Airy (Oxford, 1897), i. 26.

697 NLS, Adv. MS 31.6.20, p.132

698 *Border Papers*, [i] 491.

699 PKA, Fittis Papers, MS 2/2, file 18, p. 43; P. Drummond-Mackay, 'The Gowrie Conspiracy', *The Double Tressure: Journal of the Heraldry Society of Scotland*, 19 (1997), 35.

700 A. Lang, 'The Gowrie Conspiracy and the Gowrie Arms', *The Ancestor*, 2 (1902), 54–7.

701 *Scots Peerage*, sv 'Methven'.

702 PKA, Fittis Papers, MS 2/2, file 18, p. 42

703 There are several manuscript copies of the letter, eg,
   BL. Sloane MS 1775, fo. 58–9; Society of Antiquaries of London,
   MS SAL/MS/291, fos. 36–7. It was printed in full by McCallum,
   'Patrick Ruthven', 476–7.
704 *CSPD, 1611–18*, 190.
705 S. Gristwood, *Arbella: England's Lost Queen* (London, 2003),
   especially pp. 401–2.
706 *The Letters of Lady Arbella Stuart*, ed. S. J. Steen (Oxford, 1994),
   90–2.
707 This is most likely to have occurred in 1650, when the Ruthven
   brothers' cousin, General Patrick Ruthven, Earl of Forth and
   Brentford, stayed at Perth, probably in Gowrie House: *Ruthven
   correspondence: letters and papers of Patrick Ruthven, Earl of Forth
   and Brentford, and of his Family, AD 1615 – AD 1662*, ed.
   W. D. Macray (Roxburghe Club, Edinburgh, 1869). One of two
   urns discovered in concealed closets when Gowrie House was
   demolished was said to contain human bones, perhaps those of the
   Ruthven brothers; the other, containing ashes, was said to contain
   the remains of the Casket Letters. NAS, GD 246/75, notebook
   entitled 'A History of Gowrie House in Perth'.
708 Cowan, 60–6. Janet's son was living in Cupar, Fife, in 1943:
   letter to *The Scotsman*, 29 Nov. 1943. Cf 'Memorial to the Gowrie
   Family', *Scottish Historical Review*, 11 (1914), 119.
709 BL, Add. MSS 32,092, fo. 149.

Index